Introduction to Parallel and Vector Solution of Linear Systems

FRONTIERS OF COMPUTER SCIENCE

Series Editor: Arnold L. Rosenberg, *University of Massachusetts Amherst, Massachusetts*

INTRODUCTION TO PARALLEL AND VECTOR SOLUTION OF LINEAR SYSTEMS
James M. Ortega

A Continuation Order Plan is available for this series. A continuation order will bring delivery of each new volume immediately upon publication. Volumes are billed only upon actual shipment. For further information please contact the publisher.

Introduction to Parallel and Vector Solution of Linear Systems

James M. Ortega

University of Virginia
Charlottesville, Virginia

Plenum Press • New York and London

Library of Congress Cataloging in Publication Data

Ortega, James M., 1932-
Introduction to parallel and vector solution of linear systems / James M. Ortega.
p. cm. — (Frontiers of computer science)
Bibliography: p.
Includes index.
ISBN 0-306-42862-8
1. Equations — Numerical solutions — Data processing. 2. Parallel processing (Electronic computers) 3. Supercomputers. I. Title. II. Series.
QA218.078 1988
515′.252 — dc 19 88-721
CIP

This limited facsimile edition has been issued for the purpose of keeping this title available to the scientific community.

First Printing — March 1988
Second Printing — November 1989

A Division of Plenum Publishing Corporation
233 Spring Street, New York, N.Y. 10013

Printed in the United States of America

To SARA and SCOTT

Preface

Although the origins of parallel computing go back to the last century, it was only in the 1970s that parallel and vector computers became available to the scientific community. The first of these machines—the 64 processor Illiac IV and the vector computers built by Texas Instruments, Control Data Corporation, and then CRAY Research Corporation—had a somewhat limited impact. They were few in number and available mostly to workers in a few government laboratories. By now, however, the trickle has become a flood. There are over 200 large-scale vector computers now installed, not only in government laboratories but also in universities and in an increasing diversity of industries. Moreover, the National Science Foundation's Supercomputing Centers have made large vector computers widely available to the academic community. In addition, smaller, very cost-effective vector computers are being manufactured by a number of companies.

Parallelism in computers has also progressed rapidly. The largest supercomputers now consist of several vector processors working in parallel. Although the number of processors in such machines is still relatively small (up to 8), it is expected that an increasing number of processors will be added in the near future (to a total of 16 or 32). Moreover, there are a myriad of research projects to build machines with hundreds, thousands, or even more processors. Indeed, several companies are now selling parallel machines, some with as many as hundreds, or even tens of thousands, of processors.

Probably the main driving force for the development of vector and parallel computers has been scientific computing, and one of the most important problems in scientific computing is the solution of linear systems of equations. Even for conventional computers, this has continued to be an active area of research, especially for iterative methods. However, parallel and vector computers have necessitated a rethinking of even the most basic algorithms, a process that is still going on. Moreover, we are in the most turbulent period in the history of computer architecture. It will certainly be several years, if ever, before a single parallel architecture emerges as the machine of choice.

It follows that a book on this topic is destined to be obsolete almost before it is in print. We have attempted to mitigate this problem by not tying the book to particular machines, although the influence of the older CDC CYBER 205 and CRAY-1 will be noted. However, there are many basic approaches that are essentially machine independent and that, presumably, will survive even though particular algorithms based on them may need to be modified. It is these approaches that we have tried to stress.

This book has arisen from a second-semester first-year graduate course begun in the early 1980s. Originally the course was directed primarily toward the analysis of iterative methods, with some attention to vector computers, especially the CYBER 205. Over the years more on parallel computers has been added, but the machines used for projects have been the CYBER 205 and, more recently, the CRAY X-MP. This is reflected in the exercises, which are biased heavily toward the CYBER 205.

The organization of the book is as follows. Chapter 1 discusses some of the basic characteristics of vector and parallel computers as well as the framework for dealing with algorithms on such machines. Then many of these concepts are exemplified by the relatively simple problem of matrix multiplication. Chapter 2 treats direct methods, including LU, Choleski, and orthogonal factorizations. It is assumed that the reader has had at least a first course in numerical methods and is familiar with most of these methods. Thus, the emphasis is on their organization for vector and parallel computers. Chapter 3 deals with iterative methods. Since most introductions to numerical methods deal rather lightly, if at all, with iterative methods, we devote more time in this chapter to the basic properties of such methods, independently of the computer system. In addition, many of the standard convergence theorems and other results are collected in two appendixes for those who wish a more detailed mathematical treatment. Other than the above background in numerical methods, the main prerequisites are some programming experience and linear algebra. Very basic background material in linear algebra is summarized briefly in Appendix 4.

Many important topics are not covered, and, as mentioned previously, rather little attention is given to algorithms on current particular machines. However, each section ends with "References and Extensions," which give short summaries of related work and references to the literature. It is hoped that this will help the reader to pursue topics of interest. References are given by the format Author [year] (for example, Jones [1985]) and may be found accordingly in the bibliography.

The book should be read in the spirit of a mathematics book, not as a "how-to-do-it" manual. The incomplete code segments that are given are meant to be illustrative, not the basics of a running code. Anyone wishing to use a linear equation solver for a particular parallel or vector machine is strongly advised *not* to start from the material in this book, especially for direct methods. Rather, see what routines, especially LINPACK, are already available on that machine.

The following conventions are used. Vectors are denoted by lower case bold and matrices by upper case italic. Equation numbers are given by chapter and section; thus (3.2.4) is the fourth numbered equation in Section 3.2. Theorems and definitions are likewise numbered within a section by, for example, 3.2.6.

I am indebted to Sandra Shifflett, Beverly Martin, and especially, B. Ann Turley for typing the manuscript, and to many students and reviewers for their comments.

Charlottesville, Virginia James M. Ortega

Contents

1

Introduction

1.1. Vector and Parallel Computers

In the early 1970s, computers began to appear that consisted of a number of separate processors operating in parallel or that had hardware instructions for operating on vectors. The latter type of computer we will call a *vector computer* (or *processor*) while the former we will call a *parallel computer* (or *processor*).

Vector Computers

Vector computers utilize the concept of *pipelining*, which is the explicit segmentation of an arithmetic unit into different parts, each of which performs a subfunction on a pair of operands. This is illustrated in Figure 1.1-1 for floating point addition.

In the example of Figure 1.1-1, a floating point adder is segmented into six sections, each of which does one part of the overall floating point addition. Each segment can be working on one pair of operands, so that six pairs of operands can be in the pipeline at a given time. The advantage of this segmentation is that results are being computed at a rate that is 6 times faster (or, in general, K times, where K is the number of segments) than an arithmetic unit that accepts a pair of operands and computes the result before accepting the next pair of operands. However, in order to utilize this capability, the data must reach the arithmetic units rapidly

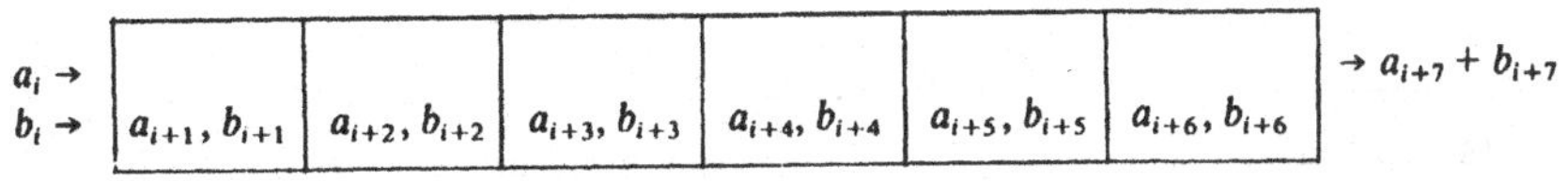

Figure 1.1-1. A floating point pipeline.

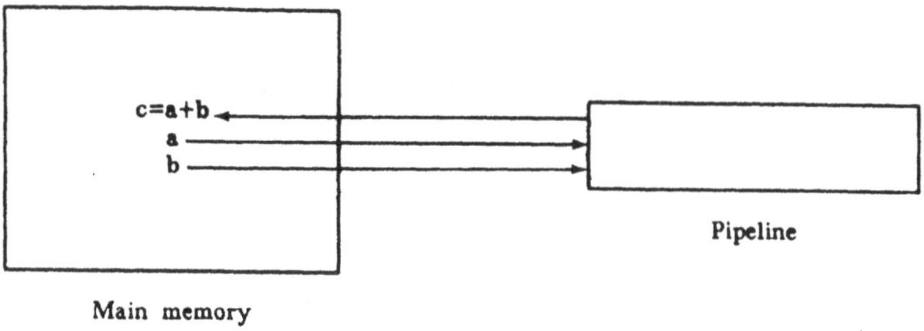

Figure 1.1-2. Memory-to-memory addition operation.

enough to keep the pipeline full. As one aspect of this, the hardware instructions for, say, vector addition eliminate the need for separate load and store instructions for the data. A single hardware instruction will control the loading of the operands and storing of the results.

Memory-to-Memory Processors

Control Data Corporation (CDC) has produced a line of vector processors starting with the STAR-100 in 1973. This machine evolved into the CYBER 203 in the late 1970s and then the CYBER 205 in the early 1980s. These machines were all *memory-to-memory* processors in that vector operations took their operands directly from main memory and stored the result back in main memory. This is illustrated in Figure 1.1-2 for a vector addition.

Register-to-Register Processors

Cray Research, Inc. has produced vector processors since the mid 1970s that are examples of *register-to-register* processors. By this we mean that the vector operations obtain their operands from very fast memory, called *vector registers*, and store the results back into vector registers. This is illustrated in Figure 1.1-3 for vector addition. In Figure 1.1-3, each vector

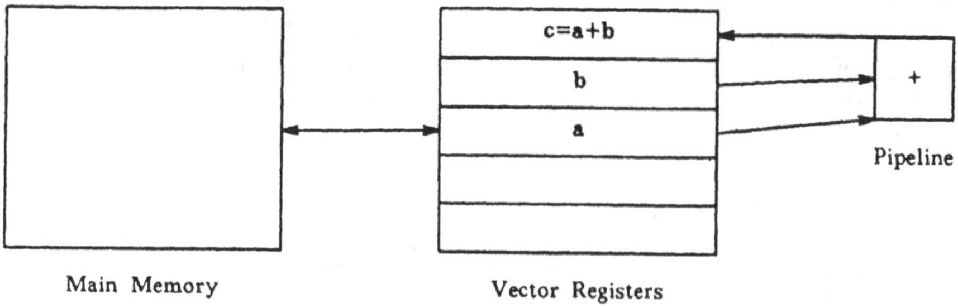

Figure 1.1-3. Register-to-register addition.

register is assumed to hold a certain number of words. For example, on the CRAY machines, there are eight vector registers, each of which holds 64 floating point numbers. Operands for a vector addition are obtained from two vector registers and the result is put into another vector register. Prior to the vector addition, the vector registers must be loaded from main memory, and, at some point, the result vector is stored back into main memory from a vector register. It is usually desirable on this type of computer to use data in the vector registers as much as possible while they are available; several examples of this will be given in later sections.

Memory Hierarchies

Vector registers play somewhat the same role as cache memory on conventional computers. More recent vector computers may have a more complex memory hierarchy. For example, the CRAY-2, in addition to vector registers, has a 16,000-word fast local memory in each processor. Other machines such as the CRAY X-MP series can have a back-up storage (the Solid-State Storage Device), which is slower than main memory but considerably faster than disk. And, of course, all the machines will have disk units. The challenge is to use these various types of storage in such a way as to have the data ready for the arithmetic units when it is needed.

Arithmetic Units

As discussed above, vector processors will have pipelined arithmetic units to handle vector operations. The form of these may differ, however. The CDC machines have used *reconfigurable* units in which a single pipeline can perform the different arithmetic operations but it must be configured for a particular operation, say addition, before that operation can begin. The CRAY machines, on the other hand, have used separate pipelines for addition and multiplication, as well as other functions. And some Japanese machines (for example, the NEC SX-2) have multiple separate pipelines (for example, four pipelines for addition, four for multiplication, etc.). There may also be multiple reconfigurable pipelines. For example, the CYBER 205 allows 1, 2, or 4 pipelines, which are used in unison on a given vector operation (rather than processing separate operations.)

Vector hardware operations are always provided for the addition of two vectors, the elementwise product of two vectors, and either the elementwise quotient of two vectors or the reciprocals of the elements of a vector. There may also be vector instructions for more complex operations such as the square roots of the elements of a vector, the inner product of two vectors, the sum of the elements of a vector, sparse vector operations, and so on. There may also be certain operations that can be handled very efficiently. A *linked triad* is an operation of the form $\mathbf{a} + \alpha\mathbf{b}$, where $\mathbf{a}$ and $\mathbf{b}$ are vectors and α is a scalar. Other forms of a linked triad are also possible such as $(\mathbf{a} + \alpha)\mathbf{b}$, where $\mathbf{a} + \alpha$ is the vector with α added to all of its components. The CYBER 205 can perform these linked triad operations at almost the same speed as a vector addition or multiplication operation. The linked triad $\mathbf{a} + \alpha\mathbf{b}$ is also known as a *saxpy* operation, and this is the more common designation, especially amongst CRAY users. We will, however, use the term "linked triad."

Machines with separate arithmetic pipelines usually allow the possibility of *chaining* arithmetic units together so that results from one unit are routed directly to another without first returning to a register. This is illustrated in Figure 1.1-4 for a linked triad operation.

Most vector computers provide separate units for scalar arithmetic. These units may also be pipelined but do not accept vector operands as the vector pipelines do. They can run concurrently with the vector pipelines, and usually produce scalar results 5–10 times slower than the maximum rates of the vector pipelines.

Vector Start-up Times

The use of vector operations incurs an overhead penalty as shown in the following approximate formula for the time T for a vector operation:

$$T = S + KN \tag{1.1.1}$$

In (1.1.1), N is the length of the vectors involved, K is the time interval at which results are leaving the pipeline, and S is the *start-up time*. S is the time for the pipeline to become full, and includes the time to initiate the fetch of the operands. This is typically much larger for memory-to-memory machines than register to register machines provided that the time to load the vector registers from main memory is not included. S also includes the time for configuring the pipeline on those machines with reconfigurable pipelines.

The result rate K is closely related to the *cycle time* (also called the clock period, clock time, or minor cycle time) of the machine. One result

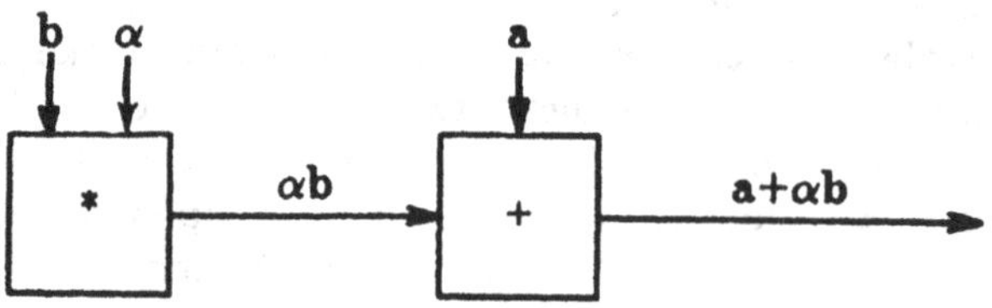

Figure 1.1-4. Chaining.

will leave a pipeline unit every cycle time once the pipeline is full. Hence, on many machines K is just the cycle time. However, on those machines with multiple reconfigurable pipelines, or multiple addition and multiplication units, K will be the cycle time divided by the number of multiple units. For example, the cycle time of the CYBER 205 is 20 ns (nanoseconds = 10^{-9} seconds) so that on a two-pipeline 205, K is 10 ns for addition and multiplication and 5 ns on a four-pipeline 205. Similarly, the cycle time of the NEC SX-2 is 6 ns and there are four units for addition and multiplication. Hence, $K = 1.5$ ns for these operations. The value of K may be larger for more complex operations such as square root or inner product.

From (1.1.1), the time per result is

$$T_R = K + S/N \tag{1.1.2}$$

which has the graph shown in Figure 1.1-5 as a function of the vector length N. Figure 1.1-5 illustrates the need to use sufficiently long vectors so as to amortize the start-up time over many results. Result rates on current vector processors are on the order of a few nanoseconds, while start-up times S range from several tens of nanoseconds on register to register machines to several hundreds of nanoseconds on memory to memory machines.

Another way of plotting the result rate is to use the number of results per time unit given by

$$R = T_R^{-1} = \frac{N}{S + KN} \tag{1.1.3}$$

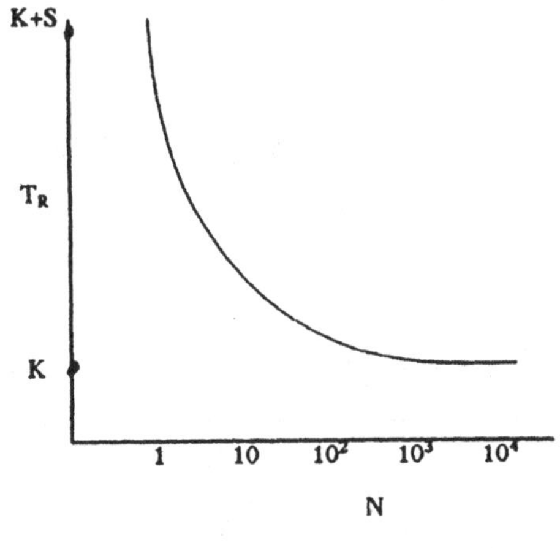

Figure 1.1-5. Time per result relation.

If $S = 0$, or as $N \to \infty$, (1.1.3) yields

$$R_\infty = \frac{1}{K} \tag{1.1.4}$$

which is called the *asymptotic result rate.* This is the (not achievable) maximum result rate when the start-up overhead is ignored. For example, if K is 10 ns, then the asymptotic rate is $R_\infty = 10^8$ results per second, or 100 mflops, where "mflops" denotes megaflops or one million floating point operations per second.

The function R of (1.1.3) is plotted in Figure 1.1-6 as a function of N under the assumption that $K = 10$ ns and $S = 100$ ns as well as $S = 1000$ ns. As illustrated in Figure 1.1-6, both curves tend to the asymptotic result rate of 100 mflops as N increases, but the approach is much more rapid initially for smaller S.

A number of some interest is $N_{1/2}$, which is defined to be the vector length for which half the asymptotic rate is achieved. For example, if $K = 10$ ns, it follows from (1.1.3) that $N_{1/2} = 100$ for $S = 1000$, while if $S = 100$, then $N_{1/2} = 10$. Another important number is the *cross-over point*, N_c, at which vector arithmetic becomes faster than scalar arithmetic. Suppose that scalar arithmetic can be done at an average rate of 10 mflops. Then the crossover point N_c is the value of N for which $R \geqslant 10$ mflops. For $S = 1000$, using (1.1.3), this is the minimum value of N for which

$$\frac{N}{(1000 + 10N)10^{-9}} \geqslant 10 \times 10^6$$

or $N_c = 12$. Thus, for vectors of length less than 12, the use of vector

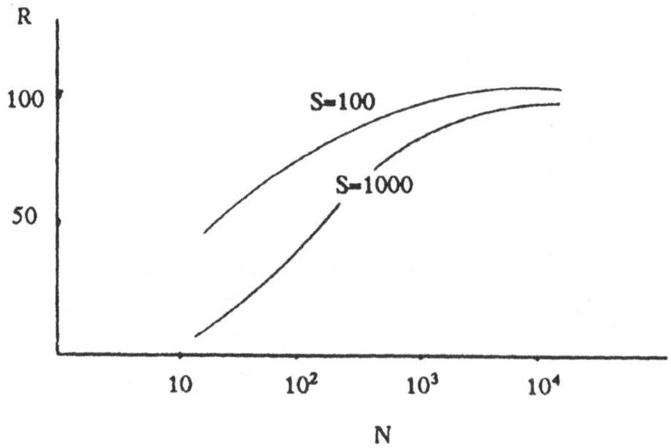

Figure 1.1-6. Result rates in mflops.

arithmetic is slower than scalar arithmetic. On the other hand, for $S = 100$, $N_c = 2$; in this case, vector operations are more efficient for all vector lengths except the trivial case of vectors of length 1. Note that the cross-over point is highly dependent on the scalar arithmetic rate. In the previous examples, if the scalar arithmetic rate was only 5 mflops, then $N_c = 6$ if $S = 1000$ and $N_c = 1$ if $S = 100$.

Vectors

On vector computers, there are restrictions on what constitutes a vector for purposes of vector arithmetic operations. On register to register machines, a vector for arithmetic instructions will be a sequence of contiguous elements in a vector register, usually starting in the first element of a register. An important consideration for these machines, then, is what constitutes a vector in main memory for the purpose of loading a vector register. This is essentially the same consideration as what constitutes a vector for arithmetic operations on memory to memory computers.

Elements that are sequentially addressable always constitute a suitable vector, and on some machines (for example, CDC machines) these are the only vectors. In the sequel, we will use *contiguous* as a synonym for sequentially addressable, although sequentially addressable elements are usually not physically contiguous in memory; rather, they are stored in different memory banks. (However, on CDC machines data are accessed in "superwords" of eight words that are physically contiguous. Here, it is superwords that are in different memory banks.) On other machines, elements with a constant stride form a vector. By *stride* we mean the address separation between elements. Thus, elements with addresses a, $a + s$, $a + 2s, \ldots$ have a constant stride equal to s. In the special case that $s = 1$, the elements are sequentially addressable.

For elements that are not stored with a constant stride, or for elements stored with a constant stride greater than one on those machines for which a vector consists only of sequentially addressable elements, it is necessary to use auxiliary hardware or software instructions to reformat the data to be an acceptable vector. A *gather* operation will map a given number of elements specified by a list of their addresses into a vector. A *merge* operation will combine two vectors into a single vector. A *compress* operation will map elements at a constant stride into a vector. All of these operations, of course, require a certain amount of time, which adds to the overhead of the vector arithmetic operations. Moreover, after the vector arithmetic is done, it may be necessary to store the results in a nonvector fashion. A *scatter* operation, the inverse of gather, stores elements of a vector into positions prescribed by an associated address list. A primary consideration in developing algorithms for vector computers is to have the data arranged so as to minimize the overhead that results from having to use the above data management operations.

Parallel Computers

The basic idea of a parallel computer is that a number of processors work in cooperation on a single task. The motivation is that if it takes one processor an amount of time t to do a task, then p processors can do the task in time t/p. Only for very special situations can this perfect "speedup" be achieved, however, and it is our goal to devise algorithms that can take as much advantage as possible, for a given problem, of multiple processors.

The processors of a parallel computer can range from very simple ones that do only small or limited tasks to very powerful vector processors. Most of our discussions will be directed towards the case in which the processors are complete sequential processors of moderate power, although attention will also be paid to having vector processors.

MIMD and SIMD Machines

A first important dichotomy in parallel systems is how the processors are controlled. In a Single-Instruction-Multiple-Data (SIMD) system, all processors are under the control of a master processor, called the *controller*, and the individual processors all do the same instruction (or nothing) at a given time. Thus, there is a single instruction stream operating on multiple data streams, one for each processor. The Illiac IV, the first large parallel system (which was completed in the early 1970s), was an SIMD machine. The ICL DAP, a commercial machine introduced in England in 1977, the Goodyear MPP, especially constructed for NASA in the early 1980s, and the Connection Machine, a commercial machine of the mid-1980s, are also machines of SIMD type, although the individual processors are relatively simple 1-bit machines: 4096 in the DAP, 16,484 in the MPP, and 64,936 in the Connection Machine. Vector computers may also be conceptually included in the class of SIMD machines by considering the elements of a vector as being processed individually under the control of a vector hardware instruction.

Most parallel computers built since the Illiac IV are Multiple-Instruction-Multiple-Data (MIMD) systems. Here, the individual processors run under the control of their own program, which allows great flexibility in the tasks the processors are doing at any given time. It also introduces the problem of synchronization. In an SIMD system, synchronization of the individual processors is carried out by the controller, but in an MIMD system other mechanisms must be used to ensure that the processors are doing their tasks in the correct order with the correct data. Synchronization will be discussed more in later sections.

Shared versus Local Memory

Another important dichotomy in parallel computers is *shared* versus *local* memory. A shared memory system is illustrated in Figure 1.1-7. Here, all the processors have access to a common memory. (In the sequel, we will use the terms "shared memory" and "common memory" interchangeably.) Each processor can also have its own local memory for program code and intermediate results. The common memory would then be used for data and results that are needed by more than one processor. All communication between individual processors is through the common memory. A major advantage of a shared memory system is potentially very rapid communication of data between processors. A serious disadvantage is that different processors may wish to use the common memory simultaneously, in which case there will be a delay until the memory is free. This delay, called *contention time*, can increase as the number of processors increases.

An alternative to shared memory systems are local memory systems, in which each processor can address only its own memory. Communication between processors takes place by *message passing*, in which data or other information are transferred between processors.

Interconnection Schemes

Probably the most important and interesting aspect of parallel computers is how the individual processors communicate with one another. This is particularly important for systems in which the processors have only local memory, but it is also important for shared memory systems since the connection to the shared memory can be implemented by different communication schemes. We shall next discuss briefly a number of the more common interconnection schemes.

Completely Connected. In a completely connected system, each processor has a direct connection to every other processor. This is illustrated

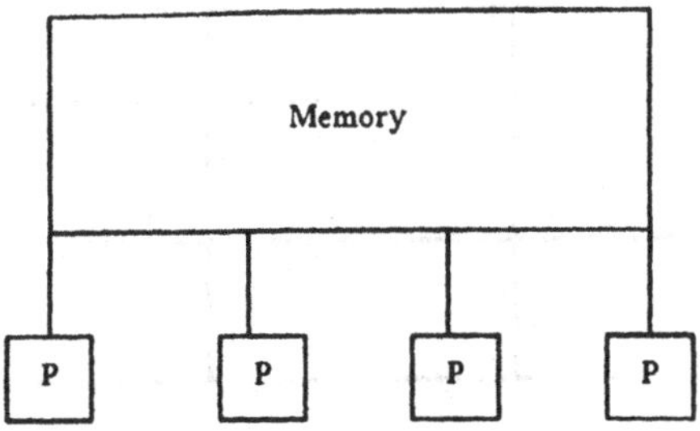

Figure 1.1-7. A shared memory system.

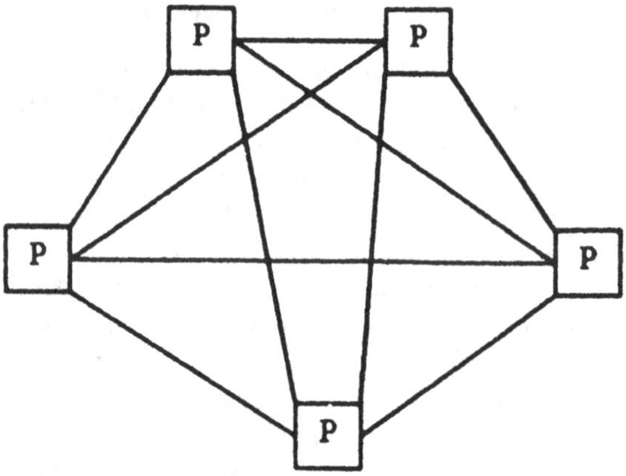

Figure 1.1-8. A completely connected system.

in Figure 1.1-8. A completely connected system of p processors requires $p - 1$ lines emanating from each processor, which is impractical if p is large.

Crossbar Switch. Another approach to a completely connected system is through a *crossbar switch* as illustrated in Figure 1.1-9. As shown there, each processor can be connected to each memory, in principle, through switches that make the connection. This has the advantage of allowing any processor access to any memory with a small number of connection lines. But the number of switches to connect p processors and p memories is p^2, which becomes impractical for large p. One early parallel system, the C.mmp developed at Carnegie-Mellon University in the early 1970s, used this scheme to connect 16 PDP-11 minicomputers.

Bus and Ring. A bus network is illustrated in Figure 1.1-10. Here, all processors are connected by a (high-speed) bus. An advantage is a very

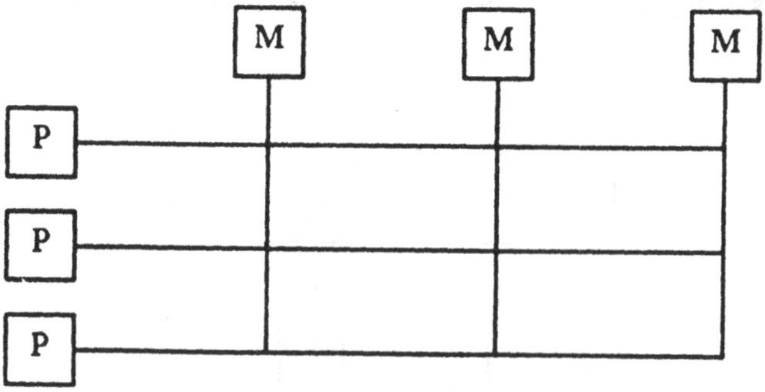

Figure 1.1-9. A crossbar switch.

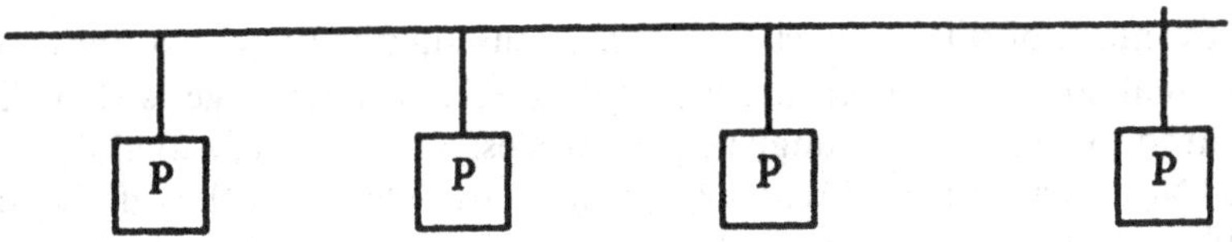

Figure 1.1-10. A bus network.

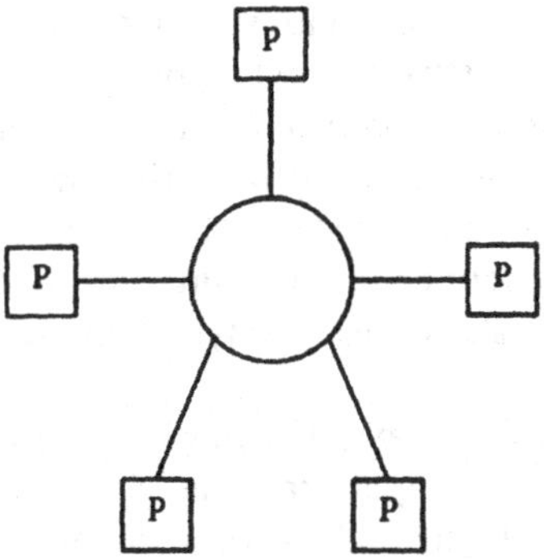

Figure 1.1-11. A ring network.

small number of connection lines, but there may be contention (*bus contention*) for use of the bus by different processors; this can become a severe problem as the number of processors increases.

A *ring network* is a closed bus network as illustrated in Figure 1.1-11. Here data move around the ring and are available to each processor in turn. Several parallel computers have used bus or ring connections of various types. Some systems have used a bus to connect processors to a global memory; an example of the mid 1980s is the Flexible Computer Corporation FLEX/32, a system with 20 processors. Other systems have used a bus to implement a local memory message passing system. An example was ZMOB, an experimental system developed at the University of Maryland in the early 1980s.

Mesh Connection. One of the most popular interconnection schemes historically has been to have each processor connected to only a few neighboring processors. The simplest example of this is a *linear array* illustrated in Figure 1.1-12. Here, each processor is connected to two nearest neighbors (except the end processors, which are connected to only one).

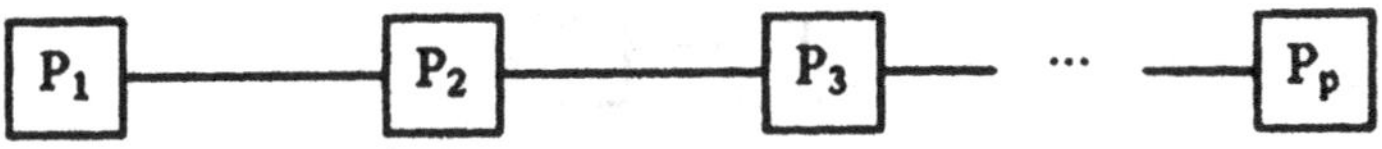

Figure 1.1-12. A linear array.

An advantage of this connection pattern is its simplicity, with at most two lines emanating from each processor. A severe disadvantage is that data may need to be passed through several processors to reach its final destination. (Note that this is different from in a bus network, although Figures 1.1-10 and 1.1-12 are rather similar.) For example, in Figure 1.1-12, if processor P_1 wishes to send data to processor P_p, the data must first be sent to P_2, and then transmitted to P_3, and so on. Thus, $p - 1$ transmissions of the data must be made. The maximum number of transmissions that must be made to communicate between any two processors of the system is called the *communication length* or *diameter* of the system. The communication length of a linear array is shortened by a ring array, illustrated in Figure 1.1-13, in which the maximum distance between processors is now about half of that for a linear connection. Communication in a ring array can be either *unidirectional* (data can move only clockwise, say, in Figure 1.1-13) or *bidirectional.*

Most mesh-connected arrays that have actually been built have used a two-dimensional connection pattern. One of the simplest such connection schemes is illustrated in Figure 1.1-14, in which the processors are laid out in a regular two-dimensional grid and each processor is connected to its north, south, east, and west neighbors. In addition, the edge processors can be connected in a wrap-around fashion. This north–south–east–west connection pattern was used by the Illiac IV, for 64 processors arranged in an 8×8 array.

The connection pattern illustrated in Figure 1.1-14 again has the virtue of simplicity. It also has the same disadvantage of a linear array in that transmission of data between distant processors must pass through a succession of intermediate processors. The communication length for p processors arranged in a square array is $O(\sqrt{p})$. This communication problem can be alleviated to some extent by adding still more connections, called *local links.* For example, in Figure 1.1-14, each processor could also be connected to four additional processors in the northeast, southeast, southwest, and northwest directions. Or, one could consider a three-dimensional

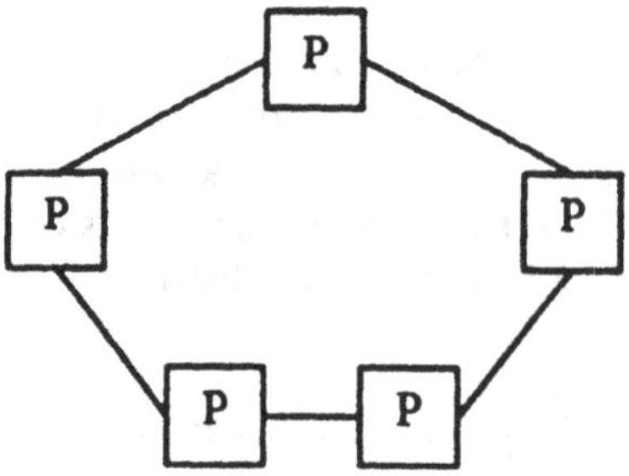

Figure 1.1-13. A ring array.

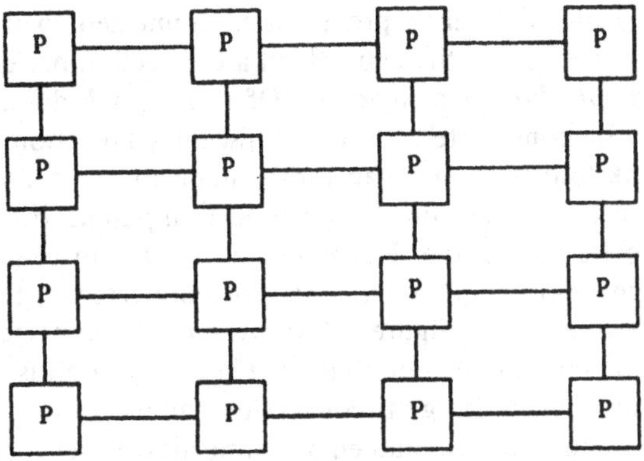

Figure 1.1-14. A mesh-connected array.

array of processors where each processor is connected to its six nearest neighbors. Clearly, the addition of more local links leads to faster average communication but at the expense of additional complexity.

Hypercube. An interesting variation of the local connection principle is to consider, conceptually, local connections in higher dimensions. Consider first the connection pattern in three dimensions illustrated in Figure 1.1-15. Here, the processors are vertices of a cube in 3-space and the edges of the cube are the local links between processors. Thus, in Figure 1.1-15, each processor is connected to its three nearest neighbors in the sense of nearest vertices on the cube.

Now imagine the analogous connection scheme using a cube in k dimensions. Again, the processors would be visualized as the 2^k vertices of

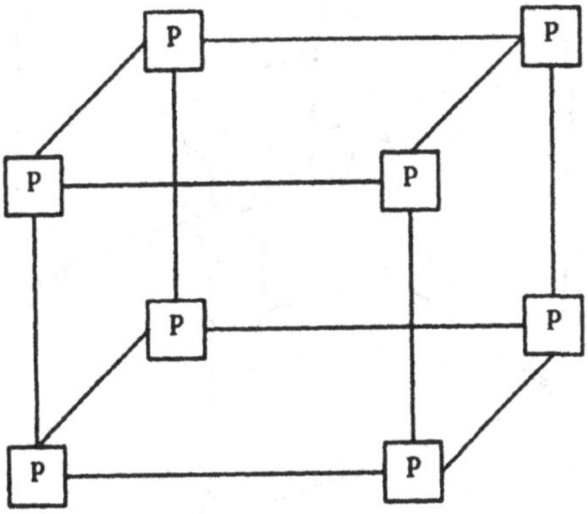

Figure 1.1-15. A 3-cube connection.

this k-dimensional cube. Each processor is connected to its k adjacent vertices, along the edges of the cube. Such a connection pattern is called a *hypercube* or *binary k-cube* connection. Of course, a k-dimensional cube cannot actually be constructed for $k > 3$ and the connection pattern must be mapped back into no more than three dimensions for fabrication. For example, Figure 1.1-15 also shows the connection pattern if the processors are assumed to lie in a plane. For a 4-cube, a cube in four dimensions, there are 16 processors, with each processor connected to four others. It turns out in this case that Figure 1.1-14 of a mesh-connected array also shows the 4-cube interconnection pattern. Figure 1.1-16 illustrates a three-dimensional way of visualizing the connection pattern for a 4-cube and also shows that the 4-cube can be obtained by connecting corresponding vertices of two 3-cubes. In general, we can construct a k-cube by connecting all corresponding processors of two $(k-1)$-cubes.

In the hypercube connection scheme, the number of connections from each processor grows as the number of processors increases and the communication length is only $\log p$. (Here, and throughout, "log" denotes $\log_2$.) For example, for 64 processors—a 6-cube—each processor is connected to six other processors and the communication length is 6, while for 1024 processors—a 10-cube—each processor is connected to ten other processors and the communication length is 10. Moreover, the hypercube contains some of the other connection patterns that have been discussed. For example, ring or mesh-connected arrays can be included by ignoring some of the local links. On the other hand, as the size of the cube is increased,

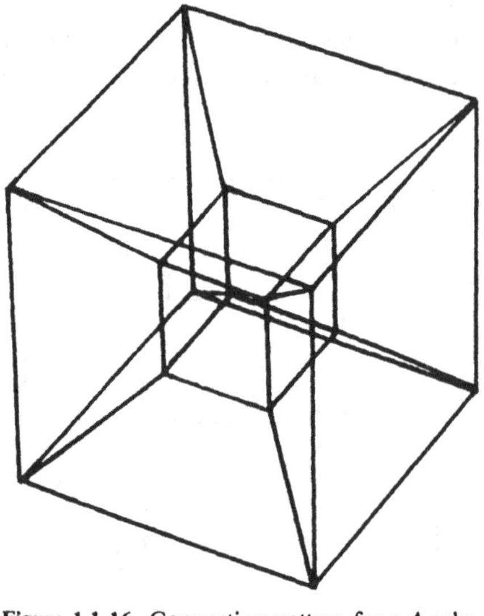

Figure 1.1-16. Connection pattern for a 4-cube.

the complexity and the number of lines emanating from each processor also increase and a practical limit to the cube size will eventually be reached.

Several systems use the hypercube connection pattern. These include the Cosmic Cube developed at the California Institute of Technology in the early 1980s and which motivated commercial versions built by Intel Corp. (the iPSC), Ncube Corp., and others.

Switching Networks. A rather general way of connecting processors, or connecting processors to memories, is by means of a *switching network.* (Switching networks are the means of connecting telephones to one another. Consider the problem of connecting all the telephones in the country by any of the previous schemes.) A simple switching network is depicted in Figure 1.1-17. On the left are shown eight processors and on the right are eight memories. Each box represents a two-way switch and the lines are the transmission links. By means of this switching network each of the processors can address any of the memories. For example, suppose P_1 wishes to address M_8. Switch 1,1 is then set to accept the link from P_1 and set the path to Switch 2,2, which sets the path to Switch 3,4, which sets the path to M_8.

Figure 1.1-17 represents a switching network implementation of a shared memory system, in the sense that each processor can access each memory. Alternatively, the memories on the right could be the processors themselves, as indicated by the processor numbers in parentheses. In this case, the figure would depict a message-passing local memory system.

Using the two-way switches shown in Figure 1.1-17, we would need $p/2$ switches at each switching stage and $\log p$ stages for a total of $\frac{1}{2}p \log p$ switches. This compares very favorably with the p^2 switches needed for the

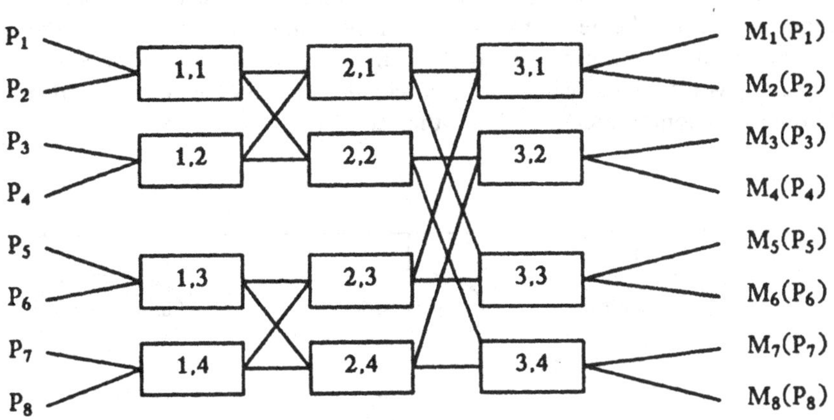

Figure 1.1-17. A switching network.

crossbar switch of Figure 1.1-9; for example, with $p = 2^{10}$, only 5×2^{10} switches would be needed, as compared with 2^{20}.

Several parallel systems have been built or designed using switching network connections (not necessarily of the form shown in Figure 1.1-17). These include the Bolt, Beranek and Newman, Inc. Butterfly and the Ultracomputer at New York University.

Hybrid Schemes. As pointed out in the discussion above, each connection scheme has certain advantages and disadvantages. This motivates the possibility of combining two or more schemes so as to obtain the major advantages of each while minimizing the disadvantages. For example, assume that the processors in the mesh-connected array of Figure 1.1-14 are also connected by a bus. Then communication between nearby processors can take place on the local links, thereby freeing the bus of this amount of traffic, while communication between more distant processors can use the bus. The Finite Element Machine developed at NASA's Langley Research Center in the late 1970s was a hybrid system of this type. Another example is the Connection Machine, in which groups of 16 processors, together with their memories, are implemented on a single chip in such a way that these processors are completely connected. These chips are connected in a hypercube fashion. A variety of other hybrid schemes could be described.

Clusters. Somewhat related to hybrid schemes is *clustering.* A cluster scheme is illustrated in Figure 1.1-18. Here there are n clusters, each consisting of m processors. Within each cluster, the processors are connected in some fashion (any of the previous schemes could be used), and then the clusters are connected by a bus. The communication within each cluster is called *local* while communication between clusters is called *global.* The hope in such a scheme is that there will be a suitable balancing of these two types of communication; that is, most communication for a given processor will be local within its own cluster and less frequently a cluster will need to communicate with another cluster.

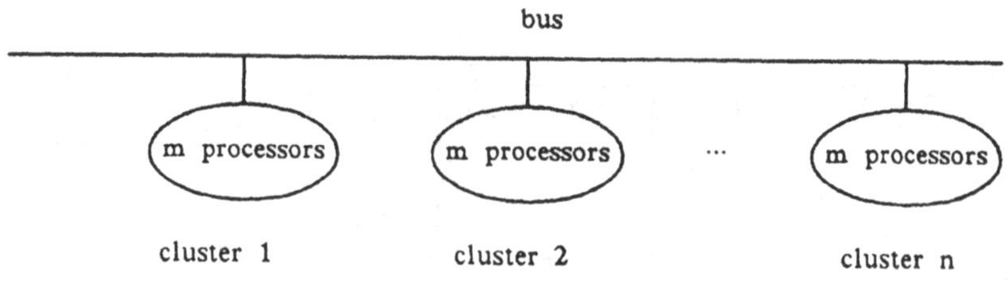

Figure 1.1-18. A cluster connection.

Clearly, there is a large number of ways a cluster scheme could be implemented. Within a cluster, the connections could be by bus, ring, mesh, hypercube, and so on. The connections between clusters could also use any of these schemes rather than the bus of Figure 1.1-18. Moreover, the clustering concept can be applied repeatedly to obtain clusters of clusters of clusters, and so on. The Cm* constructed at Carnegie-Mellon University in the mid 1970s was an early example of a system that used clustering. A current example is the Cedar system being developed at the University of Illinois.

Reconfigurable Schemes. Another way to attempt to overcome the limitations of a single communication scheme is to have the ability to *reconfigure* the connection pattern. This could be done either statically at the outset of a given program or dynamically in the middle of a program and under program control. The TRAC at the University of Texas—Austin and the Pringle at Purdue University and the University of Washington were developed in the early 1980s to demonstrate the utility of reconfigurable connection schemes.

More on Communication

We next discuss communication in local memory systems in more detail. Consider a typical problem of sending n floating point numbers from the memory of one processor, P_1, to the memory of another processor, P_2. Generally, this communication will be accomplished by a combination of hardware and software, and a typical scenario might be the following. First, the data are loaded into a buffer memory or collected into contiguous locations in memory. Then a *send* command will be executed to transfer the data to a buffer or memory of P_2. P_2 will execute a *receive* command and the data will be routed to their final location in the memory of P_2. Coprocessors may be available to relieve the main processors of much of this work.

Many details (largely dependent on the system) have been omitted in the above simplified description, but the main points are that to send the data, they must first be collected from the memory of the sending processor, information must be provided as to where they are to be sent, the data must be physically transmitted between the processors, and, finally, they must be put in the correct memory locations of the receiving processor. On many systems, the time for this communication is approximated by

$$t = s + \alpha n \tag{1.1.5}$$

where s is a start-up time and α is the incremental time necessary for each of the n words to be sent. Note that this has the same form as the time for vector instructions in (1.1.1). On local memory systems in which communication is carried out on local links between neighboring processors, it may be necessary for a message to pass through many different processors before reaching its final destination. Thus, if (1.1.5) represents the time for communication between neighbor processors than the total communication time will be much larger.

A common requirement is to send data from one processor to all others, called a *broadcast.* We illustrate one way to do this on a hypercube system when a processor can send to only one other processor at a time. Figure 1.1-19a depicts a *spanning tree* (or minimal spanning tree) of an eight-processor hypercube with the processors numbered as in (b). At the first time step, processor 1 sends to processor 2. At the second time step, processor 1 sends to processor 3 and processor 2 sends to processor 4. At the third time step, processors 1, 2, 3, and 4 send to processors 5, 6, 7, and 8, as indicated. If there are $p = 2^d$ processors, then $d = \log p$ time steps are required.

Parallel-Vector Systems

We end this section with a short discussion of parallel systems in which the processors are vector computers. Such parallel-vector systems are the current commercially available supercomputers, and this trend will probably continue into the foreseeable future. The CRAY X-MP series was introduced in 1982 with two processors, and with four processors in 1984. It is envisioned to have up to 16 processors in the near future (perhaps under the designation Y-MP). The CRAY-2 has four processors, with additional processors likely. The ETA-10, the successor to the CDC CYBER 200 series, became operational in 1987 and is designed for eight processors.

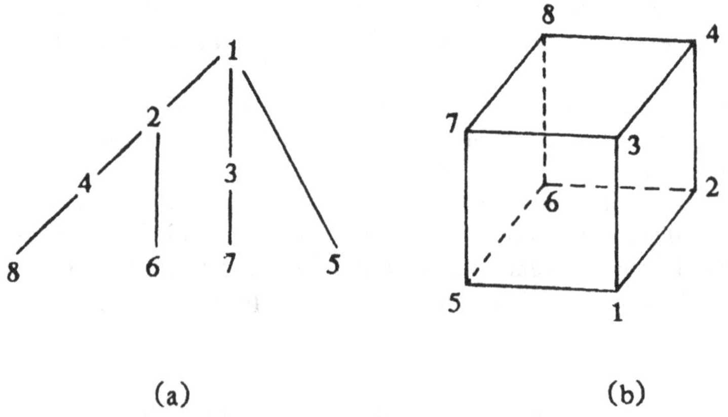

Figure 1.1-19. Spanning tree broadcast.

Parallel-vector systems are also being produced below the supercomputer level. The Intel iPSC hypercube is available with vector processors, and Alliant Corp. offers a system of eight vector processors.

References and Extensions 1.1

1. There are a number of books or anthologies on the architecture of vector computers. Kogge [1981] gives a detailed discussion of pipelining and its use in vector computers. Hockney and Jesshope [1981] discuss the CRAY-1 and CYBER 205, as well as the half-performance length, $N_{1/2}$, and related matters. (An extension of the $N_{1/2}$ concept to parallel machines is given in Hockney [1987].) More recent treatments include Fernbach [1986], which gives further information on CRAY computers as well as Japanese vector computers manufactured by Hitachi, Fujitsu and NEC, and Stone [1987], which covers design considerations for high performance computers. See also Chen [1984] and Larson [1984] for the CRAY X-MP and Lincoln [1982] for the CYBER 205.
2. Points of specific interest for particular vector computers are addressed in a number of papers. The CRAY X-MP allows chaining of both loads and stores and Dongarra and Hinds [1985] observe that for certain operations the X-MP acts as a memory to memory machine with the vector registers playing the role of storage buffers. Bucher [1983] gives performance measurements for CRAYs and other supercomputers. Hack [1986] discusses the effect on the overall computation rate of overlapping scalar and vector computations. Performance measurements on the Intel, Ncube, and Ametak hypercubes are given in Dunigan [1987].
3. Hwang and Briggs [1984] give detailed discussions of the architecture of parallel computers. Other books or anthologies dealing with various aspects of parallel computer architecture include Hockney and Jesshope [1981], Snyder *et al* [1985], Uhr [1984], and Paker [1983]. Papers discussing particular machines include Gottlieb *et al.* [1983] on the New York University Ultracomputer, Seitz [1985] on the Cosmic Cube, Storaasli *et al.* [1982] on the Finite Element Machine, and Pfister *et al.* [1985] on the IBM RP3. The dichotomy of SIMD and MIMD parallel computers was given in Flynn [1966].
4. Starting in about 1983, a number of commercial vector and/or parallel systems began to be available at relatively modest prices (in the range of \$100,000-\$1,000,000, as opposed to the roughly \$10,000,000 price of a supercomputer). Some of these are the Convex C-1, a vector computer, the Alliant FX/8, which has eight vector processors, the Flexible Computer Corp. Flex/32, the Encore, and the Sequent. The latter three are shared memory systems of roughly 8-20 sequential processors. Some performance data for an Alliant FX/8 are given in Abu-Sufah and Malony [1986].
5. Another approach to high-speed computing has been through add-on array processors such as those manufactured by Floating Point Systems, Inc. Here, a mini or mainframe computer controls the attached processor, which usually does intensive highly vectorized computation. See, for example, Clementi *et al.* [1987]

for a description of an attached processor supercomputer system. Recently, Floating Point Systems has offered a parallel system of its array processors connected in a hypercube fashion. A 16-processor system is rated at a peak speed of 256 mflops, which is close to supercomputer power.

6. Two other approaches to parallel computing have been the topic of extensive research. The first utilizes the idea of "dataflow," in which computation is controlled by the flow of data and is performed when the required data are available; for a recent review, see Veen [1986]. The second approach is that of a "systolic array," which is a lattice of usually small specialized processors. Computation proceeds by data moving through the array; for a good discussion, see Kung [1982].
7. The spanning tree approach to broadcasting in a hypercube is given in Geist and Heath [1986]. A detailed study of the topological properties of hypercubes is given in Saad and Schultz [1985].
8. A number of analyses of communication in parallel systems have been performed. For example, Saad and Schultz [1986] consider communication times for several model architectures including a bus, ring, two-dimensional grid, hypercube, and a switch. The basic data transfer operations they consider include one processor to another, one processor to all others (broadcast), every processor to every other processor (broadcast from each processor), scattering data from one processor to all others (or gathering data from all processors to one processor), and multiscattering or multigathering (scattering from every processor to all other processors). They give detailed timing estimates based on assumptions about the architectures (for example, start-up time, transmission time, etc.) and about different data transmission algorithms. For related results, see Johnsson [1985a, 1987] and Fox and Furmanski [1987]. These latter papers describe hypercube communication algorithms particularly useful for matrix computations.

1.2. Basic Concepts of Parallelism and Vectorization

In this section we will collect a number of basic concepts and measures of parallelism and illustrate them with two very simple problems. We will assume at the beginning that we have a parallel system consisting of p processors. Later, we will discuss how the parallel concepts apply to vector computers. We begin with the following definition.

1.2.1. Definition. The *degree of parallelism* of a numerical algorithm is the number of operations in the algorithm that can be done in parallel.

We will illustrate this definition in a number of ways and, in the process, refine it.

Consider first the problem of adding two n-vectors $\mathbf{a}$ and $\mathbf{b}$. The additions

$$a_i + b_i, \qquad i = 1, \ldots, n \tag{1.2.1}$$

are independent and can be done in parallel. Thus, the degree of parallelism of this algorithm is n. Note that the degree of parallelism is independent of the number of processors in our system; it is an intrinsic measure of the parallelism of the algorithm. Of course, the number of processors will affect the time required to complete the computation. For example, if $n = 1000$ and the number of processors is $p = 1000$, then (1.2.1) can be done in one time step, but if $p = 10$, we will need 100 time steps.

Next, consider the problem of summing n numbers $a_1, \ldots, a_n$. The usual serial algorithm

$$s = a_1, \qquad s \leftarrow s + a_i, \qquad i = 2, \ldots, n \tag{1.2.2}$$

is unsuitable for parallel computation. However, there is a good deal of parallelism in the problem itself. This is shown in Figure 1.2-1 by the addition of eight numbers in three stages. In the first stage, four additions are done in parallel, then two are done in the next stage, and finally one in the last stage. This illustrates the general principal of *divide and conquer*. We have divided the summation problem into smaller problems, which can be done independently.

The graph of Figure 1.2-1 is called a *fan-in graph* and is widely applicable, as we shall see in the sequel. In particular, the same idea can be used to obtain the product $a_1 a_2 \ldots a_n$ of n numbers; in Figure 1.2-1, simply replace + by ×. Similarly, to find the maximum of n numbers $a_1, \ldots, a_n$, we can replace the + operation by max; for example, in Figure 1.2-1, $a_1 + a_2$ would be replaced by $\max(a_1, a_2)$, and so on. We note that the fan-in graph of Figure 1.2.-1 is a *binary tree* and the fan-in operation is sometimes called a *tree operation.*

For $n = 2^q$ numbers, the fan-in algorithm has $q = \log n$ stages with $n/2$ additions at the first stage, $n/4$ at the second, and so on down to a single addition at the last stage. Clearly, the degree of parallelism at the first stage is $n/2$, at the second stage $n/4$, and so on. This suggests that we modify Definition 1.2.1 in order to have a parallel measure of an entire algorithm when each of its stages have differing degrees of parallelism.

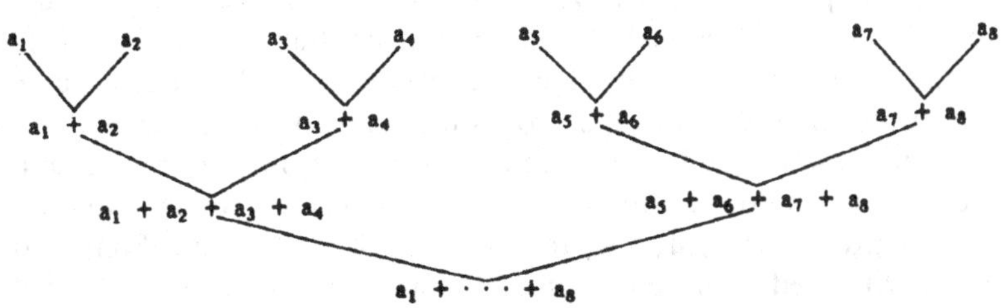

Figure 1.2-1. Fan-in for addition.

1.2.2. Definition. The *average degree of parallelism* of an algorithm is the total number of operations in the algorithm divided by the number of stages.

In the fan-in algorithm, the average degree of parallelism is

$$\frac{1}{q}\left(\frac{n}{2}+\frac{n}{4}+\cdots+1\right)=\frac{2^q-1}{q}=\frac{n-1}{\log n}=O\left(\frac{n}{\log n}\right) \tag{1.2.3}$$

while for the addition of two n vectors the average degree of parallelism is n, the same as the degree of parallelism. The latter algorithm exhibits "perfect" parallelism, while the fan-in algorithm degrades from this perfection by the factor $\log n$. Still, the fan-in algorithm is quite parallel, especially when compared with the serial algorithm (1.2.2), for which the average degree of parallelism is $(n-1)/(n-1)=1$.

Related to the degree of parallelism is the idea of *granularity. Large-scale granularity* means large tasks that can be performed independently in parallel. An example is the solution of six different large systems of linear equations, whose solutions will be combined at a later stage of the computation. *Small-scale granularity* means small tasks that can be performed in parallel; an example is the addition of two vectors where each task is the addition of two scalars.

Speedup

There are two other common measures of parallelism that we now introduce.

1.2.3. Definition. The *speedup* of a parallel algorithm is

$$S_p=\frac{\text{execution time for a single processor}}{\text{execution time using } p \text{ processors}} \tag{1.2.4}$$

For the problem of vector addition, we would expect that $S_p=p$, a perfect speedup. We note, however, that Definition 1.2.3 assumes the actual computation times. This makes it more realistic, but also more difficult to use without having these times. Let us consider the addition of n numbers by the fan-in algorithm on $n/2$ processors with local memories. Assume that a_1 and a_2 are stored in processor 1, a_3 and a_4 in processor 2, and so on. Before we can do the additions at the second stage, we need to transfer a_3+a_4 to processor 1, a_5+a_6 to processor 2, and so on. Similar data transfers will need to be made at each stage, and, of course, these data transfers increase the total time of the algorithm. Assume that the time for addition is t and the time for data transfers is αt, where α will usually be greater than 1. Then, ignoring other costs, we have for the addition algorithm

$$S_p = \frac{(n-1)t}{(\log n)(1+\alpha)t} = \frac{1}{(1+\alpha)}\frac{(n-1)}{\log n} = \frac{1}{(1+\alpha)}\frac{(2p-1)}{(1+\log p)} \qquad (1.2.5)$$

since $p = n/2$. We note that the speedup in this case is the degree of parallelism degraded by the factor $(1+\alpha)^{-1}$. If α is approximately unity, so that communication takes about as much time as arithmetic, then the speedup is roughly halved from that of the ideal with $\alpha = 0$. On the other hand, if α is large, say $\alpha = 10$, then communication time dominates the computation, and the speedup is reduced accordingly.

The speedup S_p is a measure of how a given algorithm compares with itself on one and p processors. However, the parallel algorithm may not be the best algorithm on a single processor, as we will see in several cases in later chapters. Hence, a better measure of what is gained by parallel computation is given by the following.

1.2.4. DEFINITION. The *speedup of a parallel algorithm over the best serial algorithm* is

$$S'_p = \frac{\text{execution time on a single processor of fastest serial algorithm}}{\text{execution time of the parallel algorithm on } p \text{ processors}}$$

Related to the speedup is the efficiency of a parallel algorithm.

1.2.5. DEFINITION. The *efficiency* of a parallel algorithm with respect to itself is

$$E_p = \frac{S_p}{p}$$

The *efficiency* of a parallel algorithm with respect to the best serial algorithm is

$$E'_p = \frac{S'_p}{p}$$

Since $S_p \leqslant p$, and $S'_p \leqslant S_p$ we have $E'_p \leqslant E_p \leqslant 1$. In the case in which the algorithm has perfect speedup, $S_p = p$, then $E_p = 1$.

One goal in the development of parallel algorithms is to achieve as large a speedup as possible; ideally, $S_p' = p$. However, we have already seen in the case of addition of n numbers that this ideal is not always possible. Indeed, the ideal speedup is obtainable only for essentially trivial problems. The main factors that cause a degradation from perfect speedup are as follows:

1. Lack of a perfect degree of parallelism in the algorithm and/or lack of perfect load balancing;
2. Communication, contention, and synchronization time.

We discuss these in somewhat more detail, beginning with the second. We considered previously the example of communication between processors in the case of addition of n numbers. In general, in a local memory system exchange of data between processors will be necessary at various times during an overall computation, and to the extent that processors are not doing useful computation during the communication, this constitutes an overhead that we shall try to minimize. In shared memory systems, there may be contention delays (see Section 1.1) that play the same role as communication time: processors are idle or underutilized while waiting to obtain the data necessary to continue.

Synchronization is necessary when certain parts of a computation must be completed before the overall computation can proceed. There are two aspects of synchronization that contribute to overhead. The first is the time required to do the synchronization; usually this requires that all processors do certain checks. The second aspect is that some, or even almost all, processors may become idle, waiting for clearance to proceed with the computation. We will see several examples of synchronization in later chapters.

Although synchronization, communication, and memory contention delays are quite different, their effect on the overall computation is the same: a delay while data are made ready to continue the computation. Therefore, we will sometimes consider these delay factors together according to the following.

1.2.6. Definition. The *data ready time* is the delay caused by communication, contention or synchronization in order that the data necessary to continue the computation is ready in the proper storage locations.

We next turn to the lack of a perfect degree of parallelism, which can result in different ways. In the addition of n numbers, we saw that the first stage had a perfect degree of parallelism but that this was halved in each subsequent stage; a gradual degradation of the degree of parallelism is typical in elimination algorithms for the solution of linear systems of equations, as we shall see in Chapter 2. For most problems, there will be a mix of three different degrees of parallelism, which we can term perfect, partial, and none, the latter being those portions of the algorithm that can use only a single processor. But even if there is a perfect degree of parallelism in the algorithm, it may be degraded by the problem of load balancing on a given parallel system. By *load balancing* we mean the assignment of tasks to the processors of the system so as to keep each processor doing useful work as much as possible. This assignment is sometimes called the *mapping problem*; that is, we wish to map the problem and the algorithm onto the processors to achieve maximum load balancing. Note that an algorithm may have intrinsically a high degree of parallelism but load balancing on a particular system may be difficult. For example, if we are adding vectors of length nine on a system of eight processors, we have a mismatch between the perfect degree of parallelism of the problem and the system on which it is implemented.

Load balancing may be done either statically or dynamically. In *static load balancing*, tasks (and, perhaps, data for local memory systems) are assigned to processors at the beginning of a computation. In *dynamic load balancing*, tasks (and data) are assigned to processors as the computation proceeds. A useful concept for dynamic load balancing is that of a *pool of tasks*, from which a processor obtains its next task when it is ready to do so. In general, dynamic load balancing is more efficiently implemented on shared memory systems than on local memory systems since, on the latter, data transfers between local memories may also be required as part of a task assignment.

We next consider a formal model of speedup, in which

$$S_p = \frac{T_1}{(\alpha_1 + \alpha_2/k + \alpha_3/p)T_1 + t_d} \tag{1.2.6}$$

where T_1 is the time for a single processor, α_1 is the fraction of operations done with one processor, α_2 is the fraction of operations done with average degree of parallelism $k < p$, α_3 is the fraction of operations done with degree of parallelism p, and t_d is the total time required for data ready delay. We will discuss several special cases of (1.2.6).

Case 1. $\alpha_1 = \alpha_2 = 0$, $\alpha_3 = 1$, $t_d = 0$. Here, $S_p = p$, a perfect speedup. The assumptions are that all operations are done with a perfect degree of parallelism and there are no delays.

Case 2. $\alpha_1 = \alpha_3 = 0$, $\alpha_2 = 1$, $t_d = 0$. Now, $S_p = k < p$ and the speedup is just the average degree of parallelism.

Case 3. $\alpha_2 = 0$, $t_d = 0$, $\alpha_1 = \alpha$, $\alpha_3 = 1 - \alpha$. In this case,

$$S_p = \frac{1}{\alpha + (1-\alpha)/p} \tag{1.2.7}$$

which is known as *Ware's Law* or *Amdahl's Law.* The assumption is that all operations are done either with a maximum degree of parallelism or none, and there are no delays. Although (1.2.7) is a very simplified model, it is instructive. Suppose that in a given problem, half of the operations can be done in parallel and the other half not. Then $\alpha = 1/2$ and (1.2.7) becomes

$$S_p = \frac{2}{(1 + p^{-1})} < 2$$

That is, no matter how many processors there are, and ignoring all communication, synchronization, and contention delays, the speedup is always less than 2. More generally, Figure 1.2-2 gives a plot of (1.2.7) as a function of α for $p = 100$, a nominal value. Note the very rapid decrease of S_p for small values of α. If even 1% of the operations can be done only on a single processor, the speedup is halved from 100 to 50.

Case 4. t_d Large. This case is meant to illustrate the fact that, no matter what the values of α_1, α_2, and α_3, for sufficiently large t_d we can have $S_p < 1$. Thus, in a problem with a lot of communication, contention, or synchronization it is possible that using more than one processor is actually worse than just a single processor. This is a rather extreme case, but for

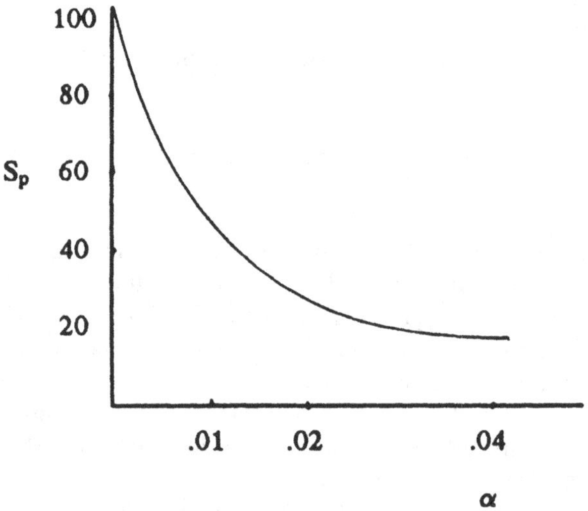

Figure 1.2-2. Degradation of speed-up.

many problems one does reach a point of diminishing returns in terms of employing additional processors.

We return now to the definitions 1.2.3 and 1.2.4 of speedup. There are several difficulties in applying these definitions in practice. On parallel machines with local memory, the more processors that are used the larger the problem that can be run. In particular, problems that can be run on a large number of processors may not fit into the memory of a single processor so that the time on a single processor would have to include I/O time to secondary memory. In one sense, this is an entirely legitimate measure of speed-up, but it may not be an appropriate one for some considerations. A related problem is that we expect to need a parallel machine only for those problems too large to run in a feasible time on a single processor. It follows that studies of speed-up of an algorithm should be done on large problems and, perhaps, on a relatively large number of processors.

Another measure of speedup, which can potentially handle both of the above problems, is to measure the computation rate as the size of the problem *and* the number of processors increases. Consider, for example, the problem of matrix-vector multiplication $A\mathbf{x}$, which will be discussed in more detail in the next section. If A is $n \times n$, then $2n^2 - n$ operations are required (n^2 multiplications and $n^2 - n$ additions). Suppose, for a nominal problem size, the computation runs at the rate of 1 mflop on a single processor. Then if we double n, the number of operations increases by a factor of about 4, for large n, and if this problem runs on four processors at a rate of 4 mflops we have achieved perfect speed-up. More generally, if a problem size is determined by a parameter n, and the operation count is $f(n)$, we can plot the computation rate (in mflops, say) as n increases and $p = \alpha f(n)$; that is, the number of processors remains proportional to the number of operations. This is illustrated in Figure 1.2.-3. In order to use this approach, we would choose a problem size n_1, suitable for a single

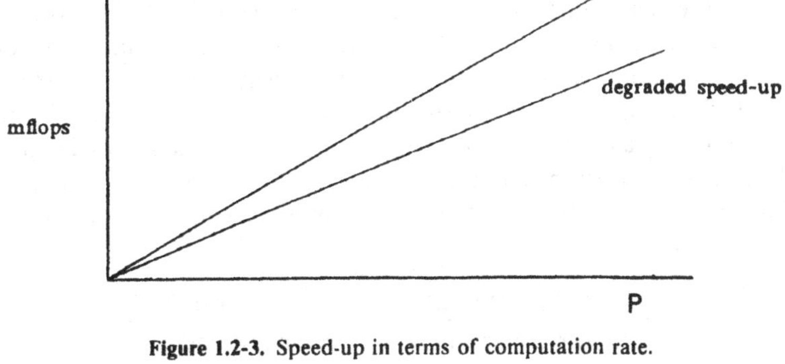

Figure 1.2-3. Speed-up in terms of computation rate.

processor. Then the commensurate problem size for p processors, n_p, would satisfy $f(n_p) = pf(n_1)$ so that the number of operations done on p processors is p times that for a single processor.

Vector Computers

So far in this section, we have limited our discussion to parallel computers, but much of what we have done has a natural analog or interpretation for vector computers. On the other hand, we will also need some additional definitions.

1.2.7. DEFINITION. The *degree of vectorization* of a computation on a vector computer is the vector length used. If different vector lengths are used in different parts of the computation, then the *average degree* is the average vector length used.

We note that the degree of parallelism in a problem is not necessarily related to the degree of vectorization. As a simple example, consider the evaluation of n functions $f_1(x_1), \ldots, f_n(x_n)$, and assume that they can be evaluated in the same amount of time. Then, the degree of parallelism of the problem is n. Moreover, if the functions are all identical and are to be evaluated at different arguments x_i, then the evaluations can be done on a vector computer using vectors of length n (see Exercise 1.2-3). Thus, the degree of vectorization is n, the same as the degree of parallelism. However, if the f_i all have a different functional form, so that we cannot vectorize across them, then the degree of vectorization will be only 1, even though the degree of parallelism is still n.

The data ready time for parallel computers has a natural analog for vector computers.

1.2.8. DEFINITION. The *data ready time* on a vector computer is the delay time required to move data to the right positions for vector operations.

For example, as discussed in the previous section, on some vector computers the data must be in sequentially addressable storage locations in memory. Data transfers may be necessary to achieve this and they cause a delay in the computation. For large problems requiring access to external storage devices, such delays can also be included in the data ready time. We note that single processor vector computers are internally synchronized, and thus synchronization is not an issue.

The speedups S_p and S_p' for parallel computers have natural analogs for vector computers:

$$S_v = \frac{\text{time for algorithm using only scalar arithmetic}}{\text{time for algorithm using vector arithmetic}} \tag{1.2.8}$$

$$S_v' = \frac{\text{time for fastest serial algorithm on serial computer}}{\text{time for vector algorithm on vector computer.}} \quad (1.2.9)$$

As with S_p, S_v is an internal measure of the speedup obtained by using vector operations when possible rather than just scalar. S_v' is the more practical definition since it is what people purchasing vector computers will want to know!

The speedup model (1.2.6) can be interpreted for vector computers as follows. Let

$$S_v = \frac{T_1}{(\alpha_1 + \alpha_2/k + \alpha_3/p)T_1 + t_d} \quad (1.2.10)$$

where now T_1 is the time for the problem using scalar arithmetic, p is the speed increase over scalar arithmetic of vector operations of optimum length, α_3 is the fraction of operations that can be done with vectors of optimum length, k is the average speedup of vector operations for vectors of non-optimum length, α_2 is the fraction of operations using vectors of non-optimum length, α_1 is the fraction of operations using scalar arithmetic, and t_d is the total data ready time.

The term "optimum length" used above must be interpreted in the following way. On many vector computers, the computation rate will continue to increase as the vector length increases, at least up to some maximum length. However, for practical purposes, we can say that vector lengths are "optimum" when they are sufficiently long to give, say, 99% or 95% of the maximum rate.

Again, it is instructive to look at the special cases discussed for parallel computers.

Case 1. $\alpha_1 = \alpha_2 = 0$, $\alpha_3 = 1$, $t_d = 0$. Here, all operations are done with vectors of optimum length and with no delays so that S_v is simply the speedup of optimum vector arithmetic over scalar arithmetic. On most vector computers, this is in the range 10–100.

Case 2. $\alpha_1 = 0$, $\alpha_2 = 1$. $\alpha_3 = 0$, $t_d = 0$. Now, the speedup is $k < p$ representing the degradation of optimum speedup caused by using average vector lengths less than optimum.

Case 3. $\alpha_2 = 0$, $t_d = 0$, $\alpha_1 = \alpha$, $\alpha_3 = 1 - \alpha$. In this case, (1.2.10) becomes

$$S_v = \frac{1}{\alpha + (1-\alpha)/p}$$

and the assumption is that a fraction α of operations is done in scalar arithmetic and the rest in optimum vector arithmetic. Figure 1.2-2 again gives the degradation in speedup under the (unreasonable) assumption that vector arithmetic is 100 times faster than scalar. For small speedup ratios, the form of the curve in Figure 1.2-2 remains the same and the important point is that even a very small amount of scalar arithmetic seriously degrades the speedup. Again, the special case $\alpha = 1/2$ is instructive. Here, $S_v < 2$, which says that if 50% of the operations must be done in scalar arithmetic, a speedup of no more than a factor of 2 over a scalar code is possible, even if the vector operations are infinitely fast.

Parallel-Vector Computers

For parallel systems whose processors are vector computers, we must combine the preceding concepts. As discussed in the previous section, many commercial systems in the near future will consist of a relatively small number (4–16) of powerful vector computers. Moreover, many parallel systems with a larger number of slower processors will also contain the capability of vector arithmetic. Efficient use of parallel-vector systems requires, ideally, the assignment to the processors of relatively large tasks which require little communication and synchronization and which can be carried out with a high degree of vectorization. In terms of granularity, our goal for parallel-vector computers is the development of parallel algorithms with large-scale granularity for tasks each of which has small-scale vectorizable granularity. Hence, our goal is not so much a high degree of parallelism as a relatively low degree of parallelism but for large tasks each of which has a high degree of vectorization.

Consistency

It may be possible to devise parallel or vector algorithms that are improvements over a scalar algorithm provided that the problem size remains sufficiently small, but that actually become worse than the scalar algorithm if the problem size becomes too large. We first embody this possibility in the following definition and then give a nontrivial example.

1.2.9. Definition. A vector algorithm for solving a problem of size n is *consistent* with the best serial algorithm for the same problem if $V(n)/S(n)$ is bounded as $n \to \infty$, where $V(n)$ and $S(n)$ are the total number of arithmetic operations in the vector and serial algorithms, respectively. The vector algorithm is *inconsistent* if $V(n)/S(n) \to \infty$ as $n \to \infty$.

A similar definition may be given for parallel algorithms.

Recursive Doubling

We next describe a potentially useful but inconsistent algorithm. Consider again the problem of summing n numbers $a_1, \ldots, a_n$, but suppose that we also wish to have the intermediate sums

$$s_i = s_{i-1} + a_i, \qquad i = 2, \ldots, n, \qquad s_1 = a_1 \tag{1.2.11}$$

If we are doing the calculation (1.2.11) serially, we obtain all the intermediate sums as a by-product of computing s_n. However, the parallel fan-in algorithm of Figure 1.2-1 computes only some of the partial sums. In order to compute all the partial sums in a parallel or vector fashion we proceed as illustrated in Figure 1.2-4, where the columns represent vectors. The same idea can be used for products (Exercise 1.2-2).

In Figure 1.2-4, $s_{ij} = a_i + \cdots + a_j$; hence, the desired partial sums are s_{1j} and these are the elements of the final vector. The first vector addition produces s_1 and s_2 (s_{11} and s_{12}) as well as several intermediate sums. The second vector addition produces s_3 and s_4 and more intermediate sums while the final addition produces s_5, s_6, s_7, and s_8. This recursive doubling algorithm is also known as the *cascade* method for partial sums.

The blanks in the vector operands in Figure 1.2-4 indicate that no operation is to be performed in these positions. Thus, the first vector operation has seven additions, the second has six, and the third has four. For $n = 2^k$, there are k vector additions for vectors of length $n - 2^i$, $i = 0, 1, \ldots, k-1$. Therefore, the average vector length of the addition is

$$\frac{1}{k}\sum_{i=0}^{k-1}(n - 2^i) = \frac{1}{k}[kn - 2^k + 1] = \frac{1}{\log n}[n(\log n - 1) + 1] \tag{1.2.12}$$

We then have the following situation. To generate all the desired sums s_{1j} requires $\log n$ vector or parallel operations with average vector lengths given by (1.2.12). Hence, the total number of results produced in the $\log n$ vector

a_1				s_{11}	s_{11}				s_{11}	s_{11}				s_{11}
a_2		a_1		s_{12}	s_{12}				s_{12}	s_{12}				s_{12}
a_3		a_2		s_{23}	s_{23}		s_{11}		s_{13}	s_{13}				s_{13}
a_4	+	a_3	=	s_{34}	s_{34}	+	s_{12}	=	s_{14}	s_{14}	+		=	s_{14}
a_5		a_4		s_{45}	s_{45}		s_{23}		s_{25}	s_{25}		s_{11}		s_{15}
a_6		a_5		s_{56}	s_{56}		s_{34}		s_{36}	s_{36}		s_{12}		s_{16}
a_7		a_6		s_{67}	s_{67}		s_{45}		s_{47}	s_{47}		s_{13}		s_{17}
a_8		a_7		s_{78}	s_{78}		s_{56}		s_{58}	s_{58}		s_{14}		s_{18}

Figure 1.2-4. Recursive doubling.

operations is $n \log n - n + 1$ as compared with $n - 1$ in the serial computation. Therefore, the algorithm is inconsistent since $(n \log n - n)/n \to \infty$ as $n \to \infty$. But this does not mean that the algorithm is not useful, as we next show.

Suppose that a vector computer performs vector additions with a timing formula of $T = s + \gamma n$ for vectors of length n, and scalar additions in time μ. Then, the time for obtaining the $n - 1$ sums s_{1j}, $j = 2, \ldots, n$, for $n = 2^k$ by the recursive doubling algorithm is, by (1.2.12),

$$T_v(n) \equiv \sum_{i=0}^{k-1} [s + \gamma(n - 2^i)] = ks + \gamma(kn - 2^k + 1)$$

$$= s \log n + \gamma(n \log n - n + 1) \tag{1.2.13}$$

and the scalar time is $T_s(n) = \mu(n - 1)$. Table 1.2-1 gives times for the vector and scalar computations, where it is assumed that $s = 1000$, $\gamma = 10$, and $\mu = 200$ (all in ns). Table 1.2-1 shows that the scalar algorithm is best until about $n = 32$ since the start-up time is dominating the vector operations for small n. For the range $n = 32$ to 2^{20}, recursive doubling is best, but for $n > 2^{21}$ the $n \log n$ term begins to dominate and the scalar algorithm again becomes the best. Thus, for a range of n that includes all sufficiently large but still practical vector lengths the recursive doubling algorithm will be superior. This conclusion depends, of course, on the particular values of s, γ, and μ used in this example. The key factor is the relative sizes of $\gamma(\log n - 1)$ and μ, the coefficients of n.

Data Flow Analysis

As we shall see in subsequent sections, it is many times fairly easy to detect the inherent parallelism in an algorithm. Other times it is not so obvious. A systematic tool for uncovering the parallelism is a *precedence graph* for the computation. This is illustrated in Figure 1.2-5 for the computation

Table 1.2.-1. Recursive Doubling Vector versus Scalar Times

n	$T_v(n)$	$T_s(n)$
8	3170	1400
32	6190	6200
128	15×10^3	25×10^3
1024	0.1×10^6	0.2×10^6
2^{20}	90×10^6	200×10^6
2^{21}	419×10^6	415×10^6

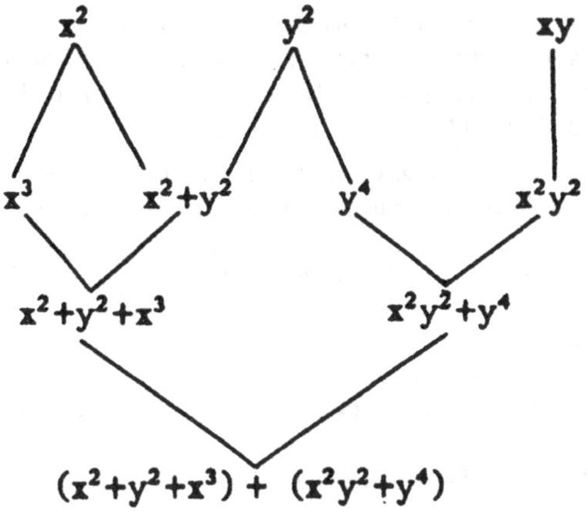

Figure 1.2-5. Precedence graph.

$$f(x, y) = x^2 + y^2 + x^3 + y^4 + x^2y^2 \tag{1.2.14}$$

The serial computation for (1.2.14) might proceed as

$$x, y, x^2, y^2, xy, x^2 + y^2, x^3, (x^2 + y^2) + x^3, y^4, x^2y^2, y^4 + x^2y^2,$$

$$(x^2 + y^2 + x^3) + (y^4 + x^2y^2)$$

which requires ten arithmetic operations. These ten operations can be done in four parallel steps as indicated in Figure 1.2-5.

The use of a graph as in Figure 1.2-5 is known as a *data flow analysis*. It shows what computations must be done to provide data to subsequent calculations. We will use this approach in Chapter 2 to analyze the inherent parallelism of certain direct methods for solving linear equations. Another aspect of data flow analysis might be called the *Data Flow Principle*: *As soon as something can be done, do it.*

Exercises 1.2

1. Formulate the fan-in algorithm of Figure 1.2-1 for the sum of $s = 2^r$ vectors $\mathbf{a}_1, \ldots, \mathbf{a}_s$ of length n. Write a pseudocode to do this on a vector machine.
2. Formulate the recursive doubling algorithm of Figure 1.2-4 for computing the products $p_i = a_1 \ldots a_i$, $i = 1, \ldots, n$.
3. Let $f(x) = x^2 + x^3$. Write a pseudocode using vectors of length n to evaluate f at the points $x_1, \ldots, x_n$.
4. Write a vector pseudocode to do the fan-in addition of Figure 1.2-1 for $s = 2^r$ numbers. Assume that vectors must be sequentially addressable storage locations

and discuss how to handle the storage. Assume that vector operations require $(1000 + 10\,m)$ ns for vectors of length m and scalar arithmetic operations require 100 ns. Find the cross-over point s_c for which the vector code is more efficient than the scalar code for (1.2.2).

5. Let $q(x) = a_0 + a_1x + \cdots + a_nx^n$ be a polynomial of degree n, where $n = r2^r$. Write a parallel code for evaluating $q(x)$ by first writing q as

$$q(x) = a_0 + q_1(x) + x^r q_2(x) + x^{2r} q_3(x) + \cdots + x^{(s-1)r} q_s(x)$$

where $s = 2r$ and

$$q_i(x) = a_k x + \cdots + a_{k+r-1} x^r, \qquad k = (i-1)2^r + 1$$

Then proceed along the following lines:

a. Compute $x^2, \ldots, x^r$ (sequentially?);
b. Compute $q_1(x), \ldots, q_s(x)$ (in parallel);
c. Compute $x^r, x^{2r}, \ldots, x^{(s-1)r}$ (sequentially?);
d. Multiply $x^r q_2(x), x^{2r} q_3(x), \ldots, x^{(s-1)r} q_s(x)$ (in parallel);
e. Add $a_0 + q_1(x) + x^r q_2(x) + \cdots + x^{(s-1)r} q_s(x)$ (by fan-in).

Adapt your parallel code to a vector computer by doing steps b, d, and e with vector operations as follows:

b′. Let $\mathbf{v}_1$ be the vector of the leading coefficients of the q_i, $\mathbf{v}_2$ the vector of the coefficients of x^2, and so on. Then form $x\mathbf{v}_1 + x^2\mathbf{v}_2 + \cdots + x^r\mathbf{v}_r$.
e′. Use Exercise 1.2-4.

References and Extensions 1.2

1. The ideas of degree of parallelism and speedup have been used for many years in one form or another. The definition 1.2.6 of data ready time is new and attempts to capture in one concept the various factors causing delay in a computation because data are not yet ready to be processed.
2. The speedup formula (1.2.7) is given in Ware [1973] and is implied in Amdahl [1967]. The more general formula (1.2.6) is new. Various interesting observations about Ware's Law are made in Buzbee [1983, 1985].
3. Early theoretical papers on speedup of parallel algorithms tended to ignore the cost of communication and synchronization. See Heller [1978] for a review of this work on linear algebra algorithms. Gentleman [1978] was one of the first to point out that communication time could be an important, even dominant, factor in actual calculations. For a more recent general treatment, see Gannon and van Rosendale [1984].
4. The idea of consistency was first put forth in Lambiotte and Voigt [1975].
5. The idea of using mflop rates to compute speedups in situations where the problem is too large to fit in the memory of a single processor is given in Moler

[1986]. This paper also introduces the notion of the *floating point utilization* in a parallel computation. It is defined by $u = \gamma/(\tau p)$, where γ is the mflop rate of the computation on p processors and τ is the mflop rate on a single processor. Clearly $u = 1$ if there is a perfect speedup.

6. Further analysis of the effects of communication costs on various elementary operations, such as summation, is given in Parkinson [1987].
7. One of the first papers to address in a general way the load balancing problem was Bokhari [1981]. Fox *et al.* [1987] discuss dynamic load balancing.
8. Recursive doubling was used by Stone [1973] as an approach to parallel algorithms for recursive relations. It was independently discovered about the same time by Harvard Lomax and Robert Downs. Lambiotte and Voigt [1975] pointed out that it led to inconsistent algorithms, as shown in the text. Further discussion of recursive doubling and the cascade method of partial sums may be found in Hockney and Jesshope [1981].
9. The reorganization of computations, such as the fan-in algorithm of Figure 1.2-1 versus the serial algorithm (1.2.2), raises the question of numerical stability. That is, if a computation is numerically stable, will it still be stable if the order of operations is changed? Rönsch [1984] addresses this problem and shows, in particular, that the fan-in algorithm is more stable than (1.2.2). See, also, Gao [1987].
10. Synchronization can be, and has been, implemented by a variety of techniques and we summarize some of the basic ideas. A good overall review may be found in Andrews and Schneider [1983]. We note that many of the concepts and terminology of synchronization have arisen in operating systems theory.

    A *critical section* of a code is a sequence of statements that must be executed as an indivisible operation without interruption. It is a sequential part of an overall code. A *fork* usually follows a critical section and initiates code sequents that operate in parallel. At a *join* these parallel segments return to a critical section. This is illustrated in the figure below:

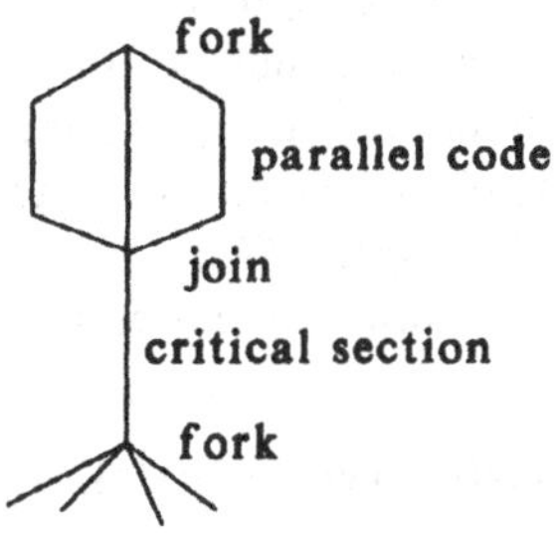

A related idea is a *barrier* (Jordan [1986], Axelrod [1986]), which is a logical point in the control flow at which all processes must arrive before any can proceed further.

On shared memory machines, synchronization is usually accomplished through the use of *shared variables*, which can be referenced by more than one process or processor. For example, in *busy-waiting*, a process tests a shared variable for a certain value that signals that it may proceed. While the process is waiting for the correct value, it is said to be *spinning* and the shared variable or variables are called *spin locks*.

11. Greenbaum [1986a] analyzes various synchronization strategies including barriers. She also considers *neighbor synchronization*, in which only the neighbors of a processor P that send data to processor P need to be synchronized for that processor. This is particularly the case for the iterative solution of linear systems on mesh-connected arrays. A refinement of neighbor synchronization is *boundary synchronization*, which recognizes that only certain data (for example, from boundary points) need be communicated in many cases. The author concludes that as long as the granularity of the program is sufficiently large so that the execution time of synchronization is small compared with the work time of each processor, then the neighbor or boundary approaches provide very attractive syncrhonization schemes.
12. How one achieves a fan-in summation on a given parallel system is dependent on the intercommunication pattern of the system. Consider, for example, the spanning tree of a hypercube as given in Figure 1.1-18. Then, a fan-in addition can be achieved by following the spanning tree in reverse order. For example, if 16 numbers are to be summed and each processor initially holds two, all processors first add these two. Then, processors 5–8 send their sums to processors 1–4 as indicated. Processors 1–4 do an addition, and then processors 3 and 4 send to processors 1 and 2. These do an addition and processor 2 sends to processor 1, which makes the final addition.

1.3. Matrix Multiplication

We consider in this section the problem of evaluation of $A\mathbf{x}$ and AB, where A and B are matrices and $\mathbf{x}$ is a vector. These basic operations will be important in the following chapters. Moreover, the study of matrix multiplication allows us to explore many of the basic issues of parallel and vector computation in the context of a very simple mathematical problem. We assume first that A and B are full matrices and then treat sparse matrices of various types later in the section. We will first work in terms of vector operations and then turn to parallel computers.

Matrix–Vector Multiplication

Assume first that A is an $m \times n$ matrix and $\mathbf{x}$ an n-vector. Then

$$A\mathbf{x} = \begin{bmatrix} (\mathbf{a}_1, \mathbf{x}) \\ \vdots \\ (\mathbf{a}_m, \mathbf{x}) \end{bmatrix} \tag{1.3.1}$$

where $\mathbf{a}_i$ is the ith row of A and $(\mathbf{x}, \mathbf{y}) = \sum_{i=1}^{n} x_i y_i$ is the usual inner product. Thus, the evaluation of $A\mathbf{x}$ requires the computation of m inner products. Before examining this approach in more detail, we consider the other standard way to view matrix-vector multiplication, as a linear combination of the columns of A. Thus,

$$A\mathbf{x} = \sum_{i=1}^{n} x_i \mathbf{a}_i \tag{1.3.2}$$

where now $\mathbf{a}_i$ denotes the ith column of A.

We note that the difference in (1.3.1) and (1.3.2) can be viewed as two different ways of accessing the data, as shown in the codes given in Figure 1.3-1. In both cases, it is assumed that the y_i are set to zero at the beginning. In Figure 1.3-1a, for each i the j loop computes the inner product of the ith row of A and $\mathbf{x}$, so that this is (1.3.1). Figure 1.3-1b corresponds to (1.3.2). Note that the final arithmetic statement is the same in both codes of Figure 1.3-1, so that the difference is in the order of the indices. We will see in the sequel that the same type of reordering of indices gives various possible algorithms for matrix-matrix multiplication and the solution of linear equations.

On some vector computers, there will be a hardware instruction for the inner product; we shall return to an example of this shortly. Otherwise, for (1.3.1) we will need to do the inner product computation

$$t_i = x_i y_i, \qquad i = 1, \ldots, n, \qquad (\mathbf{x}, \mathbf{y}) = \sum_{i=1}^{n} t_i \tag{1.3.3}$$

The first step of (1.3.3) is a vector-vector multiplication, while the second involves a summation which, as we saw in the previous section, has less than perfect parallelism. For vector computers, we would modify the fan-in addition algorithm of the previous section (Figure 1.2-1; see also Exercise 1.2-4). For example, on a vector computer for which a vector consists of sequentially addressable storage locations, we would add the first $n/2$ elements to the second $n/2$, then repeat this halving process at each stage. Note that at some point the vector length becomes less than some threshold

For $i = 1$ *to* m	For $j = 1$ to n
For $j = 1$ to n	For $i = 1$ to m
$y_i = y_i + a_{ij} x_j$	$y_i = y_i + a_{ij} x_j$

Figure 1.3-1. The ij and ji forms of matrix-vector multiplication.

for which it may be more efficient to add the remaining numbers by scalar arithmetic.

For the linear combination approach, (1.3.2), the algorithm will be

$$\mathbf{y} = 0 \qquad \text{for } i = 1 \text{ to } n \text{ do } \mathbf{y} = \mathbf{y} + x_i \mathbf{a}_i \tag{1.3.4}$$

As noted previously, an operation of the form vector plus scalar times vector is called a linked triad (or saxpy) and is particularly efficient on some vector computers.

In order to compare the two approaches, (1.3.1) and (1.3.2), we first give an example. On the CDC CYBER 205, there is a hardware instruction for the inner product of two n vectors. For a two-pipeline 205, it has an approximate timing formula of $(2300 + 20n)$ ns, so that the evaluation of m inner products requires

$$(2300m + 20nm) \text{ ns} \tag{1.3.5}$$

The timing formula for a linked triad on this machine is approximately $(1700 + 10m)$ ns for vectors of length m so that the computation (1.3.4) requires

$$(1700n + 10nm) \text{ ns} \tag{1.3.6}$$

Clearly, (1.3.5) is roughly twice as large as (1.3.6) for most values of n and m, in particular for $m = n$. However, for small values of m, (1.3.5) may be smaller. For example, for $m = 5$

$$2300 \cdot 5 + 20 \cdot 5n < 1700n + 10 \cdot 5n \qquad \text{for } n > 6$$

This simply reflects the fact that the degree of vectorization (or parallelism) of (1.3.4) is m and so is inefficient for small m.

The previous example shows that the choice of one algorithm over another may depend on the size of certain problem parameters, and we will see several examples of this in the sequel. Another extremely important consideration is the data storage. Suppose that A is stored by columns, which is the usual FORTRAN convention for storing two-dimensional arrays. (Other languages, however, such as PASCAL and PL1, store a two-dimensional array by rows.) Then the vectors required for the linear combination algorithm (1.3.2) are sequentially addressable locations in storage, while for the inner product algorithm (1.3.1), the rows of A will be vectors with a stride of m. As noted previously, on some vector computers only vectors with a stride of 1 are admissible as operands for vector arithmetic instructions, and for vectors with stride greater than 1 the data must be moved in storage before the arithmetic can proceed. On other computers, a stride greater than one is allowed but the speed of the vector operation may be degraded. In either case, if the matrix A is stored by columns, then these storage considerations make the case for the linear combination algorithm even stronger. On the other hand, if the matrix A is already stored by rows, then the storage is better for the inner product algorithm and this may dictate it to be the algorithm of choice. Only a detailed analysis for the particular machine to be used can lead to a clear choice.

Loop Unrolling

We next consider the linear combination algorithm (1.3.4) on register-to-register machines. A straightforward implementation of (1.3.4) would have the following sequence of operations:

Load $\mathbf{y} = 0$ into vector register
Load $\mathbf{a}_1$ into vector register
Multiply $x_1\mathbf{a}_1$. Result goes to register
Add $\mathbf{y} = \mathbf{y} + x_1\mathbf{a}_1$. Result goes to register
Store $\mathbf{y}$ in main memory
Load $\mathbf{y}$
Load $\mathbf{a}_2$

In the above, we have assumed that the vectors fit in the registers; if not, we would process them in segments.

The above code is very inefficient. Each cycle requires two vector loads, a store, and two vector arithmetic operations. For the arithmetic operations, we should incorporate chaining, provided the hardware allows this. Chaining was illustrated in Figure 1.1-4 and allows the result $x_1\mathbf{a}_1$ to go directly to the addition unit. Addition of $\mathbf{y}$ can then begin while the multiplications are still being carried out, so that both vector operations are being done almost concurrently. We next note that the store and load of $\mathbf{y}$ between the vector operations is unnecessary; we can simply access the current $\mathbf{y}$ from its register. Finally, most register-to-register machines will allow loads to occur concurrently with arithmetic operations. Thus, we can be loading $\mathbf{a}_2$ while the operation $\mathbf{y} + x_1\mathbf{a}_1$ is being done. (Note, however, that we would use a different vector register for $\mathbf{a}_2$ than for $\mathbf{a}_1$, so that the code must "flip-flop" on its access of the $\mathbf{a}_i$.)

With these changes, the code would be as follows:

Load $\mathbf{y} = 0$ into vector register
Load $\mathbf{a}_1$ into vector register
Form $\mathbf{y} = \mathbf{y} + x_1\mathbf{a}_1$ by chaining. Load $\mathbf{a}_2$

Form $\mathbf{y} = \mathbf{y} + x_2\mathbf{a}_2$ by chaining. Load $\mathbf{a}_3$

$$\vdots$$

Now, each cycle will require only slightly longer than the time for a single vector arithmetic operation and this code will run almost five times faster than the original.

Compilers will typically recognize when a chaining operation can be done. Unfortunately, compilers have not always recognized when intermediate results could be left in vector registers nor when loads and arithmetic operations could be overlapped. Of course, this problem can be corrected in assembly language. In FORTRAN, it can be mitigated to a large extent by the idea of *loop unrolling*. For example, if we replace the loop

$$\text{For } i = 1 \text{ to } n$$

$$\mathbf{y} = \mathbf{y} + x_i\mathbf{a}_i$$

by

$$\text{For } i = 2 \text{ to } n, \text{ steps of } 2$$

$$\mathbf{y} = \mathbf{y} + x_{i-1}\mathbf{a}_{i-1} + x_i\mathbf{a}_i$$

the vector $\mathbf{y}$ will be stored and reloaded only half as many times as in the original; moreover, the loading of $\mathbf{a}_i$ will be done concurrently with the arithmetic of $\mathbf{y} + x_{i-1}\mathbf{a}_{i-1}$. (Note that an extra statement is required to process $\mathbf{a}_n$ if n is not a multiple of 2). In this example, the loop has been unrolled to a *depth* of two. Unrolling to a depth of three is done by

$$\text{For } i = 3 \text{ to } n, \text{ steps of } 3$$

$$\mathbf{y} = \mathbf{y} + x_{i-2}\mathbf{a}_{i-2} + x_{i-1}\mathbf{a}_{i-1} + x_i\mathbf{a}_i$$

and similarly for unrolling to greater depth. (Again, additional statements are required if n is not a multiple of the depth.) Loop unrolling has been employed in practice up to depths of eight or even higher.

Multiplication of Matrices

The previous discussion of matrix-vector multiplication extends in a natural way to the multiplication of matrices, although we will see that other alternatives are now available. Let A and B be $m \times n$ and $n \times q$ matrices, respectively, so that AB is $m \times q$.

The inner product form of matrix-vector multiplication extends to the *inner product* algorithm

$$C = AB = \begin{bmatrix} \mathbf{a}_1 \\ \vdots \\ \mathbf{a}_m \end{bmatrix} (\mathbf{b}_1, \ldots, \mathbf{b}_q) = (\mathbf{a}_i\mathbf{b}_j) \tag{1.3.7}$$

Here, A is partitioned into rows and B into columns and the product AB requires the formation of the mq inner products $\mathbf{a}_i\mathbf{b}_j$ of the rows of A and columns of B. Ideally, A will be stored by rows and B by columns. Note that if $q = 1$, so that B is a vector, (1.3.7) reduces to the inner product algorithm for matrix-vector multiplication. The algorithm has the same advantages and disadvantages as the corresponding matrix-vector algorithm, and we shall not discuss it further.

The next algorithm is based on repeated matrix-vector multiplications. Let $\mathbf{a}_i$ and $\mathbf{b}_i$ denote the ith columns of A and B. Then

$$C = AB = (A\mathbf{b}_1, \ldots, A\mathbf{b}_q) = \left(\sum_{j=1}^{n} b_{j1}\mathbf{a}_j, \ldots, \sum_{j=1}^{n} b_{jq}\mathbf{a}_j \right) \tag{1.3.8}$$

The ith column of C is just A times the ith column of B, and these matrix-vector operations are done as linear combinations of the columns of A. A pseudocode for (1.3.8) is given in Figure 1.3-2. The algorithm of Figure 1.3-2 is sometimes called the *middle product algorithm*; ideally, A is stored by columns while the storage of B is immaterial. If B is stored by rows, and $\mathbf{a}_i$ and $\mathbf{b}_i$ now denote the ith rows of A and B, then an alternative, which we call the *dual middle product algorithm*, is

$$C = AB = \begin{bmatrix} \mathbf{a}_1 B \\ \vdots \\ \mathbf{a}_m B \end{bmatrix} = \begin{bmatrix} \sum a_{1j}\mathbf{b}_j \\ \vdots \\ \sum a_{mj}\mathbf{b}_j \end{bmatrix} \tag{1.3.9}$$

Here, the ith row of C is a linear combination of the rows of B. If $m = 1$ in (1.3.9), so that A is a row vector, then (1.3.9) is the linear combin ation algorithm for a row vector times a matrix.

Another algorithm is based on outer products. The *outer produc* of an m-long column vector $\mathbf{u}$ and a q-long row vector $\mathbf{v}$ is

$$\mathbf{uv} = (v_1\mathbf{u}, \ldots, v_q\mathbf{u}) = (u_i v_j) \tag{1.3.10}$$

```
Set C = 0
For i = 1 to q
    For j = 1 to n
        c_i = c_i + b_ji a_j
```

Figure 1.3-2. Middle product matrix multiplication.

The outer product can be formed by multiplication of the elements of $\mathbf{v}$ times the vector $\mathbf{u}$, and gives an $m \times q$ matrix whose i, j element is $u_i v_j$. The *outer product algorithm* for matrix multiplication based on (1.3.10) is

$$C = AB = (\mathbf{a}_1, \ldots, \mathbf{a}_n)\begin{bmatrix} \mathbf{b}_1 \\ \vdots \\ \mathbf{b}_n \end{bmatrix} = \sum_{i=1}^{n} \mathbf{a}_i \mathbf{b}_i = \sum_{i=1}^{n} (b_{i1}\mathbf{a}_i, \ldots, b_{iq}\mathbf{a}_i) \quad (1.3.11)$$

and a pseudocode is given in Figure 1.3-3.

Ideally, in Figure 1.3-3, A is stored by columns and the storage of B is immaterial. If B is stored by rows, an alternative is

$$C = AB = \sum_{i=1}^{n} \mathbf{a}_i \mathbf{b}_i = \sum_{i=1}^{n} \begin{bmatrix} a_{1i}\mathbf{b}_i \\ \vdots \\ a_{mi}\mathbf{b}_i \end{bmatrix} \quad (1.3.12)$$

which we call the *dual outer product algorithm*. In either case, C is formed as the sum of n outer products and (1.3.11) and (1.3.12) differ only in how these outer products are computed.

We note that, corresponding to Figure 1.3-1, all of the above matrix multiplication algorithms can be viewed as different orderings of the loop variables i, j, and k in the basic code

```
For ______
   For ______
      For ______
         c_ij = c_ij + a_ik b_kj
```

The six possible codes, sometimes called the *ijk forms* of matrix multiplication, are given in Exercise 1.3-3.

Comparison of Algorithms

We next wish to compare the middle and outer product algorithms under the assumption that A is stored by columns. Analogous considerations

```
Set C = 0
For i = 1 to n
    For j = 1 to q
        c_j = c_j + b_ij a_i
```

Figure 1.3-3. Outer product matrix multiplication.

apply to the dual algorithms if B is stored by rows. For the outer product algorithm, Figure 1.3-3, the inner loop forms the outer product $\mathbf{a}_i\mathbf{b}_i$, adding it to the accumulating product in C. The basic step is a linked triad for vectors of length m; hence the degree of vectorization is m. For the middle product algorithm of Figure 1.3-2, again the basic operation is a linked triad and the degree of vectorization is m. On vector computers that access data directly from memory, the algorithms are essentially equivalent. For small m, however, neither algorithm will be attractive; if B is stored by rows and $q > m$, the dual forms of the algorithms will be preferred.

On vector computers that utilize vector registers there can be an important difference between the two algorithms that we now discuss. For simplicity, we assume that the registers are of sufficient size to hold a column of A; if this is not the case, obvious modifications to the discussion can be made (Exercise 1.3-4). Note first that the inner loop of the middle product algorithm completely forms a column of C, while in the outer product algorithm the columns of C are accumulated over the whole calculation. Figures 1.3-4 and 1.3-5 illustrate the two computations on a vector register machine.

The outer product algorithm has the advantage that $\mathbf{a}_i$ is used q times once it is in a register. However, a disadvantage is that there is a delay at the end of each vector operation while the result register is stored and $\mathbf{c}_j$ is loaded. This can be alleviated to some extent by using an additional register for $\mathbf{c}_{j+1}$ and loading this register while the arithmetic operation is being performed. This decreases the delay to the time to store the result, at the expense of some additional logic to access a different register for $\mathbf{c}_j$ every other time. This strategy is useful on machines (for example, the CRAY-1) that can overlap arithmetic and memory operations but that allow only a load or a store at a given time. On machines (for example, the CRAY

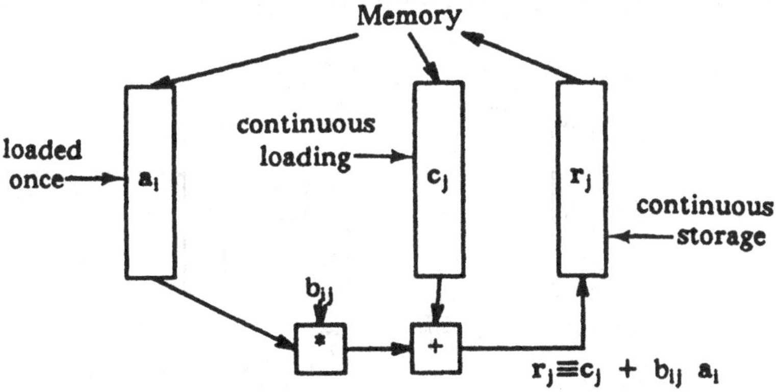

Figure 1.3-4. Outer product matrix multiplication.

X-MP) that allow load and store operations to proceed simultaneously, we can eliminate the storage delay altogether by utilizing a second result register for $\mathbf{r}_{j+1}$ as well. Now a basic step is

$$\text{compute } \mathbf{r}_j, \qquad \text{load } \mathbf{c}_{j+1}, \qquad \text{store } \mathbf{r}_{j-1}$$

with the compute, load, and store operations proceeding simultaneously.

Consider next the middle product algorithm, as illustrated in Figure 1.3-5. Note that in this case, $\mathbf{a}_j$ must be loaded before each vector operation but the result need be stored only at the end of the inner loop. However, the registers for $\mathbf{c}_i$ and $\mathbf{r}_i$ must alternate at each vector operation since the result vector becomes the input vector $\mathbf{c}_i$ at the next step. In this form, there is a delay before each vector operation while $\mathbf{a}_j$ is loaded. However, again, we can use an additional register to overlap this load with the arithmetic as indicated by

$$\text{compute } \mathbf{c}_i + b_{ji}\mathbf{a}_j, \qquad \text{load } \mathbf{a}_{j+1}$$

Note that this requires only the capability to simultaneously load and compute. In FORTRAN, we would approximate the above behavior by loop unrolling. In summary, then, we see that the middle product algorithm is preferable on those machines that allow only one memory operation to proceed simultaneously with arithmetic, while on machines that allow both load and store operations simultaneously, the two algorithms are equivalent up to, perhaps, lower-order effects.

Parallel Computers

We next discuss the previous algorithms for parallel computers with p processors. Consider first matrix-vector multiplication by the linear combination algorithm, $A\mathbf{x} = \sum_{i=1}^{n} x_i\mathbf{a}_i$, where, again, A is $m \times n$. For simplicity,

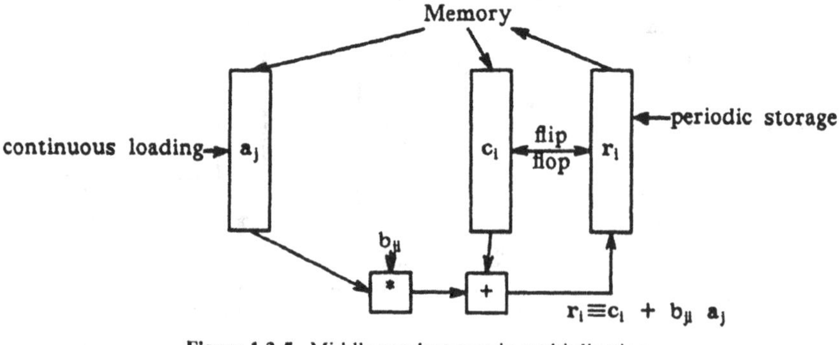

Figure 1.3-5. Middle product matrix multiplication.

assume first that $p = n$ and let x_i and $\mathbf{a}_i$ be assigned to processor i as illustrated in Figure 1.3-6. All of the products $x_i\mathbf{a}_i$ are formed with a perfect degree of parallelism, and then the additions are done by the fan-in algorithm of Section 1.2, applied now to vectors (see Exercise 1.2-1). If the parallel system is one with local memory, then we interpret Figure 1.3-6 as meaning that the indicated data are in local memories of the processors. In this case, the fan-in algorithm will require transfer of data between processors as the algorithm proceeds. On a shared memory system, we interpret Figure 1.3-6 as meaning a task assignment; that is, P_i will do the multiplication $x_i\mathbf{a}_i$. In the fan-in part of the algorithm, no data are transferred since all are in global memory.

Synchronization is needed to ensure that the necessary multiplications are complete before addition begins. On a local memory machine, this will be accomplished by the need to communicate data. For example, suppose that P_1 is to add $x_1\mathbf{a}_1$ and $x_2\mathbf{a}_2$. When P_2 has completed its multiplications it will send $x_2\mathbf{a}_2$ to P_1. P_1 will begin the addition after it has completed its multiplications, and if the data have not yet been received from P_2, it will wait. It is this wait that effects the necessary synchronization. Note that without the wait, if P_1 started adding from the memory locations reserved for $x_2\mathbf{a}_2$ before the correct data arrived, then erroneous results would be produced. In a global memory system, synchronization can be achieved in a variety of ways (Section 1.2), and the best way will depend on both the hardware and software features of the system. As an example of how the synchronization might be done, assume that when P_2 is done with its multiplication it sets a "flag" (for example, a Boolean variable can be set to True), and P_1 will then test this flag before it begins the addition.

The inner product algorithm is more attractive in some respects. Assume now that $p = m$ and that $\mathbf{x}$ and $\mathbf{a}_i$, which is now the ith row of A, are assigned to processor i as illustrated in Figure 1.3-7. Each processor does one inner product and there is a perfect degree of parallelism m. No fan-in nor data transfers are required, and synchronization is needed only at the end of the computation.

Although the inner product algorithm exhibits a perfect degree of parallelism, which of the two algorithms one uses will usually depend on other considerations. A matrix-vector multiplication will inevitably be done as part of a larger calculation and, on a local memory system, the storage

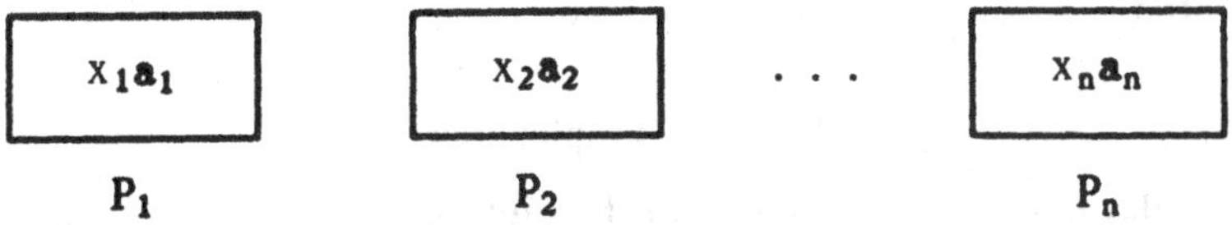

Figure 1.3-6. Parallel linear combination algorithm.

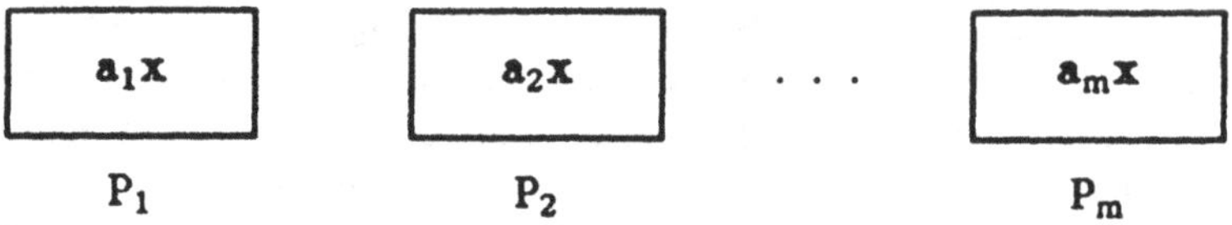

Figure 1.3-7. Parallel inner product algorithm.

of A and $\mathbf{x}$ at the time the multiplication is required will play a major role in determining the algorithm. For example, if x_i and the column $\mathbf{a}_i$ are already stored in the ith processor, as in Figure 1.3-6, the linear combination algorithm will probably be used, although its degree of parallelism is less than the other algorithm. Another consideration is the desired location of the result at the end of the multiply; the first algorithm will leave the result vector in a single processor, while the second leaves the result distributed over the processors. We note the seeming paradox, relative to the vector codes previously discussed, that the linear combination algorithm requires a fan-in while the inner product algorithm does not.

The above discussion assumes that the number of processors is equal to the number of columns or rows of A. Usually n and/or m will be considerably larger than the number of processors and each processor will be assigned many rows or columns. Ideally, for the inner product algorithm, p would divide m and m/p rows would be assigned to each processor. Mathematically, we would perform the multiplication in the partitioned form

$$A\mathbf{x} = \begin{bmatrix} A_1 \\ \vdots \\ A_p \end{bmatrix} \mathbf{x} = \begin{bmatrix} A_1\mathbf{x} \\ \vdots \\ A_p\mathbf{x} \end{bmatrix} \tag{1.3.13}$$

where A_i contains m/p rows of A. If A_i and $\mathbf{x}$ are assigned to processor i, then the products $A_1\mathbf{x}, \ldots, A_p\mathbf{x}$ are done with a perfect degree of parallelism. Note that for the multiplication $A_i\mathbf{x}$, it may not make any difference how this is carried out; it could be done by inner products or by a linear combination of columns. However, if the processors are vector processors, then our previous discussion would be relevant. Similar considerations apply to partitioning A into groups of columns (Exercise 1.3-5). If p does not divide m (or n), then we would try to distribute the rows (or columns) across the processors as evenly as possible.

Matrix Multiplication

Similar considerations apply to the multiplication of two matrices A and B, and it is left to Exercise 1.3-6 to discuss the inner product, outer product, and middle product algorithms for parallel computers. There is also the possibility of algorithms, analogous to (1.3.13), based on partitionings of A and B. Thus, if A and B are partitioned commensurately, then

$$C = AB = \begin{bmatrix} A_{11} & \cdots & A_{1r} \\ \vdots & & \vdots \\ A_{s1} & \cdots & A_{sr} \end{bmatrix} \begin{bmatrix} B_{11} & \cdots & B_{1t} \\ \vdots & & \vdots \\ B_{r1} & \cdots & B_{rt} \end{bmatrix} = \left(\sum_{k=1}^{r} A_{ik} B_{kj} \right) \tag{1.3.14}$$

which leads to a variety of possible algorithms. For example, if $p = st$, the number of blocks in C, then these st blocks can be computed in parallel provided A and B are assigned suitably to the processors (see Exercise 1.3-7). Special cases are $s = 1$, so that A is partitioned into groups of columns, and $t = 1$, where B is partitioned into groups of rows. Other special cases of interest are $s = t = 1$, which gives a "block inner product" type algorithm

$$AB = \sum_{j=1}^{r} A_{1j} B_{j1} \tag{1.3.15}$$

and $r = 1$, which gives a "block outer product" algorithm

$$AB = (A_{i1} B_{1j}) \tag{1.3.16}$$

For example, (1.3.16) would be useful if there were $p = st$ processors with A_{i1} and B_{1j} assigned to the processors as indicated in Figure 1.3-8. Here, the processor configuration mirrors the block structure of the product C and the individual products $A_{i1} B_{1j}$ are all formed in parallel.

Partitioned algorithms can also be useful for vector computers, like the CRAY-2, which have a fast local memory.

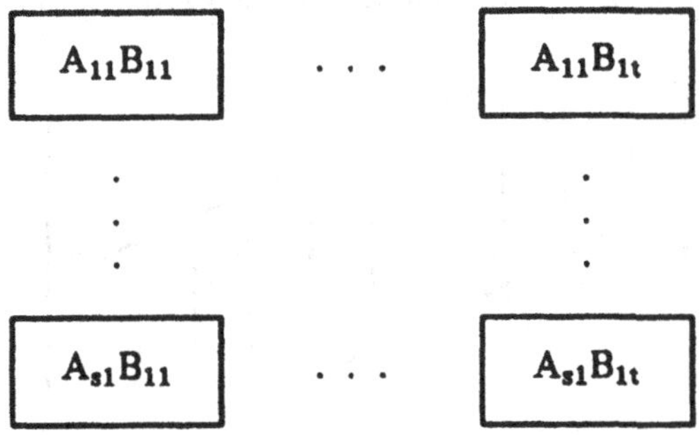

Figure 1.3-8. Parallel block multiplication.

Banded Matrices

So far in this section we have assumed that the matrices were full, that is, that all, or most, elements are nonzero. Many, if not most, matrices that arise in practice, however, are sparse, with the majority of elements being zero. We will now examine the multiplication algorithms for various types of sparse matrices and see that additional algorithms are needed in certain cases. We begin with banded matrices.

The $n \times n$ matrix A is *banded* if

$$a_{ij} = 0, \qquad i - j > \beta_1, \qquad j - i > \beta_2 \tag{1.3.17}$$

as illustrated in Figure 1.3-9. For simplicity, we will consider only the case in which A is *symmetrically banded*, $\beta_1 = \beta_2 = \beta$, and call β the *semibandwidth* (or just bandwidth). Thus, A has nonzero elements only on the main diagonal and on the 2β adjacent diagonals above and below the main diagonal. Note that a symmetrically banded matrix is not necessarily symmetric.

Consider first the matrix-vector multiplication $A\mathbf{x}$. The inner product and linear combination algorithms previously discussed are

$$A\mathbf{x} = \begin{bmatrix} (\mathbf{a}_1, \mathbf{x}) \\ \vdots \\ (\mathbf{a}_n, \mathbf{x}) \end{bmatrix} \tag{1.3.18}$$

and

$$A\mathbf{x} = \sum_{i=1}^{n} x_i \mathbf{a}_i \tag{1.3.19}$$

where in (1.3.18) $\mathbf{a}_i$ denotes the ith row of A whereas in (1.3.19) it is the ith column. Assuming that A is stored by columns, the vector lengths in (1.3.19) range from $\beta + 1$ to $2\beta + 1$. Typical values of β and n in some

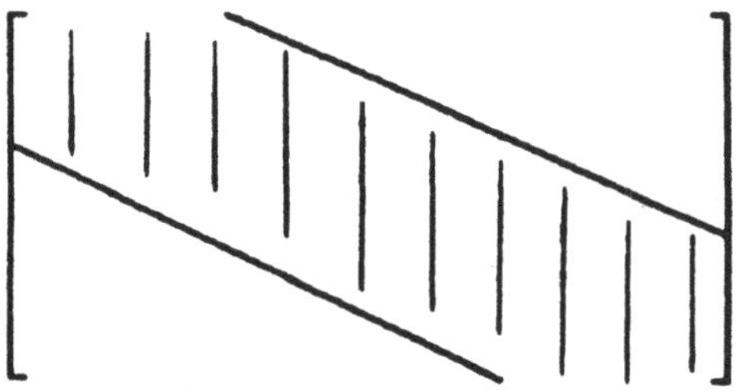

Figure 1.3-9. Banded matrix.

problems might be $n = 10^4$ and $\beta = 10^2$, in which case the vector lengths for (1.3.19) are reasonably large. On the other hand, for small β, (1.3.19) has an unsatisfactorily small degree of vectorization. In the limiting case of tridiagonal matrices, for which $\beta = 1$, the vector lengths are at most 3.

Similar considerations hold for the inner products in (1.3.18), for which the vector lengths are the same as in (1.3.19). However, (1.3.18) has a degree of parallelism of order n in the formation of the n inner products. For example, suppose that in a local memory parallel system with $p = n$ processors the ith processor holds $\mathbf{a}_i$ and $\mathbf{x}$; then all inner products can be formed in parallel. If there are $p = n/k$ processors, we would assume that the first k rows of A are handled by processor 1, the second k by processor 2, and so on; thus, the processors will be working with a maximum degree of parallelism up to the rather small loss from the fact that the lengths of the beginning and ending rows of A are shorter than the middle rows. A more careful balancing of the work load can alleviate this problem as well as the analogous one that results from n not being divisible by p. (See Exercise 1.3-10.) Hence, the inner product algorithm is potentially attractive on parallel systems, even for very small β.

Similar considerations hold for the multiplication of two banded $n \times n$ matrices. We note that if A has semibandwidth α and B has semibandwidth β, then AB will, in general, have semibandwidth $\alpha + \beta$ (Exercise 1.3-11). Consider first the middle product algorithm (1.3.8):

$$C = AB = \left(\sum_{j=1}^{\beta+1} b_{j1}\mathbf{a}_j, \ldots, \sum_{j=n-\beta}^{n} b_{jn}\mathbf{a}_j \right) \tag{1.3.20}$$

Here, if it is assumed that A is stored by columns, then the vector lengths for the linear combinations will range from $\alpha + 1$ to 2α. Hence, as before, if α is sufficiently large, this can be a viable vector algorithm. If $\alpha < \beta$, the dual form (1.3.9) of the middle product algorithm may be superior to (1.3.20), especially if B is stored by rows. Note that on parallel computers, we also have the option of evaluating the first k columns of (1.3.20) in processor 1, the second k in processor 2, and so on, and can thus achieve a high degree of parallelism; the details of this approach are left to Exercise 1.3-12.

Consider next the outer product algorithm (1.3.11):

$$C = AB = \sum_{i=1}^{n} (b_{i1}\mathbf{a}_i, \ldots, b_{in}\mathbf{a}_i) \tag{1.3.21}$$

where, again, we assume that A is stored by columns. The consideration of this algorithm is analogous to (1.3.20), with the vector lengths determined by α. Thus if $\alpha < \beta$, the dual form (1.3.12) may be preferable if B is stored by rows. The previous discussion of the relative merits of (1.3.20) and (1.3.21) on vector computers that utilize vector registers also extends immediately to banded matrices (Exercise 1.3-13). There are also various possibilities for (1.3.21) on parallel computers. With $p = n/k$ processors, k of the outer products could be formed in parallel in each processor; this would require k columns of A and k rows of B to be assigned to each processor. The summation of the outer products is then required, and after those within each processor are summed, a fan-in across the processors is performed. A more attractive possibility is to form the first k columns of C in processor 1, the next k in processor 2, and so on. This is essentially the middle product algorithm.

Consider, finally, the inner product algorithm (1.3.7):

$$C = AB = (\mathbf{a}_i \mathbf{b}_j) \tag{1.3.22}$$

in which the i, j element of C is the inner product of the ith row of A and the jth column of B. Since the semibandwidth of C is $\alpha + \beta$, only those inner products lying within C's bandwidth need to be formed, of course. As with matrix-vector multiplication, (1.3.22) is attractive for parallel computers, regardless of the bandwidths α and β.

Multiplication by Diagonals

The algorithms given so far are unattractive on vector computers for matrices with small bandwidth. This is also the case for matrices that have only a few nonzero diagonals that are not clustered near the main diagonal. An example is given in Figure 1.3-10, in which an $n \times n$ matrix is shown that has only four diagonals that contain nonzero elements. We will call a matrix that has relatively few nonzero diagonals a *diagonally sparse matrix.* Such matrices arise frequently in practice, especially in the solution of elliptic or parabolic partial differential equations by finite difference or finite element methods, as we will see in more detail in Chapter 3.

A diagonally sparse matrix may have a relatively large bandwidth, but the algorithms we have discussed so far are unsatisfactory because of the

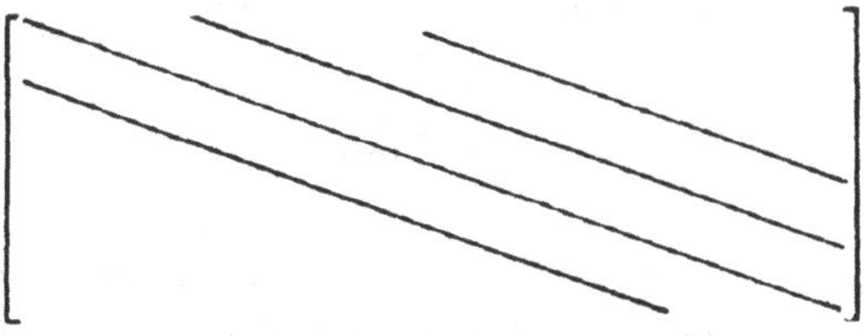

Figure 1.3-10. Diagonally sparse matrix.

large percentage of zeros in each row or column. Indeed, the storage of such matrices by row or column is unsatisfactory for that reason and a natural storage scheme is by diagonal. Thus, the nonzero diagonals of the matrix become the vectors to be used in multiplication algorithms and we next study how this multiplication can be done.

Consider first the matrix-vector multiplication $A\mathbf{x}$, where the $n \times n$ matrix A is

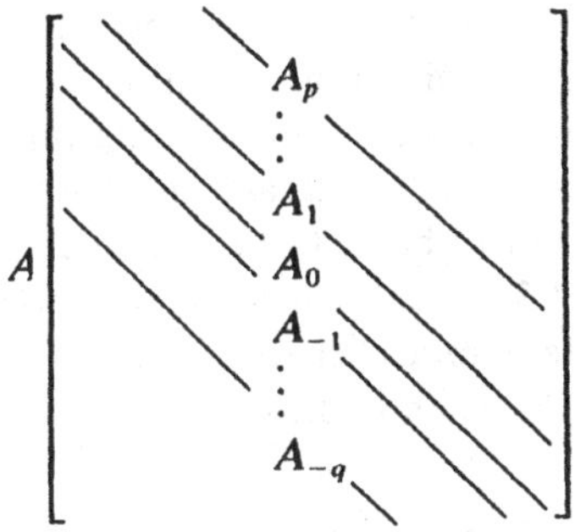

(1.3.23)

We do not assume at this point that A is diagonally sparse or symmetrically banded; indeed, A can be a full matrix. We denote in (1.3.23) the main diagonal by A_0, the diagonals below A_0 by $A_{-1}, \ldots, A_{-q}$ and the diagonals above A_0 by $A_1, \ldots, A_p$. Then it is easy to see (Exercise 1.3-14) that $A\mathbf{x}$ may be represented as

$$A\mathbf{x} = A_0\mathbf{x} \mathbin{\hat{+}} A_1\mathbf{x}^2 \mathbin{\hat{+}} \cdots \mathbin{\hat{+}} A_p\mathbf{x}^{p+1} + A_{-1}\mathbf{x}_{n-1} \mathbin{\underset{\vee}{+}} \cdots \mathbin{\underset{\vee}{+}} A_{-q}\mathbf{x}_{n-q} \tag{1.3.24}$$

where

$$\mathbf{x}^j = (x_j, \ldots, x_n), \qquad \mathbf{x}_{n-j} = (x_1, \ldots, x_{n-j}) \tag{1.3.25}$$

The multiplications in (1.3.24) are to be interpreted as elementwise vector multiplication of the vectors A_i, which are the diagonals of A, and the vectors of (1.3.25). The vectors appearing in (1.3.24) are not all the same length (for example, $A_1\mathbf{x}^2$ is $n-1$ long) and $\hat{+}$ means add the shorter vector to the first components of the longer one; for example, $A_1\mathbf{x}^2$ would add to the first $n-1$ components of $A_0\mathbf{x}$. Likewise $\underset{\vee}{+}$ denotes adding the shorter vector to the last components of the longer one.

We next discuss various special cases of (1.3.24) on vector computers. If A is a full matrix ($p = q = n-1$), then there are $2n-1$ vector multiplies in (1.3.24). Moreover, the vectors range in length from 1 to n. Thus, (1.3.24) is unattractive for full matrices compared with the linear combination algorithm. Only if A were already stored by diagonal would we consider (1.3.24), and this storage scheme for a full matrix is unlikely.

At the other extreme, suppose that A is tridiagonal so that $p = q = 1$. Then (1.3.24) reduces to

$$Ax = A_0\mathbf{x} \hat{+} A_1\mathbf{x}^2 \underset{\vee}{+} A_{-1}\mathbf{x}_{n-1} \tag{1.3.26}$$

which consists of vector lengths of n, $n - 1$, and $n - 1$ so that we have almost a perfect degree of vectorization for large n. More generally, (1.3.24) is very attractive for small bandwidth systems but becomes increasingly less so vis-à-vis the linear combination algorithm as the bandwidth increases. There will be some bandwidth β_0, depending on the computer and n, for which (1.3.24) will be the fastest algorithm for $\beta < \beta_0$ and the linear combination algorithm will be fastest for $\beta > \beta_0$. (See Exercise 1.3-15.)

The algorithm (1.3.24) is also very attractive for diagonally sparse matrices. For example, suppose that A_0, A_1, A_{30}, A_{-1}, and A_{-30} are the only nonzero diagonals. Then (1.3.24) becomes

$$A\mathbf{x} = A_0\mathbf{x} \hat{+} A_1\mathbf{x}^2 \hat{+} A_{30}\mathbf{x}^{31} \underset{\vee}{+} A_{-1}\mathbf{x}_{n-1} \underset{\vee}{+} A_{-30}\mathbf{x}_{n-30} \tag{1.3.27}$$

As with the tridiagonal case, $A_1\mathbf{x}^2$ and $A_{-1}\mathbf{x}_{n-1}$ have vector lengths of $n - 1$, while $A_{30}\mathbf{x}^{31}$ and $A_{-30}\mathbf{x}_{n-30}$ have vector lengths of $n - 30$. If n is large, these vector lengths are still quite satisfactory. On the other hand, if A_{30} and A_{-30} were replaced by A_{n-p} and $A_{-(n-p)}$ then the vector lengths for these diagonals are small if p is small, and the vector operations for $A_{n-p}\mathbf{x}^{n-p+1}$ and $A_{-(n-p)}\mathbf{x}_p$ are inefficient. However, for such a matrix the linear combination algorithm does not provide a viable alternative, and one might switch to scalar operations to process the very short vectors. The more nonzero diagonals in a diagonally sparse matrix the more the efficiency of (1.3.24) will approach the linear combination algorithm, and at some point storage considerations will be a dominant consideration in the choice of the algorithm.

On parallel computers, the computation (1.3.24) could be carried out as follows. The nonzero diagonals of A are distributed among the processors so that the total data assigned to the processors is balanced as much as possible. The vector $\mathbf{x}$, or at least that portion of it needed by each processor, will also have to be distributed. Then the multiplications of the diagonals and $\mathbf{x}$ can be done in a highly parallel fashion, but, at some point, additions must be done with a fan-in across the processors, with a loss of parallelism. Moreover, there is less motivation to consider multiplication by diagonals on parallel computers since, as we have already discussed, the implementation of the inner product algorithm can be quite satisfactory for small bandwidth systems. The same is true of diagonally sparse matrices. Here, again, the rows of A can be distributed across the processors and the inner products done in parallel. Only the nonzero elements in each row, together with an index list giving their position in the row, need be stored provided the processors are sequential computers. Thus, there would seem to be little use for the multiplication by diagonal algorithm on parallel systems unless the individual processors are themselves vector computers.

Matrix Multiplication by Diagonals

The matrix-vector multiplication by diagonal algorithm extends to the multiplication AB of matrices stored by diagonal, but the details of the algorithm become more complex. For simplicity, we assume that both A and B are $n \times n$ and we consider only the multiplication of two tridiagonal matrices:

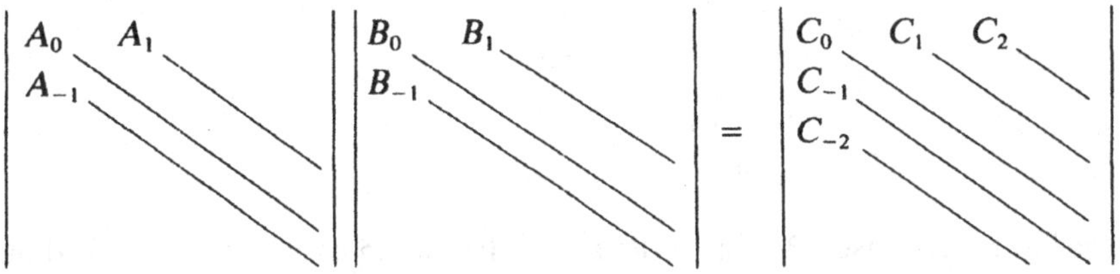

(1.3.28)

The diagonals of the product C are given by

$$C_0 = A_0B_0 + A_{-1}B_1 + A_1B_{-1}, \qquad C_1 = A_0B_1 + A_1B_0^2$$
$$C_{-1} = A_0^2B_{-1} + A_{-1}B_0, \qquad C_2 = A_1B_1^2, \qquad C_{-2} = A_{-1}^2B_{-1} \tag{1.3.29}$$

where we have used A_i^j to denote the vector starting in the jth position of A_i. We also use the convention that if the vectors are not of equal length, only the operations determined by the shorter vector are considered. For example, in the formation of C_1, A_0 is of length n and B_1 is of length $n-1$ so that A_0B_1 denotes the $n-1$ long vector in which the last element of A_0 has been ignored. To clarify this we give the following 4×4 example:

$$\begin{bmatrix} a_{11} & a_{12} & & \\ a_{21} & a_{22} & a_{23} & \\ & a_{32} & a_{33} & a_{34} \\ & & a_{43} & a_{44} \end{bmatrix} \begin{bmatrix} b_{11} & b_{12} & & \\ b_{21} & b_{22} & b_{23} & \\ & b_{32} & b_{33} & b_{34} \\ & & b_{43} & b_{44} \end{bmatrix} = \begin{bmatrix} c_{11} & c_{12} & c_{13} & \\ c_{21} & c_{22} & c_{23} & c_{24} \\ c_{31} & c_{32} & c_{33} & c_{34} \\ & c_{42} & c_{43} & c_{44} \end{bmatrix} \tag{1.3.30}$$

Then the diagonals of C are given by

$$
\begin{aligned}
&C_0: &&\begin{aligned} c_{11} &= a_{11}b_{11} + a_{12}b_{21} \\ c_{22} &= a_{21}b_{12} + a_{22}b_{22} + a_{23}b_{32} \\ c_{33} &= a_{32}b_{23} + a_{33}b_{33} + a_{34}b_{43} \\ c_{44} &= a_{43}b_{34} + a_{44}b_{44} \end{aligned} \\
&C_1: &&\begin{aligned} c_{12} &= a_{11}b_{12} + a_{12}b_{22} \\ c_{23} &= a_{22}b_{23} + a_{23}b_{33} \\ c_{34} &= a_{33}b_{34} + a_{34}b_{44} \end{aligned} \\
&C_{-1}: &&\begin{aligned} c_{21} &= a_{21}b_{11} + a_{22}b_{21} \\ c_{32} &= a_{32}b_{22} + a_{33}b_{32} \\ c_{43} &= a_{43}b_{33} + a_{44}b_{43} \end{aligned} \\
&C_2: &&\begin{aligned} c_{13} &= a_{12}b_{23} \\ c_{24} &= a_{23}b_{34} \end{aligned} \\
&C_{-2}: &&\begin{aligned} c_{31} &= a_{32}b_{21} \\ c_{42} &= a_{43}b_{32} \end{aligned}
\end{aligned}
\tag{1.3.31}
$$

It is left to Exercise 1.3-16 to write a pseudocode to carry out the algorithm (1.3.28), (1.3.29).

The formulas corresponding to (1.3.29) for general banded matrices are easy to derive in principle, but rather complex in detail. Exercise 1.3-17 considers the case of a tridiagonal matrix and a five-diagonal matrix.

It is part of the folklore of parallel and vector computing that matrix multiplication is "easy." As we have seen in this section, this is true only if proper attention is paid to the structure of the matrices and if we adapt our algorithms to that structure.

Exercises 1.3

1. Find the values of m and n for which (1.3.5) is smaller than (1.3.6).
2. Write pseudocodes, corresponding to Figures 1.3-2 and 1.3-3, for the dual algorithms (1.3.9) and (1.3.12).
3. The matrix multiplication $C = AB$, where A is $m \times n$ and B is $n \times q$, can be described by any one of the six loops

for $i = 1$ to m	for $j = 1$ to q	for $i = 1$ to m
for $j = 1$ to q	for $i = 1$ to m	for $k = 1$ to n
for $k = 1$ to n	for $k = 1$ to n	for $j = 1$ to q
ijk form	*jik* form	*ikj* form

for $j = 1$ to q	for $k = 1$ to n	for $k = 1$ to n
for $k = 1$ to n	for $i = 1$ to m	for $j = 1$ to q
for $i = 1$ to m	for $j = 1$ to q	for $i = 1$ to m
jki form	*kij* form	*kji* form

where the arithmetic statement in all cases is $c_{ij} = c_{ij} + a_{ik}b_{kj}$. Show that the *ijk*, *ikj*, and *kij* forms correspond to the inner product, middle product, and outer product algorithms, respectively, while the *jki* and *kji* forms correspond to the dual middle product and outer product algorithms. Show also that the *jik* form gives a "dual inner product" algorithm that was not discussed in the text.

4. Assume that the vector registers are of length s. Discuss the necessary changes to the outer and middle product algorithms of Figures 1.3-4 and 1.3-5 for arbitrary sizes of m, n, and q, where A is $m \times n$ and B is $n \times q$.
5. Formulate the algorithm illustrated by Figure 1.3-6 in the case that $p \neq n$.
6. Discuss in detail the inner, middle, and outer product algorithms for matrix multiplication on p processors.
7. Discuss the storage requirements to carry out the algorithm (1.3.14) efficiently on $p = st$ processors.
8. Let A be an $m \times n$ matrix and B an $n \times q$ matrix. Assume that there are $p = nmq$ processors. Give a storage distribution of A and B across the processors so that all nmq multiplications needed to form AB can be done in parallel. (Note that this will require the elements of A and/or B to be stored in more than one processor.) Then show that $O(\log n)$ fan-in addition steps are required to form the necessary sums. Hence, conclude that the matrix multiplication can be done in $1 + O(\log n)$ parallel steps.
9. Formulate the recursive doubling algorithm of Section 1.2 for sums and products of matrices.
10. Assume that a parallel system has p processors. Discuss the distribution of work for the inner product algorithm (1.3.18) for a matrix A of bandwidth β so as to achieve maximum utilization of the processors. Consider, in particular, the case that p does not divide n.
11. Let A and B be $n \times n$ matrices with semibandwidths α and β, respectively. Show that AB will, in general, have semibandwidth $\alpha + \beta$.
12. For $n \times n$ banded matrices A and B with semibandwidths α and β, organize the computation (1.3.20) on a parallel computer with p processors so as to obtain a maximum degree of parallelism.
13. Discuss the relative merits of (1.3.20) and (1.3.21) on vector computers that utilize vector registers and (a) allow only a load or store operation concurrently with arithmetic; or (b) allow both load and store operations concurrently with arithmetic.
14. Verify (1.3.24).
15. Determine the semibandwidth β for which the algorithm (1.3.24) for matrix-vector multiplication ceases to be better than the linked triad algorithm. Assume

that A is symmetrically banded, the storage is suitable for both algorithms, and the vector instructions obey the timing formula $T = (1000 + 10)$ ns.

16. Write a pseudocode to carry out the multiplication (1.3.28) of two tridiagonal matrices using the vector operations (1.3.29). Assume that A is stored as the linear array A_0, A_1, A_{-1}, B is stored as the linear array B_0, B_1, B_{-1}, and C is stored as the linear array C_0, C_1, C_2, C_{-1}, C_{-2}.
17. Give the formulas corresponding to (1.3.31) for $C = AB$, where A is an $n \times n$ tridiagonal matrix and B is an $n \times n$ pentadiagonal matrix. (The main diagonal and the two diagonals on each side are nonzero.)

References and Extensions 1.3

1. Further discussion of many of the algorithms of this section may be found in Hockney and Jesshope [1981], where the term "middle product algorithm" is used.
2. The different loop formulations of Figure 1.3-1 and Exercise 1.3-3 are given in Dongarra, Gustavson, and Karp [1984]. Also, see this paper for a discussion of memory bank conflicts on CRAY-1 computers that can influence timing degradation in inner product computations, chaining of stores, etc. This paper also introduces the term *gaxpy* (generalized saxpy) to denote a linear combination of vectors.
3. Sorensen [1984] points out that the computation of $A\mathbf{x} + \mathbf{y}$ by $\mathbf{y} + \sum x_i \mathbf{a}_i$ may not be good on some parallel machines because of the need to synchronize access to $\mathbf{y}$. This paper also considers the possibility of buffering to improve performance in matrix-vector multiplication.
4. The terms "symmetrically banded" and "diagonally sparse" are not standard, but no other suitable terms are in common use for matrices of these kinds.
5. The multiplication by diagonals algorithm was developed by Madsen *et al.* [1976], and more details on the process may be found in this paper. Another advantage of storing a matrix by diagonals is that its transpose is much more readily available than if the matrix is stored by rows or columns. Indeed, the transpose may be obtained simply by changing the pointers to the first elements of the diagonals and no change in storage of the matrix elements need be made.
6. McBryan and van de Velde [1985, 1986a, 1987] consider several approaches to matrix multiplication on parallel machines. In [1986b], they also consider a storage scheme that packs the $2n - 1$ diagonals of an $n \times n$ matrix into n one-dimensional arrays by suitable "wrapping around."
7. Melham [1987a, b] considers an interesting generalization of diagonals that he calls *stripes*. Roughly speaking, stripes may be considered to be "bent" diagonals. He then gives matrix multiplication algorithms based on this type of storage scheme.
8. Hayes and Devloo [1986] give a matrix-vector multiplication algorithm predicated on the matrix A being of the form $A = \sum A_i$. (The primary motivation

for this is when the A_i arise from individual element matrices in a finite element problem.)

9. Jalby and Meier [1986] consider the problem of effectively utilizing a two-level memory (main memory plus fast local or cache memory) on vector machines. They consider in some detail the problem of matrix multiplication by blocks where the block sizes are to be determined so as to minimize total time. They address this problem by minimizing memory time and computation time separately and then obtain a compromise. Fox *et al.* [1987] also give a block oriented algorithm, primarily for a hypercube architecture.

10. Algorithms for banded matrix multiplication on several VLSI architectures are considered in Cheng and Sahni [1987].

11. Parallel and vector algorithms for matrix multiplication of arbitrarily sparse matrices are intrinsically more difficult than the algorithms we have discussed. For some work on this problem, see Reed and Patrick [1984; 1985a, b].

12. Loop unrolling is discussed in Dongarra and Hinds [1979]. As pointed out in this paper, it is also a useful technique for serial computers since it can reduce loop overhead as well as give other benefits. See Cowell and Thompson [1986] for a more general discussion in the context of a set of tools for transforming DO loops.

13. The BLAS are a collection of subroutines for basic linear algebra operations such as inner products. The BLAS are continuously being extended to include more operations, such as matrix-vector multiplication. See Dongarra and DuCroz *et al.* [1986] for further information and references, and Louter-Nool [1987] for timing results for the BLAS on the CYBER 205. The use of the BLAS will help portability of codes between different machines. For another approach to the portability problem, see Dongarra and Sorensen [1987].

14. Dave and Duff [1987] give timing results for matrix-vector and matrix-matrix multiplication on a CRAY-2. They report mflop rates as high as 432 on a single processor for multiplication of two 500×500 matrices.

2

Direct Methods for Linear Equations

We now begin the study of the solution of linear systems of equations by direct methods. In Sections 2.1 and 2.2 we assume that the coefficient matrix is full, and we study Gaussian elimination, Choleski factorization, and the orthogonal reduction methods of Givens and Householder. In Section 2.1, we deal only with vector computers and then consider the same basic algorithms for parallel computers in Section 2.2. In Section 2.3 we treat the same algorithms, as well as others, for banded systems.

2.1. Direct Methods for Vector Computers

We consider the linear system of equations

$$A\mathbf{x} = \mathbf{b} \tag{2.1.1}$$

where A is a nonsingular $n \times n$ matrix. We assume in this section that A is a full dense matrix, and restrict our attention to vector computers.

Gaussian Elimination and LU Decomposiion

The most common form of Gaussian elimination subtracts multiples of rows of A from other rows in order to reduce (2.1.1) to an upper triangular system, which is then solved by back substitution. This is mathematically equivalent to first forming the decomposition $A = LU$, where L is lower triangular with 1's on the main diagonal and U is upper triangular. Then, the solution is obtained by solving the triangular systems

$$L\mathbf{y} = \mathbf{b}, \qquad U\mathbf{x} = \mathbf{y}, \tag{2.1.2}$$

which are called the *forward* and *back substitutions*.

We concentrate first on the LU decomposition, which is the time-consuming part of the process, and return to the solution of the triangular systems shortly. A pseudocode for the decomposition is given in Figure 2.1-1.

The j loop in Figure 2.1-1 subtracts multiples of the kth row of the current A from succeeding rows. These are linked triad operations in which the vectors are rows of A. Hence, on vector computers that require vectors to be sequentially addressable elements, it is assumed that A will be stored by rows. These linked triad operations perform *updating* of the rows of A and constitute the bulk of the work in the LU decomposition. At the kth stage of the algorithm, there are $n-k$ vector operations and the vector lengths are $n-k$. Therefore, the average vector length for the updating operations is

$$\frac{(n-1)(n-1)+(n-2)(n-2)+\cdots+1}{n-1+n-2+\cdots+1}=O(2n/3) \qquad (2.1.3)$$

where the verification of the equality is left to Exercise 2.1-1. [Here, and henceforth, we use the more or less common notation that $O(cn^p)$ is the highest-order term in the expression; in many cases, it is the constant c that plays a key role.] Hence, the average degree of vectorization of the vector instructions is $O(2n/3)$, and this is degraded somewhat by the scalar divisions to form the multipliers at each stage. On some vector computers it may be advantageous to switch from vector to scalar arithmetic when the vector length drops below a certain threshold, although this will complicate the code.

A further degradation in the speed will be caused by pivoting, if this is needed. For the partial pivoting strategy applied to the first stage, we must search the first column for the maximum element in absolute value. Although some vector computers have vector instructions to facilitate this search, the elements of the first column are not in contiguous storage locations. Thus, the search might have to be carried out by scalar operations or by a gather operation followed by a vector maximum operation. Once

```
For k = 1 to n − 1
  For i = k + 1 to n
    l_ik = a_ik / a_kk
    For j = k + 1 to n
      a_ij = a_ij − l_ik a_kj
```

Figure 2.1-1. Row oriented *LU* decomposition.

the location of the maximum element is known, the corresponding row can be swapped with the first row by vector operations or the indexing can be modified. How the pivoting strategy will be done will depend on the particular vector computer.

The right-hand side **b** of (2.1.1) may also be processed as part of the reduction to triangular form in order to achieve the forward substitution part of (2.1.2). If A is stored by rows, it is useful to append b_i to the ith row, if other storage considerations permit this. Then, in Figure 2.1-1, the j loop would run to $n+1$, and the vector lengths would increase by one.

If A is stored by columns, we modify the LU decomposition algorithm as shown in Figure 2.1-2. At the kth stage, the algorithm of Figure 2.1-2 first forms the kth column of L; this can be done by a vector divide. The innermost loop, the i loop, subtracts a multiple of this kth column of L from the $n-k$ long jth column of the current A. Hence, the basic vector operation is again a linked triad, but now the vectors are columns of L and columns of the current A. The right hand side **b** can be processed in the same manner as the columns of A to effect the forward substitution of (2.1.2).

Not counting the formation of the multiplier vector or processing the right-hand side, there are again $n-k$ linked triad operations at the kth stage with vector lengths of $n-k$. Hence, (2.1.3) gives the average vector length so that the average degree of vectorization is again $O(2n/3)$. Only a more detailed analysis for a particular machine (see, e.g., Exercise 2.1-2) can determine whether the row form is more efficient than the column form, but the formation of the multipliers by a vector operation will probably show that the column form is the best. A deciding factor on which to use will be the way that A may already be stored.

The incorporation of pivoting is somewhat more difficult in the column form, however. The search for the pivot element can now be done by vector operations on those machines with that capability, but the interchange of rows presents a problem. The elements of the rows can be interchanged by vector operations with a stride of n, by gathers followed by vector operations,

```
For k = 1 to n − 1
   For s = k + 1 to n
      l_sk = a_sk / a_kk
   For j = k + 1 to n
      For i = k + 1 to n
         a_ij = a_ij − l_ik a_kj
```

Figure 2.1-2. Column-oriented *LU* decomposition.

or by scalar operations. Hence, if pivoting is required and if A can be easily stored by rows, the row-oriented algorithm will probably be preferable.

Register-to-Register Machines

The above discussion applies to both memory-to-memory and register-to-register vector machines, but for register-to-register machines additional discussion is needed. Also, on some register-to-register machines an alternative approach is desirable.

We examine first the load/store pattern for the inner loop of the column algorithm of Figure 2.1-2. For simplicity, we assume that entire columns of A can be held in a vector register (see Exercise 2.1-4), and we consider first the case when only a register load or a store can be done concurrently with computation. The following gives the first few operations:

Form first column of L	(2.1.4a)
Load second column of A	(2.1.4b)
Modify second column of A; load third column of A	(2.1.4c)
Store modified second column	(2.1.4d)
Modify third column; load fourth column of A	(2.1.4e)

$$\vdots$$

As indicated in (2.1.4c), we can overlap the load of the next column of A with the modification of the current column. But then we have a delay while the modified second column is stored into memory from its register.

We can modify the algorithm to eliminate the delay caused by the store in (2.1.4d). The new algorithm is similar to the middle product algorithm for matrix multiplication; the idea is to do all of the processing for the jth column before moving to the $(j + 1)$st. Thus, the updating of the remaining columns of A is delayed until such time as a column is to be completed. A pseudocode for this algorithm is given in Figure 2.1-3. The first few steps of the jth stage of the computation showing the load/store pattern are

Load first column of L	(2.1.5a)
Load jth column of A	(2.1.5b)
Modify jth column of A; load second column of L	(2.1.5c)
Modify jth column of A; load third column of L	(2.1.5d)

$$\vdots$$

Note that in (2.1.5) there are no stores until all work on the jth column of

```
For j = 2 to n
  For s = j to n
    l_{s,j-1} = a_{s,j-1}/a_{j-1,j-1}
  For k = 1 to j - 1
    For i = k + 1 to n
      a_ij = a_ij - l_ik a_kj
```

Figure 2.1-3. Column-oriented delayed update *LU* decomposition.

A has been completed. The columns of *L* must be continuously loaded into registers, but this can be overlapped with the computation. Only at the beginning and end of each stage is there extra delay for loads and/or stores. As in Section 1.3, it is likely that the compiler will not recognize that the current *j*th column can be retained in a register, and the desired effect of Figure 2.1-3 will have to be approximated by loop unrolling or achieved by assembly language coding. Another potential problem in implementing this algorithm is that the vector lengths in the updates are not equal. That is, at the *j*th stage, we update the *j*th column using the $n - 1$ last elements of column 1, the $n - 2$ last elements of column 2, and so on.

The delayed update algorithm is not as necessary on those register-to-register machines that allow both a load and a store to proceed concurrently. In this case, (2.1.4d) would be eliminated and (2.1.4e) would be changed to:

modify third column of *A*; load fourth column of *A*; store second column of *A*

Thus, the store of the second column of *A* would proceed concurrently with the load of the fourth column. We note that the delayed update algorithm is not necessary for memory-to-memory machines, although even there it may have some advantages.

The *ijk* Forms of LU Decomposition

It is instructive to view the above algorithms in terms of a triple For loop as done in Section 1.3 for matrix multiplication:

$$\begin{array}{l} \text{For } \_\_\_\_ \\ \quad \text{For } \_\_\_\_ \\ \quad\quad \text{For } \_\_\_\_ \\ \quad\quad\quad a_{ij} = a_{ij} - l_{ik}a_{kj} \end{array} \qquad (2.1.6)$$

This shows the basic arithmetic operation, which remains the same in all forms (we do not show the formation of the multipliers l_{ik}), and three For loops where the blanks are to be filled with some permutation of the indices i, j, k. For example,

$$\begin{aligned} &\text{For } k = 1 \text{ to } n-1 \\ &\quad \text{For } i = k+1 \text{ to } n \\ &\qquad \text{For } j = k+1 \text{ to } n \end{aligned} \tag{2.1.7}$$

corresponds to the algorithm of Figure 2.1-1 while

$$\begin{aligned} &\text{For } j = 2 \text{ to } n \\ &\quad \text{For } k = 1 \text{ to } j-1 \\ &\qquad \text{For } i = k+1 \text{ to } n \end{aligned} \tag{2.1.8}$$

corresponds to Figure 2.1-3. The algorithm of Figure 2.1-2 is the *kji* form. Note that the algorithms in Figures 2.1-1–2.1-3 are not as simple as is suggested by (2.1.6). This is especially so for the other three algorithms, which are given in detail in Appendix 1.

We next summarize some of the properties of the *ijk* forms and refer to Appendix 1 for further details. One important property is that the different forms use different basic vector operations, as defined by the innermost loop. The vector operation of the *kji* and *kij* forms is a linked triad. In these forms, rows (or columns) are updated as soon as the multipliers are available, and we call these *immediate update algorithms*. In the *jki* form, which is Figure 2.1-3, columns are updated only just before that column is to be zeroed; the *ikj* form is the corresponding row-oriented version. We call these *delayed update* algorithms. The vector operation is again a linked triad but is applied repeatedly to accumulate a linear combination. The *ijk* and *jik* forms are also delayed update algorithms, but the vector operation is an inner product.

The six different forms of (2.1.6) have different patterns of data access of the elements of A and of L. The *kji* and *jki* forms are column oriented; they access columns of both A and L. The *kij* and *ikj* forms access A by rows and only scalar elements of L. The *ijk* and *jik* forms have mixed access: A by columns and L by rows. Since we assume that L overwrites the lower triangular position of A, this mixed access will require access to vectors with stride greater than one. The data access patterns are given in Figure 2.1-4, and show which parts of the matrices are being accessed during a given stage.

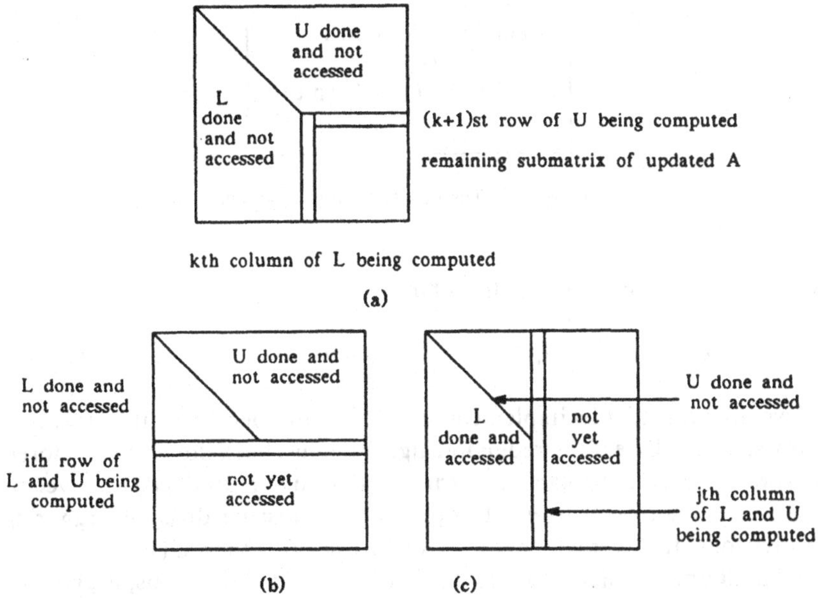

Figure 2.1-4. Data access patterns of the *ijk LU* forms. (a) *kij, kji*; (b) *ikj, ijk*; (c) *jki, jik*.

Table 2.1-1 summarizes the basic properties of the *ijk* forms. It is doubtful that the last two forms, *ijk* and *jik*, are of interest on vector computers, but the other four all have a role under the right circumstances.

Triangular Systems

At the end of the reduction stage of Gaussian elimination, we must solve a triangular system of equations

$$\begin{bmatrix} u_{11} & \cdots & u_{1n} \\ & u_{22} & \vdots \\ & \ddots & \\ & & u_{nn} \end{bmatrix} \begin{bmatrix} x_1 \\ \vdots \\ x_n \end{bmatrix} = \begin{bmatrix} c_1 \\ \vdots \\ c_n \end{bmatrix} \tag{2.1.9}$$

Table 2.1-1. The *ijk* Forms of *LU* Decomposition.

Form	Operation	Update	A access	L access
kij	Linked triad	Immediate	Row	Scalar
kji	Linked triad	Immediate	Column	Column
ikj	Lin. comb.	Delayed	Row	Scalar
jki	Lin. comb.	Delayed	Column	Column
ijk	Inner product	Delayed	Column	Row
jik	Inner product	Delayed	Column	Row

```
For j = n down to 1
  x_j = c_j/u_jj
  For i = j - 1 down to 1
    c_i = c_i - x_j u_ij
```

Figure 2.1-5. The column sweep algorithm.

One usual back substitution algorithm is

$$x_i = (c_i - u_{ii+1}x_{i+1} - \cdots - u_{in}x_n)/u_{ii}, \qquad i = n, \ldots, 1 \qquad (2.1.10)$$

and we now consider its implementation in vector operations. If U is stored by rows, as it will be if the reduction algorithm has been done with A stored by rows, then (2.1.10) can be carried out by inner products with vector lengths ranging from 1 to $n - 1$, together with n scalar divisions. Ignoring the divisions, the average degree of vectorization is then $O(n/2)$.

An alternative algorithm, useful if U is stored by columns, is given by the pseudocode in Figure 2.1-5, which is known as the *column sweep* (*or vector sum*) *algorithm.* After x_n is computed, the quantities $x_n u_{in}$, $i = 1, \ldots, n - 1$, are computed and subtracted from the corresponding c_i; thus, the contribution of x_n to the other solution components is made before moving to the next stage. The ith stage consists of a scalar division followed by a linked triad of length $i - 1$. Hence, the average degree of vectorization is again $O(n/2)$, but now the vector operations are linked triads. Which of the two algorithms we use will almost certainly be dictated by the storage pattern of U, if this has been determined by the LU decomposition.

Both the inner product and the column sweep algorithms are easily formulated for lower triangular systems. (See Exercise 2.1-5.)

Matrix–Vector Forms of LU Decomposition

Although the *ijk* forms give six different organizations of LU decomposition, there are still others that are potentially useful for vector computers. Even when one of the *ijk* forms is theoretically suited for a particular vector computer, there may be problems in implementing it, especially in a high-level language. The following organizations are based on operations involving submatrices and have the potential to be more easily implemented and to be more portable to other machines.

The simplest of these other organizations is based on the idea of *bordering.* Let A_j be the jth leading principal submatrix of A, and assume that we have the decomposition $L_{j-1}U_{j-1}$ of the $(j - 1)$st leading principal submatrix A_{j-1}. Then the decomposition of A_j satisfies

$$\begin{bmatrix} L_{j-1} & 0 \\ \mathbf{l}_j & 1 \end{bmatrix} \begin{bmatrix} U_{j-1} & \mathbf{u}_j \\ 0 & u_{jj} \end{bmatrix} = \begin{bmatrix} A_{j-1} & \mathbf{a}_j \\ \hat{\mathbf{a}}_j & a_{jj} \end{bmatrix}$$

where $\mathbf{l}_j$ and $\hat{\mathbf{a}}_j$ are row vectors and $\mathbf{u}_j$ and $\mathbf{a}_j$ are column vectors. This gives the relations

$$L_{j-1}\mathbf{u}_j = \mathbf{a}_j, \qquad \mathbf{l}_j U_{j-1} = \hat{\mathbf{a}}_j, \qquad \mathbf{l}_j\mathbf{u}_j + u_{jj} = a_{jj} \tag{2.1.11}$$

Thus, the vectors $\mathbf{u}_j$ and $\mathbf{l}_j$ can be computed by solving the lower triangular systems

$$L_{j-1}\mathbf{u}_j = \mathbf{a}_j, \qquad U_{j-1}^T\mathbf{l}_j^T = \hat{\mathbf{a}}_j^T \tag{2.1.12}$$

and then u_{jj} is computed from the third relation of (2.1.11).

There are two natural ways to carry out the bordering form of LU decomposition. The first solves the triangular systems by the column sweep algorithm while the second uses the inner product algorithm. The decomposition codes for these two approaches are given in Figure 2.1-6. The first i loop in Figure 2.1-6a does the updating of the jth column of A and thus computes the jth column of U. The second i loop updates the jth row of A and computes the jth row of L. The updates can be done by linear combinations but the vector lengths vary. Note that when $i = j$ in the second i loop, we are updating the (j, j) element of A and thereby computing u_{jj} as in (2.1.11).

In the second form of the bordering algorithm, Figure 2.1-6b, the first jk loop computes the ith row of L by first updating the elements of A with inner products of rows of L and columns of U. Together with the division, this is equivalent to solving the system $U_{i-1}^T\mathbf{l}_i^T = \hat{\mathbf{a}}_i^T$. Note that when $j = i$,

(a)	(b)
For $j = 2$ to n	For $i = 2$ to n
For $k = 1$ to $j - 2$	For $j = 2$ to i
For $i = k + 1$ to $j - 1$	$l_{ij-1} = a_{ij-1}/a_{j-1,j-1}$
$a_{ij} = a_{ij} - l_{ik}a_{kj}$	For $k = 1$ to $j - 1$
For $k = 1$ to $j - 1$	$a_{ij} = a_{ij} - l_{ik}a_{kj}$
$l_{jk} = a_{jk}/a_{kk}$	For $j = 2$ to $i - 1$
For $i = k + 1$ to j	For $k = 1$ to $j - 1$
$a_{ji} = a_{ji} - l_{jk}a_{ki}$	$a_{ji} = a_{ji} - l_{jk}a_{ki}$

Figure 2.1-6. Bordering algorithms for LU decomposition: (a) Column sweep; (b) inner products.

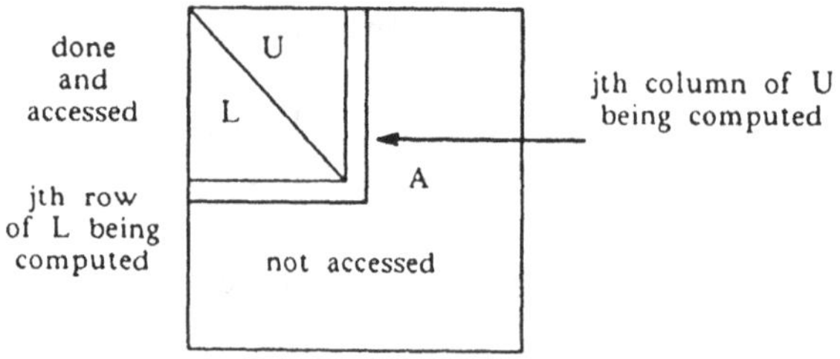

Figure 2.1-7. Data access pattern for bordering forms.

we are updating the (i, i) element of A and this pertains to the calculation of the ith column of U. The second jk loop updates the ith column of A by, again, inner products of rows of L and columns of U. Equivalently, we are solving the triangular system $L_{i-1}\mathbf{u}_i = \hat{\mathbf{a}}_i$ for the ith column of U.

Both forms of the bordering approach have the same data access pattern, which is shown in Figure 2.1-7. Note that both forms require access to A by both rows and columns, and therefore will be unsatisfactory on vector computers that require contiguous elements.

The key part of the bordering algorithm is the solution of the triangular systems (2.1.12). These are matrix-vector operations that could be implemented as subroutines and made as efficient as possible for particular machines. The next organization, which we call the *Dongarra-Eisenstat* algorithm, has the advantage that its basic operations are matrix-vector multiplications. The algorithm can be described mathematically as follows. Let A, L, and U be partitioned as

$$\begin{bmatrix} A_{11} & \mathbf{a}_{12} & A_{13} \\ \mathbf{a}_{21} & a_{22} & \mathbf{a}_{23} \\ A_{31} & \mathbf{a}_{32} & A_{33} \end{bmatrix} = \begin{bmatrix} L_{11} & & \\ \mathbf{l}_{21} & 1 & \\ L_{31} & \mathbf{l}_{32} & L_{33} \end{bmatrix} \begin{bmatrix} U_{11} & \mathbf{u}_{12} & U_{13} \\ & u_{22} & \mathbf{u}_{23} \\ & & U_{33} \end{bmatrix} \quad (2.1.13)$$

where $\mathbf{a}_{21}$, $\mathbf{a}_{23}$, $\mathbf{l}_{21}$, and $\mathbf{u}_{23}$ are row vectors and $\mathbf{a}_{12}$, $\mathbf{a}_{32}$, $\mathbf{l}_{32}$, and $\mathbf{u}_{12}$ are column vectors. Assume that A_{11} has been factored into $L_{11}U_{11}$ and that $\mathbf{l}_{21}$, L_{31}, $\mathbf{u}_{12}$, and U_{13} are known. Then at the next stage we wish to compute $\mathbf{l}_{32}$, the next column of L, as well as u_{22} and $\mathbf{u}_{23}$, the next row of U. By equating corresponding elements in (2.1.13), these are obtained by

$$u_{22} = a_{22} - \mathbf{l}_{21}\mathbf{u}_{12}, \quad \mathbf{u}_{23} = \mathbf{a}_{23} - \mathbf{l}_{21}U_{13}, \quad \mathbf{l}_{32} = (\mathbf{a}_{32} - L_{31}\mathbf{u}_{12})/u_{22} \quad (2.1.14)$$

The data access pattern for this is shown in Figure 2.1-8.

The main operations in (2.1.14) are multiplications by rectangular matrices. We may carry out these multiplications either by inner products or by linear combinations, and this gives rise to the two different forms shown in Figure 2.1-9. In Figure 2.1-9a the first kj loop carries out the successive updates of the ith row of A, which then becomes the ith row of U at the termination of the k loop. These updates may be viewed as doing

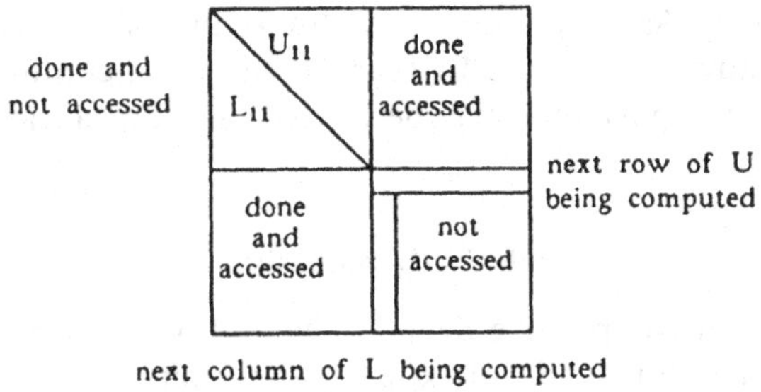

Figure 2.1-8. Data access pattern for the Dongarra–Eisenstat algorithm.

the vector–matrix multiplication $\mathbf{l}_{21}U_{13}$ of (2.1.14) by linear combinations of the rows of U. Note that when $j = i$ we are doing the update leading to the first quantity of (2.1.14). The second kj loop does updates of the ith column of A, which may be interpreted in terms of the matrix–vector multiplication $L_{31}\mathbf{u}_{12}$ of (2.1.14) as linear combinations of the columns of L. At the termination of the k loop, the updated ith column is divided to obtain the ith column of L. Note that, as opposed to the delayed update algorithm of Figure 2.1-3, the linear combinations may be done by operations in which the vectors are the same length. The second index statement for k could be removed and the code would still be correct, but we have inserted it to emphasize the linear combination operations. Note also that the first kj loop accesses A by row while the second kj loop accesses it by column. Hence, this is an unsatisfactory form for vector computers that require contiguous elements for vectors.

The algorithm given in Figure 2.1-9b uses inner products. At the jth stage, the first ik loop computes the jth column of L, except for the final division, by updating the jth column of A with inner products of rows of L and the jth column of U. The second ik loop computes the jth row of U by updating the jth row of A with inner products of the jth row of L

```
For i = 1 to n
  For k = 1 to i - 1
    For j = i to n
      a_ij = a_ij - l_ik a_kj
  For k = 1 to i - 1
    For j = i + 1 to n
      a_ji = a_ji - l_jk a_ki
  For s = i + 1 to n
    l_si = a_si / a_ii
```

```
For j = 1 to n
  For i = j + 1 to n
    For k = 1 to j - 1
      a_ij = a_ij - l_ik a_kj
  For i = j to n
    For k = 1 to j - 1
      a_ji = a_ji - l_jk a_ki
  For s = j + 1 to n
    l_sj = a_sj / a_jj
```

Figure 2.1-9. The Dongarra–Eisenstat LU decomposition algorithms. (a) Linear Combinations; (b) inner products.

and columns of U. Again, access to A by both row and column is required. The potential advantage of the Dongarra–Eisenstat algorithms is that the matrix–vector multiplications may be carried out very efficiently on some vector computers.

Choleski Decomposition

If A is symmetric positive definite, then an often used alternative to Gaussian elmination is the Choleski decomposition

$$A = LL^T \tag{2.1.15}$$

where L is a lower triangular matrix, followed by the forward and back substitutions

$$L\mathbf{y} = \mathbf{b}, \qquad L^T\mathbf{x} = \mathbf{y} \tag{2.1.16}$$

to complete the solution of the linear system $A\mathbf{x} = \mathbf{b}$.

One implementation of (2.1.15) is given in Figure 2.1-10. Since A is symmetric, it is necessary to store only the lower (or upper) triangular part of A. The innermost loop, the i loop, in Figure 2.1-10, modifies columns of A by subtracting multiples of columns of L. Hence, the basic vector operation is again a linked triad.

At the jth stage there are $j - 1$ linked triads using vectors of length $n - j + 1$. Hence, the average vector length is (see Exercise 2.1.6)

$$\frac{n - 1 + 2(n-2) + \cdots + (n-1)1}{1 + 2 + \cdots + n - 1} = O\left(\frac{n}{3}\right) \tag{2.1.17}$$

which is only half that of LU decomposition. This is to be expected since in the Choleski algorithm we are using the symmetry of the coefficient matrix to reduce the serial computational work by a factor of 2. On vector machines with large start-up time, the relative speed advantage of Choleski over LU decomposition is much less than the nominal factor of 2 for serial computers. For example, using the results of Exercises 2.1-2 and 2.1-8, the

```
l_11 = a_11^{1/2}
For j = 2 to n
   For s = j to n
      l_{s,j-1} = a_{s,j-1}/l_{j-1,j-1}
   For k = 1 to j - 1
      For i = j to n
         a_ij = a_ij - l_ik l_jk
   l_jj = a_jj^{1/2}
```

Figure 2.1-10. Column-oriented Choleski decomposition.

ratio of times is approximately 0.8 for $n = 100$ and 0.7 for $n = 500$. Only for very large n does the ratio approach the serial computer value of 0.5.

The *ijk* Choleski forms

We have used in Figure 2.1-10 only one possible organization of a Choleski algorithm. As with *LU* decomposition, we can give other organizations based on the nested loops

For ______
  For ______
    For ______

Again, there are six permutations of the loop indices *ijk*, which give six different organizations of the algorithm. These are given in detail in Appendix 1, and we summarize some of the main aspects of the different organizations in Table 2.1-2.

We note that several of the forms listed in Table 2.1-2 have mixed storage access; that is, rows of A and columns of L, or vice versa, are required. Since we are assuming that L will overwrite A, or at least be stored in the same fashion, this mixed data access will be bad for vector computers requiring contiguous elements.

The algorithm of Figure 2.1-10 is the *jki* form, with access to both A and L by column. It corresponds to Figure 2.1-3 for *LU* decomposition but now the vector lengths in the updates at the jth stage are the same. The *kji* form also accesses both A and L by column and is very satisfactory for other vector computers. Figure 2.1-11 shows the data access patterns for the six Choleski forms of Table 2.1-2.

Multiple Right-Hand Sides

In some problems, we are required to solve several systems of equations

$$A\mathbf{x}_i = \mathbf{b}_i, \qquad i = 1, \ldots, q \tag{2.1.18}$$

Table 2.1-2. The *ijk* Forms of Choleski Factorization

Form	Operation	Update	A-access	L-access
kij	Linked triad	Immediate	Row	Column
kji	Linked triad	Immediate	Column	Column
ikj	Linear combination	Delayed	Row	Column
jki	Linear combination	Delayed	Column	Column
ijk	Inner product	Delayed	Column	Row
jik	Inner product	Delayed	Scalar	Row

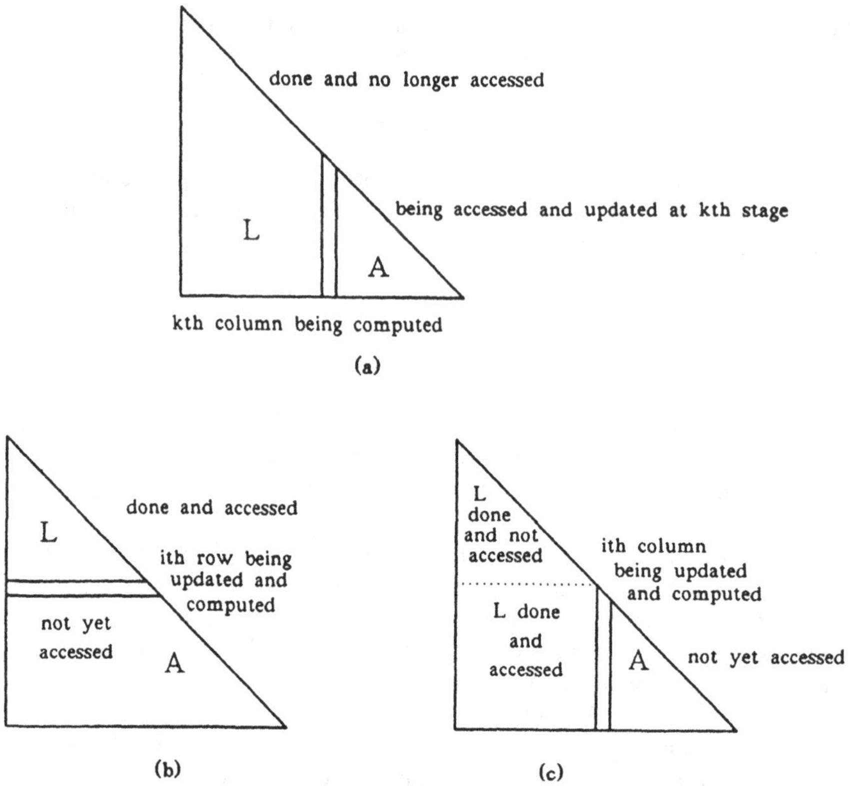

Figure 2.1-11. Data access patterns of Choleski *ijk* forms. (a) *kij*, *kji*; (b) *ikj*, *ijk*; (c) *jki*, *jik*.

with different right-hand sides $\mathbf{b}_i$ but the same coefficient matrix A. This occurs, for example, in structural analysis problems in which a given structure is being tested for several different load configurations, which are represented by the vectors $\mathbf{b}_i$. It also occurs in computing the inverse of A, in which case $q = n$ and $\mathbf{b}_i$ is the vector with 1 in the ith position and 0 elsewhere.

We can write (2.1.18) in an equivalent way as $AX = B$, where X and B are $n \times q$ matrices. The column-oriented algorithm of Figure 2.1-2 can be modified so as to process all the columns of B by considering them as additional columns of A. The vector lengths remain $n - j$ at the jth stage, but now there are $n - j + q$ vector operations. Thus, the average vector length is (Exercise 2.1.6)

$$\frac{(n-1+q)(n-1) + \cdots + (1+q)}{(n-1+q) + \cdots + (1+q)} = O\left(\frac{2n^2 + 3qn}{3n + 6q}\right) \qquad (2.1.19)$$

which decreases slightly as a function of q and for $q = n$ is $O(5n/9)$ compared with $O(2n/3)$ for $q = 1$.

On the other hand, we can modify the row-oriented algorithm of Figure 2.1-1 by appending the rows of B to the rows of A, so that the vector lengths at the jth stage are $n - j + q$. Since there are still only $n - j$ vector operations, the average vector length is (Exercise 2.1.6)

$$\frac{(n-1)(n-1+q)+\cdots+(1+q)}{(n-1)+\cdots+1} = O(\tfrac{2}{3}n + q) \qquad (2.1.20)$$

which is now an increasing function of q, and for $q = n$ is $O(5n/3)$, over twice that for $q = 1$. We conclude that the row-oriented algorithm, although possibly slightly inferior for $q = 1$, becomes increasingly satisfactory as q increases.

There remains the back substitution, and if there are sufficiently many right-hand sides, it may be beneficial to use the following scheme. Let the systems be given by $UX = C$, where X and C are $n \times q$ and $\mathbf{x}_i$ and $\mathbf{c}_i$ denote the ith rows. Then, the algorithm

$$\mathbf{x}_i = (\mathbf{c}_i - u_{ii+1}\mathbf{x}_{i+1} - \cdots - u_{in}\mathbf{x}_n)/u_{ii}, \qquad i = n, n-1, \ldots, 1 \quad (2.1.21)$$

computes the rows $\mathbf{x}_n, \mathbf{x}_{n-1}, \ldots$ by using linked triad operations on vectors of length q. This is just the inner product algorithm (2.1.10) applied "simultaneously" to compute the ith components of all the solution vectors "at once." Thus, the basic vector operation is a linked triad and not an inner product. Whether this is preferable to the inner product algorithm applied to each right-hand side will depend on the size of q and n, as well as on the particular computer. (See Exercise 2.1-7.)

Orthogonal Reduction

An alternative to LU decomposition is the reduction

$$A = QR \qquad (2.1.22)$$

where Q is an orthogonal matrix and R is upper triangular. There are two usual approaches to obtaining the factorization (2.1.22): Householder transformations and Givens transformations. On serial computers, (2.1.22) has an operation count of $O(4n^3/3)$ using Householder transformations and $O(2n^3)$ using Givens transformations. Thus, they are approximately two times and three times as slow as LU decomposition, respectively. They have the property that they are numerically stable without any row interchanges, but this does not overcome the operation count advantage of LU decomposition, even with pivoting, and as a consequence they are rarely used on serial computers in the context of solving nonsingular systems of equations. They are, however, widely used for eigenvalue detemination, least-squares problems, orthogonalization of vectors, and other purposes. For many of these uses, A will be a rectangular matrix but, for simplicity, we will restrict our attention to $n \times n$ matrices.

A *Householder transformation* is a matrix of the form $I - \mathbf{w}\mathbf{w}^T$ where $\mathbf{w}$ is a real column vector with $\mathbf{w}^T\mathbf{w} = 2$. It is easy to see (Exercise 2.1-11) that a Householder transformation is symmetric and orthogonal. We use such matrices to perform the reduction (2.1.22) in the following way. Let $\mathbf{a}_1$ be the first column of A and define

$$\mathbf{u}^T = (a_{11} - s, a_{21}, \ldots, a_{n1}), \qquad \mathbf{w} = \mu\mathbf{u} \tag{2.1.23}$$

where

$$s = \pm(\mathbf{a}_1^T\mathbf{a}_1)^{1/2}, \qquad \gamma = (s^2 - a_{11}s)^{-1}, \qquad \mu = \gamma^{1/2} \tag{2.1.24}$$

and the sign of s is chosen to be opposite that of a_{11} for numerical stability. Then

$$\mathbf{w}^T\mathbf{w} = \mu^2\left[(a_{11} - s)^2 + \sum_{i=2}^{n} a_{i1}^2\right] = \mu^2(\mathbf{a}_1^T\mathbf{a}_1 - 2a_{11}s + s^2) = 2$$

which shows that $I - \mathbf{w}\mathbf{w}^T$ is a Householder transformation. Moreover,

$$\mathbf{w}^T\mathbf{a}_1 = \mu\left[(a_{11} - s)a_{11} + \sum_{i=2}^{n} a_{i1}^2\right] = \mu(s^2 - a_{11}s) = \frac{1}{\mu}$$

so that

$$a_{11} - w_1\mathbf{w}^T\mathbf{a}_1 = a_{11} - \frac{\mu(a_{11} - s)}{\mu} = s$$

and

$$a_{i1} - w_i\mathbf{w}^T\mathbf{a}_1 = a_{i1} - \frac{a_{i1}\mu}{\mu} = 0, \qquad i = 2, \ldots, n$$

Therefore,

$$A_1 = P_1A = \begin{bmatrix} s & a'_{12} & \cdots & a'_{1n} \\ 0 & & & \\ \vdots & \vdots & & \vdots \\ 0 & a'_{n2} & \cdots & a'_{nn} \end{bmatrix}, \qquad P_1 = I - \mathbf{w}\mathbf{w}^T \tag{2.1.25}$$

and the effect of the Householder transformation applied to A is to produce a new matrix that has zeros in the first column below the main diagonal. We now repeat the process with a vector $\mathbf{w}_2$ that is zero in its first position and is otherwise defined as in (2.1.23) and (2.1.24) using now the last $n-1$ elements in the second column of the matrix A_1. With $P_2 = I - \mathbf{w}_2\mathbf{w}_2^T$, P_2A_1 retains the zero elements in the first column and introduces zeros in the second column in the last $n-2$ positions. We continue in this way to successively zero elements below the main diagonal by Householder matrices $P_i = I - \mathbf{w}_i\mathbf{w}_i^T$. Thus

$$P_{n-1}\cdots P_1A = R$$

where R is upper triangular. The matrices P_i are all orthogonal so that $P = P_{n-1}\cdots P_1$ and P^{-1} are also orthogonal and $Q = P^{-1}$ is the orthogonal matrix of (2.1.22).

The bulk of the work in carrying out the Householder reduction to triangular form is in updating the nonzero columns of A at each stage, and we next examine (2.1.25) more closely. If $\mathbf{a}_1, \ldots, \mathbf{a}_n$ are the columns of A, we have

$$A_1 = (I - \mathbf{w}\mathbf{w}^T)A = A - \mathbf{w}\mathbf{w}^TA = A - \mathbf{w}(\mathbf{w}^T\mathbf{a}_1, \mathbf{w}^T\mathbf{a}_2, \ldots, \mathbf{w}^T\mathbf{a}_n) \quad (2.1.26)$$

so that the ith column of A_1 is

$$\mathbf{a}_i - \mathbf{w}^T\mathbf{a}_i\mathbf{w} = \mathbf{a}_i - \gamma\mathbf{u}^T\mathbf{a}_i\mathbf{u} \quad (2.1.27)$$

We can then summarize the Householder reduction by the vector pseudocode in Figure 2.1-12.

At the kth stage, the computation of s_k requires an inner product of length $n-k+1$, and scalar operations are then needed for γ_k and $a_{kk} - s_k$.

For $k = 1$ to $n-1$

$$s_k = -\text{sgn}(a_{kk})\left(\sum_{l=k}^{n} a_{lk}^2\right)^{1/2}, \quad \gamma_k = (s_k^2 - s_k a_{kk})^{-1}$$

$\quad \mathbf{u}_k^T = (0, \ldots, 0, a_{kk} - s_k, a_{k+1,k}, \ldots, a_{nk})$

$\quad a_{kk} = s_k$

$\quad$ For $j = k+1$ to n

$\quad\quad \alpha_j = \gamma_k\mathbf{u}_k^T\mathbf{a}_j$

$\quad\quad \mathbf{a}_j = \mathbf{a}_j - \alpha_j\mathbf{u}_k$

Figure 2.1-12. Column-oriented Householder reduction. Inner products.

The inner loop is an inner product followed by a linked triad, and the vector lengths are $n - k + 1$. Thus the average vector length is the same as for LU decomposition, $O(2n/3)$, and the inner loop requires linked triads of the same form. The major difference, of course, is that the inner loop also requires the inner products $\mathbf{u}_k^T\mathbf{a}_j$.

On register-to-register machines, it is important to organize the computation of Figure 2.1-12 so that unnecessary references to memory are not made. Consider the first stage, $k = 1$, and assume first that n is no more than the length of the vector registers. Then, to start the updating, $\mathbf{u}_1$ and $\mathbf{a}_2$ are loaded into vector registers and α_2 is computed. Since $\mathbf{u}_1$ and $\mathbf{a}_2$ are still in the registers, $\mathbf{a}_2$ can now be updated with no additional register loads. For $j = 3$, only $\mathbf{a}_3$ need be loaded since $\mathbf{u}_1$ remains in a register, and so on. Thus, the first stage, $k = 1$, requires only n vector loads.

In the likely event that n exceeds the length of a vector register, the situation is quite different. Since α_2 must be computed before $\mathbf{a}_2$ can be updated, all of $\mathbf{u}_1$ and $\mathbf{a}_2$ must be loaded, in parts, to compute α_2 and then all of $\mathbf{u}_1$ and $\mathbf{a}_2$ must be loaded again to update $\mathbf{a}_2$. If the same is done for $\mathbf{a}_3, \ldots, \mathbf{a}_n$, a total of $2(n - 1)$ loads of $\mathbf{u}_1$ and two loads each of $\mathbf{a}_2, \ldots, \mathbf{a}_n$ must be done for a total of $4(n - 1)$ loads of the complete vectors in the first stage.

A better strategy may be to compute all of the α_i before beginning the updating. In this case, we load the first part of $\mathbf{u}_1$ into a register and compute all of the partial inner products with the corresponding parts of $\mathbf{u}_1, \mathbf{a}_2, \mathbf{a}_3, \ldots, \mathbf{a}_n$. Then, the second parts of $\mathbf{u}_1$ and the $\mathbf{a}_i$ are loaded and the inner products are continued, and so on. For the updating, we again load the first part of $\mathbf{u}_1$ and then update the corresponding parts of $\mathbf{a}_2, \ldots, \mathbf{a}_n$. Then, the second part of $\mathbf{u}_1$ is loaded, the corresponding parts of $\mathbf{a}_2, \ldots, \mathbf{a}_n$ are updated, and so on. The advantage of this approach is that $\mathbf{u}_1$ needs to be loaded only twice so there are now a total of $2n$ complete vector loads in the first stage. A disadvantage is that additional storage for the α_i must be provided.

We next consider an alternative form of the Householder reduction. If $\mathbf{a}_i$ now denotes the ith row of A, the updating (2.1.26) may also be written in the form

$$A_1 = A - \mathbf{w}\mathbf{z}^T, \qquad \mathbf{z}^T = \mathbf{w}^T A = \mu \sum_{i=1}^{n} u_i \mathbf{a}_i = \mu \mathbf{v}^T \tag{2.1.28a}$$

so that the new ith row of A is

$$\mathbf{a}_i - w_i \mathbf{z}^T = \mathbf{a}_i - \gamma u_i \mathbf{v}^T \tag{2.1.28b}$$

This is sometimes called the *rank one* update form since $\mathbf{w}\mathbf{z}^T$ is a rank

For $k = 1$ to $n - 1$

$$s_k = -\text{sgn}(a_{kk})\left(\sum_{l=k}^{n} a_{lk}^2\right)^{1/2}, \gamma_k = (s_k^2 - s_k a_{kk})^{-1}$$

$$\mathbf{u}_k^T = (0, \ldots, 0, a_{kk} - s_k, a_{k+1,k}, \ldots, a_{nk})$$

$$\mathbf{v}_k^T = \sum_{l=k}^{n} u_{lk}\mathbf{a}_l$$

$$\hat{\mathbf{v}}_k^T = \gamma_k \mathbf{v}_k^T$$

For $j = k$ to n

$$\mathbf{a}_j = \mathbf{a}_j - u_{jk}\hat{\mathbf{v}}_k^T$$

Figure 2.1-13. Row-oriented Householder reduction. Rank one updates.

one matrix. The updating can be done entirely with linked triad or linear combination operations, and the overall algorithm is given in Figure 2.1-13.

The average vector length in this algorithm is again $O(2n/3)$, and the vector operations are now all linked triads. Note, however, that the computation of the s_k is now less satisfactory since the elements of the columns of A are not in contiguous locations if A is stored by rows. The number of array references is essentially the same as in the alternative organization of the inner product algorithm. At the first stage, the computation of $\mathbf{v}_1$ allows all of the $\mathbf{a}_i$ to be used with $\mathbf{v}_1$ (or parts of $\mathbf{v}_1$) left in a vector register. Hence $O(2n)$ loads of complete vectors are required in the first stage.

The code of Figure 2.1-13 for the rank one update form is predicated on storage of A by rows. It may be desirable to use this form when A is stored by columns and we can achieve this on vector computers requiring contiguous storage by using Householder transformations on the right,

$$A(I - \mathbf{w}\mathbf{w}^T) \tag{2.1.29}$$

The first transformation introduces zeros above the main diagonal in the last column and successive transformations give zeros in columns $n - 1$, $n - 2$, and so on. Thus, in place of the QR decomposition of A the sequence of transformations $AP_1P_2 \cdots P_{n-1} = L$ gives an LQ decomposition, where L is lower triangular and Q is orthogonal. This is equivalent to doing the QR decomposition of A^T, but without performing an explicit transposition of A. The details of an LQ algorithm corresponding to Figure 2.1-13 are left to Exercise 2.1-10.

Givens Reduction

A Givens transformation is a plane rotation matrix of the form

$$P_{ij} = \begin{bmatrix} 1 & & & & & & & & \\ & \ddots & & & & & & & \\ & & 1 & & & & & & \\ & & & \cos\theta_{ij} & & & \sin\theta_{ij} & & \\ & & & & 1 & & & & \\ & & & & & \ddots & & & \\ & & & & & & 1 & & \\ & & & -\sin\theta_{ij} & & & \cos\theta_{ij} & & \\ & & & & & & & 1 & \\ & & & & & & & & \ddots \\ & & & & & & & & & 1 \end{bmatrix} \tag{2.1.30}$$

with sine and cosine elements in the ith and jth rows and columns as indicated. It is easy to see (Exercise 2.1-12) that any plane rotation matrix is orthogonal. Viewed as a linear transformation, P_{ij} causes a rotation through the angle θ_{ij} in the (i, j) plane.

We now use the matrices P_{ij} in the following way to achieve the QR reduction (2.1.22). Consider

$$A_1 = P_{12}A = \begin{bmatrix} c_{12}\mathbf{a}_1 + s_{12}\mathbf{a}_2 \\ -s_{12}\mathbf{a}_1 + c_{12}\mathbf{a}_2 \\ \mathbf{a}_3 \\ \vdots \\ \mathbf{a}_n \end{bmatrix} \tag{2.1.31}$$

where $c_{12} = \cos\theta_{12}$, $s_{12} = \sin\theta_{12}$ and $\mathbf{a}_i$ is the ith row of A. We choose θ_{12} so that

$$-a_{11}s_{12} + a_{21}c_{12} = 0 \tag{2.1.32}$$

Thus, A_1 has a zero in the $(2, 1)$ position and the elements in the first two rows now differ, in general, from those of A, while the remaining rows are the same. Next, we compute $A_2 = P_{13}A_1$, which modifies the first and third rows of A_1 while leaving all others the same; in particular, the zero produced in the $(2, 1)$ position in the first stage remains zero. The angle θ_{13} is now chosen so that the $(3, 1)$ element of A_2 is zero. We continue in this fashion, zeroing the remaining elements in the first column, one after another, and then zeroing elements in the second column in the order $(3, 2)$,

$(4, 2), \ldots, (n, 2)$, and so on. In all, we will use $(n-1)+(n-2)+\cdots+1$ plane rotation matrices and the result is that

$$PA \equiv P_{n-1,n} \cdots P_{12}A = R \tag{2.1.33}$$

is upper triangular. The matrices P_{ij} are all orthogonal so that P and P^{-1} are also orthogonal. With $Q = P^{-1}$, (2.1.33) is then the QR decomposition (2.1.22).

We note that we do not actually compute the rotation angles θ_{ij} but only their sines and cosines so as to achieve the desired zeroing of elements. For example, for (2.1.32),

$$c_{12} = a_{11}(a_{11}^2 + a_{21}^2)^{-1/2}, \qquad s_{12} = a_{21}(a_{11}^2 + a_{21}^2)^{-1/2} \tag{2.1.34}$$

The Givens reduction has a natural parallelism in the updating of the rows at each stage. At the first stage, after c_{12} and s_{12} are computed by scalar operations, the first two rows are modified as shown in (2.1.31). This requires a scalar-vector multiplication followed by a linked triad. Note that the vector lengths are $n-1$ because we know that the new $(2, 1)$ element is zero. Since the Euclidean length of the first column must be preserved under multiplication by P_{12}, we also know that the new $(1, 1)$ element is $(a_{11}^2 + a_{21}^2)^{1/2}$, which has already been computed. Thus, to zero the elements in the first column requires $4(n-1)$ vector operations with vector lengths of $n-1$. Similarly, zeroing elements in the jth column will require $4(n-j)$ vector operations with vector lengths of $n-j$ so that the average vector length for the entire reduction will be (Exercise 2.1-6),

$$\frac{4(n-1)(n-1)+4(n-2)(n-2)+\cdots+4}{4(n-1)+4(n-2)+\cdots+4} = O(2n/3) \tag{2.1.35}$$

the same as LU decomposition and the Householder reduction.

A pseudocode for the above Givens algorithm is given in Figure 2.1-14. Note that in the update of $\mathbf{a}_i$ it is the current $\mathbf{a}_k$ that is used, not the new $\mathbf{a}_k$ which has just been computed and is denoted by $\hat{\mathbf{a}}_k$.

```
For k = 1 to n
    For i = k + 1 to n
        Compute s_ki, c_ki
        â_k = c_ki a_k + s_ki a_i
        a_i = -s_ki a_k + c_ki a_i
```

Figure 2.1-14. Row-oriented Givens reduction.

The Givens algorithm has twice as many vector operations as the Householder algorithms. However, on register-to-register machines these can be accomplished with only half the number of memory references as the Householder algorithms. Consider the first stage, consisting of zeroing the first column of A. The vectors $\mathbf{a}_1$ and $\mathbf{a}_2$ (or parts of them) are loaded into vector registers and then the necessary arithmetic is done. The updated $\mathbf{a}_1$ is left in a register so that the zeroing of the (3, 1) element requires only the loading of $\mathbf{a}_3$. Thus, the zeroing of the $n-1$ elements in the first column requires only a single load of each of the rows of A, for a total of n complete vector loads. This compares with $O(2n)$ loads for the Householder algorithms, and Givens will be more competitive on such vector machines than a simple operation count would indicate.

The Givens algorithm of Figure 2.1-14 is row oriented. A column-oriented algorithm is given in Figure 2.1-15. At the beginning of the kth stage, all of the sine–cosine pairs for the kth column are computed. This requires continual updating of the (k, k) element so that this preparatory l loop is entirely scalar arithmetic. The first arithmetic statement in the ji loop is the updating of the (k, j) element, which is modified each time through the i loop. Here, the superscripts indicate that the value of the (k, j) element is from the previous pass through the i loop. In terms of vector operations, the inner i loop may be written as

$$\mathbf{p} = \mathbf{s}_k\mathbf{a}_j, \qquad \mathbf{r} = \mathbf{c}_k\mathbf{a}_j$$

$$\text{For } i = k+1 \text{ to } n$$

$$a_{kj}^{(i+1)} = c_{ki}a_{kj}^{(i)} + p_i$$

$$q_i = s_{ki}a_{kj}^{(i)}$$

$$\mathbf{a}_j = \mathbf{r} - \mathbf{q}$$

where the formation of $\mathbf{p}$ and $\mathbf{r}$ is by elementwise vector multiplication.

```
For k = 1 to n - 1
  For l = k + 1 to n
    Compute s_kl, c_kl
    a_kk = c_kl a_kk + s_kl a_lk
  For j = k + 1 to n
    For i = k + 1 to n
      a_kj^(i+1) = c_ki a_kj^(i) + s_ki a_ij
      a_ij = -s_ki a_kj^(i) + c_ki a_ij
```

Figure 2.1-15. Column-oriented Givens algorithm.

Thus, the inner loop may be written in terms of three vector operations (two vector–vector multiplies and one vector add) plus a scalar loop. It is clear that this column-oriented algorithm does not vectorize as well as the row-oriented algorithm of Figure 2.1-14.

Exercises 2.1

1. Verify by induction the summation formulas

$$\sum_{i=1}^{n} i = \tfrac{1}{2} n(n+1), \qquad \sum_{i=1}^{n} i^2 = \tfrac{1}{6} n(n+1)(2n+1)$$

Use these to show that the expression in (2.1.3) is

$$\frac{1}{3}\,\frac{n(n-1)(2n-1)}{n(n-1)} = \tfrac{1}{3}(2n-1) = O(2n/3)$$

2. Assume that a vector computer has timing formulas of $(1000 + 10m)$ ns for addition, $(1600 + 10m)$ ns for linked triads and $(1600 + 70m)$ ns for division for vectors of length m, and 100 ns for scalar operations. Show that the total times for the LU decompositions of Figures 2.1-1 and 2.1-2 are

$$T_R \doteq (\tfrac{10}{3} n^3 + 850n^2) \text{ ns}, \qquad T_C \doteq (\tfrac{10}{3} n^3 + 835n^2) \text{ ns}$$

for a system of size n.

3. Assume that a vector computer has the characteristics of Exercise 2 and, in addition, can perform inner products with a timing formula of $(2000 + 20m)$ ns on vectors of length m. Ascertain which of the algorithms (2.1.10) and Figure 2.1-4 is more efficient for solving triangular systems as a function of the system size n.

4. Assume that on a register-to-register machine, the registers are of length 64 words. Discuss modifications of (2.1.4) and (2.1.5) to take this into account.

5. Formulate the inner product and column sweep algorithms for the solution of a lower triangular system of equations $L\mathbf{x} = \mathbf{b}$.

6. Use the summation formulas of Exercise 1 to verify (2.1.17), (2.1.19), (2.1.20), and (2.1.35).

7. Assume that a vector computer has the characteristics of Exercises 2 and 3. For an $n \times n$ system with q right-hand sides, ascertain for which values of q and n the algorithm (2.1.21) for the back substitution is more efficient than (2.1.10) applied to each right-hand side.

8. Assume that a vector computer has the characteristics of Exercise 2 and that square roots require 500 ns. Show that the total time for the Choleski decomposition algorithm of Figure 2.1-10 is

$$T \doteq (\tfrac{5}{3} n^3 + 835n^2) \text{ ns}$$

9. Change (2.1.13) to correspond to $A = LL^T$ and then give Dongarra-Eisenstat-type formulations of Choleski decomposition.
10. Give a rank-one update algorithm corresponding to Figure 2.1-13 for computing the LQ decomposition of A based on right-handed Householder transformations of the form (2.1.29).
11. Let $P = I - \mathbf{w}\mathbf{w}^T$, where $\mathbf{w}$ is a real column vector. Show that P is symmetric and is also orthogonal if and only if $\mathbf{w}^T\mathbf{w} = 2$.
12. Show that a plane rotation matrix of the form (2.1.30) is orthogonal.
13. Extend the Dongarra-Eisenstat algorithm to a block form by replacing (2.1.13) by

$$\begin{bmatrix} A_{11} & A_{12} & A_{13} \\ A_{21} & A_{22} & A_{23} \\ A_{31} & A_{32} & A_{33} \end{bmatrix} = \begin{bmatrix} L_{11} & & \\ L_{21} & L_{22} & \\ L_{31} & L_{32} & L_{33} \end{bmatrix} \begin{bmatrix} U_{11} & U_{12} & U_{13} \\ & U_{22} & U_{23} \\ & & U_{33} \end{bmatrix}$$

where A_{22}, L_{22}, and U_{22} are now matrices, and L_{22} has 1's on its main diagonal, Equate corresponding elements in this block factorization to obtain the formulas, corresponding to (2.1.14), that determine L_{22}, L_{32}, U_{22}, and U_{23} given L_{11}, L_{21}, L_{31}, U_{11}, U_{12}, U_{13}.

References and Extensions 2.1

1. Dongarra, Gustavson, and Karp [1984] discuss in some detail how to handle vectors that are longer than the length of the vector registers, as well as important issues of chaining and overlapping. This paper also introduces in a systematic way the *ijk* forms of LU decomposition. Earlier, Moler [1972] had advocated the *kji* form for serial computers with virtual memory and Fong and Jordan [1977] had observed that the *jki* form was highly suitable for the CRAY-1. See also Ortega [1987b] for a more detailed treatment of the *ijk* forms for LU and Choleski decomposition and a generalized formulation that includes the bordering and Dongarra-Eisenstat algorithms. Appendix 1 is partially based on this paper.
2. The Dongarra-Eisenstat algorithm is given in Dongarra and Eisenstat [1984], which also discusses bordering algorithms. The inner-product form of the Dongarra-Eisenstat algorithm is essentially the *Doolittle reduction* (see for example, Stewart [1973]). We have preferred to call it the Dongarra-Eisenstat algorithm to recognize their emphasis on the matrix-vector multiplication aspect of the algorithm.
3. Calahan [1986] has extended the Dongarra-Eisenstat algorithm to a block form (see Exercise 2.1-13) in which the basic operation is matrix-matrix multiplication, rather than matrix-vector. Results on a single processor CRAY-2 are given. Other block algorithms for LU decomposition are discussed, primarily for the Alliant FX/8, in Gallivan *et al.* [1987]. Their results are impressive and it is

becoming clear that the block approach will probably lead to the best algorithms on machines with hierarchical memories.

4. Dongarra and Hewitt [1986] discuss a combination *jki* and *kji* LU decomposition in which a few (for example, four) columns of L are computed and then used to update all remaining columns. Excellent results are reported for a four processor CRAY X-MP. Dave and Duff [1987] give timing results for a similar algorithm on the CRAY-2. Other papers considering the CRAY X-MP include Calahan [1985] and Dongarra and Hinds [1985], which reports timing results for LU and Choleski factorization on the CRAY X-MP and two Japanese machines.
5. There are a variety of points of view regarding the problem of interchanges in Gaussian elimination. Lambiotte [1975] recommends doing the interchanges by scalar operations on CDC machines if A is stored by columns. Also for CDC machines, Kascic [1979] recommends interchange by gather–scatter operations if A is stored by columns and recommends finding the maximum element by a gather followed by a vector maximum operation if A is stored by rows. For CRAY machines, Dongarra, Gustavson, and Karp [1984] recommend interchanging rows. Hay and Gladwell [1985] observe that doing implicit interchanges gives rise to indirect addressing, which may be bad for vector machines.
6. A variation of Gaussian elimination is the Gauss–Jordan algorithm, which reduces A to a diagonal matrix, rather than upper triangular. At the kth stage, the partially reduced matrix has the form

$$\begin{array}{cccccc}
a_{11} & & & \hat{a}_{1k} & \cdots & \hat{a}_{1n} \\
 & \ddots & & \vdots & & \vdots \\
 & & \hat{a}_{k-1,k-1} & & & \\
 & & & \hat{a}_{kk} & \cdots & \hat{a}_{kn} \\
 & & & \vdots & & \vdots \\
 & & & \hat{a}_{nk} & \cdots & \hat{a}_{nn}
\end{array}$$

where the carets indicate that the elements have probably been changed from their original values. Assuming that $\hat{a}_{kk} \neq 0$, a multiple of the kth row is then subtracted from all other rows so as to eliminate all entries in the kth column, except the diagonal one. The basic update step is the linked triad $\mathbf{a}_j - a_{kj}\mathbf{m}_k$ where $\mathbf{a}_j$ is the current column of A and $\mathbf{m}_k$ is the vector of multipliers a_{ik}/a_{kk} with the kth component of $\mathbf{m}_k$ set to zero. The potential advantage of the Gauss–Jordan algorithm on vector machines is that the vector lengths remain n throughout the computation, rather than decrease in length as the reduction proceeds. However, the serial operation count is $O(n^3)$ rather than the $O(2n^3/3)$ of Gaussian elimination and the extra operations tend to cancel out the advantage of the longer vector lengths. Moreover, there are potential problems of numerical stability. Overall, in spite of the seeming attractiveness of the long vector lengths, there seems to be little reason to prefer this algorithm over Gaussian elimination.
7. Dongarra, Kaufman, and Hammarling [1986] give times on a CRAY-1 for solving triangular systems with q right-hand sides by the column sweep algorithm, the column sweep algorithm with loops unrolled to a depth of two,

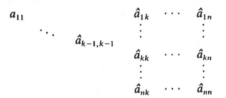

and the "inner product" algorithm (2.1.21). A subset of their results is given below in units of 10^{-3} seconds.

n	q	CS	UCS	IP
100	25	12.5	8.32	6.92
	100	49.9	33.3	14.4
200	25	38.6	25.5	24.1
	200	308	202	93.7
300	25	78.5	51.1	51.8
	300	940	613	290

Note that the unrolled column sweep algorithm is always about 50% faster than the original version.

8. An excellent summary of Choleski's method (for serial computers) is given in George and Liu [1981], and the data access pattern figures in this section follow their examples. A review of the implementation of Choleski's method on the first generation of vector computers such as the TI-ASC, CRAY-1 and CDC STAR-100 is given in Voigt [1977].

9. The algorithms of this section do not make explicit use of zeros in the coefficient matrix A; Section 2.3 will address this question. We note here only that zeros in A may well become nonzeros during the course of LU decomposition or the other algorithms; this is called *fill-in*. One of the simplest examples of how extensive fill-in can occur is given by a matrix of the form

$$\begin{bmatrix} * & * & \cdots & * \\ * & \ddots & & \\ \vdots & & & \\ * & & & * \end{bmatrix}$$

which is zero except for nonzeros in the first row and column and main diagonal. All of the zero positions in the lower triangle will, in general, become nonzero during the course of LU decomposition. On the other hand, the matrix

$$\begin{bmatrix} * & & & * \\ & \ddots & & \vdots \\ & & \ddots & * \\ * & \cdots & & * \end{bmatrix}$$

suffers no fill and the L and U factors have the same nonzero structure as the corresponding parts of the original matrix.

10. Mattingly, Meyer, and Ortega [1987] have discussed the "*ijk* forms" of Householder and Givens reduction, in analogy with LU and Choleski factorization. The row-oriented Givens algorithm given in the text corresponds to the *kij* form. There are also natural *kji*, *jki*, and *ikj* forms, but the other two forms

do not lead to viable vector algorithms. For Householder reduction, the rank one update algorithm of Figure 2.1-13 is the *kij* form, whereas the inner product algorithm of Figure 2.1-12 is the *kji* form. There is also a delayed update *jki* form, but the other three *ijk* forms are not useful.

11. To minimize round-off error, the computation of the sines and cosines in Givens method as given in (2.1.34) can be replaced by

$$\text{if } |a_{21}| \geq |a_{11}|, \qquad r = a_{11}/a_{21}, \qquad s_{12} = (1 + r^2)^{-1/2}, \qquad c_{12} = s_{12}r$$

$$\text{if } |a_{21}| < |a_{11}|, \qquad r = a_{21}/a_{11}, \qquad c_{12} = (1 + r^2)^{-1/2}, \qquad s_{12} = c_{12}r$$

Similarly, in the Householder reduction, it is possible that overflow or underflow could occur in the computation of s_k in Figure 2.1-12. This problem can be eliminated by scaling; see, for example, Stewart [1973].

12. Dongarra, Kaufman, and Hammarling [1986] suggest combining two Householder transformations in a single step to reduce the number of memory references. This idea has been extended by Bischof and van Loan [1987] to block Householder methods in which the basic operations are matrix-matrix multiplication. As with the *LU* decomposition, such block methods will probably to the best on machines with hierarchical memories.

2.2. Direct Methods for Parallel Computers

We next consider the implementation of the algorithms of Section 2.1, as well as others, on parallel computers. As in the previous section, we will assume that the $n \times n$ coefficient matrix A is full.

LU Decomposition

We assume at first that we have a local memory system and that the number of processors $p = n$. Then one possible organization of *LU* decomposition is the following. Assume that the *i*th row of A is stored in processor *i*. At the first stage, the first row of A is sent to all other processors and then the computations

$$l_{i1} = a_{i1}/a_{11}, \qquad a_{ij} = a_{ij} - l_{i1}a_{1j}, \qquad j = 2, \ldots, n \tag{2.2.1}$$

can be done in parallel in the processors $P_2, \ldots, P_n$. The computation is continued by sending the new second row of the reduced matrix from processor P_2 to processors $P_3, \ldots, P_n$, then doing the calculations in parallel, and so on. The first two stages are shown in Figure 2.2-1, in which $\mathbf{a}_i$ denotes the current *i*th row of A. Note that this approach has two major drawbacks:

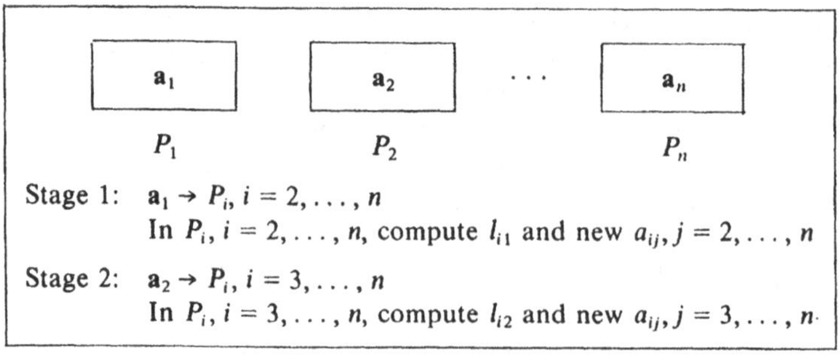

Figure 2.2-1. *LU* decomposition in n processors.

there is considerable communication of data between each stage, and the number of active processors decreases by one at each stage.

An alternative to storing by rows is to store column i of A in processor i. In this case, at the first stage, the multipliers l_{i1} are all computed in processor 1 and then sent to all processors. The updates

$$a_{ij} = a_{ij} - l_{i1}a_{1j}, \qquad j = 2, \ldots, n \tag{2.2.2}$$

are then computed in parallel in processors $2, \ldots, n$. Processor 1 ceases to be active after computing the multipliers l_{i1}, and, in general, one more processor becomes idle at each stage, the same load-balancing problem as in the row-oriented algorithm.

Interleaved Storage

In the more realistic situation that $p \ll n$, the above load-balancing problems are mitigated to some extent. Suppose that $n = kp$, and, in the storage by rows strategy, assign the first k rows of A to processor 1, the second k to processor 2, and so on. This is called *block* storage. Again, the first row will be sent from processor 1 to the other processors and then the computation (2.2.1) will be done but in blocks of k sets of operations in each processor. As before, processors will become idle as the computation proceeds, but the overall ratio of computation time to data transmission and idle time will be an increasing function of k.

A more attractive scheme is to interleave the storage of the rows among the processors. Assuming still that $n = kp$, rows $1, p + 1, 2p + 1, \ldots$ are stored in processor 1, rows $2, p + 2, 2p + 2, \ldots$ in processor 2, and so on, as illustrated in Figure 2.2-2. We will call this storage pattern *wrapped interleaved storage.* It greatly alleviates the problem of processors becoming idle

processor 1	processor 2	...	processor p
rows 1, p+1, ⋯, (k−1)p+1	rows 2, p+2, ⋯, (k−1)p+2	...	rows p, 2p, ⋯, kp

Figure 2.2-2. Wrapped interleaved row storage.

since, for example, processor 1 will be working almost until the end of the reduction, in particular, until processing of row $(k-1)p+1$ is complete. There will, of course, still be some imbalances in the workloads of the processors. For example, after the first stage, row 1 is no longer needed and processor 1 will have one less row to process at the next stage than the other processors. A similar kind of imbalance will result in the likely event that n is not a multiple of the number of processors.

A similar interleaving may also be done in storage by columns where now processor 1 would hold columns $1, p+1, \ldots, (k-1)p+1$, processor 2 would hold columns $2, p+2, \ldots, (k-1)p+2$, and so on. Again, all processors would be working, with minor imbalances, almost to the end of the reduction. Comparisons of the two algorithms are given in Exercises 2.2-1 and 2.2-3.

A variation of row (or column) wrapped storage is *reflection interleaved storage.* Here, the rows are distributed as illustrated in Figure 2.2-3 for the case of four processors and sixteen rows. In general, the first p rows are distributed to the p processors in order, the next p rows are distributed in reverse order, and so on. Wrapped and reflection storage have many of the same properties, but wrapped storage does have some advantages. We will consider only it in the sequel, and use the terms "wrapped," "interleaved," and "wrapped interleaved" as synonomous.

The notion of interleaved storage is motivated primarily by local memory systems. It can also be used on global memory systems as a means of assigning tasks to processors. That is, with row interleaved storage, processor 1 will do the updates (2.2.2) on rows $p+1, 2p+1, \ldots$ and so on. However, on global memory systems, dynamic load balancing can also be achieved by using the idea of a pool of tasks. Such dynamic load balancing is less satisfactory for a local memory machine because of the need to reassign storage from one processor to another.

processor 1	processor 2	processor 3	processor 4
rows 1, 8, 9, 16	rows 2, 7, 10, 15	rows 3, 6, 11, 14	rows 4, 5, 12, 13

Figure 2.2-3. Reflection interleaved row storage.

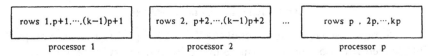

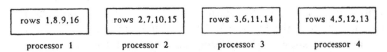

Send-ahead and Compute-ahead

We now discuss in more detail the *LU* decomposition using wrapped interleaved row storage. We assume first a local memory system. Consider the first stage, in which zeros are introduced into the first column. If we proceed in the usual serial fashion, the multipliers l_{i1} are computed, the corresponding rows updated, and then the second stage is begun. At the beginning of the second stage, the processor holding the second row must transmit this row to all other processors. Hence, there is a delay while this transmission takes place. An obvious solution to this problem is for processor 2 to transmit the updated second row as soon as it is ready. We call this a *send-ahead* strategy. If computation and communication can be overlapped, all of the processors can be carrying out the updating of the first stage while this transmission takes place. The same will be done at each stage: at the kth stage, the $(k+1)$st row will be transmitted as soon as it is updated. How well this strategy works on a given machine will depend on the communication properties of the system.

This send-ahead strategy also has application on shared-memory systems. Here, a straightforward implementation would have a synchronization after each stage so that no processor would begin the next stage until all processors have finished the current one. During the kth stage, the processor to which row $k+1$ is assigned will have at least as much work as any other processor since it is assigned at least as many rows. Thus, other processors may have to wait until this processor is done before they can begin the next stage. The send-ahead strategy, which is now really a *compute-ahead* strategy, modifies this by marking the $(k+1)$st row "done" as soon as it has been updated. Then, as soon as other processors have completed their work on the kth stage, they may immediately start the $(k+1)$st stage if the $(k+1)$st row has been marked "done". This marking serves to carry out the necessary synchronization without unnecessary delays. We note that send-ahead and compute-ahead are also called *pipelining*.

Partial Pivoting

The use of partial pivoting to maintain numerical stability introduces additional considerations into the storage question. Suppose, first, that A is stored by column wrapped storage. Then the search for the pivot element takes place in a single processor. This has the virtue of simplicity but also the potential for all other processors to be idle while the search is done. This problem can potentially be mitigated by a compute-and-send-ahead strategy in which, at the kth stage, the pivot element in the $(k+1)$st column is determined as soon as the column has been updated. In any case, after the pivot row is determined, this information must be transmitted to all other processors. Then an interchange of rows can be done in parallel within all the processors (or the interchange can be handled implicitly by indexing).

The situation with row-wrapped storage is rather different. Now the search for the maximum element in the current column (say the kth) must take place across the processors. This can be done by a fan-in mechanism as indicated in Section 1.2 (See Exercise 2.2-3). At the end of the fan-in, a single processor will know the next pivot row and this information must be sent to all other processors. Again, we must decide whether to physically interchange rows. If we do interchange, only two processors are involved and all others may be idle during the interchange. On the other hand, if we do not interchange, then we deviate from row wrapped storage in the subsequent calculations. Indeed, the more interchanges that are required but not done physically, the more the storage pattern will look like a random scattering of the rows to local memories.

The *ijk* Forms and Parallel-Vector Computers

The *ijk* forms of LU decomposition discussed in the previous section, and in more detail in Appendix 1, provide a number of other possible organizations of LU decomposition that might be useful on parallel systems. More importantly, they provide alternative organizations for parallel-vector systems (the processors are vector computers). A detailed analysis of these *ijk* forms for parallel and parallel-vector systems is given in Appendix 1, and we summarize in Table 2.2-1 the main conclusions of that appendix.

In Table 2.2-1, *kij*,r denotes the *kij* form using wrapped interleaved row storage, whereas *kij*,c uses wrapped interleaved column storage; similarly, for the other forms. We have listed the basic problems with each method as well as comments on the vector lengths. "Full vector lengths"

Table 2.2-1. The *ijk* Forms of LU Decomposition on Parallel-Vector Systems

kij, r:	Minimum delays	Full vector lengths
kij, c:	Multiplier and transmission delays	Partial vector lengths
kji, r:	Minimum delays	Partial vector lengths
kji, c:	Minimum delays	Full vector lengths but delays
ikj, r:	Very poor load balancing	
ikj, c:	Multiplier and transmission delays	Partial vector lengths
jki, r:	High communication costs	Partial vector lengths
jki, c:	Multiplier and transmission delays	Full vector lengths but delays
ijk, r:	High communication costs	
ijk, c:	High communication costs	
jik, r:	High communication costs	
jik, c:	High communication costs	

means that the maximum vector lengths possible at a given stage of LU decomposition can be used; for example, at the kth stage, these vector lengths would be $O(n-k)$. "Partial vector lengths" means that the corresponding data are distributed across the processors and, consequently, the vector lengths are divided by the number of processors. As indicated in the table, in the case of *kji*,c and *jki*,c we can achieve full vector lengths but only at the expense of delays in acquring the elements of the vector. The *ijk* and *jik* forms have very poor data distribution and seem unsuitable for all parallel systems. The *kij*,r *kji*,r and *kji*,c forms seem most promising. In particular, the *kij*,r form is the algorithm described above under "send-ahead and compute-ahead."

Fine Grain Algorithms and Data Flow Organization

The parallel organizations of LU decomposition discussed so far have used rows (or columns) as the basic entity, and are called *medium grain* algorithms. They essentially mirror the vector algorithms of the previous section. However, there is inherently more parallelism in the decomposition and this can be utilized if sufficiently many processors are available. We next discuss some of these algorithms, which are called *small* or *fine grain*.

We first note that LU decomposition may, in principle, be carried out as in Figure 2.2-4, where each step performs in parallel the computations that are indicated. Since each element update requires two operations (a multiply and an add), the process is completed in $3(n-1)$ time steps. (We have made the usually unrealistic assumption that a divide can be performed in the same time as a multiply or add.)

The above scheme assumes that there are at least $(n-1)^2$ processors available so that all of the computations of step 2 proceed in parallel. However, the important question of communication is not addressed. It is assumed at each step that the necessary data (multipliers and/or updated matrix elements) are available in the proper processors. For this to be true

Step 1. Compute first column of multipliers l_{i1}, $i = 2, \ldots, n$
Step 2. Compute updated elements $a_{ij}^1 = a_{ij} - l_{i1}a_{1j}$, $i = 2, \ldots, n$, $j = 2, \ldots, n$
Step 3. Compute second column of multipliers l_{i2}, $i = 3, \ldots, n$
Step 4. Compute updated elements $a_{ij}^2 = a_{ij}^1 - l_{i2}a_{2j}^1$, $i = 3, \ldots, n$, $j = 3, \ldots, n$
⋮
Step $2n-3$. Compute last multiplier $l_{n,n-1}$
Step $2n-2$. Update (n, n) element

Figure 2.2-4. LU decomposition with maximum parallelism.

on a local memory system these data will need to be transmitted from the processors where they are computed to those that will use them at the next step. We next discuss one way to do this.

Assume that there are $(n-1)^2$ processors, which are numbered according to the matrix element they will update; that is, processor P_{ij} will update a_{ij}. Then the following transmissions need to be added to the scheme of Figure 2.2-4:

Step 1. Compute l_{i1} in processor P_{i1}, $i = 2, \ldots, n$

Step 1a. Transmit l_{i1} to processors P_{ij}, $i = 2, \ldots, n$, $j = 2, \ldots, n$

Step 2. Compute a_{ij}^1 in processor P_{ij}, $i = 2, \ldots, n$, $j = 2, \ldots, n$

Step 2a. Transmit a_{2j}^1 to P_{ij}, $i = 3, \ldots, n$, $j = 2, \ldots, n$

$$\vdots$$

If we assume that the necessary transmissions at each step can be done in one time step, the total number of time steps increases to $O(5n)$. However, it is quite unrealistic that the transmission could be done this rapidly.

We next examine another approach, which is a *data flow algorithm.* We again assume that there are n^2 processors that are arranged in a square lattice with a four-nearest-neighbor connection (see Figure 1.1-14). We assume that each processor can transmit one word of data in the same time as a floating point operation and that transmission and computation can take place concurrently. (Both of these assumptions are highly optimistic.) The initial steps of the algorithm we wish to discuss are given in Figure 2.2-5.

We now consider the above computation in more detail. Figure 2.2-6 shows the situation at the end of step 4. At the end of this step, $l_{21}a_{12}$ has been computed in processor P_{22}. The multipliers have been sent to processors P_{23} and P_{32} but the computations using these multipliers have not

Step 1.	Send a_{1j} from P_{1j} to $P_{2j}, j = 1, \ldots, n$.
Step 2.	Send a_{1j} from P_{2j} to $P_{3j}, j = 1, \ldots, n$. Compute l_{21}.
Step 3.	Send a_{1j} from P_{3j} to $P_{4j}, i = 1, \ldots, n$. Send l_{21} to P_{22}. Compute l_{31}.
Step 4.	Send a_{1j} from P_{4j} to $P_{5j}, j = 1, \ldots, n$. Send l_{21} to P_{23}. Send l_{31} to P_{32}. Compute l_{41}. Compute $l_{21}a_{12}$ in P_{22}.
Step 5.	Send a_{1j} from P_{5j} to $P_{6j}, j = 1, \ldots, n$. Send l_{21} to P_{21}. Send l_{31} to P_{33}. Send l_{41} to P_{42}. Compute l_{51}. Compute $a_{22}^1 = a_{22} - l_{21}a_{12}$ in P_{22}. Compute $l_{21}a_{13}$ in P_{23}. Compute $l_{31}a_{12}$ in P_{32}.

Figure 2.2-5. A data flow organization of *LU* decomposition.

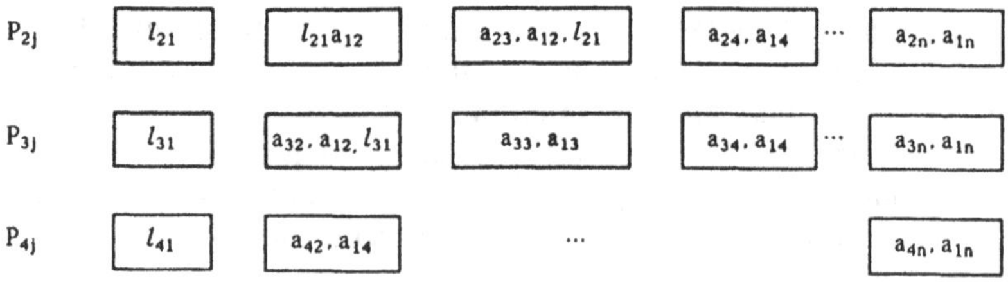

Figure 2.2-6. End of step 4 of data flow.

yet been done. The multiplier l_{41} has just been computed in processor P_{41} and the first row has been transmitted to all processors in the fifth row. To continue the process, Figure 2.2-7 shows the computation and transmission occuring *during* step 5.

The pattern should now be clear. At each step, one more multiplier is computed, while the previous multipliers are all transmitted to the next processor to the right. Simultaneously, matrix elements are updated by those processors that have the necessary data. The computation thus moves through the matrix (equivalently, the array of processors) in a diagonal wavefront manner. Hence, this is sometimes called a *wavefront* organization of *LU* decomposition. Note that as soon as the updated (2, 2) element is computed, it can be transmitted to processor P_{32}, and when the updated (3, 2) element is ready, the multiplier l_{32} can be computed. This starts a new wavefront, which computes the updates of the second stage of *LU* decomposition. After a while, several wavefronts will be moving through the matrix simultaneously.

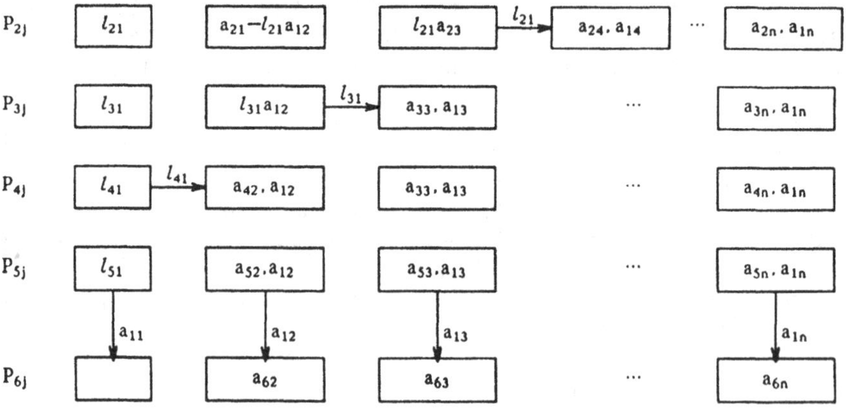

Figure 2.2-7. Step 5 of data flow.

We next examine the number of time steps needed to complete the factorization. Consider the second row. At the end of the fifth time step, the updated element a_{22}^1 has been computed, l_{21} is in P_{24}, and $l_{21}a_{13}$ has been computed in P_{23}. At each subsequent time step, one additional updating is completed so the second row is finished after $5 + n - 2 = n + 3$ time steps. The updating of the third row during the first stage is one time step behind the second row and the second stage is four time steps behind the first stage. To see this, consider the (3, 3) element. At the time the (2, 3) element is complete the (3, 2) element has just completed and the (2, 2) element received in processor P_{32}. Then the following steps are needed to complete the (3, 3) element: compute l_{32}; send l_{32}; compute $l_{32}a_{23}^1$; compute $a_{33}^1 = a_{33} - l_{32}a_{23}^1$. Therefore, the third row is complete at time $n + 7$. Continuing in this fashion, we see that the overall factorization is complete at the end of $n + 3 + 4(n - 2) = 5n - 5$ time steps.

On the basis on this number of time steps, the speed-up of the data flow LU decomposition algorithm is

$$S_p = \frac{O(\frac{2}{3}n^3)}{O(5n)} = O(n^2)$$

Hence, for large n this algorithm gives very high speed-up, under the assumption of a very large number of processors. For the linear systems for which we would wish to use parallel computers we might expect n to be in the range $10^3 \leq n \leq 10^6$. Even for $n = 10^3$, the above algorithm requires 10^6 processors. Therefore, the algorithm as described is mainly of theoretical interest, although combinations of the data flow approach with the medium grained algorithms discussed previously could be potentially useful. For example, several matrix elements, rather than just one, could be assigned to each processor. Then the algorithm could be potentially useful on systems such as the Connection Machine (Section 1.1), which currently has 65,000 processors.

Choleski Decomposition

If A is symmetric positive definite, we can consider the Choleski decomposition $A = LL^T$, where now we assume that only the lower triangular part of A will be stored. As with LU decomposition, we use interleaved wrapped storage, either by rows or by columns. The *ijk* forms of Choleski decomposition provide a guide to several possible organizations, and these are discussed in some detail in Appendix 1 for both parallel and parallel-vector computers. We summarize in Table 2.2-2 the main conclusions of that appendix. As before, *kij*,r and *kij*,c denote the *kij* form

Table 2.2-2. The *ijk* Forms of Choleski on Parallel-Vector Systems

kij, r:	High communication costs	Full vector lengths but delays
kij, c:	Not competitive	
kji, r:	High communication costs	Partial vector lengths
kji, c:	Minimum delays	Full vector lengths but delays
ikj, r:	Not competitive	
ikj, c:	Not competitive	
jki, r:	Fairly high communication costs	Partial vector lengths
jki, c:	Not competitive	
ijk, r:	Poor load balancing	
ijk, c:	High communication cost	
jik, r:	Delays for transmits	Full vector lengths
jik, c:	Not competitive	

with row and column interleaved wrapped storage, respectively, and similarly for the other algorithms.

The most promising of these forms on parallel systems would seem to be *kji*,c and *jki*,r. Of these, only *kji*,c permits long vector lengths on parallel-vector systems but at the expense of delays to accumulate the data for the vectors.

Solution of Triangular Systems

After the LU or Choleski decompositions, we need to solve triangular systems of equations, as discussed in the previous section. We will consider only upper triangular systems $U\mathbf{x} = \mathbf{c}$; the treatment of lower triangular systems is similar (Exercise 2.2-8). The basic methods will again be the column sweep and inner product algorithms, discussed in Section 2.1, and given in Figure 2.2-8.

We consider first local memory systems. Assuming that the triangular system has resulted from a prior LU or Choleski decomposition, the storage of U is already determined by the storage for the decomposition. For example, if we have used the row wrapped interleaved storage of Figure 2.2-2, then the storage of U will have the same row interleaved pattern. We

(a)	(b)
For $j = n$ down to 1	For $i = n$ down to 1
$x_j = c_j u_{jj}$	For $j = i + 1$ to n
For $i = 1$ to $j - 1$	$c_i = c_i - u_{ij} x_j$
$c_i = c_i - x_j u_{ij}$	$x_i = c_i / u_{ii}$

Figure 2.2-8. Algorithms for $U\mathbf{x} = \mathbf{c}$. (a) Column sweep; (b) inner product.

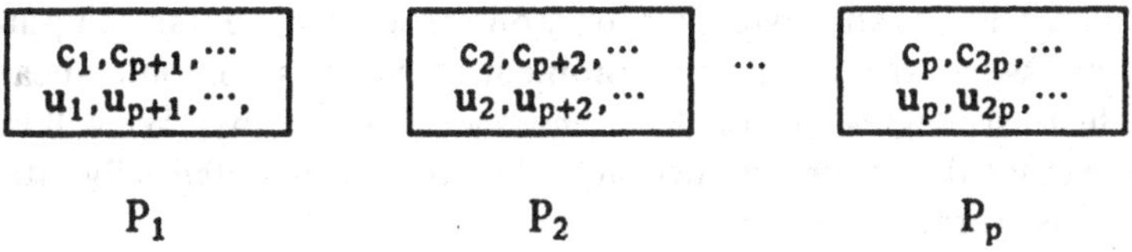

Figure 2.2-9. Wrapped interleaved row storage for $U\mathbf{x} = \mathbf{c}$.

will assume that the right-hand side $\mathbf{c}$ also is stored by interleaved rows so that the storage of the system is as shown in Figure 2.2-9, where $\mathbf{u}_i$ denotes the ith row of U. The column sweep algorithm can then be implemented as in Figure 2.2-10. At the first step, c_n and u_{nn} are in the same processor. After x_n is transmitted to all processors, each processor updates the right-hand side components that it holds and then x_{n-1} is computed in the processor holding the $(n-1)$st row. The process is now repeated to obtain x_{n-2}, then x_{n-3}, and so on. The work of updating the c_i will be fairly well balanced until the current triangular system becomes small; indeed, in the final stages, an increasing number of processors will become idle.

One bad aspect of the column sweep algorithm as shown in Figure 2.2-10 is that the computation of x_i takes place in a single processor while all other processors are idle. Thus, it may be beneficial to try to overlap the computation of the subsequent x_i by the following compute-ahead strategy. The processor that holds the $(n-1)$st row will update c_{n-1} and then compute and transmit x_{n-1} before updating the other c_i. Hence, x_{n-1} will be available to all processors at the time they are ready to begin the next update. This will cause the processor that computed x_{n-1} to finish its first updates behind the other processors, but this imbalance should average out since each processor in turn will be subject to this delay as the subsequent x_i are computed.

If U is stored by column wrapped interleaved storage, a straightforward implementation of the column sweep algorithm results in essentially a serial code. Assume that $P(n)$, the processor holding the last column of U, also holds $\mathbf{c}$. Then $P(n)$ computes x_n, updates $\mathbf{c}$, and transmits the new $\mathbf{c}$ to $P(n-1)$. $P(n-1)$ then computes x_{n-1}, updates $\mathbf{c}$, transmits to $P(n-2)$,

Compute $x_n = c_n / u_{nn}$ in $P(n)$
Send x_n to all processors
Compute $c_i = c_i - u_{in} x_n$, $i = 1, \ldots, n-1$,
Compute $x_{n-1} = c_{n-1} / u_{n-1,n-1}$ in $P(n-1)$
Send x_{n-1} to all processors
Compute $c_i = c_i - u_{i,n-1} x_{n-1}$, $i = 1, \ldots, n-2$
$\vdots$

Figure 2.2-10. Parallel column sweep algorithm for U stored by rows.

and so on. Thus, at any given time, only one processor is doing computation. There are ways to alleviate this problem by various compute-ahead and send-ahead strategies (see the References and Extensions). We will instead next consider the inner product algorithm since it is potentially attractive when U is stored by columns.

In the inner product algorithm of Figure 2.2-8b, the computation of x_i requires the inner product of the ith row of U, excluding the main diagonal, and the vector with components $x_{i+1}, \ldots, x_n$. We assume that these components have been computed so that $x_j \in P(j)$. Thus, processor $P(j)$ can compute $\sum u_{ij}x_j$ for all the x_j that it holds since the corresponding u_{ij} are also in $P(j)$. After these partial inner products have been computed in parallel in all processors, they can be summed by a fan-in so that the inner product is in $P(i)$. We assume that the right-hand side has been stored so that $c_i \in P(i)$, and then $P(i)$ computes x_i. We summarize this inner product algorithm in Figure 2.2-11.

For large n and i, there is almost perfect parallelism in the computation of the partial inner products. The fan-in is less satisfactory. It will involve communication and an increasing number of processors will become idle. Moreover, in the initial stages, when i is close to n, there is very little parallelism even in the computation of the partial inner products. Some of these problems can potentially be alleviated by compute-ahead strategies. For example, during the ith stage, as soon as processor P_j has finished its computations required in this stage, it could begin its partial inner product for the next stage.

We note that an intrinsic difficulty in solving triangular systems on local memory systems is that there are only $O(n^2)$ arithmetic operations over which to amortize the communication costs. This is in contrast to the factorization, in which there are $O(n^3)$ operations.

After the Choleski decomposition, we must solve the triangular systems $L^T\mathbf{y} = \mathbf{b}$ and $L\mathbf{x} = \mathbf{y}$. If the storage of A has been by rows, then the storage of L will be the same and a column sweep algorithm analogous to Figure 2.2-10 can be done for $L\mathbf{x} = \mathbf{y}$, the only difference being that we now solve for the unknowns in the order $x_1, \ldots, x_n$ (see Exercise 2.2-8). For the solution of $L^T\mathbf{y} = \mathbf{b}$, storage of L by rows corresponds to storage of L^T by columns. If A has been stored by columns, then L will be stored by columns and L^T by rows. Thus, in either case, solutions of triangular systems with both row and column storage will be required.

```
For i = n down to 1
    All processors compute their portion of ith inner product
    Fan-in partial inner products to P(i)
    P(i) computes x_i
```

Figure 2.2-11. Parallel inner product algorithm.

```
If (row n assigned to this processor)
  x_n = c_n/u_nn
  mark x_n as done
For j = n - 1 down to 1
  wait for x_{j+1} to be marked done
  If (row j assigned to this processor)
    c_j = c_j - u_{jj+1}x_{j+1}
    x_j = c_j/u_jj
    mark x_j as done
For i = 1 to j - 1
  If (row i assigned to this processor)
    c_i = c_i - u_{ij+1}x_{j+1}
```

Figure 2.2-12. Shared-memory column sweep for $U\mathbf{x} = \mathbf{c}$.

For Gaussian elimination, it is usual to perform the forward substitution (the solution of $L\mathbf{y} = \mathbf{b}$) as part of the factorization. The elements of $\mathbf{b}$ can be appended to the rows of A if row storage is being used, or considered as another column of A if column storage is used.

The solution of triangular systems on shared memory machines can be carried out by either dynamic allocation of tasks or a static allocation. For example, we can use a row or column wrapped interleaved assignment scheme in which processor i is assigned the work associated with columns (or rows) i, $i+p$, $i+2p, \ldots$. Assuming assignment by rows, a pseudocode for each processor is given in Figure 2.2-12.

In Figure 2.2-12, the necessary synchronization is achieved by marking the unknowns x_i "done" as they are computed. Processors wait until the x_i needed for the next computations are done and thus available. The marking and waiting can be implemented in different ways, depending on the system. In order to be available to other processors as soon as possible, the x_i are computed before completing the current update of the right-hand side.

Householder Reduction

In the previous section, we discussed the Givens and Householder orthogonal reductions for vector computers and we now wish to consider their implementation on parallel systems. We treat the Householder reduction first and assume that A is stored by wrapped interleaved column storage. We start from the vector code of Figure 2.1-12, which we reproduce in Figure 2.2-13 for convenience (recall that $\mathbf{a}_i$ is the ith column of the current A).

The first stage of a parallel code on a local memory system might be implemented as shown in Figure 2.2-14. The steps in Figure 2.2-14 have been organized to achieve good load balancing. For example, while s_1 is

For $k = 1$ to $n - 1$

$$s_k = -\text{sgn}(a_{kk})\left(\sum_{l=k}^{n} a_{lk}^2\right)^{1/2}, \quad \gamma_k = (s_k^2 - s_k a_{kk})^{-1}$$

$\mathbf{u}_k^T = (0, \ldots, 0, a_{kk} - s_k, a_{k+1,k}, \ldots, a_{nk})$

$a_{kk} = s_k$

For $j = k + 1$ to n

$\alpha_j = \gamma_k \mathbf{u}_k^T \mathbf{a}_j$

$\mathbf{a}_j = \mathbf{a}_j - \alpha_j \mathbf{u}_k$

Figure 2.2-13. Inner product form of Householder reduction.

1. Send first column of A to all processors.
2. Compute s_1 in processor 1. Start computation of the $\mathbf{u}_1^T \mathbf{a}_j$ in other processors. Send s_1 to all processors.
3. Compute γ_1 and $a_{11} - s_1$ in all processors. Continue computation of the $\mathbf{u}_1^T \mathbf{a}_j$. Replace a_{11} by s_1 in processor 1.
4. Compute $\alpha_i = \gamma_1 \mathbf{u}_1^T \mathbf{a}_i$ in all processors.
5. Compute $\mathbf{a}_i - \alpha_i \mathbf{u}_1$ in all processors.

Figure 2.2-14. First stage of parallel inner product form of Householder.

being computed in processor 1, the other processors can begin the computation of the inner products $\mathbf{u}_1^T \mathbf{a}_i$, although they cannot be completed, of course, until s_1 is available in all processors. We also elect to compute γ_1 and $a_{11} - s_1$ in all processors rather than computing them in processor 1 and then sending them. Thus, the only communication in this stage is the broadcast of the first column and s_1 to all processors. This is a major delay in the first stage, and for the second stage it may be advantageous to do the transmission of the second column as soon as it is complete. The bulk of the work in each Householder stage is the updating of the columns, and we see that this has excellent load-balancing properties until the final stages.

We next consider the rank one update form of Householder reduction as given in Figure 2.1-13. We reproduce the code in Figure 2.2-15 without explicit statements for s_j, μ_j and $\mathbf{u}_j$, which are the same as in the inner product code. The first stage of the corresponding parallel code is shown in Figure 2.2-16.

In Figure 2.2-15, the $\mathbf{a}_i$ denote the rows of A. But since we are assuming that A is stored by columns, the computation in step 4 of Figure 2.2-16 is the same as in step 4 of Figure 2.2-14. That is, the computation of $\hat{\mathbf{v}}^T$ is just γ_1 times the inner products of $\mathbf{u}_1$ and the columns of A held by each processor. Similarly, the computations in step 5 of both figures are the same. Thus, the parallel forms given in Figures 2.2-14 and 2.2-16 are identical.

For $k = 1$ to $n - 1$
  $s_k, \gamma_k, \mathbf{u}_k$
  $\mathbf{v}_k^T = \sum_{j=k}^{n} u_{jk}\mathbf{a}_j$
  $\hat{\mathbf{v}}_k^T = \gamma_k \mathbf{v}_k^T$
  For $j = k + 1$ to n
    $\mathbf{a}_j = \mathbf{a}_j - u_{jk}\hat{\mathbf{v}}_k^T$

Figure 2.2-15. Rank one update form of Householder reduction.

1. Send first column of A to all processors.
2. Compute s_1 in procesor 1. Start computation of $\mathbf{v}_1$ in other processors. Send s_1 to all processors.
3. Compute γ_1 and $a_{11} - s_1$ in all processors. Continue computation of $\mathbf{v}_1$ in all processors. Replace a_{11} by s_1 in processor 1.
4. Compute $\hat{\mathbf{v}}_1$ in all processors.
5. Compute $\mathbf{a}_j - u_{j1}\hat{\mathbf{v}}_1^T$ in all processors.

Figure 2.2-16. First stage of parallel rank one form of Householder.

If A is stored by interleaved wrapped row storage, the parallel algorithms are not nearly as satisfactory as with column storage. Consider first the inner product form. Here, we need the inner products $\mathbf{u}_j^T\mathbf{a}_i$. The partial inner products obtained from the elements already in each processor are first computed, but a fan-in across the processors is needed to complete the inner product. Then each of these inner products must be sent to all processors. The rank one form suffers from the same problem. Here, we must compute the vector $\mathbf{v}_j^T$, which is a linear combination of rows of A, and in order to complete this we again need to fan-in across the processors and then transmit the result to all processors. We conclude that column storage is better than row storage for the Householder reduction.

Givens Reduction

Recall from the previous section that in the first step of the Givens reduction the first two rows of A are modified by

$$\hat{\mathbf{a}}_1 = c_{12}\mathbf{a}_1 + s_{12}\mathbf{a}_2, \qquad \hat{\mathbf{a}}_2 = -s_{12}\mathbf{a}_1 + c_{12}\mathbf{a}_2 \tag{2.2.3}$$

where s_{12} and c_{12} are the sine and cosine defined by (2.1.34). This step produces a zero in the (2, 1) position of A. Subsequent steps zero the remaining elements of the first column, then the subdiagonal elements of the second column, and so on.

1. Compute c_{12} and s_{12} in processor 1. Send to all processors.
2. Begin update of rows 1 and 2 in all processors.
3. Compute c_{13} and s_{13} in processor 1. Send to all processors.
4. Complete update of rows 1 and 2 in all processors.
5. Begin update of rows 1 and 3 in all processors.

   ⋮

Figure 2.2-17. Column form of parallel Givens.

Assume that A is stored by column wrapped interleaved storage. Then the initial steps of a parallel algorithm are shown in Figure 2.2-17. Note that there is a delay at the outset in computing the first sine–cosine pair and transmitting them to all processors. In subsequent stages, we compute and transmit the next sine–cosine pair as soon as the data are ready; for example, as soon as processor 1 has updated its $(1,1)$ element in step 2 it can perform step 3 while the other processors continue their updates of rows 1 and 3. During the first stage, processor 2 has the additional work of computing all the sine–cosine pairs so that it will complete the first stage after the other processors. However, column 1 is now complete and processor 1 has one less column so it will begin to catch up while processor 2 falls behind on the next stage, and so on. All in all, this form of the Givens reduction has good parallel properties.

The same is not true if we use row wrapped interleaved storage in a straightforward way. At the first step only processors 1 and 2 will be active in processing rows 1 and 2; at the second step only processors 2 and 3 will be active, and so on. This problem is alleviated by another type of parallelism that is inherent in the Givens method, and which we now discuss.

The above discussion has been predicated on the usual order of zeroing the elements in the lower triangular part of A. This ordering has the important property that once a zero is produced, it remains zero in subsequent steps. However, other orderings, which we will call *annihilation patterns*, also have this property and we wish to consider annihilation patterns that allow the simultaneous zeroing of more than one element. One such ordering is illustrated in Figure 2.2-18. In the first stage, rows 1 and 2 are combined to produce a zero in the first position of row 2. Simultaneously, rows 3 and 4 are combined, rows 5 and 6, and so on. At the second stage, rows 1 and 3 are combined, rows 5 and 7, and so on. Hence, each stage zeros half of the remaining nonzero elements in the first column. Although highly parallel in the first stages, in the latter stages successively fewer processors will be used. However, at the point that processors would begin to be not utilized, we can begin zeroing elements in column 2, using rows that have already been zeroed in the first position.

*	*
0	0
*	0
0	0
*	*
0	0
.	0
.	0
.	*
First Stage	Second Stage

Figure 2.2-18. Simultaneous zeroing in Givens method.

One difficulty with the above arrangement is that a good deal of data must be transmitted. For example, if processor 1 is to perform the combination of rows 1 and 2, then row 2 must be sent from processor 2 to processor 1 and then the modified second row sent back to processor 2. This problem can be alleviated to some extent if we begin by combining rows that a processor already holds. For example, processor 1 will hold rows 1 and $p + 1$ and these can be combined with no interchange of data. Then at the next stage, rows 1 and $2p + 1$ can be combined and so on, with analogous combinations in the other processors. However, at some point, rows in different processors will have to be combined. But even with the above modifications, row storage does not seem to be competitive with column storage.

We next consider a quite different annihilation pattern for Givens reduction. It is illustrated in Figure 2.2-19 for an 8×8 matrix. The numbers

row							
2	7						
3	6	8					
4	5	7	9				
5	4	6	8	10			
6	3	5	7	9	11		
7	2	4	6	8	10	12	
8	1	3	5	7	9	11	13

Figure 2.2-19. Sameh-Kuck annihilation pattern.

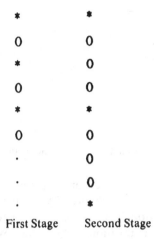

row					
2	$n-1$				
3	$n-2$	n			
·	·	$n-1$	$n+1$		
·	·		n		
·	·			$\ddots$	
n	1	3	5	$\cdots$	$2n-3$

Figure 2.2-20. Sameh-Kuck Annihilation Pattern for even n.

indicate the stage that the corresponding element in the strictly lower triangular part of A can be annihilated by a Givens transformation while retaining all zeros previously produced. At stage 1, rows 7 and 8 are combined to yield a zero in position (8, 1). Then, rows 6 and 7 are combined to produce a zero in position (7, 1). At the third stage, rows 5 and 6 can be combined to produce a zero in position (6, 1) and simultaneously rows 7 and 8 can produce a zero in position (8, 2), and so on. The maximum degree of parallelism occurs at the seventh stage when four zeros can be produced in parallel. For general (even) n, the maximum degree of parallelism is $n/2$ at stage $n-1$ as shown in Figure 2.2-20, in which there are $2n-3$ stages. This will be true for either even or odd n. However, for odd n, both stages $n-1$ and n exhibit a maximum degree of parallelism of $(n-1)/2$.

The Sameh-Kuck annihilation pattern provides the possibility of large speed-up if sufficiently many processors are available. For example, we can envision an array of processors holding the matrix A as indicated below for $p = n^2/2$ processors:

$$P_1 - P_n: \qquad \text{rows } 1, 2, 3$$

$$P_{n+1} - P_{2n}: \qquad \text{rows } 3, 4, 5$$

$$\vdots$$

$$P_{p-n+1} - P_p: \qquad \text{rows } n-1, n$$

That is, P_i holds the elements in the ith column of rows 1, 2, and 3. P_{n+i} holds the elements in the ith column of rows 3, 4, and 5, and so on. The Sameh-Kuck annihilation pattern is used, but now the updating of the rows at each stage can be done in parallel. Hence, ignoring the computation of the sines and cosines and the communication, the average degree of parallelism will be $O(n^2/4)$.

Multiple Right-Hand Sides

We end this section with a few comments on the system $AX = B$, where X and B are $n \times q$. Suppose that any of the methods of this section has produced a decomposition $A = SU$, where U is upper triangular and S will depend on the decomposition used. Then we need to solve the systems

$$SY = B, \qquad UX = Y \tag{2.2.4}$$

Consider first the system $UX = Y$. Assume that there are q processors, that U is stored in each processor, and that the ith column of Y is stored in processor i. Then the q systems $U\mathbf{x}_i = \mathbf{y}_i$ can be solved in parallel, and the analogous computations can be done for $SY = B$. Thus, these computations can be done with a perfect degree of parallelism, and we next discuss the practicality of this approach.

As mentioned previously, there are two main cases in which multiple right sides arise. The first is when $B = I$, $q \doteq n$, and $X = A^{-1}$. The second is where there may be different loads to be analyzed in a structures problem or analogous situations for other problems. In this case, q may vary from small to very large. Clearly, the above approach is not viable if $q \ll p$, where p is the number of processors, since $p - q$ processors are left idle. In this case, we would solve the systems with, for example, the column sweep algorithm. For example, if $q = 5$ and $p = 20$ we might allocate four processors to each system.

On the other hand, if $p \ll q$, then the solution of q/p systems in each processor is potentially attractive. The main difficulty is that if the reduction has been carried out by, for example, LU decomposition with interleaved row storage, then U will be distributed across the processors with the same interleaved row storage and it will be necessary to collect all of U in each processor before doing the computations. Only a more detailed analysis for a particular parallel system can ascertain if this is more efficient than solving each system $U\mathbf{x}_i = \mathbf{y}_i$ across the processors.

Exercises 2.2

1. Assume that a parallel system requires t time units to do arithmetic operations and αt time units to send one word of data from one to arbitrarily many processors. Assume that the number of processors $p = n$, the size of the system. Without pivoting, compute the total time for the LU decomposition using storage by rows and storage by columns as discussed in the text. Conclude which is best as a function of α.
2. Discuss in detail a fan-in procedure for determining the maximum of m numbers distributed across p processors.

3. Assume that a parallel system has the characteristics of Exercise 1 and that the comparison of the magnitude of two numbers also requires t time units. Compare the two algorithms with partial pivoting added.
4. Assume that a parallel system has the characteristics of Exercise 1, and assume that $n = kp$. Compare the number of time steps for LU decomposition, without pivoting, if (a) the first k rows of A are stored in processor 1, the second k in processor 2, and so on, and (b), if the storage of the rows is interleaved as shown in Figure 2.2-2. Repeat the analysis if partial pivoting is added.
5. Repeat Exercise 4 if A is stored by columns.
6. Carry out in detail the data flow algorithm of Figure 2.2-5 for the matrix

$$A = \begin{bmatrix} 4 & 1 & 1 & 1 \\ 1 & 4 & 1 & 1 \\ 1 & 1 & 4 & 1 \\ 1 & 1 & 1 & 4 \end{bmatrix}$$

7. Write out a code for the *kji* form of Choleski decomposition without consulting Appendix 1. Then compare your code with the one given in Appendix 1.
8. Discuss the column sweep and inner product algorithms of Figure 2.2-8 for a lower triangular system.
9. Show that a straightforward implementation of the column sweep algorithm on a shared memory machine with assignment of tasks by interleaved columns has very poor load balancing. Discuss ways to improve the implementation.

References and Extensions

1. The idea of interleaved storage was considered independently by O'Leary and Stewart [1985], who call it *torus assignment*, Ipsen *et al.* [1986], who call it *scattering*, and Geist and Heath [1986], who call it a *wrapped* mapping. O'Leary and Stewart [1985] also consider reflection storage.
2. There have been a number of LU or Choleski factorization implementations reported for various real or assumed parallel systems. Saad [1986b] considers two implementations of Gaussian elimination on hypercubes. The first broadcasts the pivot row to all processors that need it. The second pipelines the send of the pivot row in the following way. As each processor receives the pivot row, it first passes it to another processor and then proceeds computing. It is concluded that pipelining can be more efficient even if broadcasting takes advantage of the hypercube topology. LeBlanc [1986] reports on experiments on Gaussian elimination on a 128 processor BBN Butterfly. (The processors did not have floating point hardware so that arithmetic time was simulated by integer arithmetic.) The goal of this study was to compare message passing versus shared memory, both of which can be implemented on the Butterfly. Davis [1986] gives

an implementation, which includes pivoting and a compute-and-send-ahead strategy, of *LU* decomposition using wrapped column storage for the Intel iPSC hypercube. George, Heath, and Liu [1986], motivated by the Denelcor HEP, have given implementations of Choleski factorization particularly suitable for shared memory machines. They consider implementations based on several of the *ijk* forms of Choleski; see also Heath [1985]. Geist and Heath [1986] have given a detailed study of the *kji*,c form of Choleski factorization on an Intel iPSC hypercube. (They call their form *jki*, but in the final algorithm do immediate updates.) They consider different storage assignments of columns including block wrapping and random scattering and conclude experimentally that wrapped column storage is the best of those tried. In particular, for a system of 512 equations on 32 processors, they give the following execution times: column wrapped: 79.4 s, wrapped blocks (4 columns per block): 92.1 s; wrapped blocks (16 columns per block): 174.7 s; random: 94.1 s. They also consider various communication strategies, for example, a broadcast implemented by a send to each receiving processor, and a broadcast implemented by embedding a minimal spanning tree in the hypercube. The latter has the advantage that only $O(\log p)$ steps are required while the others take $O(p)$ steps. (However, the other implementations have advantages in certain circumstances.)

3. There have been a number of analyses of *LU* decomposition that attempt to understand its basic properties on parallel systems. Saad [1986a] considers the communication complexity of Gaussian elimination for several possible architectures. One of the main results is that for bus and ring local memory systems, the *LU* decomposition requires a communication time of at least $O(n^2)$ for an $n \times n$ matrix, regardless of the number of processors. See also Ipsen *et al.* [1986] for related results. Romine [1986] gives a detailed analysis of the *ijk* forms of *LU* decomposition. He concludes that under certain assumptions on the parallel system, the *kij* form is optimal among all medium-grained algorithms that use row wrapped storage. He also gives a similar, less complete analysis of Choleski factorization. See also Ortega and Romine [1987], on which the parallel portion of Appendix 1 is based.

4. Geist and Romine [1987] do an extensive study of pivoting strategies on a hypercube. They consider four basic approaches: row storage with row pivoting, column storage with row pivoting, row storage with column pivoting, and column storage with column pivoting. For each basic approach, they also consider various possible enhancements (for example, compute-ahead, loop unrolling to minimize index computations, and so on). As mentioned in the text, if rows are not actually interchanged the row wrapped storage pattern is lost. At the extreme, there is essentially a random distribution of rows, and Geist and Heath [1986] have given some experimental results on an Intel iPSC hypercube showing that such a distribution causes a 5%–15% degradation in speed compared with wrapped storage (see Note 2). On the other hand, Chu and George [1987] have considered explicitly interchanging rows. They mitigate the problem of idle processors by broadcasting the pivot row before doing the interchange; thus, other processors will have the information to begin updating their rows. They also use a dynamic load balancing scheme. See also Chamberlain [1987], who

uses column pivoting rather than row pivoting, and Sorensen [1985], who considers pairwise pivoting in which only two rows are considered for interchanging at each step.

5. The data flow approach to LU decomposition discussed in the text is based on a similar organization of the Choleski factorization given by O'Leary and Stewart [1985]. See also Funderlic and Geist [1986]. It exemplifies the general question of how much speed-up can be achieved in an algorithm if an arbitrary or unlimited number of processors are available. Much of the early research in parallel algorithms was along this line and typically ignored communication time. For a good summary of this early work for linear algebra algorithms see Heller [1978]. More recent papers that have considered LU decomposition for a large number of processors [usually $O(n)$ or $O(n^2)$ for an $n \times n$ system] include Bojanczyk, Brent, and Kung [1984], Kumar and Kowalik [1984], and Neta and Tai [1985].

6. The data flow approach in the text also exemplifies wavefront-type algorithms, which have been used on systolic arrays and other parallel systems that are feasible to implement in VLSI. For a review of such algorithms on systolic arrays, see H. Kung [1984], and for wavefront algorithms, in particular, see S. Kung [1984]. More recent papers dealing with this approach include Onaga and Takechi [1986].

7. A method closely related to LU decomposition, which was introducd for parallel computation, is the Quadrant Interlocking Factorization (QIF) method analyzed in Shanehchi and Evans [1982]. The basic idea of the method is to eliminate from both the top and bottom of the matrix. This leads to a decomposition of the form

$$A = \begin{bmatrix} * & & O & & 0 \\ \vdots & \ddots & & & * \\ \cdot & & * \;\; * & \iddots & \cdot \\ \cdot & \iddots & * & & \cdot \\ * & & & \ddots & \cdot \\ 0 & & O & & * \end{bmatrix} \begin{bmatrix} * & & \cdots & & * \\ & \ddots & & \iddots & \\ O & & * & & O \\ & \iddots & & \ddots & \\ * & & \cdots & & * \end{bmatrix}$$

8. When the coefficient matrix A has a special structure, the system $A\mathbf{x} = \mathbf{b}$ can sometimes be solved much faster by special algorithms. For example, a *Toeplitz* matrix has constant diagonals and the system can be solved in $O(n^2)$ operations rather than $O(n^3)$. For a review of parallel methods for Toeplitz systems (with emphasis on systolic arrays), see Delosme and Ipsen [1987]. See, also, Gohberg *et al.* [1987] for other Toeplitz-like matrices, and Grear and Sameh [1981].

9. It was thought that the solution of triangular systems on local memory systems using column storage was an intrinsically difficult problem. Romine and Ortega [1988] then pointed out that the inner product algorithm was potentially very good, and Li and Coleman [1987a] gave an efficient implementation of the column sweep algorithm. Heath and Romine [1987] analyzed these as well as

"wavefront" implementations of the column sweep algorithm with column storage and the inner product algorithm with row storage. These wavefront algorithms are based on overlapping work as much as possible, and are implemented by sending "segments" of partially computed results from one processor to the next in a ring arrangement. "Cyclic" algorithms also use a segment but of fixed size $p - 1$; the Li-Coleman algorithm is a cyclic implementation of the column sweep algorithm with column storage, and a similar approach by Chamberlain [1987] is an implementation of the inner product algorithm with row storage. Heath and Romine performed extensive experiments on hypercube systems. Their conclusions were as follows:

a. For row or column wrapped interleaved storage the cyclic approach was best for a small number (16) of processors.
b. For row or column wrapped interleaved storage the wavefront approach was best for a large number of processors.
c. For random column interleaved storage, the inner product algorithm with fan-in done by the minimal spanning tree of the cube was best.

A more recent modification of the cyclic algorithm by Li and Coleman [1987b] has shown much better performance for a large number of processors (see also Eisenstat *et al.* [1987]). In any case, good algorithms now exist for either row or column storage.

10. A version of Householder reduction has been described by Sameh [1985] for a ring of processors. The matrix begins in processor 1 (or the columns of A are loaded one by one from a central memory into processor 1). The first Householder transformation and the updating of the second column are done in processor 1. The new second column (from the main diagonal down) is then sent to processor 2, which computes the second Householder transformation. Simultaneously, processor 1 continues updating the columns of A and sending them to processor 2 (from the second position down). Processor 2 updates these columns and sends them to processor 3, and so on. At the end of the reduction, processor i will hold rows $i, i + p, \ldots$ of the upper triangular matrix U so that U is stored by interleaved rows.

11. Another approach to a parallel Givens algorithm, called "pipelined Givens," has been given by Dongarra, Sameh, and Sorensen [1986] for shared memory systems with relatively small synchronization overhead time. The idea is to overlap the processing of rows in such a way that several rows are being processed simultaneously, each slightly behind the previous one so that the proper sequencing of operations is maintained. See also Heath and Sorensen [1986] for a pipelined Givens method for sparse matrices.

12. It was observed by Gentleman [1975] that the Givens reduction has a natural parallelism in that several elements can be zeroed at once. The particular annihilation pattern of Figure 2.1-19 was given by Sameh and Kuck [1978], but a number of others have been proposed. For example, Lord *et al.* [1980] gave a "zig-zag" pattern predicated on using $O(n/2)$ processors, one for each two subdiagonals of the matrix, and a "column sweep" pattern when the number

of processors is small. See also Modi and Clarke [1984], and Cosnard and Robert [1986] for other annihilation patterns and some results on optimality.

13. Other recent papers on parallel Givens or Householder methods include Bowgen and Modi [1985], who compare implementations of both methods on the ICL DAP and conclude that Householder is 1.5–2.3 times faster than Givens; Barlow and Ipsen [1984], and Ispen [1984], who consider a "scaled" Givens method and a "fast" Givens method, respectively; Pothen *et al.* [1987], who compare several different versions of Givens method; Golub *et al.* [1986], who consider block orthogonal factorization methods for least squares problems; and Luk [1986].

2.3. Banded Systems

In the previous two sections we assumed that the matrix A was full; now we treat banded systems. For simplicity, as in Section 1.3, we shall consider explicitly only symmetrically banded systems with semibandwidth β but most of the discussion extends in a natural way to general banded systems.

LU Decomposition

We begin with LU decomposition. The pseudocodes of Figures 2.1-1 and 2.1-2 adapted to a system with bandwidth β are given in Figure 2.3-1. Adaptations of the other *ijk* forms of LU decomposition in Section 2.1 are easily given (Exercise 2.3-1).

In Figure 2.3-2, we have indicated schematically the first few steps of the *kij* algorithm for a matrix with $\beta = 3$. For $k = 1$, multiples of the first row are subtracted from rows 2 through $\beta + 1$. Since the first row and column have $\beta + 1$ elements, only the first $\beta + 1$ rows and columns of A participate in this first stage, as indicated in Figure 2.3-2 by the submatrix marked 1. Similarly, for $k = 2$, only elements 2 through $\beta + 2$ of rows 2 through $\beta + 2$ participate, and so on. As the decomposition proceeds, we

```
For k = 1 to n − 1
  For i = k + 1 to min(k + β, n)
    l_ik = a_ik / a_kk
    For j = k + 1 to min(k + β, n)
      a_ij = a_ij − l_ik a_kj
```

```
For k = 1 to n − 1
  For s = k + 1 to min(k + β, n)
    l_sk = a_sk / a_kk
  For j = k + 1 to min(k + β, n)
    For i = k + 1 to min(k + β, n)
      a_ij = a_ij − l_ik a_ij
```

Figure 2.3-1. Banded LU decomposition.

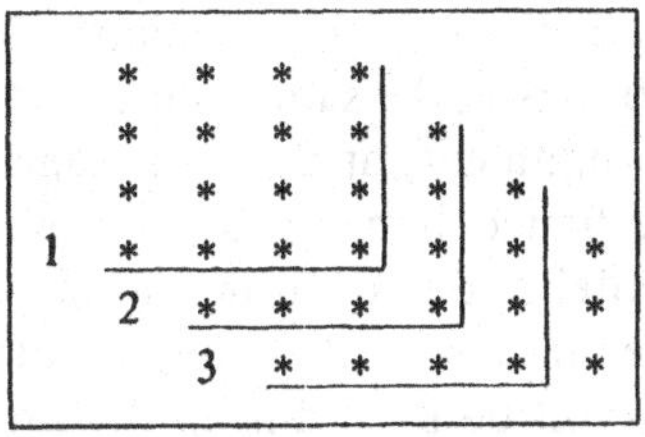

Figure 2.3-2. First stages of banded LU decomposition.

will reach the point that a $\beta \times \beta$ submatrix remains, and then the decomposition proceeds as for a full matrix.

On serial computers, it is common to store a banded matrix by diagonals, but this is not very satisfactory for vector computers. For example, for the *kij* algorithm of Figure 2.3-1, the natural storage is by rows. However, we do not wish to use a full $n \times n$ two-dimensional array for the storage since much of this space would be wasted, especially when β is small. An alternative is to store the rows in a one-dimensional array as indicated in Figure 2.3-3 in which $\mathbf{a}_i$ denotes the ith row and the corresponding row length is shown. Figure 2.3-3 also provides a schematic for column storage if $\mathbf{a}_i$ is interpreted as the ith column.

The row or column updates in the last loops of Figure 2.3-1 can utilize vectors of length β until the final $\beta \times \beta$ submatrix is reached and the lengths decrease by 1 at each subsequent stage. Thus, when β is suitably large, Figure 2.3-1 provides the basis for potentially satisfactory algorithms for vector computers, but they are increasingly inefficient as β becomes small. In particular, for tridiagonal systems, for which $\beta = 1$, they are totally inadequate. We will consider other algorithms for small bandwidth systems later in this section.

Parallel Implementation

We treat next the parallel implementation of LU decomposition. As in the previous section, we assume that we will use row or column wrapped interleaved storage, as illustrated in Figure 2.2-2. The general considerations of Section 2.2 for LU decomposition are relevant also to the banded case, but the major issue now is the effect of the bandwidth on the parallelism.

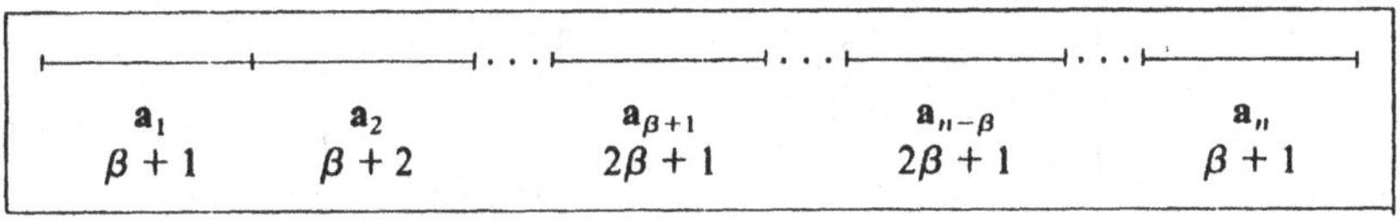

Figure 2.3-3. Row (column) storage for banded matrix.

For the algorithms of Figure 2.3-1, the basic degree of parallelism of the updates of the last loop is β, the same as the vector length. In particular, with row interleaved assignment, at the first stage rows $2, \ldots, \beta + 1$ will have an element in the first column to be eliminated. These β rows can then be updated in parallel in the *kij* form and the corresponding columns in the *kji* form. Hence, if $\beta < p$, the number of processors, then only processors $2, \ldots, \beta + 1$ will be used during the first stage. Thus, we need $\beta \geqslant p$ in order to utilize fully all the processors. Moreover, there is more potential for load imbalance with banded systems even if $\beta \geqslant p$. For example, suppose that we have 50 processors and $n = 10{,}032$. Then 32 processors will have 201 rows and 18 will have 200. For a full system, this would be a very small imbalance. Suppose, however, that $\beta = 75$. Then the number of rows each processor holds is still 201 or 200 but, with a straightforward implementation of the *kij* algorithm, only half of the processors would be active during the second part of a stage. Clearly, the worse case is when $\beta = p + 1$ so that only one processor would be active during the second part of the stage. This load imbalance problem can be alleviated to a large extent by a compute-ahead strategy. For example, during the kth stage, as soon as row $k + 1$ has been updated it will be sent to all other processors. Then, when a processor finishes its work on the kth stage it will immediately start the $(k + 1)$st stage.

Choleski Decomposition

The same considerations apply to the Choleski decomposition for algorithms analogous to those of Figure 2.3-1. In particular, if $\beta < p$, then some processors will be inactive in all stages of the decomposition, using either row or column interleaved storage. A more detailed discussion of Choleski algorithms is left to Exercises 2.3-5 and 2.3-6.

Triangular Systems

The treatment in Section 2.1 of the solution of triangular systems on vector computers goes over immediately to banded systems. Consider first the solution of the triangular system $U\mathbf{x} = \mathbf{c}$, where U has an upper semibandwidth of β as shown below:

$$\begin{bmatrix} u_{11} & \cdots & u_{1\beta+1} & & \\ & \ddots & & \ddots & \\ & & \ddots & & u_{n-\beta,n} \\ & & & & \vdots \\ & & & & u_{nn} \end{bmatrix} \begin{bmatrix} x_1 \\ \vdots \\ x_n \end{bmatrix} = \begin{bmatrix} c_1 \\ \vdots \\ c_n \end{bmatrix} \tag{2.3.1}$$

For $i = n$ down to 1
$x_i = c_i / u_{ii}$
$\mathbf{c} = \mathbf{c} - x_i \mathbf{u}_i$

Figure 2.3-4. Column sweep algorithm.

If U is stored by its columns within the band, the column sweep algorithm of Figure 2.1-5 may be written as in Figure 2.3-4. In Figure 2.3-4, $\mathbf{u}_i$ consists of the elements in the ith column from the edge of the band to the main diagonal, but not including the main diagonal element. These vectors all have length β until $i \leq \beta$ at which point the vector lengths decrease to 1 as i decreases to 2. Thus, the vector lengths of the linked triad operations are β for most of the computation, decreasing to 1 in the final stages.

If U is stored by rows, we would use the inner product algorithm (2.1.10) which now becomes

$$x_i = (c_i - u_{ii+1}x_{i+1} - \cdots - u_{i,i+\beta+1}x_{i+\beta+1})/u_{ii}, \qquad i = n - \beta, \ldots, 1 \quad (2.3.2)$$

For $i = n, \ldots, n - \beta + 1$, (2.3.2) would be modified to reflect a row length less than $\beta + 1$. An algorithm based on (2.3.2) consists of inner products of vectors of length β, while the corresponding inner products for $i = n, \ldots, n - \beta + 1$ use vectors of lengths $1, \ldots, \beta - 1$.

As with full matrices, the column sweep algorithm may be appealing on some vector computers because of the linked triad operations as opposed to the inner products in the row algorithm. Moreover, for the row-oriented *kij* algorithm of Figure 2.3-1, and with storage as indicated by Figure 2.3-3, the element b_i of the right-hand side of the system cannot just be appended to the ith row of A, as was the case for full systems. This points more strongly towards the use of storage by columns than is the case for full matrices. However, for small β and several right-hand sides, this is no longer the case, as will be discussed later.

Consider, next, local memory parallel machines and assume that U is stored by wrapped interleaved row storage. The parallel column sweep

Compute $x_n = c_n/u_{nn}$. Send x_n to all processors
Compute $c_i = c_i - u_{in}x_n$, $i = n - \beta, \ldots, n - 1$
Compute $x_{n-1} = c_{n-1}/u_{n-1,n-1}$. Send x_{n-1} to all processors
Compute $c_i = c_i - u_{i,n-1}x_{n-1}$, $i = n - \beta - 1, \ldots, n - 2$
⋮

Figure 2.3-5. Parallel column sweep algorithm for banded systems.

algorithm given in Figure 2.2-10 is modified for banded systems as shown in Figure 2.3-5. Clearly, the degree of parallelism in this algorithm in the beginning stages is β. If $\beta < p$, then $p - \beta$ processors are not used. Even if $\beta > p$ it is likely that there will be an imbalance in the workload unless a compute-ahead strategy is included, as previously discussed for the reduction phase. All in all, however, this is a potentially satisfactory algorithm. If U is stored by wrapped interleaved column storage, then the inner product algorithm in Figure 2.2-11 is easily adapted to banded systems.

Interchanges

The LU or Choleski decompositions preserve the bandwidth; that is, the upper triangular matrix U will have the same bandwidth as A. But the row interchanges needed for partial pivoting increase the bandwidth with consequences somewhat more severe for vector and parallel computers than for serial ones. Suppose that at the first stage, an interchange is made of the kth and first rows as illustrated below for a matrix with bandwidth 4 and $k = 5$.

```
* * * * * * * * *
* * * * * *
* * * * * * *
* * * * * * * *
* * * * *
```

As a consequence of this interchange, there will now be fill in the second, third, and fourth rows, as well as the new fifth row, as the decomposition proceeds. Thus, the bandwidth above the main diagonal has effectively doubled, and this can persist if additional "worst-case" interchanges are needed.

One way to handle this problem is simply to allow enough extra storage at the outset. Thus, if A is stored by rows, we would modify Figure 2.3-3 as shown in Figure 2.3-6, so that β extra storage locations are allowed for each row down to row $n - 2\beta$, at which point the storage requirement

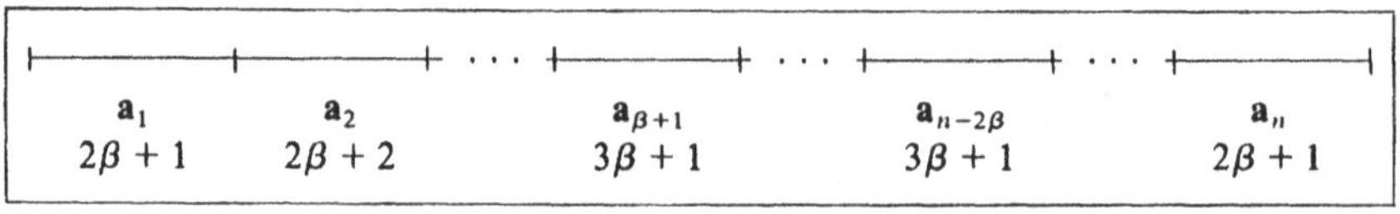

Figure 2.3-6. Row storage for interchanges.

decreases by one for each row. In the LU decomposition using this storage pattern, we would like to use vector lengths that are no longer than necessary. Thus, for example, if there is no interchange at the first stage, then vector lengths of only β are required, as before. In general, whenever there is an interchange, we will set the vector lengths for the subsequent operations accordingly. This adds both overhead and program complexity but is probably preferable to using the maximum vector lengths of Figure 2.3-6 when there are few interchanges or when the interchanges introduce relatively few extra nonzero elements. The considerations for storage by column are similar.

Orthogonal Reduction

Orthogonal reduction by means of Householder or Givens transformations also expands the bandwidth above the main diagonal. Consider first a Householder transformation $I - \mathbf{w}\mathbf{w}^T$ applied to A in order to zero elements in the first column of A below the main diagonal. Then, $\mathbf{w}$ is of the form $\mathbf{w}^T = (*, \ldots, *, 0, \ldots, 0)$ in which the first $\beta + 1$ elements are, in general, nonzero. By (2.1.27), the new ith column of A is $\mathbf{a}_i - \mathbf{w}^T\mathbf{a}_i\mathbf{w}$, and the effect on the bandwidth of A is illustrated in Figure 2.3-7 for $\beta = 3$. The first Householder transformation introduces, in general, nonzero elements outside the original band. These are indicated to the right of the dotted line in Figure 2.3-7. No further nonzero elements are introduced since, on the first transformation $\mathbf{w}^T\mathbf{a}_i = 0$ for $i > 2\beta + 1$. On the second Householder transformation, nonzeros will be introduced into the $2\beta + 2$ column, starting in the second element. At each subsequent transformation nonzeros will be introduced in one more column so that at the end of the triangular reduction the upper triangular matrix will have a bandwidth of $2\beta + 1$.

The same occurs with Givens' method. As we zero the elements in the first column by Givens transformations, we successively introduce β nonzero elements outside the band in the first row. In zeroing the elements of the

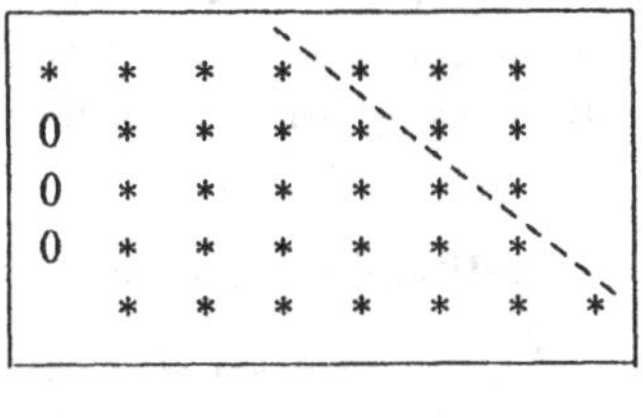

Figure 2.3-7. Structure of A after first Householder transformation.

*	*	*	*	1	2	3	
1	*	*	*	*	4	5	6
2	4	*	*	*	*		
3	5	*	*	*	*	*	
	6						*

Figure 2.3-8. Bandwidth expansion for Givens reduction.

second column we introduce nonzero elements outside the band in the second row, and so on. This is illustrated for $\beta = 3$ in Figure 2.3-8, where the numbers indicate the introduction of nonzero elements at the time of zeroing the corresponding element in the first two columns. Although the nonzero elements outside the band are introduced in a somewhat different way than by Householder transformations, the net result is the same: the bandwidth of the upper triangular part of A increases to $2\beta + 1$.

Multiple Right-Hand Sides

With multiple right-hand sides $B = (\mathbf{b}_1, \ldots, \mathbf{b}_q)$ and storage of A and B by columns, the algorithm of Figure 2.3-1b may be modified to process the q right-hand sides during the reduction. This adds q linked triad operations during each stage of the reduction, just as with full matrices.

If A is stored by rows, we would like to append the rows of B to the rows of A. As discussed in Section 2.1 for full matrices A, this increases the vector lengths during the reduction by q. For banded systems, however, we encounter the problem illustrated below:

$$\begin{array}{cccccccc} a_{11} & \cdots & a_{1\beta+1} & b_{11} & & \cdots & b_{1q} & \\ a_{21} & \cdots & a_{2\beta+1} & a_{2\beta+2} & b_{21} & \cdots & & b_{2q} \end{array}$$

Because of the varying lengths of the rows of A, the columns of B do not align properly. If β and q are both reasonably large, we can forego the idea of appending the rows of B and operate on A and B separately.

A case of some interest is when β is small, but q is sufficiently large that vector operations of length q are efficient. In this case it may well be most efficient to do the decomposition of A in scalar arithmetic and then do vector operations for processing all right-hand sides "at once."

Partitioning Methods

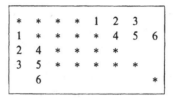

The methods discussed so far are satisfactory for banded systems as long as the bandwidth β is sufficiently large. For small β, however, the vector lengths are too small or, on a parallel system, the processors become underutilized. In contrast to matrix–vector multiplication, as discussed in Section 1.3, there are no efficient elimination algorithms based on diagonal storage of A.

We next consider a class of methods predicated on partitioning of the coefficient matrix A. We write the banded system in the block form

$$\begin{bmatrix} A_1 & B_1 & & \\ C_2 & A_2 & B_2 & \ddots \\ & \ddots & \ddots & B_{p-1} \\ & & C_p & A_p \end{bmatrix} \begin{bmatrix} \mathbf{x}_1 \\ \mathbf{x}_2 \\ \vdots \\ \mathbf{x}_p \end{bmatrix} = \begin{bmatrix} \mathbf{b}_1 \\ \mathbf{b}_2 \\ \vdots \\ \mathbf{b}_p \end{bmatrix} \tag{2.3.3}$$

where we assume, for simplicity, that $q = n/p$ is an integer and the A_i in (2.3.3) are all $q \times q$. We illustrate in Figure 2.3-9 in more detail the composition of the matrices A_i, B_i, and C_i for $\beta = 2$. In general, the B_i are lower triangular and the C_i are upper triangular.

We assume that the A_i are nonsingular and have a stable LU decomposition; this is the case, in particular, if A is symmetric positive definite or nonsingular and diagonally dominant. We then solve the systems

$$A_i W_i = B_i, \qquad A_i V_i = C_i, \qquad A_i \mathbf{d}_i = \mathbf{b}_i \tag{2.3.4}$$

using the decompositions

$$A_i = L_i U_i \tag{2.3.5}$$

If we multiply the system (2.3.3) by $\mathrm{diag}(A_1^{-1}, \ldots, A_p^{-1})$, the resulting system

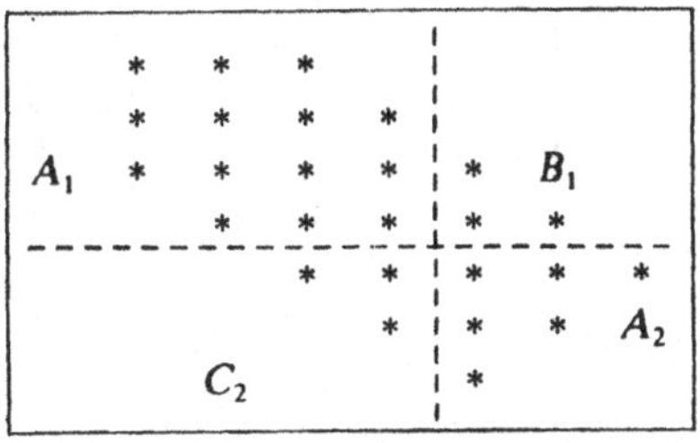

Figure 2.3-9. Partitioning for $\beta = 2$.

is

$$\begin{bmatrix} I & W_1 & & & \\ V_2 & I & W_2 & & \\ & \ddots & \ddots & \ddots & W_{p-1} \\ & & & V_p & I \end{bmatrix} \begin{bmatrix} \mathbf{x}_1 \\ \mathbf{x}_2 \\ \vdots \\ \mathbf{x}_p \end{bmatrix} = \begin{bmatrix} \mathbf{d}_1 \\ \mathbf{d}_2 \\ \vdots \\ \mathbf{d}_p \end{bmatrix} \tag{2.3.6}$$

Thus, by solution of the systems (2.3.4), we reduce the original system (2.3.3) to (2.3.6).

The jth column of W_i is A_i^{-1} times the jth column of B_i. Even though A_i is banded, its inverse will, in general, be full and the jth column of W_i will be full whenever the corresponding column of B_i is nonzero; that is, the W_i "fill-in" the nonzero columns of B_i. Likewise, the nonzero columns of the C_i "fill-in." The matrix of (2.3.6) then has the structure shown in Figure 2.3-10 for $\beta = 2$.

Only the first β columns of each W_i and the last β columns of each V_i are nonzero and we write these matrices in the form

$$W_i = \begin{bmatrix} W_{i1} & 0 \\ W_{i2} & 0 \\ W_{i3} & 0 \end{bmatrix}, \qquad V_i = \begin{bmatrix} 0 & V_{i1} \\ 0 & V_{i2} \\ 0 & V_{i3} \end{bmatrix}, \qquad \mathbf{x}_i = \begin{bmatrix} \mathbf{x}_{i1} \\ \mathbf{x}_{i2} \\ \mathbf{x}_{i3} \end{bmatrix}, \qquad \mathbf{d}_i = \begin{bmatrix} \mathbf{d}_{i1} \\ \mathbf{d}_{i2} \\ \mathbf{d}_{i3} \end{bmatrix}$$

where the W_{i1}, W_{i3}, V_{i1}, and V_{i3} are $\beta \times \beta$ and the W_{i2} and V_{i2} are $(q - 2\beta) \times \beta$. (We are assuming that $q > 2\beta$.) We also partition the vectors $\mathbf{x}_i$ and $\mathbf{d}_i$ of (2.3.6) in the same fashion, as shown above. With these partitionings, the first block equation of (2.3.6), $\mathbf{x}_1 + W_1\mathbf{x}_2 = \mathbf{d}_1$, can be written as

$$\begin{bmatrix} \mathbf{x}_{11} \\ \mathbf{x}_{12} \\ \mathbf{x}_{13} \end{bmatrix} + \begin{bmatrix} W_{11} \\ W_{12} \\ W_{13} \end{bmatrix} \mathbf{x}_{21} = \begin{bmatrix} \mathbf{d}_{11} \\ \mathbf{d}_{12} \\ \mathbf{d}_{13} \end{bmatrix} \tag{2.3.7}$$

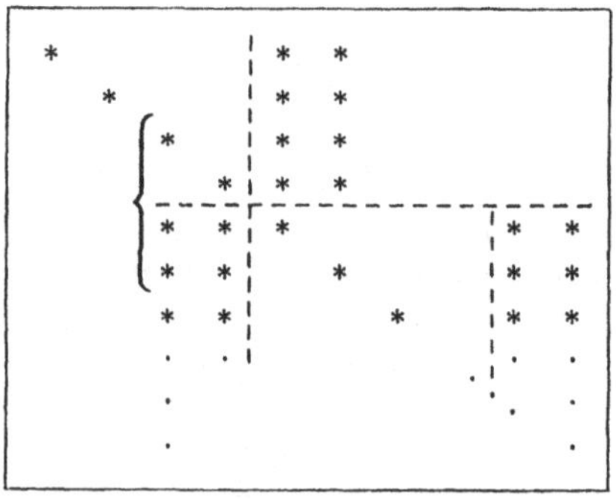

Figure 2.3-10. Structure of reduced system.

Similarly, the second block equation, $V_2\mathbf{x}_1 + \mathbf{x}_2 + W_2\mathbf{x}_3 = \mathbf{d}_2$ can be written as

$$\begin{bmatrix} V_{21} \\ V_{22} \\ V_{23} \end{bmatrix} \mathbf{x}_{13} + \begin{bmatrix} \mathbf{x}_{21} \\ \mathbf{x}_{22} \\ \mathbf{x}_{23} \end{bmatrix} + \begin{bmatrix} W_{21} \\ W_{22} \\ W_{23} \end{bmatrix} \mathbf{x}_{31} = \begin{bmatrix} \mathbf{d}_{21} \\ \mathbf{d}_{22} \\ \mathbf{d}_{23} \end{bmatrix} \tag{2.3.8}$$

and so on for the remaining block equations.

We now note that the equations

$$\begin{aligned} \mathbf{x}_{13} + W_{13}\mathbf{x}_{21} &= \mathbf{d}_{13} \\ V_{21}\mathbf{x}_{13} + \mathbf{x}_{21} + W_{21}\mathbf{x}_{31} &= \mathbf{d}_{21} \\ V_{23}\mathbf{x}_{13} + \mathbf{x}_{23} + W_{23}\mathbf{x}_{31} &= \mathbf{d}_{23} \\ &\vdots \end{aligned} \tag{2.3.9}$$

are independent from the equations involving the $\mathbf{x}_{i2}$; that is, none of the equations in the system (2.3.9) contains any of the variables $\mathbf{x}_{12}, \mathbf{x}_{22}, \mathbf{x}_{32}, \ldots$. Therefore, the system (2.3.9) can be solved independently of the $\mathbf{x}_{i2}$. We call (2.3.9) the *reduced system.* (The reader may wish to work Exercise 2.3-9 at this point.) Once (2.3.9) has been solved, the $\mathbf{x}_{i2}$ can be obtained from the second equations of (2.3.7) and (2.3.8) as

$$\mathbf{x}_{12} = \mathbf{d}_{12} - W_{12}\mathbf{x}_{21}, \qquad \mathbf{x}_{22} = \mathbf{d}_{22} - V_{22}\mathbf{x}_{13} - W_{22}\mathbf{x}_{31}$$

and, in general,

$$\mathbf{x}_{i2} = \mathbf{d}_{i2} - V_{i2}\mathbf{x}_{i-1,3} - W_{i2}\mathbf{x}_{i+1,3} \tag{2.3.10}$$

The unknown $\mathbf{x}_{11}$ does not appear in the reduced system and may be obtained from the first equation of (2.3.7): $\mathbf{x}_{11} = \mathbf{d}_1 - W_{11}\mathbf{x}_{21}$. Similarly for $\mathbf{x}_{p3}$, which also does not appear in the reduced system.

The overall procedure is then shown in Figure 2.3-11. Clearly, steps 1 and 3 are highly parallel. Assuming that we have p processors, the decompositions (2.3.5) and solutions (2.3.4) would be carried out in the ith processor. Similarly, for the final step (2.3.10). The potential bottleneck is solving the reduced system (2.3.9) and we next ascertain the size of this system.

Step 1.	Do the *LU* decompositions (2.3.5) and solve the systems (2.3.4).
Step 2.	Solve the system (2.3.9) to obtain the $\mathbf{x}_{i1}$ and $\mathbf{x}_{i3}$.
Step 3.	Obtain the $\mathbf{x}_{i2}$ from (2.3.10), and obtain $\mathbf{x}_{11}$ and $\mathbf{x}_{p3}$.

Figure 2.3-11. Lawrie–Sameh partitioning algorithm.

Table 2.3-1. Size of Reduced System (2.3.9) for Several Values of p and β.

p	β: 1	2	10	20	50
2	2	4	20	40	100
10	18	36	180	360	900
20	38	76	380	760	1900
50	98	196	980	1960	4900

The vectors $\mathbf{x}_{i1}$ and $\mathbf{x}_{i3}$ are β long. Hence, the system (2.3.9) contains $2\beta(p-2)+2\beta = 2\beta(p-1)$ unknowns (Exercise 2.3-10). We tabulate in Table 2.3-1 the size of this reduced system for various values of β and p. We also note that the coefficient matrix of (2.3.9) is block pentadiagonal and has semibandwidth 3β (Exercise 2.3-10).

Suppose, for example that $n = 10{,}000$, $p = 20$, and $\beta = 2$. Then $q = 500$, so that the matrices A_i are 500×500. The size of the reduced system is 76×76 with semibandwidth 6. On the other hand, if $p = 50$ and $\beta = 10$ the A_i are only 200×200 and the size of the reduced system is 980, with semibandwidth 30.

We next discuss a different type of partitioning in which the reduced system is only half as large. Again, we assume that $q = n/p$ is an integer and we partition the A_i in (2.3.3) as

$$A_i = \begin{bmatrix} A_{i,1} & A_{i,2} \\ A_{i,3} & A_{i,4} \end{bmatrix} \tag{2.3.11}$$

where $A_{i,4}$ is $\beta \times \beta$ and $A_{i,1}$ is $(q-\beta)\times(q-\beta)$. The B_i, C_i, $\mathbf{x}_i$ and $\mathbf{b}_i$ in (2.3.3) are partitioned accordingly as

$$B_i = \begin{bmatrix} 0 & 0 \\ B_{i,1} & B_{i,2} \end{bmatrix}, \quad C_i = \begin{bmatrix} 0 & C_{i,1} \\ 0 & C_{i,2} \end{bmatrix}, \quad \mathbf{x}_i = \begin{bmatrix} \mathbf{x}_{i,1} \\ \mathbf{x}_{i,2} \end{bmatrix}, \quad \mathbf{b}_i = \begin{bmatrix} \mathbf{b}_{i,1} \\ \mathbf{b}_{i,2} \end{bmatrix} \tag{2.3.12}$$

We note that if $2\beta \leq q$, then the $B_{i,2}$ and $C_{i,2}$ are zero.

We now do the LU decompositions $A_{i,1} = L_{i,1}U_{i,1}$, and by means of these decompositions solve the systems

$$A_{i,1}A^1_{i,2} = A_{i,2}, \qquad A_{i,1}C^1_{i,1} = C_{i,1}, \qquad A_{i,1}\mathbf{b}^1_{i,1} = \mathbf{b}_{i,1} \tag{2.3.13}$$

The effect of these solutions is to multiply the original system by $\operatorname{diag}(A^{-1}_{1,1}, I, A^{-1}_{21}, I, \ldots)$ to obtain a new system, which we illustrate in (2.3.14) for $p = 3$:

$$\begin{bmatrix} I & A^1_{1,2} & & & & \\ A_{1,3} & A_{1,4} & B_{1,1} & B_{1,2} & & \\ & C^1_{2,1} & I & A^1_{2,2} & & \\ & C_{2,2} & A_{2,3} & A_{2,4} & B_{2,1} & B_{2,2} \\ & & & C^1_{3,1} & I & A^1_{3,2} \\ & & & C_{3,2} & A_{3,3} & A_{3,4} \end{bmatrix} \begin{bmatrix} \mathbf{x}_{1,1} \\ \mathbf{x}_{1,2} \\ \mathbf{x}_{2,1} \\ \mathbf{x}_{2,2} \\ \mathbf{x}_{3,1} \\ \mathbf{x}_{3,2} \end{bmatrix} = \begin{bmatrix} \mathbf{b}^1_{1,1} \\ \mathbf{b}_{1,2} \\ \mathbf{b}^1_{2,1} \\ \mathbf{b}_{2,2} \\ \mathbf{b}^1_{3,1} \\ \mathbf{b}_{3,2} \end{bmatrix} \tag{2.3.14}$$

We next multiply the first block equation of (2.3.14) by $A_{1,3}$ and the third block equation by $B_{1,1}$ and subtract these from the second block equation to give the new equation

$$A^1_{1,4}\mathbf{x}_{1,2} + B^1_{1,2}\mathbf{x}_{2,2} = \mathbf{b}^1_{1,2}$$

where

$$A^1_{1,4} = A_{1,4} - A_{1,3}A^1_{1,2} - B_{1,1}C^1_{2,1}$$

$$B^1_{1,2} = B_{1,2} - B_{2,1}A^1_{1,2}, \qquad \mathbf{b}^1_{1,2} = \mathbf{b}_{1,2} - A_{1,3}\mathbf{b}^1_{1,1} - B_{1,1}\mathbf{b}^1_{2,1}$$

Continuing in this way, we multiply the third block equation by $A_{2,3}$ and the fifth block equation by $B_{2,1}$ and subtract both from the fourth block equation. Finally, we multiply the fifth block equation by $A_{3,3}$ and subtract from the sixth block equation to obtain the system

$$\begin{bmatrix} I & A^1_{1,2} & & & & \\ & A^1_{1,4} & 0 & B^1_{1,2} & & \\ & C^1_{2,1} & I & A^1_{2,2} & 0 & \\ & C^1_{2,2} & 0 & A^1_{2,4} & 0 & B^1_{2,2} \\ & & & C^1_{3,1} & I & A^1_{3,2} \\ & & & C^1_{3,2} & 0 & A^1_{3,4} \end{bmatrix} \begin{bmatrix} \mathbf{x}_{1,1} \\ \mathbf{x}_{1,2} \\ \mathbf{x}_{2,1} \\ \mathbf{x}_{2,2} \\ \mathbf{x}_{3,1} \\ \mathbf{x}_{3,2} \end{bmatrix} = \begin{bmatrix} \mathbf{b}^1_{1,1} \\ \mathbf{b}^1_{1,2} \\ \mathbf{b}^1_{2,1} \\ \mathbf{b}^1_{2,2} \\ \mathbf{b}^1_{3,1} \\ \mathbf{b}^1_{3,2} \end{bmatrix} \tag{2.3.15}$$

We now note that the even-numbered block equations in (2.3.15) are independent of the others and form the reduced system

$$\begin{bmatrix} A^1_{1,4} & B^1_{1,2} & \\ C^1_{2,2} & A^1_{2,4} & B^1_{2,2} \\ & C^1_{3,2} & A^1_{3,4} \end{bmatrix} \begin{bmatrix} \mathbf{x}_{1,2} \\ \mathbf{x}_{2,2} \\ \mathbf{x}_{3,2} \end{bmatrix} = \begin{bmatrix} \mathbf{b}^1_{1,2} \\ \mathbf{b}^1_{2,2} \\ \mathbf{b}^1_{3,2} \end{bmatrix} \tag{2.3.16}$$

Step 1.	Form the decompositions $A_{i1} = L_{i1}U_{i1}$ and solve the systems (2.3.13)
Step 2.	Solve the reduced system (2.3.16) (in general, $p \times p$ block tridiagonal)
Step 3.	Obtain the remaining unknowns $\mathbf{x}_{i,1}$ from (2.3.17)

Figure 2.3-12. Johnsson's partitioning method.

Once (2.3.16) is solved, the $\mathbf{x}_{i,1}$ are obtained from the odd-numbered equations of (2.3.15) by

$$\mathbf{x}_{i,1} = \mathbf{b}_{i,2}^1 - A_{i,2}^1\mathbf{x}_{i,2} - C_{i,1}^1\mathbf{x}_{i-1,2}, \qquad i = 1, \ldots, p \tag{2.3.17}$$

where for $i = 1$, the last term is not present.

The equations (2.3.14)–(2.3.16) exhibit the above computation for $p = 3$ but the extension to general p should be clear. In particular, the reduced system (2.3.16) is a $p \times p$ block tridiagonal system with block sizes $\beta \times \beta$; thus, its semibandwidth is $2\beta - 1$. We summarize the overall procedure in Figure 2.3-12. As in the Lawrie–Sameh method, steps 1 and 3 are highly parallel but step 2 is a potential bottleneck. However, the reduced system for Johnsson's method has only βp equations as opposed to $2\beta(p - 1)$ with the Lawrie–Sameh partitioning.

Domain Decomposition Methods

We next discuss another class of methods, which are similar in some respects to the partitioning methods. We will illustrate the basic idea by means of the tridiagonal matrix

$$A = \begin{bmatrix} 2 & -1 & & & \\ -1 & & \ddots & & \\ & & \ddots & & \\ & \ddots & & & -1 \\ & & & -1 & 2 \end{bmatrix} \tag{2.3.18}$$

This matrix arises, for example, in the solution of a two-point boundary value problem for the differential equation

$$x''(t) = f(t), \qquad a \leqslant t \leqslant b, \qquad x(a) = \alpha, \qquad x(b) = \gamma \tag{2.3.19}$$

The interval $[a, b]$ is discretized by equally spaced grid points x_i as shown in Figure 2.3-13. The second derivative in (2.3.19) is discretized by the usual central difference formula to give the approximating equations at each grid point

$$x_{i+1} - 2x_i + x_{i-1} = h^2 f_i, \qquad i = 1, \ldots, n \tag{2.3.20}$$

where h is the spacing between grid points. Since x_0 and x_{n+1} are known

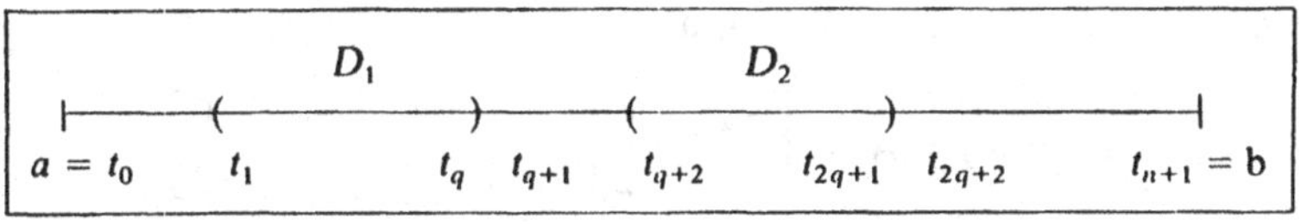

Figure 2.3-13. Grid points and domain decomposition.

boundary values, (2.3.20) is a system of n equations in the n unknowns $x_1, \ldots, x_n$, which approximate the solution of (2.3.19) at the grid points. If we multiply (2.3.20) by -1, then (2.3.18) is the coefficient matrix of the system (2.3.20).

We now partition the grid points t_i as indicated in Figure 2.3-13. We call D_1 the points $t_1, \ldots, t_q$, D_2 the points $t_{q+2}, \ldots, t_{2q+1}$, and so on. For simplicity, we assume that $n = pq + p - 1$. Then there are p sets $D_1, \ldots, D_p$ each containing q points and $p - 1$ points $t_{q+1}, t_{2q+2}, \ldots$, which are between the sets D_i. These $p - 1$ points constitute the *separator set* S. We then order the unknowns x_i by numbering those points in the separator set last. For example, for $q = 2$ and $p = 3$, the ordering of the unknowns corresponding to the grid points is shown in Figure 2.3-14.

We now write the equations corresponding to (2.3.20) using this new ordering of the unknowns as

$$
\begin{array}{ll}
x_0 - 2x_1 + x_2 = h^2 f_1, & x_8 - 2x_5 + x_6 = h^2 f_5 \\[1mm]
x_1 - 2x_2 + x_7 = h^2 f_2, & x_5 - 2x_6 + x_9 = h^2 f_6 \\[1mm]
x_7 - 2x_3 + x_4 = h^2 f_3, & x_2 - 2x_7 + x_3 = h^2 f_7 \\[1mm]
x_3 - 2x_4 + x_8 = h^2 f_4, & x_4 - 2x_8 + x_5 = h^2 f_8
\end{array}
\tag{2.3.21}
$$

Note that we have written the equations corresponding to the separator points last. We can write the system (2.3.21) in the matrix form

$$
\begin{bmatrix}
A_1 & & & & B_1 \\
 & A_2 & & & B_2 \\
 & & \ddots & & \vdots \\
 & & & A_p & B_p \\
C_1 & C_2 & \cdots & C_p & A_S
\end{bmatrix}
\begin{bmatrix}
x_1 \\ x_2 \\ \vdots \\ x_p \\ x_S
\end{bmatrix}
=
\begin{bmatrix}
b_1 \\ b_2 \\ \vdots \\ b_p \\ b_S
\end{bmatrix}
\tag{2.3.22}
$$

x_0	x_1	x_2	x_7	x_3	x_4	x_8	x_5	x_6	x_9
	D_1		S	D_2		S	D_3		

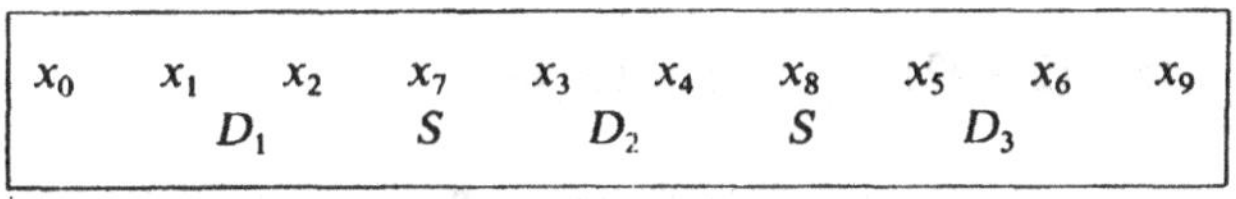

Figure 2.3-14. Reordering of unknowns.

where $p = 3$, $C_i = B_i^T$, $i = 1, 2, 3$, and

$$A_1 = A_2 = A_3 = \begin{bmatrix} -2 & 1 \\ 1 & -2 \end{bmatrix}, \qquad A_S = \begin{bmatrix} -2 & 0 \\ 0 & -2 \end{bmatrix}$$

$$B_1 = \begin{bmatrix} 0 & 0 \\ 1 & 0 \end{bmatrix}, \qquad B_2 = \begin{bmatrix} 1 & 0 \\ 0 & 1 \end{bmatrix}, \qquad B_3 = \begin{bmatrix} 0 & 1 \\ 0 & 0 \end{bmatrix}$$

More generally, the A_i will be $q \times q$ tridiagonal matrices, A_S will be a $(p-1) \times (p-1)$ diagonal matrix, and the B_i will be $q \times (p-1)$ matrices. The matrix in (2.3.22) is sometimes called the *arrowhead* matrix.

Before discussing the properties of the system (2.3.22) further, we first return to the case of a general banded matrix with bandwidth β. Such a matrix may or may not arise from the discretization of a differential equation but we can still proceed as above. We divide the unknowns into $p+1$ sets $D_1, \ldots, D_p$ and S such that each D_i has q unknowns and the unknowns in S "separate" the unknowns in the D_i in the following way. Analogous to Figure 2.3-13, we can imagine the unknowns lined up and partitioned as

$$D_1 \quad S_1 \quad D_2 \quad S_2 \quad \cdots \quad S_{p-1} \quad D_p \tag{2.3.23}$$

Each set S_i in (2.3.23) contains β unknowns. The jth equation in the system $A\mathbf{x} = \mathbf{b}$ is of the form

$$a_{jj}x_j + \sum_{k=j-\beta}^{j+\beta} a_{jk}x_k = b_j \tag{2.3.24}$$

Therefore, if $x_j \in D_i$, none of the unknowns in the equation (2.3.24) are in any of the other D_k. The sets S_i separate the unknowns in the D_i so that each equation in the system contains unknowns in only one D_i.

If we now renumber the unknowns so that those in the separator sets are numbered last, and write the equations in the corresponding order, we obtain a new system of the form (2.3.22) in which $A_1, \ldots, A_p$ are $q \times q$ and A_S is $s \times s$, where $s = \beta(p-1)$ is the number of unknowns in the separator set $S = \bigcup S_i$. Then the B_i are $q \times s$ and the C_i are $s \times q$. We have assumed, for simplicity, that $n = pq + s$ and will return to this point shortly.

Now let

$$A_I = \operatorname{diag}(A_1, \ldots, A_p), \qquad B^T = (B_1^T, \ldots, B_p^T), \qquad C = (C_1, \ldots, C_p) \tag{2.3.25}$$

Then the system (2.3.22) can be written as

$$A_I\mathbf{x}_I + B\mathbf{x}_S = \mathbf{b}_I \tag{2.3.26a}$$

$$C\mathbf{x}_I + A_S\mathbf{x}_S = \mathbf{b}_S \tag{2.3.26b}$$

where $\mathbf{x}_I^T = (\mathbf{x}_1^T, \ldots, \mathbf{x}_p^T)$ and $\mathbf{b}_I^T = (\mathbf{b}_1^T, \ldots, \mathbf{b}_p^T)$. We assume that A_I is nonsingular. Then if we multiply (2.3.26a) by CA_I^{-1} and subtract from (2.3.26b) we obtain the equation

$$\hat{A}\mathbf{x}_S = \hat{\mathbf{b}}, \qquad \hat{A} = A_S - CA_I^{-1}B, \qquad \hat{\mathbf{b}} = \mathbf{b}_S - CA_I^{-1}\mathbf{b}_I \tag{2.3.27}$$

Note that this is just block Gaussian elimination for the system (2.3.26). The matrix $\hat{A}$ is called a *Gauss transform* or *Schur complement*. Once the system (2.3.27) is solved for $\mathbf{x}_S$, the remaining $\mathbf{x}_i$ can be obtained by solving the systems

$$A_i\mathbf{x}_i = \mathbf{b}_i - B_i\mathbf{x}_S, \qquad i = 1, \ldots, p \tag{2.3.28}$$

We now discuss the computation in more detail. We assume that the A_i have stable LU decompositions

$$A_i = L_iU_i, \qquad i = 1, \ldots, p \tag{2.3.29}$$

We then solve the systems

$$L_iY_i = B_i, \qquad L_i\mathbf{y}_i = \mathbf{b}_i, \qquad i = 1, \ldots, p \tag{2.3.30}$$

$$U_iZ_i = Y_i, \qquad U_i\mathbf{z}_i = \mathbf{y}_i, \qquad i = 1, \ldots, p. \tag{2.3.31}$$

Since

$$C_iA_i^{-1}B_i = C_i(L_iU_i)^{-1}B_i = C_iU_i^{-1}Y_i = C_iZ_i$$

and, similarly, $C_iA_i^{-1}\mathbf{b}_i = C_i\mathbf{z}_i$, we can write

$$\hat{A} = A_S - \sum_{i=1}^{p} C_iA_i^{-1}B_i = A_S - \sum_{i=1}^{p} C_iZ_i \tag{2.3.32}$$

and

$$\hat{\mathbf{b}} = \mathbf{b}_S - \sum_{i=1}^{p} C_iA_i^{-1}\mathbf{b}_i = \mathbf{b}_S - \sum_{i=1}^{p} C_i\mathbf{z}_i \tag{2.3.33}$$

which shows how $\hat{A}$ and $\hat{\mathbf{b}}$ are to be obtained. The overall procedure can then be summarized as shown in Figure 2.3-15.

It is clear that Steps 1, 2, 4, and 5 are highly parallel. For example, on a local memory system, assume that A_i, B_i, C_i, and $\mathbf{b}_i$ are assigned to

Step 1.	Form the decompositions (2.3.29) and solve the systems (2.3.30) and (2.3.31).
Step 2.	Form $C_i Z_i$ and $C_i \mathbf{z}_i$, $i = 1, \ldots, p$.
Step 3.	Form $\hat{A}$ and $\hat{\mathbf{b}}$ and solve $\hat{A}\mathbf{x}_S = \hat{\mathbf{b}}$.
Step 4.	Form $\mathbf{c}_i = \mathbf{b}_i - B_i \mathbf{x}_S$, $i = 1, \ldots, p$.
Step 5.	Solve $A_i \mathbf{x}_i = \mathbf{c}_i$, $i = 1, \ldots, p$ using the decompositions (2.3.29).

Figure 2.3-15. Domain decomposition algorithm.

processor i. Then, the computations in each of the steps 1 and 2 are parallel and with no communication. The potential bottleneck is in Step 3. One possibility is to solve the system $\hat{A}\mathbf{x}_S = \hat{\mathbf{b}}$ in a single processor, say, P_1. In this case, the summations of (2.3.32, 33) would be done by a fan-in across the processors with the final sums arriving in P_1. Alternatively, we could use Gaussian elimination with interleaved storage. Then, we would wish to do the fan-in additions of (2.3.32) in such a way that the first row of $\hat{A}$ is in processor 1, the second row in processor 2, and so on. In any case, after $\mathbf{x}_S$ has been obtained, we need to send copies of it to all processors. Then, steps 4 and 5 can be carried out in parallel with no further communication.

We noted previously that A_S is $s \times s$, with $s = \beta(p-1)$. This compares to $2\beta(p-1)$ for the reduced system (2.3.9) in the Lawrie-Sameh partitioning method, and to βp in Johnsson's method.

We next summarize the changes to the domain decomposition algorithm in the important special case that A is symmetric positive definite. Since the matrix of (2.3.22), call it $\bar{A}$, arises from A by interchanges of equations and unknowns, it is related to A by $\bar{A} = PAP^T$, where P is a permutation matrix. Hence, $\bar{A}$ is symmetric positive definite and, thus, so are the A_i and A_S. In step 1 of Figure 2.3-15, we would probably now use Choleski decompositions $A_i = L_i L_i^T$. Then, since $C_i = B_i^T$ by the symmetry, we have

$$\hat{A} = A_S - \sum_{i=1}^{p} B_i^T A_i^{-1} B_i, \qquad \hat{\mathbf{b}} = \mathbf{b}_S - \sum_{i=1}^{p} B_i^T A_i^{-1} \mathbf{b}_i$$

But

$$B_i^T A_i^{-1} B_i = B_i^T (L_i L_i^T)^{-1} B_i = Y_i^T Y_i$$

so that with $\mathbf{y}_i = L_i^{-1}\mathbf{b}_i$

$$\hat{A} = A_S - \sum_{i=1}^{p} Y_i^T Y_i, \qquad \hat{\mathbf{b}} = \mathbf{b}_S - \sum_{i=1}^{p} Y_i^T \mathbf{y}_i \tag{2.3.34}$$

An important point to note is that the matrix $\hat{A}$ is symmetric positive definite whenever A itself is. Clearly, it is symmetric. For the positive definiteness, let $\mathbf{x}_2$ be any nonzero vector of length s, and set $\mathbf{x}_1 = -A_I^{-1} B\mathbf{x}_2$.

Step 1.	Do the Choleski decompositions $A_i = L_i L_i^T$ and solve the systems $L_i Y_i = B_i$, $L_i \mathbf{y}_i = \mathbf{b}_i$, $i = 1, \ldots, p$
Step 2.	Form $\hat{\mathbf{A}}$ and $\hat{\mathbf{b}}$ by (2.3.34) and solve $\hat{\mathbf{A}}\mathbf{x}_S = \hat{\mathbf{b}}$
Step 3.	Form $\mathbf{c}_i = \mathbf{b}_i - B_i \mathbf{x}_S$ and solve the systems $A_i \mathbf{x}_i = \mathbf{c}_i$, $i = 1, \ldots, p$.

Figure 2.3-16. Symmetric positive definite domain decomposition.

Then

$$0 < (\mathbf{x}_1^T, \mathbf{x}_2^T) \begin{bmatrix} A_I & B \\ B^T & A_S \end{bmatrix} \begin{bmatrix} \mathbf{x}_1 \\ \mathbf{x}_2 \end{bmatrix}$$

by the positive definiteness of A. Expanding this out gives

$$0 < \mathbf{x}_1^T A_I \mathbf{x}_1 + 2\mathbf{x}_1^T B \mathbf{x}_2 + \mathbf{x}_2^T A_S \mathbf{x}_2 = \mathbf{x}_2^T \hat{A} \mathbf{x}_2$$

which shows that $\hat{A}$ is positive definite. We summarize the domain decomposition algorithm for symmetric positive definite matrices in Figure 2.3-16. As with the previous algorithms, Steps 1 and 3 are highly parallel and Step 2 is the possible bottleneck.

There is a very close relation between the domain decomposition methods and Johnsson's partitioning method as given in Figure 2.3-12. Indeed, Johnsson's method can be viewed as a domain decomposition method in which there is one additional separator set at the end [that is, (2.3.23) would end with S_p rather than D_{p-1}], and in which no reordering of the unknowns is done. It follows (See Exercise 2.3-13) that the reduced system of Johnsson's method is symmetric positive definite if the original matrix is. The same is not necessarily true for the Lawrie–Sameh method of Figure 2.3-11. We note also that in the Lawrie–Sameh method there are no separator sets.

Tridiagonal Systems and Cyclic Reduction

The partitioning and domain decomposition methods all apply in principle to tridiagonal systems. (See Exercise 2.3-14). We next describe another approach to the solution of tridiagonal systems, which we write in the form

$$\begin{aligned} a_1x_1 + b_1x_2 &= d_1 \\ c_2x_1 + a_2x_2 + b_2x_3 &= d_2 \\ c_3x_2 + a_3x_3 + b_3x_4 &= d_3 \\ &\vdots \\ c_nx_{n-1} + a_nx_n &= d_n \end{aligned} \qquad (2.3.35)$$

We multiply the first equation of (2.3.35) by c_2/a_1 and subtract it from the second equation to eliminate the coefficient of x_1 in the second equation; this is just the usual first step of Gaussian elimination. But next we multiply the third equation by b_2/a_3 and also subtract it from the second equation to eliminate the coefficient of x_3 in the second equation. This produces a new second equation of the form

$$a_2'x_2 + b_2'x_4 = d_2'$$

We now do the same thing with equations 3, 4 and 5, subtracting multiples of equations 3 and 5 from equation 4 to produce a new equation of the form

$$c_3'x_2 + a_4'x_4 + b_4'x_6 = d_4'$$

in which the coefficients of x_3 and x_5 have been eliminated from the original fourth equation. We continue in this way, working with overlapping groups of three equations to produce new middle equations in which the odd numbered variables have been eliminated. This is illustrated schematically in Figure 2.3-17 for $n = 7$. Assuming that n is odd, we have at the end of the process a modified system

$$\begin{aligned} a_2'x_2 + b_2'x_4 &= d_2' \\ c_2'x_2 + a_4'x_4 + b_4'x_6 &= d_4' \\ &\vdots \end{aligned} \tag{2.3.36}$$

involving only the variables $x_2, x_4, \ldots, x_{n-1}$. (Note that we have already done this process for the block tridiagonal matrix (2.3.3) in deriving the reduced system (2.3.16) of Johnsson's method.)

The system (2.3.36) is tridiagonal in the variables $x_2, x_4, \ldots,$ and we can repeat the process to obtain a new system containing only the variables $x_4, x_8, \ldots$. We continue in this fashion until no further reduction is possible. In particular, if $n = 2^q - 1$, the algorithm will terminate with a single final equation. This final equation is solved and then a back

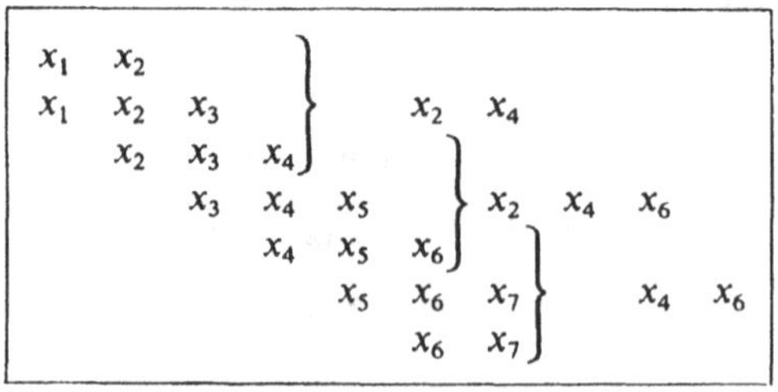

Figure 2.3-17. Cyclic reduction.

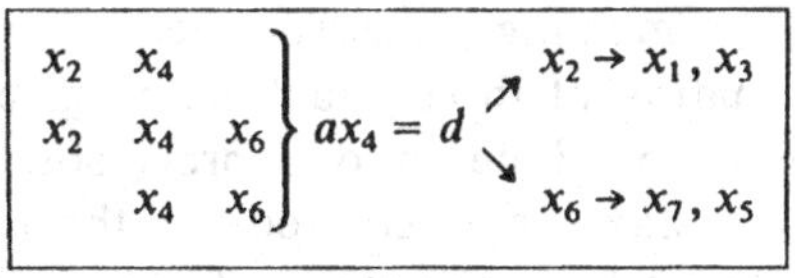

Figure 2.3-18. Back substitution.

substitution is initiated. This is illustrated in Figure 2.3-18 for $n = 7$, which continues the schematic of Figure 2.3-17. In Figure 2.3-18, the three equations obtained from the first step, as shown in Figure 2.3-17, are combined to yield a final equation in the single unknown x_4. This is solved and then the first and last reduced equations can be solved for x_2 and x_6. The original first and last equations can then be solved for x_1 and x_7 and the original third and fifth equations may be solved for x_3 and x_5.

If $n \neq 2^q - 1$, the process can be terminated in a system with a small number of variables which can be solved separately before the back substitution begins. An alternative is simply to add dummy equations of the form $x_i = 1$ to the system so that the total number of variables becomes $2^q - 1$, for some q.

The above process is known as *cyclic* or *odd–even reduction.* Although it was devised originally without parallel computing in mind, it has considerable inherent parallelism, which we now examine. Note first that the operations leading to the new equations for $x_2, x_4, \ldots, x_{n-1}$ are independent and can be done in parallel. Suppose that there are $p = (n-1)/2$ processors with the storage pattern illustrated in Figure 2.3-19. The processors could then do in parallel the operations leading to the first reduced system containing the even-numbered unknowns. At the end of this step, each processor would contain the coefficients for exactly one new equation, and before the next step the coefficients for two additional equations would have to be transmitted to other processors. One natural scheme is that each "middle" processor receives this information as indicated below:

$$P_1 \to P_2 \leftarrow P_3 \to P_4 \leftarrow P_5$$

The odd-numbered processors are now finished and the even-numbered processors do the next elimination step. The process is continued with

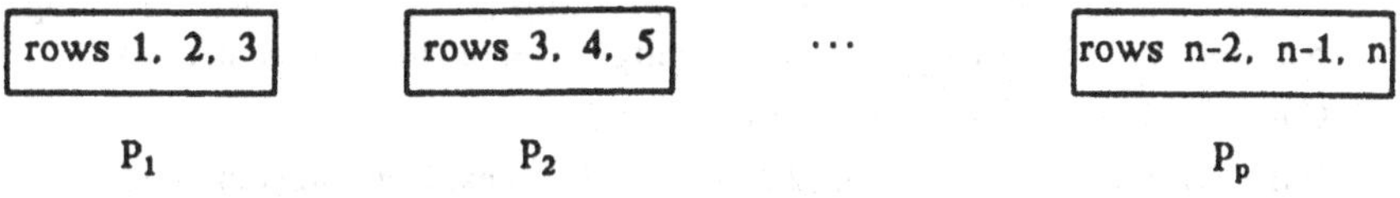

Figure 2.3-19. Processor assignment for cyclic reduction.

essentially half of the remaining processors becoming inactive after each step; the final combination of three equations to give one equation in a single unknown would be done in one processor. Note that $q - 1 = \log[(n+1)/2]$ parallel stages are required for the reduction. The back substitution essentially works in the reverse fashion. The final equation is solved in one processor and then additional processors can be used as the back substitution proceeds.

In the more realistic case that $p \ll n$, several rows would be distributed to each processor initially and processors would work with high efficiency until the final stages, when data transmission would be required and the processors would start to become inactive as above.

Exercises 2.3

1. Give adaptations of the other LU decomposition pseudocodes of Section 2.1 for the case of banded systems. Show that the maximum vector length for any of these codes is β.
2. Assume that a vector computer requires 200 ns for scalar operators and $1000 + 10n$ for vector operations of length n, except linked triads, which require $1600 + 10n$. Do operation counts in both vector and scalar arithmetic for the LU decomposition of Figure 2.3-1b and for the column sweep algorithm of Figure 2.3-4 for a banded system of bandwidth β, assumed to be stored by columns. Ascertain for what values of the bandwidth it is better to use just scalar arithmetic.
3. For the vector computer of Exercise 2, ascertain if it is better to use the algorithm of Figure 2.3-1a or the algorithm of Figure 2.3-1b, assuming optimum storage for each. Next, add the solution of the triangular systems for forward and back substitution using the inner product algorithm or the column sweep algorithm as appropriate. Conclude which is the better overall algorithm.
4. Let A be a 1000×1000 banded system of bandwidth β. For $\beta = 20$, 45, and 75, discuss the load balancing of LU decomposition with row wrapped interleaved storage for 10, 50, and 100 processors.
5. Let A be a symmetric positive definite matrix with bandwidth β. Adapt the Choleski code of Figure 2.1-10 to banded systems. Discuss the vector lengths.
6. For the matrix of Exercise 5, discuss the parallel implementation of Choleski's method for both row and column wrapped interleaved storage. Follow the discussion of LU decomposition in the text.
7. Let A be a 1000×1000 matrix with bandwidth $\beta = 100$. Discuss the storage requirements for solving $A\mathbf{x} = \mathbf{b}$ assuming that interchanges are needed.
8. Complete Figures 2.3-9 and 2.3-10 for $p = 3$.
9. Write out the systems (2.3.7), (2.3.8), and (2.3.9) explicitly in component form for $p = 3$, $\beta = 2$, and $q = 5$.

10. Show that the size of the reduced system (2.3.9) is $2\beta(p-1)$. Show also that the coefficient matrix of (2.3.9) is block pentadiagonal and has semibandwidth 3β.
11. Write out explicitly the matrix of (2.3.14) for $\beta = 2$ and $q = 3$. Do the same for the matrix of (2.3.16).
12. Write out explicitly the matrix of (2.3.22) for $p = 3$, $\beta = 2$, $q = 4$, and $s = 2$.
13. Reorder the system in Johnsson's method by numbering all the unknowns $\mathbf{x}_{i,2}$ of (2.3.12) last and writing the equations in the corresponding order. Show that the coefficient matrix has the form of (2.3.22). Show next that the reduced system [corresponding to (2.3.16) in the case $p = 3$] corresponds to the system $\hat{A}\mathbf{x}_S = \hat{\mathbf{b}}$ of the domain decomposition method. Conclude, following the argument in the text for domain decomposition, that the reduced system of Johnsson's method is symmetric positive definite if A is.
14. Formulate the partitioning and domain decomposition methods of Figures 2.3-11, 2.3-12, 2.3-15, and 2.3-16 for tridiagonal systems ($\beta = 1$). Write out explicitly the reduced systems in each case, noting their size. Discuss the parallel properties of each method as a function of p and n.

References and Extensions 2.3

1. The recognition that the degree of vectorization or parallelism of LU or Choleski decomposition depended on the bandwidth of the system motivated considerable early research on narrow banded systems, especially tridiagonal systems. Stone [1973] gave an algorithm for tridiagonal systems based on recursive doubling (Section 1.2). Lambiotte and Voigt [1975] showed that this algorithm was inconsistent and gave a consistent version, as did Stone [1975], but these methods have not been widely used.
2. The cyclic reduction algorithm, or one of its variants, has probably been the most preferred method for tridiagonal systems on both parallel and vector computers. It was originally proposed by G. Golub and R. Hockney for special block tridiagonal systems (See Hockney [1965]), but it soon became apparent (Hockney [1970]) that it could be applied to general tridiagonal systems. Heller [1976] showed, under certain assumptions, that during the cyclic reduction process the off-diagonal elements decrease in size relative to the diagonal elements at a quadratic rate; this allows termination before the full $\log n$ steps have been performed. It was also recognized by several authors (see, for example, Lambiotte and Voigt [1975]) that cyclic reduction is just Gaussian elimination applied to the matrix PAP^T for a suitable permutation matrix P. Thus, if A is symmetric positive definite, so is PAP^T and cyclic reduction is numerically stable. However, it is still necessary to handle the right-hand side carefully in order to retain the numerical stability; see Golub and van Loan [1983]. Note also that when Gaussian elimination is applied to PAP^T there is fill-in which does not occur with the original tridiagonal system; consequently, the arithmetic operation count of cyclic reduction is roughly twice that of Gaussian elimination applied to the tridiagonal

system. For further discussion of cyclic reduction and its variants, see Hockney and Jesshope [1981]. For a recent analysis of cyclic reduction and related methods on several parallel architectures, see Johnsson [1987b]. For an analysis of communication on hypercubes, see Lakshmivarahan and Dhall [1987].

3. There have been a number of other parallel methods proposed for tridiagonal systems. Traub [1974] (see also Heller *et al.* [1976]) proposed an iterative method by turning the three basic recursion relations in *LU* factorization into iterations. Swarztrauber [1979] considered a method based on Cramer's rule. Sameh and Kuck [1978] use Given's transformations for a QR reduction, which is numerically stable without interchanges. This, and a partitioning method of Wang [1981], were the precursors of the partitioning methods discussed in the text. Other papers proposing or analyzing parallel methods for tridiagonal systems include Gao [1986], who bases an algorithm on parallel methods for linear recurrence relations, Opsahl and Parkinson [1986], who consider almost tridiagonal systems on SIMD machines such as the ICL DAP and the MPP, and van der Vorst [1986].
4. For $\beta = 1$, the Lawrie-Sameh partitioning algorithm of Figure 2.3-11 is based on the method of Wang [1981] for tridiagonal systems. The QR method of Sameh and Kuck [1978] used a similar partitioning and Lawrie and Sameh [1984] extended the partitioning idea to give the algorithm of Figure 2.3-11 for *LU* decomposition of banded systems. A similar method was developed by Meier [1985]. Since the solution of the reduced system (2.3.9) is a potential bottleneck in this algorithm, Dongarra and Sameh [1984] considered using iterative methods for the reduced system. The partitioning algorithm of Figure 2.3-12 was given by Johnsson [1985b], who analyzed its basic properties and gave complexity estimates for a number of communication topologies, including hypercubes, binary trees, and linear arrays. See also Dongarra and Johnsson [1987] for further analysis and experimental results for partitioning methods. A variant of the Lawrie-Sameh method was used by Gannon and van Rosendale [1984] as an example in a study of communication complexity.
5. The idea of domain decomposition has a long history in the engineering community, independent of parallel methods, where it is usually called *substructuring.* The original motivation was to break up a large problem into small parts which could be solved separately, and then the final solution obtained from these subproblems (see, for example, Noor *et al.* [1978]). Under the name "one-way dissection," George and Liu [1981] discuss domain decomposition from the point of view of utilizing sparsity in the matrices B_i of (2.3.22). The idea of exploiting substructuring in parallel computing is reviewed in Adams and Voigt [1984].
6. The substructuring process can be continued by substructuring the subproblems. For example, if the original system has bandwidth β, then so do the matrices A_i in (2.3.22) and the substructuring approach can be applied to each of them. The process can then be repeated again, and so on. This idea was developed by A. George in the early 1970s (see George [1977] and George and Liu [1981]) and called *nested dissection.* It is particularly useful for certain problems arising from partial differential equations. Some of the properties of nested dissection on parallel and vector computers have been studied in George *et al.* [1978] and Gannon [1980].

7. Other papers dealing with banded systems on parallel or vector computers include Ashcraft [1985a], Cleary *et al.* [1986], who discuss LU and Choleski factorization on a parallel computer with local and shared memory, Gannon [1986], who considers Gaussian elimination on a parallel-vector machine, Bjorstad [1987], who describes a large-scale finite element code that uses repeated substructuring, Schreiber [1986], who gives a QR factorization algorithm for systolic arrays, Kapur and Browne [1984], who deal with the solution of block tridiagonal systems on a reconfigurable array of processors, and Saad and Schultz [1987].
8. We noted in the text the fact that interchanges in Gaussian elimination increase the bandwidth. The same is true of Gauss–Jordan elimination, even without interchanges. More precisely, in eliminating the superdiagonal elements in the ith column, all elements above the diagonal in the $(i + \beta)$ column become nonzero, in general. This increases the amount of computation considerably and makes the Gauss–Jordan algorithm even less attractive for banded systems than for full ones.
9. The methods discussed in this section are not suitable for general sparse matrices. For such matrices, there are well-developed methods for serial computers (see, for example, George and Liu [1981]). For parallel computers, George and Heath *et al.* [1986] consider Choleski factorization assuming that suitable preprocessing (permutation and symbolic factorization) has already been done. They give a column-oriented factorization algorithm in which the basic operations are to modify the jth column using the kth column when $l_{jk} \neq 0$ $(j > k)$, and divide the jth column by a scalar. See also George, Liu, and Ng [1987] and George and Heath *et al.* [1987a, b]. Peters [1984] discusses parallel pivoting algorithms. Lewis and Simon [1986] treat Gaussian elimination on vector computers, especially the CRAY X-MP series. The basic operation is a sparse linked triad which is difficult to vectorize. However, the X-MP series, as opposed to the CRAY-1, has hardware gather/scatter operations and the use of these allows mflop rates up to 78 for assembly language coding. Other papers dealing with methods for sparse matrices include Duff [1984] for implementations on CRAY machines, Duff [1986], who proposes a multifrontal method, Dave and Duff [1987], who report on the performance of a sparse frontal method on the CRAY-2, Liu [1986, 1987] on sparse Choleski factorization, Greenbaum [1986b], who considers triangular systems on a shared memory machine, Wing and Huang [1977, 1980], and Alaghband and Jordan [1985].

3

Iterative Methods for Linear Equations

3.1. Jacobi's Method

We consider in this section one of the simplest iterative methods: Jacobi's method. Although Jacobi's method is not a viable method for most problems, it provides a convenient starting point for our discussion of iterative methods. It will also be useful as a subsidiary method later.

Let A be an $n \times n$ nonsingular matrix and

$$A\mathbf{x} = \mathbf{b} \tag{3.1.1}$$

the system to be solved. We assume that the diagonal elements, a_{ii}, of A are all nonzero. Then Jacobi's method is

$$x_i^{k+1} = \frac{1}{a_{ii}}\left(-\sum_{j \neq i} a_{ij}x_j^k + b_i\right), \qquad i = 1, \ldots, n, \qquad k = 0, 1, \ldots \tag{3.1.2}$$

where the superscript indicates the iteration number and it is assumed, as in all iterative methods, that $x_1^0, \ldots, x_n^0$ is a given approximation to the solution of (3.1.1).

For many purposes it is convenient to rewrite (3.1.2) in matrix form. Let $D = \operatorname{diag}(a_{11}, \ldots, a_{nn})$ be the diagonal matrix containing the diagonal elements of A, and let $B = D - A$ so that $A = D - B$ is the splitting of A into its diagonal and off-diagonal elements. Then we can write (3.1.2) as

$$\mathbf{x}^{k+1} = H\mathbf{x}^k + \mathbf{d}, \qquad k = 0, 1, \ldots, \qquad H = D^{-1}B, \qquad \mathbf{d} = D^{-1}\mathbf{b} \tag{3.1.3}$$

The Jacobi method does not, of course, always converge. Two standard convergence theorems are the following, whose proofs are given in Appendix 2.

3.1.1. THEOREM. *If A is strictly or irreducibly diagonally dominant, then the Jacobi iteration converges for any* $\mathbf{x}^0$.

3.1.2. THEOREM. *If $A = D - B$ is symmetric and positive definite, then the Jacobi iteration converges for any* $\mathbf{x}^0$ *if and only if $D + B$ is positive definite.*

The basic operation of (3.1.3) is a matrix-vector multiply and for this we can consider any of the techniques of Section 1.3. As we saw there, an effective parallel or vector implementation of matrix-vector multiplication depends very much on the structure of H. Iterative methods will generally be used only when A, and hence H, is a large sparse matrix of the type that, for example, results from the discretization of elliptic boundary value problems by finite difference or finite element methods. We next describe a model problem of this type.

Poisson's Equation

We consider the elliptic partial differential equation, known as *Poisson's equation*,

$$u_{xx} + u_{yy} = f, \tag{3.1.4}$$

where $(x, y) \in \Omega = [0, 1] \times [0, 1]$ and u is given on the boundary of the domain Ω. f is a given function of x and y and if $f \equiv 0$, (3.1.4) is *Laplace's equation.* We discretize the unit square as illustrated in Figure 3.1-1 with mesh spacing h. If u_{ij} denotes an approximation to the solution of (3.1.4) at the grid point (ih, jh), then by approximating the derivatives of (3.1.4) by the usual second-order difference approximations we obtain the system of equations

$$u_{i+1,j} + u_{i-1,j} + u_{i,j+1} + u_{i,j-1} - 4u_{ij} = h^2 f_{ij}, \qquad i, j = 1, \ldots, N \tag{3.1.5}$$

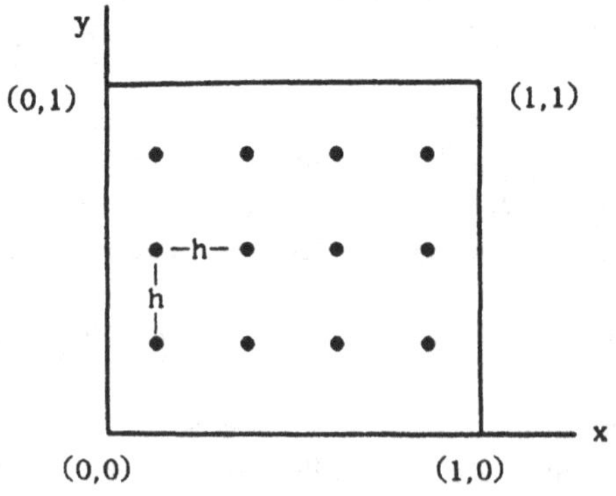

Figure 3.1-1. Mesh points on the unit square.

where $(N+1)h = 1$. By our assumption that u is given on the boundary of the domain, only the N^2 variables u_{ij}, $i, j = 1, \ldots, N$, at the interior grid points are unknowns in (3.1.5); hence, this is a linear system of $n = N^2$ equations, the solution of which gives approximations at the grid points to the solution of (3.1.4).

We can write the system in the form $A\mathbf{x} = \mathbf{b}$ by letting $x_k = u_{k1}$, $k = 1, \ldots, N$, be the unknowns on the first line of grid points, $x_k = u_{k-N,2}$, $k = N+1, \ldots, 2N$, be-the unknowns on the second line, and so on. That is,

$$\mathbf{x}^T = (u_{11}, \ldots, u_{N1}, u_{12}, \ldots, u_{N2}, \ldots, u_{1N}, \ldots, u_{NN}) \tag{3.1.6}$$

The coefficient matrix A can be written in the block form

$$A = \begin{bmatrix} T & -I & & \\ -I & \ddots & \ddots & \\ & \ddots & \ddots & -I \\ & & -I & T \end{bmatrix}, \qquad T = \begin{bmatrix} 4 & -1 & & \\ -1 & \ddots & \ddots & \\ & \ddots & \ddots & -1 \\ & & -1 & 4 \end{bmatrix} \tag{3.1.7}$$

where I is the $N \times N$ identity matrix and T is $N \times N$. The right-hand side $\mathbf{b}$ of the system consists of the quantities $-h^2 f_{ij}$ as well as the known boundary values in the proper positions.

Note that (3.1.7) is an example of a diagonally sparse matrix, as discussed in Section 1.3, and consists of only five nonzero diagonals, regardless of the size of N. However, such a matrix would rarely be stored, even in diagonal form, especially to carry out something like the Jacobi iteration. Rather, we would apply the Jacobi method to (3.1.5) in the form

$$\begin{aligned} u_{ij}^{k+1} &= \tfrac{1}{4}[u_{i+1,j}^k + u_{i-1,j}^k + u_{i,j+1}^k + u_{i,j-1}^k - h^2 f_{ij}], \\ & i, j = 1, \ldots, N, \qquad k = 0, 1, \ldots \end{aligned} \tag{3.1.8}$$

For Laplace's equation, $(f \equiv 0)$, (3.1.8) shows that the next iterate at the (i, j) grid point is just the average of the previous iterates at the neighboring north, south, east, and west grid points.

Jacobi's Method in Parallel

It is clear from (3.1.8) that, in principle, all of the u_{ij}^{k+1} can be computed in parallel; it is for this reason that Jacobi's method is sometimes considered to be a prototypical parallel method. However, various details need to be considered in implementing it on vector or parallel computers. We consider next some of the simplest issues for parallel systems, for the moment remaining with the discrete Poisson equation (3.1.5).

Suppose first that the parallel system consists of a mesh connected array of $p = q^2$ processors P_{ij} arranged in a two-dimensional lattice with each connected to its north, south, east, and west neighbors as illustrated in Figure 3.1-2. Suppose that $N^2 = mp$. Then it is natural to assign m unknowns to each processor and there are a variety of ways to accomplish this. One of the simplest is to imagine the array of processors overlaid on the grid points of Figure 3.1-1, as illustrated in Figure 3.1-2 for four unknowns per processor. We assume that those processors that contain interior points adjacent to a boundary hold the corresponding known boundary values.

On a local memory system, at the end of each iteration the new iterates at certain grid points will need to be transmitted to adjacent processors. We next discuss this in more detail. A limiting case of the above arrangement is when there are $p = N^2$ processors, and each processor contains exactly one unknown. In this case, the computation in an interior processor will proceed as

$$\begin{aligned} &\text{compute } u_{ij}^{k+1} \text{ in processor } P_{ij} \\ &\text{send } u_{ij}^{k+1} \text{ to processors } P_{i+1,j}, P_{i-1,j}, P_{i,j+1}, P_{i,j-1} \end{aligned} \tag{3.1.9}$$

that is, at each stage a compute step, using (3.1.8) in the case of Poisson's equation, is followed by transmissions of the updated iterates to the processors that need them for the next iteration. Although this arrangement exhibits the perfect parallelism of Jacobi's method, the requirement of N^2 processors is generally unrealistic, and, moreover, a good deal of time may be spent in communication.

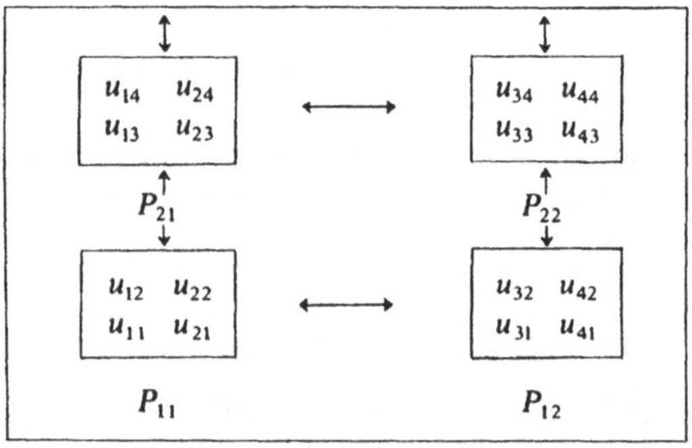

Figure 3.1-2. Grid point assignments.

A more common situation is when $N^2 = mp$ and each processor holds m unknowns. This was illustrated in Figure 3.1-2 for $m = 4$, but a more realistic case might be $N = 100$ and $p = 20$, which implies that $m = 500$. Each processor will proceed to compute iterates for the unknowns it holds. For example, for the situation of Figure 3.1-2 the computation in processor P_{22} would be

$$\text{compute } u_{33}^{k+1},\ u_{43}^{k+1};\ \text{send to } P_{12}$$

$$\text{compute } u_{34}^{k+1},\ \text{send } u_{33}^{k+1},\ u_{34}^{k+1} \text{ to } P_{21} \tag{3.1.10}$$

$$\vdots$$

with analogous computations proceeding in parallel in the other processors.

We denote by "internal boundary values" those values of u_{ij} that are needed by other processors at the next iteration and must be transmitted. This is illustrated in Figure 3.1-3 for a single processor. If there are $m = q^2$ unknowns in a processor, then all m must be updated but at most $4q$ are transmitted. Thus, if we have a fixed number of processors, then the larger the problem, the higher will be the ratio of computation time to communication. In particular, the number of interior grid points for which no data

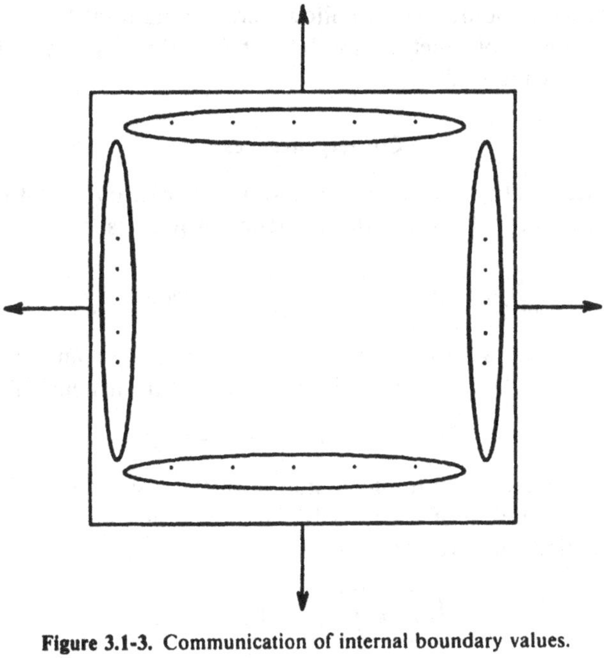

Figure 3.1-3. Communication of internal boundary values.

communication is required grows quadratically as a function of the number of unknowns, whereas the number of grid points for which communication is required grows only linearly. Hence, for sufficiently large problems, the data communication time becomes increasingly negligible relative to the computation time.

Synchronous and Asynchronous Methods

In the computation scheme indicated by (3.1.10), it is necessary to add a synchronization mechanism to ensure that the Jacobi iteration is carried out correctly. For example, the computation of u_{22}^{k+1} cannot be completed until u_{32}^{k} and u_{23}^{k} have been received from the neighboring processors. As discussed in Section 1.2, the time necessary to carry out the synchronization, as well as the time that a processor must wait until its data is ready to continue the computation, adds an overhead to the computation.

For certain iterative methods, such as Jacobi's method, a potentially attractive alternative is to allow the processors to proceed asynchronously, that is, without any synchronization. In this case, some iterates may be computed incorrectly. For example, in the situation of Figure 3.1-2 suppose that at the time u_{12}^{k+1} is to be computed, u_{13}^{k} has not yet been received from processor P_{12}. Then the previous value, u_{13}^{k-1}, will be used in the computation of u_{12}^{k+1}, and this new iterate is not the Jacobi iterate defined by (3.1.8). However, this need not be detrimental to the overall iteration and it may be cost-effective in some cases to allow iterative methods to proceed asynchronously. The Jacobi method implemented in this fashion will be called an *asynchronous* method.

Convergence Tests

In carrying out any iterative method, it is necessary to test for convergence of the iterates. If $\{\mathbf{x}^k\}$ is the sequence of iterates, two common tests are

$$\|\mathbf{x}^{k+1} - \mathbf{x}^k\| \leqslant \varepsilon \quad \text{or} \quad \|\mathbf{x}^{k+1} - \mathbf{x}^k\| \leqslant \varepsilon \|\mathbf{x}^k\| \tag{3.1.11}$$

where $\| \quad \|$ denotes a vector norm. It is also relatively common to use the residual, $\mathbf{r}^k = \mathbf{b} - A\mathbf{x}^k$, of the kth iterate and require instead of (3.11) that

$$\|\mathbf{r}^k\| \leqslant \varepsilon \quad \text{or} \quad \|\mathbf{r}^k\| \leqslant \varepsilon \|\mathbf{r}^0\| \tag{3.1.12}$$

We next consider the implementation of the tests (3.1.11) for Jacobi's method in the situation of Figure 3.1-2. Two common norms are the l_2 and l_∞ norms defined for a vector $\mathbf{x}$ by

$$\|\mathbf{x}\|_2 = \left(\sum_{i=1}^{n} x_i^2\right)^{1/2}, \qquad \|\mathbf{x}\|_\infty = \max_{1\leqslant i\leqslant n} |x_i| \tag{3.1.13}$$

The use of the l_2 norm requires the computation of an inner product across the processors, which was discussed in Section 1.3. On the other hand, the first test of (3.1.11) can be implemented in the l_∞ norm in the following way. Each processor tests its unknowns at each iteration to see if they all satisfy

$$|u_{ij}^{k+1} - u_{ij}^{k}| \leq \varepsilon$$

If so, a "flag" is set indicating that the processor's iterates have converged and then some mechanism is required to examine the flags of all processors. If they are all set, the iteration has converged and is stopped; if not, the iteration proceeds. Thus, this procedure is very much like a synchronization mechanism. Note that the vector norm is not actually computed in order to carry out the convergence test.

The second test of (3.1.11) is a relative error test and is useful when the magnitude of the solution is not known a priori so as to guide in the choice of ε. However, this test requires the computation of a norm across the processors followed by a transmission of the norm back to the processors and is more costly to implement.

Vectorization

We turn next to the implementation of Jacobi's method on vector computers. Again, at first, we will restrict attention to the discrete Poisson equation and the iteration (3.1.8). Then, Jacobi's method would be implemented by the pseudocode of Figure 3.1-4. Here, U and UN are $(N+2) \times (N+2)$ two-dimensional arrays that hold the iterates on the grid as well as the boundary values, and G is an $N \times N$ two-dimensional array that holds $h^2 f$. Figure 3.1-4 depicts only one iteration; at the next iteration the roles of U and UN would be reversed. Note that we allow zero indices in order to retrieve the boundary values.

Consider first the implementation of Figure 3.1-4 on a vector computer that utilizes vector registers. Assuming, for simplicity, that $N+2$ is the length of a register, we could proceed as illustrated in Figure 3.1-5. A schematic of the register layout is given in Figure 3.1-6. The statements in

```
For J = 1 to N
  For I = 1 to N
     UN(I, J) = 0.25*[U(I - 1, J) + U(I + 1, J) + U(I, J + 1)
                  + U(I, J - 1) - G(I, J)]
```

Figure 3.1-4. Code segment for Jacobi's method.

```
 Load U( ,0) (boundary column)
[Load U( ,2) (second column)
[Compute UN( ,1) = U( ,0) + U( ,2)
[Load U( ,1) (first column)
[Compute UN( ,1) = UN( ,1) + U( ,1)+1
 Compute UN( ,1) = UN( ,1) + U( ,+1)-1
 Load G( ,1)
 Compute UN( ,1) = UN( ,1) - G( ,1)
 Compute UN( ,1) = 0.25 * UN( ,1)
 Load U( ,3)
[Store UN( ,1)
[ :
  :
```

Figure 3.1-5. Jacobi's method on a register computer.

Figure 3.1-5 compute the new iterates in the first column of grid points. $U(,1)$ denotes the vector of length N containing the current iterates corresponding to the first column of the grid, and $U(,1)_{\pm 1}$ denotes the corresponding vector translated by one in the up or down directions. The bracket on the second and third statements indicates that on some vector computers these operations can be overlapped after a short delay. Similarly, the second bracket indicates that the load instruction for the next column of data can be done concurrently with the previous computation, and the next bracket indicates that the final store instruction can be done concurrently with the next computation. This section of code would, of course, be part of an overall loop that would index on the columns of U and UN. Additional code complexity would be required to utilize efficiently data

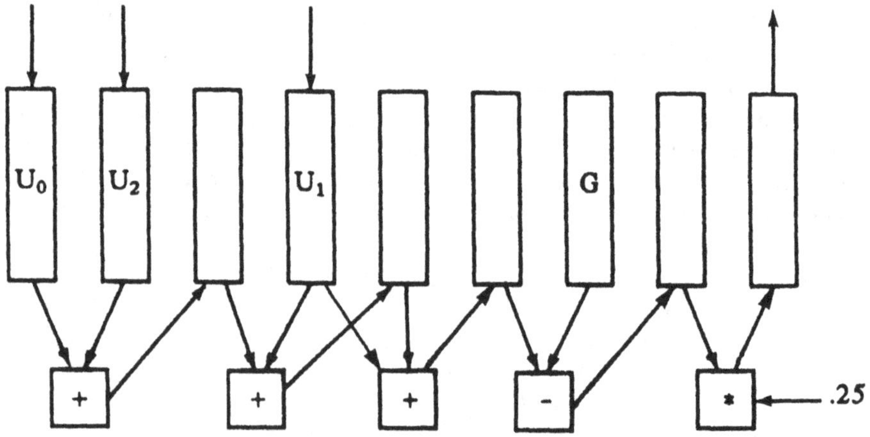

Figure 3.1-6. Register utilization for Jacobi's method.

$$
\begin{array}{l}
\vdots \\
U(N+3) \quad U(N+4) \quad \cdots \\
\quad U(1) \qquad U(2) \qquad U(3) \quad \cdots \quad U(N+2)
\end{array}
$$

Figure 3.1-7. Storage as one-dimensional array.

currently in the registers and, of course, when $N + 2$ is larger than the length of the vector registers, it will be necessary to do each column in appropriate segments. The important point is that with proper handling of the vector registers, the computation vectorizes nicely.

Long Vectors

We consider next the implementation on vector computers that obtain their vector operands directly from memory and are most efficient for long vector lengths. The code of Figure 3.1-4 can be implemented easily one column at a time, but the vector lengths will be $O(N)$. It is possible, however, to reorganize the computation so that the vector lengths are $O(N^2)$. In order to do this, it is convenient to think in terms of the iterates and boundary values being stored by rows, left to right, bottom to top, in one-dimensional arrays of length $(N + 2)^2$. This is illustrated in Figure 3.1-7.

We will use the notation that $U(I; K)$ denotes a K-long vector starting in the Ith position of U, and let $M1 = (N + 1)(N + 2) - 1$, $M2 = N(N + 2) - 2$. Then one stage of the Jacobi iteration is carried out as shown in Figure 3.1-8. In Figure 3.1-8, T is a temporary vector of the same length as U. The first statement computes the pairwise "diagonal" sums as indicated in Figure 3.1-9. The dotted line in Figure 3.1-9 coupling $U(N + 3)$ and

$$T(2; M1) = U(2; M1) + U(N + 3; M1)$$

$$U(N + 4; M2) = T(2; M2) + T(N + 5; M2)$$

$$U(N + 4; M2) = 0.25*(U(N + 4; M2) - G(N + 4; M2))$$

Figure 3.1-8. Jacobi long vector code.

$$
\begin{array}{llll}
U(2N+5) & U(2N+6) & & \\
U(N+3) & U(N+4) & \cdots \quad U(2N+3) & U(2N+4) \\
\quad U(2) & \quad U(3) & \qquad\qquad U(N+2) & \quad U(N+3)
\end{array}
$$

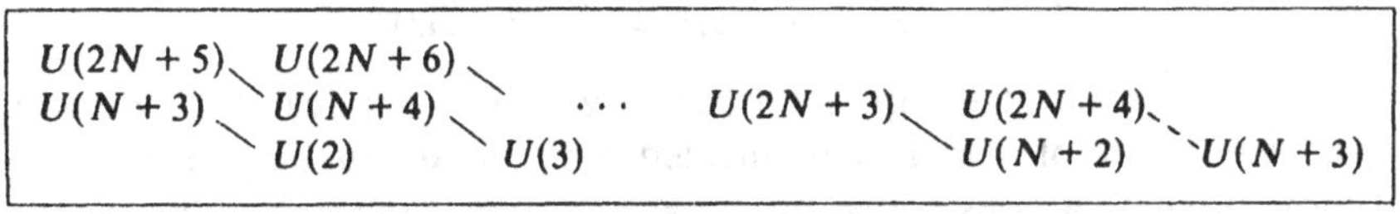

Figure 3.1-9. Pairwise sums.

$$\begin{array}{l} U(2) + U(N+3) + U(N+5) + U(2N+6) \\ U(3) + U(N+4) + U(N+6) + U(2N+7) \\ \vdots \end{array}$$

Figure 3.1-10. Sums from second statement.

$U(2N + 4)$ indicates that this is an unnecessary computation that we will discuss in a moment. The last sum produced by the first statement is $U((N + 1)(N + 2)) + U((N + 2)^2 - 1)$. The second statement yields the sum of the neighboring values for each grid point, as shown in Figure 3.1-10.

A potential difficulty with the second statement of Figure 3.1-8 is that it overwrites the boundary values with spurious results. On some vector computers (for example, the CYBER 205) there is the capability to suppress storage by means of a bit vector, and this capability is very useful here; no time is added to the computation but storage for $(N + 2)^2$ bits is required. The final statement subtracts h^2f and divides by 4. It is assumed that G is also an $(N + 2)^2$-long array, and the suppression of storage onto the boundary positions is needed in this statement also. An alternative to suppressing storage is to restore the boundary values after each iteration, which would be much more time consuming. We also note that the code in Figure 3.1-8 contains only three vector additions as opposed to the four that would seem to be implied by Figure 3.1-4. This is because we obtain the effect of a fan-in addition; that is, in the first statement of Figure 3.1-8 we compute the sums $U(2) + U(N + 3)$ and $U(N + 5) + U(2N + 6)$; then, in the second statement, we add these sums.

To summarize the above discussion, we are able to achieve maximum vector lengths of $O(N^2)$ and eliminate one vector addition but at the expense of a more complicated code, additional storage for the boundary positions in both the T and G arrays (as well as for the bit vector if that capability is used), and additional redundant calculations corresponding to the boundary values. We note that it is not possible to do a code of the type in Figure 3.1-8 using a vector of only the values at the interior grid points (Exercise 3.1-11).

Vectorization by Matrix Multiplication

The approach of Figure 3.1-8 has very limited applicability. We will give an example of a more complicated differential equation in the next section to which it does apply, but, in general, one cannot deviate very far from the Poisson equation. Even for the Poisson equation, if the region is not a square (or a rectangle) or if uneven spacing of the grid points in either the x or y direction is taken, it does not work (Exercise 3.1-12). The approach of Figure 3.1-8 has two benefits: long vector lengths, and a reduction in the amount of computation by reducing four vector additions to three. A much more generally applicable approach, to be described next, can achieve the long vector lengths but not the arithmetic reduction.

For many problems, the iteration matrix H of the Jacobi iteration (3.1.3) is diagonally sparse but does not have constant diagonals as with the Poisson equation (3.1.5). We illustrate this by the "generalized Poisson" equation

$$(au_x)_x + (bu_y)_y = f \tag{3.1.14}$$

where a and b are positive functions of x and y. Again, for simplicity, we shall assume that the domain of (3.1.14) is the unit square and the solution u is prescribed on the boundary. A standard finite difference discretization of (3.1.14) is

$$\begin{aligned} a_{i-1/2,j}u_{i-1,j} + a_{i+1/2,j}u_{i+1,j} + b_{i,j-1/2}u_{i,j-1} \\ + b_{i,j+1/2}u_{i,j+1} - c_{ij}u_{ij} = h^2 f_{ij} \end{aligned} \tag{3.1.15}$$

where

$$c_{ij} = a_{i-1/2,j} + a_{i+1/2,j} + b_{i,j-1/2} + b_{i,j+1/2} \tag{3.1.16}$$

In (3.1.15) the coefficients a and b are evaluated at the midpoints of the intervals between grid points. For example, $a_{i-1/2,j} = a(ih - \frac{1}{2}h, jh)$ and similarly for the others. This assures symmetry of the coefficient matrix, as seen below. Note that (3.1.15) reduces to (3.1.5) if $a = b = 1$.

It is easy to see (Exercise 3.1-13) that the equations (3.1.15) can be written in the form $A\mathbf{x} = \mathbf{b}$, where $\mathbf{x}$ is the vector of unknowns u_{ij} as given in (3.1.6), $\mathbf{b}$ is the vector containing boundary values and $-h^2 f_{ij}$, and

$$A = \begin{bmatrix} T_1 & B_1 & & \\ B_1 & \ddots & \ddots & \\ & \ddots & \ddots & B_{N-1} \\ & & B_{N-1} & T_N \end{bmatrix} \tag{3.1.17}$$

where

$$T_j = \begin{bmatrix} c_{1j} & -a_{1/2,j} & & & \\ -a_{1/2,j} & c_{2j} & -a_{3/2,j} & & \\ & \ddots & \ddots & \ddots & \\ & & & & -a_{N-1/2,j} \\ & & & -a_{N-1/2,j} & c_{Nj} \end{bmatrix}$$

$$B_j = \begin{bmatrix} -b_{1,j+1/2} & & \\ & \ddots & \\ & & -b_{N,j+1/2} \end{bmatrix}$$

The matrix A of (3.1.17) has five nonzero diagonals. The Jacobi iteration matrix H has the same structure, as shown schematically in (3.1.18):

$H =$ 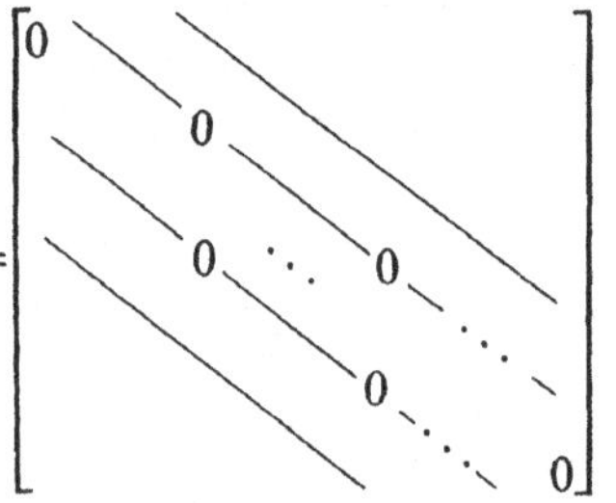 (3.1.18)

We assume that H is stored by diagonals and that the multiplication $H\mathbf{x}^k$ in the Jacobi iteration is carried out by the multiplication by diagonals procedure of Section 1.3. Thus the vector lengths in carrying out the Jacobi iteration are $O(N^2)$. More precisely, the main diagonal of H is of length N^2, the close off-diagonals are of length $N^2 - 1$, and the far off-diagonals are of length $N^2 - N$. Hence, the storage of the matrix H requires $2N^2 - N - 1$ words since, by symmetry, we need only store the upper triangular part. There is wasted storage of $N - 1$ words for the zeros on the close-in diagonal, indicated in (3.1.18), but this is necessary to obtain the desired long vector length.

The above method of implementing the Jacobi iteration in terms of long vector operations is efficient for those problems with variable coefficients for which the equivalent of the matrix H must be stored in any case. However, for the Poisson equation, the explicit storage of H is unnecessary, as we have already seen. Moreover, the approach of Figure 3.1-8 is much more efficient if it can be carried out (see Exercise 3.1-14).

On parallel machines, the implementation of the Jacobi method for the equations (3.1.15) follows the previous discussion for Poisson's equation but with the important difference that the coefficients a, b, and c must now be stored and used. If, again, the grid points are assigned to processors as shown in Figure 3.1-2, then on a local memory system we wish the corresponding a, b, and c to be stored in the memory of the processor that requires them. For example, from (3.1.15), the next Jacobi iterate for u_{ij} is given by

$$u_{ij}^{k+1} = c_{ij}^{-1}(a_{i-1/2,j}u_{i-1,j}^{k} + a_{i+1/2,j}u_{i+1,j}^{k} + b_{i,j-1/2}u_{i,j-1}^{k} + b_{i,j+1/2}u_{i,j+1}^{k} - h^2 f_{ij})$$

and we would want all of the indicated coefficients, including f_{ij}, to be stored in the processor that does this computation. Note that this will require storing a few of these coefficients in more than one processor. For example, in the situation depicted in Figure 3.1-2, the iterations for u_{33} and u_{23} both require the coefficient $a_{5/2,3}$, which we would want to be stored in both of the processors P_{12} and P_{22}. Similarly, the iterations for u_{33} and u_{32} will both require the coefficient $b_{3,5/2}$.

Block Methods

Let a given matrix A be partitioned into submatrices as

$$A = \begin{bmatrix} A_{11} & \cdots & A_{1q} \\ \vdots & & \vdots \\ A_{q1} & \cdots & A_{qq} \end{bmatrix} \tag{3.1.19}$$

where each A_{ii} is assumed to be nonsingular. Then the *block Jacobi method* for the solution of $A\mathbf{x} = \mathbf{b}$, relative to this partitioning, is

$$A_{ii}\mathbf{x}_i^{k+1} = -\sum_{j\neq i} A_{ij}\mathbf{x}_j^k + \mathbf{b}_i, \qquad i = 1, \ldots, q, \qquad k = 0, 1, \ldots \tag{3.1.20}$$

where $\mathbf{x}$ and $\mathbf{b}$ are partitioned commensurately with A. Thus, to carry out one block Jacobi iteration requires the solution of the q systems of (3.1.20) with coefficient matrices A_{ii}. Note that in the special case that each A_{ij} is 1×1, (3.1.20) reduces to the Jacobi method previously discussed. It is known that in certain cases block methods are faster than point methods on serial computers.

As an example of a block Jacobi method, consider again the discrete Poisson equation (3.1.5) and the corresponding matrix representation (3.1.7). In this case, $q = N$, $A_{ii} = T$, $i = 1, \ldots, N$, $A_{ii+1} = A_{i+1,i} = -I$, and all other A_{ij} are zero. Thus (3.1.20) becomes

$$T\mathbf{x}_i^{k+1} = \mathbf{x}_{i+1}^k + \mathbf{x}_{i-1}^k + \mathbf{b}_i, \qquad i = 1, \ldots, N \tag{3.1.21}$$

where we assume that $\mathbf{x}_0^k$ and $\mathbf{x}_{N+1}^k$ contain the boundary values along the bottom and top boundaries, respectively, and the vectors $\mathbf{b}_i$ contain the

$$\mathbf{d}_i^k = \mathbf{x}_{i+1}^k + \mathbf{x}_{i-1}^k + \mathbf{b}_i, \qquad i = 1, \ldots, N$$
$$\text{Solve } L\mathbf{y}_i^k = \mathbf{d}_i^k, \qquad i = 1, \ldots, N$$
$$\text{Solve } U\mathbf{x}_i^{k+1} = \mathbf{y}_i^k, \qquad i = 1, \ldots, N$$

Figure 3.1-11. Line Jacobi method.

boundary values on the sides of the region as well as the h^2f values. In terms of the grid of Figure 3.1-1, the effect of (3.1.21) is to update all unknowns on each row of grid points simultaneously using the values of the unknowns from the previous iteration at the adjacent grid lines. Thus (3.1.21) is known as a *line Jacobi method.*

We would implement (3.1.21) by doing a Choleski or LU decomposition of T once and for all at the outset, and then use the factors to solve the systems of (3.1.21). Thus, if $T = LU$, then (3.1.21) is carried out as shown in Figure 3.1-11. The systems for the $\mathbf{y}_i^k$ are independent and can be solved in parallel; similarly for the $\mathbf{x}_i^{k+1}$ once the $\mathbf{y}_i^k$ are known. Thus, for example, if there are $p = N$ processors, we can assign one pair of systems to each processor as illustrated in Figure 3.1-12. As also illustrated in Figure 3.1-12, after each iteration the new iterates $\mathbf{x}_i^{k+1}$ must be transmitted to each of the neighboring processors P_{i-1} and P_{i+1}. Note that this arrangement is ideal for a linearly connected array of processors.

The more general block matrix (3.1.19) can be handled in much the same way. Since each A_{ii} is assumed to be nonsingular, it has a decomposition L_iU_i where, if interchanges are required in the decomposition, L_i need not be lower triangular. These decompositions may be done in parallel at the outset as is illustrated in Figure 3.1-13, where the dashed line separates these one-time decompositions from the subsequent iterative process, and it is assumed that there are q processors. From (3.1.20), the vector $\mathbf{d}_i^k$ in Figure 3.1-13 are

$$\mathbf{d}_i^k = -\sum_{j \neq i} A_{ij}\mathbf{x}_j^k + \mathbf{b}_i \tag{3.1.22}$$

Hence, in general, $\mathbf{x}_i^{k+1}$ would have to be transmitted to every other processor before the next iteration. However, it is highly unlikely that an iterative

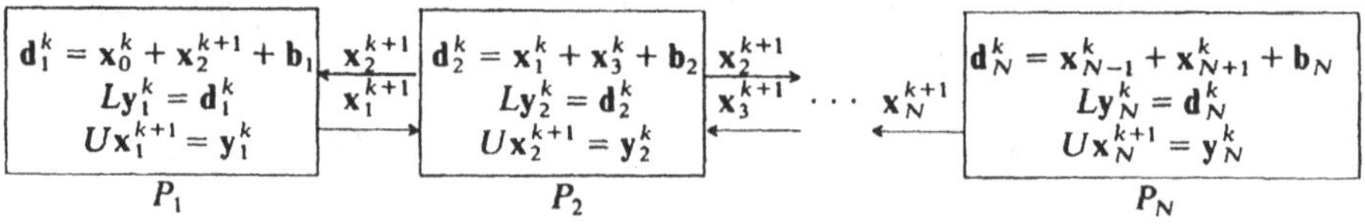

Figure 3.1-12. Parallel line Jacobi.

$$\boxed{\begin{array}{c} A_1 = L_1 U_1 \\ \hline L_1 y_1^k = d_1^k \\ U_1 x_1^{k+1} = y_1^k \end{array}} \quad \cdots \quad \boxed{\begin{array}{c} A_q = L_q U_q \\ \hline L_q y_q^k = d_q^k \\ U_q x_q^{k+1} = y_q^k \end{array}}$$
$$\qquad P_1 \qquad\qquad\qquad\qquad\qquad P_q$$

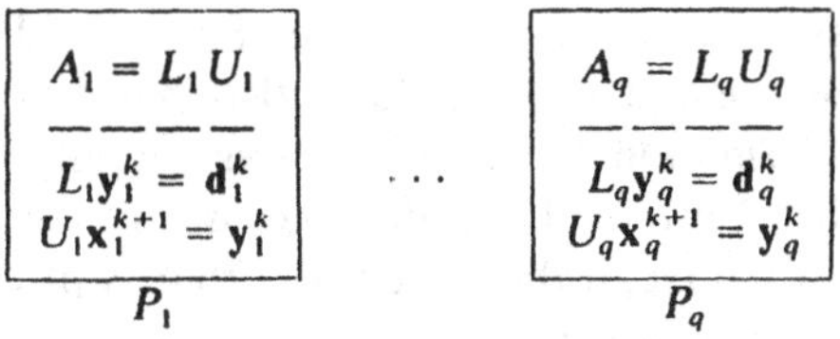

Figure 3.1-13. Parallel block Jacobi.

method would be used for a matrix with this full block structure. It is more likely that A arises from some decomposition of the domain of a partial differential equation. Two such decompositions are illustrated in Figure 3.1-14.

We assume that the subdomains contain some specified portion of the grid points on the interior boundaries between subdomains, so that all interior grid points are associated with one and only one subdomain. For example, in Figure 3.1-14a we might assume that each subdomain contains the points on its top interior boundary. A limiting case of Figure 3.1-14a is when each strip contains only one line of grid points so that we again obtain the line Jacobi method. More generally, if we assume that any unknown associated with the ith strip is coupled with unknowns only in strips $i-1$ and $i+1$, then A will have the block tridiagonal form

$$A = \begin{bmatrix} A_{11} & A_{12} & & & \\ A_{21} & & \ddots & & \\ & \ddots & \ddots & \ddots & \\ & & \ddots & & A_{q-1,q} \\ & & & A_{qq-1} & A_{qq} \end{bmatrix} \qquad (3.1.23)$$

In this case x_i^{k+1} needs to be transmitted only to processors P_{i-1} and P_{i+1}, just as in Figure 3.1-12. We assume, of course, that the workload is balanced

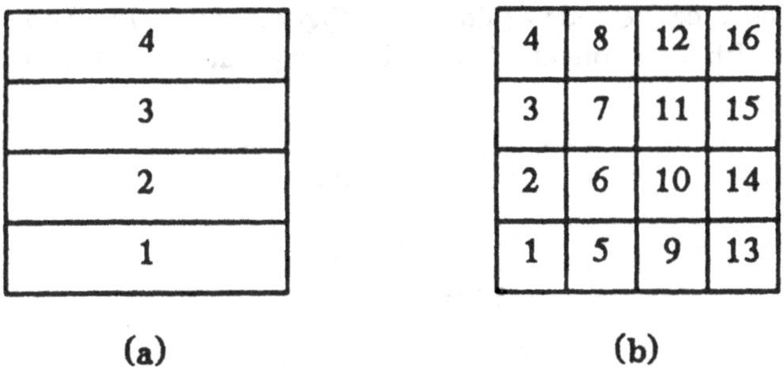

Figure 3.1-14. Domain decompositions. (a) Strips; (b) subsquares.

among the processors as much as possible. This would be the case if the A_{ii} are all the same size and structure (and also that the off-diagonal blocks are such that the formation of the $\mathbf{d}_i$ requires roughly the same time). If not, a different distribution of the data across the processors would be considered. And, of course, if there are fewer than q processors, more than one subsystem would be assigned to each processor. In Figure 3.1-14b, it is possible that unknowns in an interior subsquare will be coupled with unknowns in any of the surrounding subsquares. In this case, the block form of the matrix will no longer be tridiagonal but neither will it be full as in (3.1.19). Block methods may be run asynchronously, just as previously discussed for point methods, but now there is the potential for whole blocks of unknowns to fail to be updated in time for the next iteration, depending upon how the data transmission is accomplished.

Vectorization of Block Methods

We consider next the implementation of the block Jacobi method (3.1.20) on vector computers, and we begin with the special case of (3.1.21). Assume that T has been factored into LU where L is a lower bidiagonal matrix with unit diagonal. Then the forward and back substitutions of Figure 3.1-11 can be accomplished by "vectorizing across the systems" as illustrated in Figure 3.1-15. A pseudocode to accomplish this is given in Figure 3.1-16. In Figure 3.1-16, it is assumed that $L1$ is a one-dimensional array that holds the elements of L in the first diagonal below the main diagonal and y is a two-dimensional array such that $y(\ , J)$ is the N-long vector of the Jth components of all of the solution vectors. Similarly, $d(\ , J)$ is the N-long vector of the Jth components of the right-hand sides. Thus, the vector lengths in Figure 3.1-16 are all N. The back substitution $U\mathbf{x} = \mathbf{y}$ can be handled in an analogous way (Exercise 3.1-15).

At each iteration it is also necessary to determine the new right-hand sides as given by (3.1.21). These can also be computed using vectors across the $\mathbf{x}_i$; indeed, this storage of the $\mathbf{x}_i$ is what is produced by the back substitution since the code analogous to Figure 3.1-15 will give $x(\ , J)$, the vectors of Jth components. Thus, the computation of the next set of

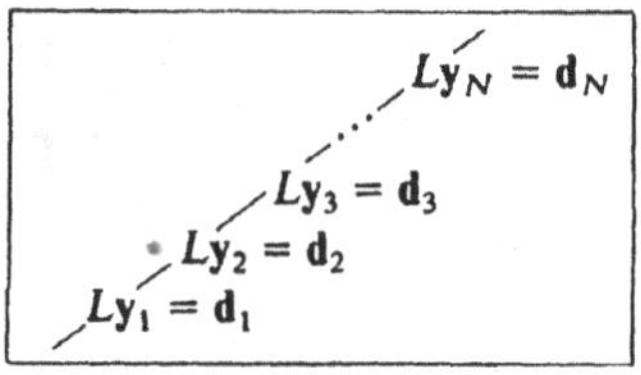

Figure 3.1-15. Vectorizing across systems.

```
y( ,1) = d( ,1)
For J = 2, N
  y( ,J) = -L1(J)*y( ,J - 1) + d( ,J)
```

Figure 3.1-16. Vector forward substitution for several systems.

right-hand sides would be accomplished by

$$\text{for } J = 1 \text{ to } N$$

$$d(\ ,J) = x(\ ,J)_{-1} + x(\ ,J)_{+1} + b(\ ,J)$$

where $x(\ ,J)_{\pm 1}$ denotes the vector $x(\ ,J)$ shifted up or down one position.

Consider, next, the more general matrix (3.1.23) [or (3.1.19)]. If we assume that the diagonal blocks A_{ii} are all the same dimension and have the same structure (for example, they all have the same semibandwidth) then we can vectorize the LU decompositions $A_{ii} = L_i U_i$ across the systems. For each fixed j and k, we assume that the (j, k) components of all the A_{ii} are stored as a vector. These factorizations can be done once and for all at the beginning of the Jacobi iteration and the factors stored. Note that in the case that all A_{ii} are identical (as in (3.1.21) in which $A_{ii} = T$, $i = 1, \ldots, N$) nothing is gained by vectorizing the decomposition in this way; rather, the decomposition would be done by one of the techniques discussed in Section 2.3. It could also just be done in scalar arithmetic since this single decomposition will usually be only a small part of the total time for the Jacobi iteration.

With the factors L_i and U_i known, the forward and back substitutions in the Jacobi iteration can be done in a manner analogous to Figure 3.1-16 after the new right-hand sides are computed. These right-hand sides are given by (3.1.22) and their computation can also be vectorized across the A_{ij} provided that, in the case of (3.1.23), the $A_{i,i+1}$, $i = 1, \ldots, q-1$, all have the same size and structure; likewise for the $A_{i-1,i}$, $i = 2, \ldots, q$. In this case, the vector lengths for all parts of the computation—the decomposition, formation of the right-hand sides, forward and back substitutions—will be q and the size of q will determine whether this is a viable approach on a particular vector computer.

ADI Methods

We end this section with a brief discussion of *alternating direction implicit* (ADI) methods. Probably the most central of these is the *Peaceman–Rachford method,* which we will describe first for the discrete Poisson equation (3.1.5) on a square.

At the $(k+1)$st stage of the Peaceman–Rachford iteration there are two steps:

Step 1: For some parameter α_k solve the N linear systems for $j = 1, \ldots, N$

$$(2+\alpha_k)u_{i,j}^{k+1/2} - u_{i-1,j}^{k+1/2} - u_{i+1,j}^{k+1/2} = (-2+\alpha_k)u_{i,j}^{k} + u_{i,j+1}^{k} + u_{i,j-1}^{k} + h^2 f_{ij},$$
$$i = 1, \ldots, N \quad (3.1.24a)$$

Step 2: Solve the N linear systems for $j = 1, \ldots, N$

$$(2+\alpha_k)u_{i,j}^{k+1} - u_{i,j-1}^{k+1} - u_{i,j+1}^{k+1} = (-2+\alpha_k)u_{i,j}^{k+1/2} + u_{i+1,j}^{k+1/2} + u_{i-1,j}^{k+1/2} + h^2 f_{ij},$$
$$i = 1, \ldots, N \quad (3.1.24b)$$

The first step, (3.1.24a), produces intermediate values $u^{k+1/2}$ that are then used in the second step, (3.1.24b), to obtain the final values of the iterates at the $(k+1)$st stage.

The systems in (3.1.24a) are $N \times N$ and tridiagonal and are the same as for the line Jacobi method, with the exception of the parameter α_k and the fact that half of the term u_{ij} has been moved to the right-hand side and evaluated at the previous iterate value. In any case, as in the line Jacobi method, (3.1.24a) amounts to solving for new values of u on each line while holding values of u on the adjacent lines at their previous iterate value. In (3.1.24b), the directions of the lines are changed to vertical so that new values along each vertical line of the grid are obtained, using values on the adjacent vertical lines just obtained at the previous half step; hence the name "alternating directions." The directions are shown in Figure 3.1-17.

We next formulate (3.1.24) in matrix terms. With $n = N^2$, let H and V be the $n \times n$ matrices

$$H = \begin{bmatrix} C & & \\ & \ddots & \\ & & C \end{bmatrix}, \qquad V = \begin{bmatrix} 2I & -I & & \\ -I & \ddots & \ddots & \\ & \ddots & \ddots & -I \\ & & -I & 2I \end{bmatrix} \quad (3.1.25)$$

where all the identities are $N \times N$ and C is the $N \times N$ matrix

$$C = \begin{bmatrix} 2 & -1 & & \\ -1 & \ddots & \ddots & \\ & \ddots & \ddots & -1 \\ & & -1 & 2 \end{bmatrix} \quad (3.1.26)$$

Then

$$A = H + V \quad (3.1.27)$$

Figure 3.1-17. Alternating directions. (a) Horizontal directions; (b) vertical directions.

where A is the coefficient matrix of the discrete Poisson system as given by (3.1.7). It is easy to see (Exercise 3.1-22) that (3.1.24) is equivalent to

$$(\alpha_k I + H)\mathbf{x}^{k+1/2} = (\alpha_k I - V)\mathbf{x}^k + \mathbf{b} \tag{3.1.28a}$$

$$(\alpha_k I + V)\mathbf{x}^{k+1} = (\alpha_k I - H)\mathbf{x}^{k+1/2} + \mathbf{b} \tag{3.1.28b}$$

where $\mathbf{x}$ is the vector of the unknowns at the interior grid points, as in (3.1.6), and $\mathbf{b}$ contains the boundary values as well as the forcing function f.

If H and V are given by (3.1.25), it is clear from (3.1.28a) that $\mathbf{x}^{k+1/2}$ is obtained by solving N tridiagonal systems with coefficient matrix $\alpha_k I + C$. The systems in (3.1.28b) are not tridiagonal but there is a permutation matrix P such that $PVP^T = H$ (Exercise 3.1-23). Hence, the systems in (3.1.28b) are permutationally similar to tridiagonal systems and can be solved, in essence, as tridiagonal systems.

Since the matrix C of (3.1.26) is positive definite (Exercise 3.1-19), so is H. Thus, so is V, since it is a permutation of H. Therefore, for $\alpha_k \geq 0$, the coefficient matrices of (3.1.28) are positive definite and hence nonsingular. It is this positive definite property that is the key to convergence of the iteration. We state the following theorem, whose proof is given in Appendix 2.

3.1.3. THEOREM. *ADI Convergence. Let A, H, and V be symmetric positive definite $n \times n$ matrices such that* (3.1.27) *holds, and let $\alpha_k = \alpha > 0$, $k = 0, 1, \ldots.$ Then the iterates* (3.1.28) *are well defined and converge to the unique solution of $A\mathbf{x} = \mathbf{b}$ for any $\mathbf{x}^0$.*

Theorem 3.1.3 applies to any positive definite matrix A. However, the matrices H and V must be chosen so that the systems (3.1.28) are suitably "easy" to solve. That $\alpha > 0$ is critical, and the iteration is not convergent with the α_k of (3.1.28) all zero (Exercise 3.1-24). Theorem 3.1.3 can be extended to a variable sequence of positive α_k. The role of a variable sequence of α_k is to give very rapid convergence of the iterates when the α_k are chosen in a certain way. However, the restrictive condition that $HV = VH$ is required. This commutativity property is satisfied (Exercise

3.1-25) for the H and V of (3.1.25), but, in general, it will be true only for certain elliptic boundary value problems and suitable discretizations.

The parallel and vector implementation of (3.1.24) can be done as follows. The N tridiagonal systems of (3.1.24a) are independent and can be solved in parallel or by vectorizing across the systems, just as with the line Jacobi method. The same can be done, in principle, with the systems (3.1.24b). However, if the storage of the iterates is correct for the solution of the systems (3.1.24a), then it is not correct for the systems (3.1.24b) and must be rearranged by essentially a matrix transpose before the solution of (3.1.24b) can be vectorized. However, the storage is correct to solve the tridiagonal systems of (3.1.24b) by the cyclic reduction algorithm of Section 2.3.

Exercises 3.1

1. Verify that (3.1.2) can be written in the matrix form (3.1.3).
2. Let

$$A = \begin{bmatrix} 1 & \alpha & \alpha \\ \alpha & 1 & \alpha \\ \alpha & \alpha & 1 \end{bmatrix}$$

   Show that A is positive definite when $-1 < 2\alpha < 2$ but that the conditions of 3.1.2 for the convergence of the Jacobi iteration are satisfied only for $-1 < 2\alpha < 1$.
3. Write out the system (3.1.7) completely for $N = 2$, 4, and 6.
4. Assume a local memory parallel system of p processors in which arithmetic computation requires α time units per result and transmittal of one word of data between any two processors requires β time units. Assume that $N^2 = mp$ so that m unknowns are assigned to each processor. Ascertain the time for one Jacobi iteration for the discrete Poisson equation.
5. Write out the details of the computation described by Figures 3.1-4, 3.1-5, and 3.1-6 for $N = 4$.
6. Write out the details of the computation of Figure 3.1-8 for $N = 4$.
7. Assume that a vector computer requires $(1000 + 10n)$ ns (nanoseconds) for arithmetic operations on vectors of length n and 200 ns for scalar operations. Estimate the time required for one Jacobi iteration for (a) the algorithm of Figure 3.1-4 and (b) the algorithm of Figure 3.1-8. Compare these estimates for $N = 50, 100, 200$.
8. For the vector computer of Exercise 7, estimate the amount of time lost to redundant calculations in the algorithm of Figure 3.1-8 for $N = 50, 100, 200$.
9. Assuming the parallel system of Exercise 4 with $p = N$, estimate the time for the line Jacobi iteration as described in (3.1.21), Figure 3.1-11, and Figure 3.1-12.

10. For the vector computer of Exercise 7, estimate the time required to do the line Jacobi iteration for (3.1.21) using the vectorization of Figure 3.1-14.
11. Show that a code of the form of Figure 3.1-8 cannot give correct results on the Poisson (or even Laplace) equation if the array U contains only the interior points.
12. If the Poisson equation (3.1.4) is discretized by finite differences using a grid spacing Δx in the x direction and Δy in the y direction, the equation (3.1.5) is replaced by

$$(\Delta x)^{-2}(u_{i+1,j} - 2u_{ij} + u_{i-1,j}) + (\Delta y)^{-2}(u_{i,j+1} - 2u_{ij} + u_{i,j-1}) = f_{ij}$$

or

$$u_{i+1,j} + u_{i-1,j} + c(u_{i,j+1} + u_{i,j-1}) - 2(1+c)u_{ij} = (\Delta x)^2 f_{ij}$$

where $c = (\Delta x)^2/(\Delta y)^2$. The Jacobi iteration is then

$$u_{ij}^{k+1} = (2+2c)^{-1}[u_{i+1,j}^k + u_{i-1,j}^k + c(u_{i,j+1}^k + u_{i,j-1}^k) - (\Delta x)^2 f_{ij}]$$

Show that the code of Figure 3.1-8 cannot be modified to carry out this Jacobi iteration for $\Delta x \neq \Delta y$.

13. Verify that (3.1.15) can be written in the form $A\mathbf{x} = \mathbf{b}$ where A is given by (3.1.17).
14. For the discrete Poisson equation (3.1.5) on a square, show that the Jacobi iteration matrix is

$$H = \frac{1}{4}\begin{bmatrix} T_0 & I & & \\ I & T_0 & I & \\ & \ddots & \ddots & I \\ & & I & T_0 \end{bmatrix}, \qquad T_0 = \begin{bmatrix} 0 & 1 & & \\ 1 & \ddots & \ddots & \\ & \ddots & \ddots & 1 \\ & & 1 & 0 \end{bmatrix}$$

where the submatrices are $N \times N$. Show that the matrix-vector multiplication $H\mathbf{x}$, where $\mathbf{x}$ is given by (3.1.6), can be written as

$$H\mathbf{x} = 0.25\begin{bmatrix} u_{11} \\ \cdot \\ u_{N-1,1} \\ 0 \\ u_{12} \\ \vdots \end{bmatrix} + 0.25\begin{bmatrix} u_{21} \\ \vdots \\ u_{N1} \\ 0 \\ u_{22} \\ \vdots \end{bmatrix} + 0.25\begin{bmatrix} u_{11} \\ \vdots \end{bmatrix} + 0.25\begin{bmatrix} u_{12} \\ \vdots \end{bmatrix}$$

(starts N in; stops one short; stops N short)

Discuss how to implement this calculation using linked triad operations and storage suppression. Assuming that the timing formulas for vectors of length m

are $(1000 + 10m)$ ns for addition and multiplication and $(1700 + 10m)$ ns for linked triads, show that the time for one Jacobi iteration is approximately $(50N^2 - 40N + 7000)$ ns. Show, however, that the time for one Jacobi iteration using Figure 3.1-8 is approximately $(40N^2 + 100N + 4000)$ ns, and for Poisson's equation and using the average instruction (for the CYBER 205), this can be reduced to $(20N^2 + 50N + 2000)$ ns.

15. Write a pseudocode analogous to Figure 3.1-16 for the back substitution $U\mathbf{x} = \mathbf{y}$.

16. Consider the Poisson equation $u_{xx} + u_{yy} = 4$ on the unit square with the condition that $u(x, y) = x^2 + y^2$ on the boundary. Show that the exact solution of this problem is $u(x, y) = x^2 + y^2$. For the discrete equations (3.1.5), show that the exact solution is $u_{ij} = x_i^2 + y_j^2$; that is, there is no discretization error.

17. For the discrete problem of Exercise 16, implement the Jacobi iteration of Figure 3.1-6 in a column-oriented way as exemplified by Figure 3.1-5, and in a "long-vector" way as exemplified by Figure 3.1-8. Estimate the time per iteration and the storage required for each method.

18. For the problem of Exercise 17, compare the three convergence tests $\|\mathbf{x}^{k+1} - \mathbf{x}^k\|_2 \leq \varepsilon$, $\|\mathbf{x}^{k+1} - \mathbf{x}^k\|_\infty \leq \varepsilon$, $\|\mathbf{b} - A\mathbf{x}^{k+1}\|_2 \leq \varepsilon$. Which test requires the most time to implement on your machine?

19. Show that the eigenvalues of the $N \times N$ matrix

$$S = \begin{bmatrix} 2 & -1 & & & \\ -1 & & -1 & & \\ & \ddots & & \ddots & \\ & & & & -1 \\ & & & -1 & 2 \end{bmatrix}$$

are $2 - 2\cos[k\pi/(N+1)]$, $k = 1, \ldots, N$ with corresponding eigenvectors

$$\left(\sin\frac{k\pi}{N+1}, \ldots, \sin\frac{Nk\pi}{N+1}\right)^T$$

Hint: Use the trigonometric identity $\sin(\alpha \pm \beta) = \sin\alpha\cos\beta \pm \cos\alpha\sin\beta$ to verify that $S\mathbf{x} = \lambda\mathbf{x}$.

20. A *Kronecker product* of two $n \times n$ matrices B and C is the $n^2 \times n^2$ matrix defined by

$$B \otimes C = \begin{bmatrix} b_{11}C & \cdots & b_{1n}C \\ \vdots & & \\ b_{n1}C & \cdots & b_{nn}C \end{bmatrix}$$

The *Kronecker sum* of B and C is defined by $A = (I \otimes B) + (C \otimes I)$, where I is the $n \times n$ identity matrix. It is known (see, e.g., Ortega [1987a; Theorem 6.3.2]) that the eigenvalues of the Kronecker sum A are $\mu_i + \nu_j$, $i, j = 1, \ldots, n$, where $\mu_1, \ldots, \mu_n$ and $\nu_1, \ldots, \nu_n$ are the eigenvalues of B and C, respectively. Show that the matrix A of (3.1.7) is the Kronecker sum $(I \otimes S) + (S \otimes I)$ where S is the matrix given in Exercise 19. Then use the result of Exercise 19 to show that the eigenvalues of A are

$$4 - 2\left(\cos\frac{k\pi}{N+1} + \cos\frac{j\pi}{N+1}\right), \qquad j, k = 1, \ldots, N.$$

21. Use the results and/or methods of Exercise 20 to show that the eigenvalues of the Jacobi iteration matrix of Exercise 14 are

$$\frac{1}{2}\left(\cos\frac{k\pi}{N+1} + \cos\frac{j\pi}{N+1}\right), \qquad j, k = 1, \ldots, N.$$

22. Show that (3.1.24) and (3.1.28) are equivalent if H and V are given by (3.1.25).
23. Find a permutation matrix P such that $PVP^T = H$ where H and V are the matrices of (3.1.25). Hint: Consider ordering the grid points bottom to top, left to right.
24. Let $A = H + V$ where A, H, and V are symmetric positive definite. Show that the iteration (3.1.28) with $\alpha_k = 0$, $k = 0, 1, \ldots$, is not convergent.
25. Let H and V be given by (3.1.25). Show that $HV = VH$.

References and Extensions 3.1

1. The Jacobi iteration is described in numerous books. Definitive treatments on its basic properties are given, for example, in Varga [1962] and Young [1971]. Because of its nearly ideal parallel properties, the Jacobi iteration has been implemented by many authors on parallel and vector machines; see, for example, Lambiotte [1975] for a review of earlier work and the use of the long vector approach exemplified by Figure 3.1-8. The long vector approach by means of matrix multiplication was used by E. Wachspress.
2. We have only considered in the text the simplest kind of partitioning of the grid points to the processors in a parallel system. More difficult problems include irregular regions, nonuniform grids, and dynamically changing grids. For these and other questions, see Bokhari [1985], Berger and Bokhari [1985], Gropp [1986], McBryan and van de Velde [1985, 1986a], and Morison and Otto [1987]. The latter paper considers mappings of irregular domains to hypercubes (or other mesh-connected arrays) by *scattered decomposition.*
3. The idea of asynchronous iterations dates back at least to the "chaotic relaxation" of Chazan and Miranker [1969]. A detailed study of asynchronous iterations, including numerical experiments, was done by Baudet [1978]; see also Barlow and Evans [1982], Deminet [1982], and Dubois and Briggs [1982].
4. Block Jacobi methods are classical and a detailed treatment of line methods and their rate of convergence is given in Varga [1962]. More recent work on block

methods (not necessarily just Jacobi) includes Parter and Steurwalt [1980, 1982], and Fergusson [1986].

5. ADI methods date back to the 1950s. See Varga [1962] for a good discussion of the methods and their convergence properties. Implementations on vector computers have been given by Lambiotte [1975], Oppe and Kincaid [1987], and Kincaid, Oppe, and Young [1986a, b]. Chan [1987] has considered the implementation of an ADI method on a hypercube by a strategy that avoids transposing the data. See, also, Saied *et al.* [1987].
6. Although the discrete Poisson equation (3.1.5) has long been a standard model problem for iterative methods, it can be solved very efficiently by direct methods, referred to as "fast Poisson solvers." For a short review of such methods on vector and parallel computers, and further references, see Ortega and Voigt [1985]. For recent work on fast Poisson solvers using domain decomposition, see Chan and Resasco [1987a,b].

3.2. The Gauss–Seidel and SOR Iterations

We now consider other iterative methods for the system $A\mathbf{x} = \mathbf{b}$, where, again, we assume that the diagonal elements of A are nonzero. After computing the new Jacobi iterate for x_1,

$$x_1^{k+1} = \frac{1}{a_{11}}\left(-\sum_{j=2}^{n} a_{1j}x_j^k + b_1\right)$$

it is reasonable to use this updated value in place of x_1^k in the computation of the subsequent x_i^{k+1}. The *Gauss–Seidel principle* is to use new information as soon as it is available, and the *Gauss–Seidel iteration* is then

$$x_i^{k+1} = \frac{1}{a_{ii}}\left(-\sum_{j<i} a_{ij}x_j^{k+1} - \sum_{j>i} a_{ij}x_j^k + b_i\right), \qquad i = 1, \ldots, n, \qquad k = 0, 1, \ldots \tag{3.2.1}$$

Let

$$A = D - L - U \tag{3.2.2}$$

where D is the diagonal of A and $-L$ and $-U$ are the strictly lower and strictly upper triangular parts of A. Then it is easy to see (Exercise 3.2-1) that (3.2.1) may be written as

$$D\mathbf{x}^{k+1} = L\mathbf{x}^{k+1} + U\mathbf{x}^k + \mathbf{b}$$

or

$$\mathbf{x}^{k+1} = H\mathbf{x}^k + \mathbf{d}, \qquad k = 0, 1, \ldots, \qquad H = (D - L)^{-1}U,$$
$$\mathbf{d} = (D - L)^{-1}\mathbf{b} \tag{3.2.3}$$

Since $D - L$ is just the lower triangular part of A, its inverse exists by the assumption that the diagonal elements of A are nonzero.

An important modification to the Gauss-Seidel iteration is the following. Let $\hat{x}_i^{k+1}$ denote the right-hand side of (3.2.1), the Gauss-Seidel iterate, and define

$$x_i^{k+1} = x_i^k + \omega(\hat{x}_i^{k+1} - x_i^k) \tag{3.2.4}$$

Substituting the representation of $\hat{x}_i^{k+1}$ into (3.2.4) and rearranging terms shows that the x_i^{k+1} satisfy

$$a_{ii}x_i^{k+1} + \omega \sum_{j<i} a_{ij}x_j^{k+1} = (1 - \omega)a_{ii}x_i^k - \omega \sum_{j>i} a_{ij}x_j^k + \omega b_i \tag{3.2.5}$$

or, in terms of the matrices of (3.2.2),

$$\mathbf{x}^{k+1} = (D - \omega L)^{-1}[(1 - \omega)D + \omega U]\mathbf{x}^k$$
$$+ \omega(D - \omega L)^{-1}\mathbf{b}, \qquad k = 0, 1, \ldots \tag{3.2.6}$$

This defines the *successive overrelaxation (SOR) iteration.* Note that if $\omega = 1$, this reduces to the Gauss-Seidel iteration. Note, also, that $D - \omega L$ is nonsingular by the assumption on the diagonal elements of A.

While (3.2.6) and (3.2.3) provide useful matrix representations of the SOR and Gauss-Seidel iterations, the actual computations are to be done by (3.2.1) and (3.2.4). In any case, the next iterate is obtained by solving a lower triangular system of equations with coefficient matrix $D - \omega L$. The equations (3.2.1) and (3.2.4) are just an explicit representation of this solution.

Convergence Theorems

We next state a few main theorems about the convergence of the Gauss-Seidel and SOR iterations. Proofs of these and additional results, as well as definitions, are given in Appendix 2. We assume throughout that A is nonsingular.

3.2.1. THEOREM. *If A is strictly or irreducibly diagonally dominant, or if A is an M matrix, then the Gauss-Seidel iterates converge for any* $\mathbf{x}^0$.

The following result shows that, no matter what the matrix, the real parameter ω in SOR must be restricted to the interval $(0, 2)$ in order to have convergence.

3.2.2. KAHAN'S LEMMA. *The SOR iteration cannot converge for every* $\mathbf{x}^0$ *unless* $\omega \in (0, 2)$.

The previous result by no means implies convergence if $\omega \in (0, 2)$. However, for an important class of matrices, this is indeed the right interval.

3.2.3. OSTROWSKI-REICH THEOREM. *If A is symmetric positive definite and* $\omega \in (0, 2)$, *then the SOR iteration converges for every* $\mathbf{x}^0$.

We note that the introduction of the parameter ω has been made in order to enhance the rate of convergence of the Gauss-Seidel iteration. This is discussed in Appendix 2.

Block SOR

We next consider two variations of the SOR iteration that will be important in the sequel. As with the Jacobi iteration, we can apply the Gauss-Seidel iteration to a partitioned matrix

$$A = \begin{bmatrix} A_{11} & \cdots & A_{1q} \\ \vdots & & \vdots \\ A_{q1} & \cdots & A_{qq} \end{bmatrix} \tag{3.2.7}$$

to obtain the *block Gauss-Seidel method*

$$\begin{gathered} A_{ii}\mathbf{x}_i^{k+1} = -\sum_{j<i} A_{ij}\mathbf{x}_j^{k+1} - \sum_{j>i} A_{ij}\mathbf{x}_j^k + \mathbf{b}_i, \\ i = 1, \ldots, q, \qquad k = 0, 1, \ldots \end{gathered} \tag{3.2.8}$$

where $\mathbf{x}^k$ and $\mathbf{b}$ are partitioned commensurately with A. It is assumed here that the A_{ii} are all nonsingular. The parameter ω is introduced analogously to (3.2.4) by

$$\mathbf{x}_i^{k+1} = \mathbf{x}_i^k + \omega(\hat{\mathbf{x}}_i^{k+1} - \mathbf{x}_i^k) \tag{3.2.9}$$

where $\hat{\mathbf{x}}_i^{k+1}$ is the Gauss-Seidel iterate produced by (3.2.8); this gives the *block SOR iteration.* As an example of these block methods, consider again the matrix (3.1.7) corresponding to the discrete Poisson equation on the unit square. In this case, (3.2.8) reduces to

$$T\mathbf{x}_i^{k+1} = \mathbf{x}_{i-1}^{k+1} + \mathbf{x}_{i+1}^{k} + \mathbf{b}_i, \qquad i = 1, \ldots, N \tag{3.2.10}$$

As with the corresponding line Jacobi method, the new iterates on a line of the grid are updated simultaneously, the difference now being that these new iterates are used as soon as we move to the next line. Thus, (3.2.10) is called a *line Gauss-Seidel method* and the corresponding SOR iteration is generally called a *successive line overrelaxation* (*SLOR* or *LSOR*) *method.*

SSOR

Another important modification of the SOR iteration is the *symmetric SOR* (*SSOR*) method. This is a double step method in which an SOR step is followed by an SOR step in the reverse order. We consider it first for the Gauss-Seidel method to obtain the *symmetric GS* (*SGS*) iteration. In the kth stage, the Gauss-Seidel iterate is obtained by

$$\mathbf{x}^{k+1/2} = (D - L)^{-1}U\mathbf{x}^k + (D - L)^{-1}\mathbf{b} \tag{3.2.11}$$

and we have labeled this Gauss-Seidel iterate $\mathbf{x}^{k+1/2}$. We now proceed through the equations in reverse order using the values of $\mathbf{x}^{k+1/2}$ just computed:

$$x_i^{k+1} = \frac{1}{a_{ii}}\left(-\sum_{j>i} a_{ij}x_j^{k+1} - \sum_{j<i} a_{ij}x_j^{k+1/2} + b_i\right), \qquad i = n, n-1, \ldots, 1$$

In terms of the matrices D, L, and U, this can be written as

$$D\mathbf{x}^{k+1} = U\mathbf{x}^{k+1} + L\mathbf{x}^{k+1/2} + \mathbf{b}$$

or

$$\mathbf{x}^{k+1} = (D - U)^{-1}L\mathbf{x}^{k+1/2} + (D - U)^{-1}\mathbf{b} \tag{3.2.12}$$

Thus, the roles of L and U reverse on this step. One SGS iteration is then the combination of (3.2.11) and (3.2.12):

$$\mathbf{x}^{k+1} = (D - U)^{-1}L(D - L)^{-1}U\mathbf{x}^k + \hat{\mathbf{d}} \tag{3.2.13}$$

where

$$\hat{\mathbf{d}} = (D - U)^{-1}L(D - L)^{-1}\mathbf{b} + (D - U)^{-1}\mathbf{b}$$

For the SSOR iteration, one simply inserts the relaxation parameter ω, as in (3.2.4)-(3.2.6), on both steps. The matrix representation of the SSOR iteration is then

$$\mathbf{x}^{k+1} = (D - \omega U)^{-1}[(1 - \omega)D + \omega L](D - \omega L)^{-1} \times [(1 - \omega)D + \omega U]\mathbf{x}^k + \hat{\mathbf{d}} \tag{3.2.14}$$

where now

$$\hat{\mathbf{d}} = \omega(D - \omega U)^{-1}\{[(1 - \omega)D + \omega L](D - \omega L)^{-1} + I\}\mathbf{b}$$

Computationally, of course, SSOR is carried out by the simple formulas analogous to (3.2.1) and (3.2.4) and the rather formidable expression (3.2.14) is only the matrix representation of this process. In terms of a discrete partial differential equation, the symmetric Gauss-Seidel or SSOR iterations amount to sweeping through the grid points on one step and then sweeping through again in exactly the reverse order on the second step.

A basic convergence theorem for the SSOR iteration corresponds to the Ostrowski-Reich Theorem 3.2.3. The proof is given in Appendix 2.

3.2.4. THEOREM. *SSOR Convergence. If A is symmetric positive definite and* $\omega \in (0, 2)$, *then the SSOR iteration converges for every* $\mathbf{x}^0$.

The Red–Black Ordering

We turn now to the parallel and vector implementation of the methods discussed so far in this section. We begin with the Gauss-Seidel iteration.

By (3.2.3), a Gauss-Seidel iteration can be viewed as solving a lower triangular system of equations, a problem discussed at some length in the previous chapter, in which it was noted that parallel methods are only moderately satisfactory. However, the Gauss-Seidel (or SOR) iteration will in practice only be used for sparse systems of equations, and in this case the methods of the previous chapter for triangular systems may be totally unsatisfactory.

One approach to successful parallel implementation of the SOR method is to reorder the equations in such a way that the solution of the lower triangular system can be done efficiently in parallel. Note that, as opposed to the Jacobi iteration, the Gauss-Seidel iteration depends on the order in which the equations are solved. Thus, given the equations

$$\sum_{j=1}^{n} a_{ij}x_j = b_i, \qquad i = 1, \ldots, n$$

we can elect to apply the Gauss-Seidel principle to these equations in any order, not necessarily the order $i = 1, \ldots, n$. Equivalently, we can apply Gauss-Seidel in the usual order to the equations $PA\mathbf{x} = P\mathbf{b}$, where P is a permutation matrix that gives us the order of the equations that we desire. However, our basic assumption in applying the Gauss-Seidel method is that the diagonal elements a_{ii} are all nonzero and we wish to maintain this property under reorderings. Thus, instead of only interchanging the equations, we will also make a corresponding renumbering of the unknowns. This is equivalent to considering new coefficient matrices PAP^T, where P is a permutation matrix. For a given system of n equations there are $n!$ possible reorderings of this type and $n!$ corresponding Gauss-Seidel (and SOR) methods. Our general problem, then, is to ascertain for a given matrix A which, if any, of these $n!$ possible orderings leads to a form of PAP^T that is suitable for parallel and vector computing.

In order to establish an approach to this problem, we concentrate first on the discrete Poisson equation (3.1.5) on a square grid. Corresponding to (3.2.1), the update at a grid point by the Gauss-Seidel iteration is shown schematically in Figure 3.2-1. If we assume that we are moving through the grid points left to right, bottom to top, Figure 3.2-1 depicts the situation at the i, j grid point: iterates already computed on this sweep, labeled "new," combine with iterates from the previous sweep, labeled "old," to give the new iterate at the i, j point. A direct vectorization of this computation, as was done for Jacobi's method, is not suitable, although we will discuss a variation of it later.

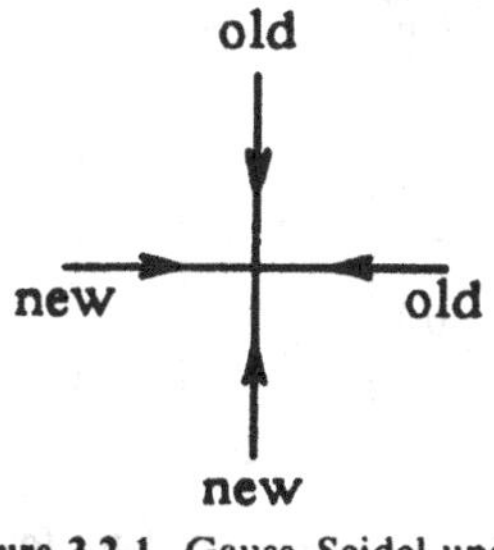

Figure 3.2-1. Gauss-Seidel update.

$\dot{B}6$	$\dot{R}6$	$\dot{B}7$	$\dot{R}7$	$\dot{B}8$
$\dot{R}3$	$\dot{B}4$	$\dot{R}4$	$\dot{B}5$	$\dot{R}5$
$\dot{B}1$	$\dot{R}1$	$\dot{B}2$	$\dot{R}2$	$\dot{B}3$

Figure 3.2-2. The red-black ordering of grid points.

In line with our previous discussion of reordering the equations, we now renumber the grid points and the corresponding unknowns. An important classical ordering is the *red-black* (or *checkerboard*) ordering illustrated in Figure 3.2-2. The grid points are first divided into two classes, red and black, and then ordered within each class. In Figure 3.2-2 is shown the ordering left to right, bottom to top within each class. The unknowns at the grid points are ordered analogously so that, for example, u at $R1$ will be the first unknown, u at $R2$ the second, and so on until the red points are exhausted; the ordering then continues with the black points. This is illustrated in Figure 3.2-3 by writing out the equations (excluding the right-hand sides) for $N = 2$ for Poisson's equation.

For general N, at any interior point, red grid points will be coupled only with black grid points and conversely, as illustrated in Figure 3.2-4. Thus when we write the equations with all of the unknowns at red points ordered first, the system will be of the form

$$\begin{bmatrix} D_R & C \\ C^T & D_B \end{bmatrix} \begin{bmatrix} \mathbf{u}_R \\ \mathbf{u}_B \end{bmatrix} = \begin{bmatrix} \mathbf{b}_1 \\ \mathbf{b}_2 \end{bmatrix} \tag{3.2.15}$$

Here $D_R = 4I_R$ and $D_B = 4I_B$, where I_R is the identity matrix of size equal to the number of red interior grid points and similarly for I_B. The matrix C contains the interactions between the red and the black unknowns. The special case of (3.2.15) for $N = 2$ has been illustrated in Figure 3.2-3. Note that the coefficient matrix of (3.2.15) must be symmetric since it is of the form PAP^T and A is symmetric.

Now consider the Gauss-Seidel iteration applied to (3.2.15):

$$\begin{bmatrix} D_R & 0 \\ C^T & D_B \end{bmatrix} \begin{bmatrix} \mathbf{u}_R^{k+1} \\ \mathbf{u}_B^{k+1} \end{bmatrix} = \begin{bmatrix} \mathbf{b}_1 \\ \mathbf{b}_2 \end{bmatrix} - \begin{bmatrix} 0 & C \\ 0 & 0 \end{bmatrix} \begin{bmatrix} \mathbf{u}_R^{k} \\ \mathbf{u}_B^{k} \end{bmatrix} \tag{3.2.16}$$

$$\begin{bmatrix} 4 & 0 & -1 & -1 \\ 0 & 4 & -1 & -1 \\ -1 & -1 & 4 & 0 \\ -1 & -1 & 0 & 4 \end{bmatrix} \begin{bmatrix} u_{R1} \\ u_{R2} \\ u_{B1} \\ u_{B2} \end{bmatrix} = \begin{bmatrix} \\ \\ \\ \\ \end{bmatrix}$$

$\dot{B}2$	$\dot{R}2$
$\dot{R}1$	$\dot{B}1$

Figure 3.2-3. Red-black equations for four unknowns.

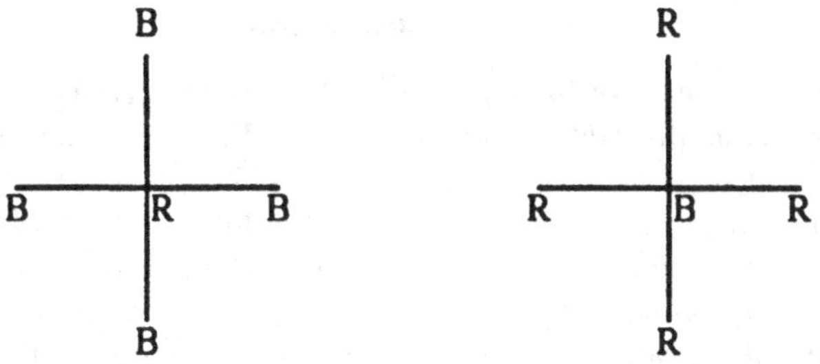

Figure 3.2-4. Red–black stencils.

This uncouples into the two separate parts

$$\mathbf{u}_R^{k+1} = D_R^{-1}(\mathbf{b}_1 - C\mathbf{u}_B^k), \qquad \mathbf{u}_B^{k+1} = D_B^{-1}(\mathbf{b}_2 - C^T\mathbf{u}_R^{k+1}) \qquad (3.2.17)$$

Thus, although (3.2.16) still requires the solution of a lower triangular system of equations to advance one iteration, because D_R and D_B are diagonal the solution of this system reduces to the matrix-vector multiplications indicated in (3.2.17).

For the SOR iteration we add the parameter ω in the usual way. Thus, applying (3.2.6) to (3.2.16), we obtain

$$\begin{bmatrix} D_R & 0 \\ \omega C^T & D_B \end{bmatrix}\begin{bmatrix} \mathbf{u}_R^{k+1} \\ \mathbf{u}_B^{k+1} \end{bmatrix} = \begin{bmatrix} \omega\mathbf{b}_1 \\ \omega\mathbf{b}_2 \end{bmatrix} + \begin{bmatrix} (1-\omega)D_R & -\omega C \\ 0 & (1-\omega)D_B \end{bmatrix}\begin{bmatrix} \mathbf{u}_R^k \\ \mathbf{u}_B^k \end{bmatrix}$$

or

$$\begin{aligned} \mathbf{u}_R^{k+1} &= D_R^{-1}[\omega\mathbf{b}_1 + (1-\omega)D_R\mathbf{u}_R^k - \omega C\mathbf{u}_B^k] \\ \mathbf{u}_B^{k+1} &= D_B^{-1}[\omega\mathbf{b}_2 + (1-\omega)D_B\mathbf{u}_B^k - \omega C^T\mathbf{u}_R^{k+1}] \end{aligned} \qquad (3.2.18)$$

This is the matrix representation of an SOR step, but the actual computation need not utilize explicitly these matrix formulas. Rather, the Gauss–Seidel values at the red points, $\hat{\mathbf{u}}_R^{k+1}$, can first be computed and then the SOR values are

$$\mathbf{u}_R^{k+1} = \mathbf{u}_R^k + \omega(\hat{\mathbf{u}}_R^{k+1} - \mathbf{u}_R^k) \qquad (3.2.19)$$

Using these updated values at the red points, the new values at the black points are obtained in an analogous way. The new Gauss–Seidel iterate for the red points is the same as the Jacobi iterate for these points, and similarly for the black points. Thus, the SOR iteration is implemented by using two Jacobi sweeps through the grid, each on roughly half of the grid points.

Parallel Implementation

Suppose first that we have $p = N^2/2$ processors arranged in a mesh-connected array as illustrated in Figure 3.1-2. We assign one red and one black interior grid point to these processors as shown in Figure 3.2-5. The processors holding grid points adjacent to the boundary will be assumed to hold the corresponding boundary values. In order to do one Gauss–Seidel iteration, all processors will first update their, say, red values in parallel and then their black values. As noted previously, these are just the computations for Jacobi iterations. The relaxation parameter ω will be inserted after each half step to yield the SOR values. For the red points, this is the computation (3.2.19) and similarly for the black points.

In the more realistic case that $p \ll N^2$, the unknowns would be suitably packed into the available processors. For example, if $N^2 = 2mp$, then m red points and m black points would be assigned to each processor. If p is not an even multiple of N^2, then we will assign as close as possible the same number of red and black points to each processor, but there will necessarily be some imbalance in the assignment. Note that the extreme case of $p = N^2$ processors with one unknown per processor, as discussed for the Jacobi iteration, is not beneficial here since half the processors would be idle at any given time while the computations for the unknowns of the other color were progressing.

The above SOR iteration involves the same considerations as in the Jacobi method concerning communication on local memory machines, convergence testing, and synchronization. The synchronization here would be done after each Jacobi step; that is, all new black values would be computed and passed to the processors that need them before the computation on the red values would proceed, and conversely. Alternatively, just as with the Jacobi iteration, the iteration may be carried out asynchronously and we will call this the *asynchronous red–black SOR iteration.*

Vectorization

The vectorization of the red-black SOR iteration is done in essentially the same way as for Jacobi's method. Consider first a vector computer that

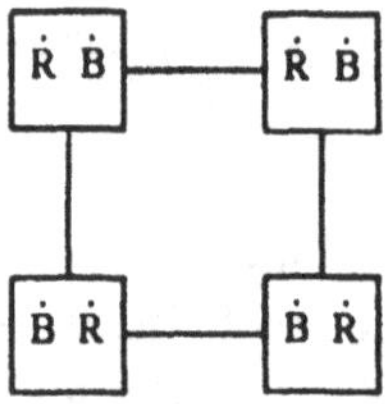

Figure 3.2-5. Red–black processor assignments.

uses vector registers and for which $N/2$ is a suitable vector length. We assume that the red unknowns at each row of the grid are stored as vectors and likewise for the black unknowns. Then, for the Poisson equation, a Gauss–Seidel updating of the red unknowns on the ith grid line is accomplished by

$$\begin{aligned} UR(I,\ ) = 0.25[&UB(I,\ )_{-1} + UB(I,\ )_{+1} \\ &+ UB(I-1,\ ) + UB(I+1,\ )] \end{aligned} \tag{3.2.20}$$

where the notation $UB(I,\ )_{-1}$ denotes the vector of black values on the ith line starting one position to the left and, similarly, $UB(I,\ )_{+1}$ starts one position to the right. It is assumed that all UB and UR vectors also hold the boundary values for their rows and that vectors with 0 or $N+1$ in the first position hold the boundary values at the bottom and top of the grid. If the forcing function f for Poisson's equation is nonzero, it would be added to (3.2.20) and the relaxation factor ω for the SOR iteration would be incorporated in an obvious way. A vector register schematic corresponding to Figure 3.1-5 is left to Exercise 3.2-5.

For a vector computer for which it is desirable to use vector lengths as long as possible, we again follow the procedures used for Jacobi's method. Corresponding to the approach of Figure 3.1-8, we now will have two vectors, each of length $O(N^2/2)$, one containing all red values and one containing all black values. Each will also contain red or black boundary values. This is illustrated in (3.2.21) for the grid of Figure 3.2-2, where now we assume that the outermost points on the two sides and bottom are boundary points. Equation (3.2.21) then indicates the computation to obtain new red Gauss–Seidel values from black ones:

$$T = \begin{bmatrix} B_2 \\ B_3 \\ B_4 \\ B_5 \\ B_6 \\ \vdots \end{bmatrix} + \begin{bmatrix} B_4 \\ B_5 \\ B_6 \\ B_7 \\ B_8 \\ \vdots \end{bmatrix}, \qquad R = \begin{bmatrix} T_1 \\ T_2 \\ T_3 \\ \vdots \\ \\ \end{bmatrix} + \begin{bmatrix} T_4 \\ T_5 \\ T_6 \\ \vdots \\ \\ \end{bmatrix} = \begin{bmatrix} B_2 + B_4 + B_5 + B_7 \\ B_3 + B_5 + B_6 + B_8 \\ B_4 + B_6 + B_7 + B_9 \\ \vdots \\ \\ \end{bmatrix}^* \tag{3.2.21}$$

After (3.2.21), R is multiplied by 0.25 to obtain the new red values. Similar computations give new black values from red ones. The SOR parameter and values of a forcing function f are easily incorporated into this scheme. As with Jacobi's method, (3.2.21) will overwrite boundary values unless this is suppressed by a suitable control function. The asterisk in (3.2.21) indicates such a spurious value.

The scheme of (3.2.21) illustrates the computation for the grid of Figure 3.2-2 for which $N = 3$. It extends immediately and obviously to a grid for which N is odd but not to a grid with even N. This is illustrated in Figure 3.2-6 for the grid with four interior grid points $B3$, $R4$, $R5$, and $B6$. The computation corresponding to (3.2.21) is then

$$T = \begin{bmatrix} B_2 \\ B_3 \\ B_4 \\ B_5 \\ \vdots \end{bmatrix} + \begin{bmatrix} B_3 \\ B_4 \\ B_5 \\ B_6 \\ \vdots \end{bmatrix},$$

$$R = \begin{bmatrix} T_1 \\ T_2 \\ T_3 \\ T_4 \\ \vdots \end{bmatrix} + \begin{bmatrix} T_3 \\ T_4 \\ T_5 \\ \vdots \end{bmatrix} = \begin{bmatrix} B_2 + B_3 + B_4 + B_5 \\ B_3 + B_4 + B_5 + B_6 \\ \vdots \\ \\ \end{bmatrix}$$

which is incorrect. In many cases, the value of N is up to the problem solver and can be chosen to be odd. If N must be even, a simple artifice is to extend the grid with an additional column of "boundary" values. Thus the grid of Figure 3.2-6 would be changed to that of Figure 3.2-2. There are still only four interior grid points, labeled now $B4$, $R4$, $R6$, and $B7$. The values of u on the right-most column are arbitrary values; these enter the computation but not in a substantive way. The calculation of (3.2.21) now produces the correct values at the interior grid points. This introduction

$R7$	$B7$	$R8$	$B8$
$B5$	$R5$	$B6$	$R6$
$R3$	$B3$	$R4$	$B4$
$B1$	$R1$	$B2$	$R2$

Figure 3.2-6. Four interior grid points.

of artificial grid points causes some inefficiency, both in computation time as well as storage (see Exercise 3.2-7), and it would be desirable to choose N to be odd when possible.

The matrix multiplication approach to long vectors, discussed for Jacobi's method for the equation (3.1.14), also extends to the red-black SOR method. This is based on the formulas (3.2.17) or (3.2.18). However, the average vector lengths will now be less than half that for Jacobi's method since the red-black ordering tends to distribute long diagonals in the Jacobi iteration matrix into several shorter diagonals in the matrix C.

Multicoloring

The implementation of the SOR iteration by means of the red-black ordering of grid points is limited to rather simple partial differential equations, such as Poisson's equation, and rather simple discretizations, as we will now illustrate.

Consider the equation

$$u_{xx} + u_{yy} + au_{xy} = 0 \tag{3.2.22}$$

again on the unit square, where a is a constant. This is just Laplace's equation with an additional mixed derivative term. The standard finite difference approximation to u_{xy} is

$$u_{xy} \doteq \frac{1}{4h^2}[u_{i+1,j+1} - u_{i-1,j+1} - u_{i+1,j-1} + u_{i-1,j-1}] \tag{3.2.23}$$

which combined with the previous approximation (3.1.5) for Laplace's equation gives the system of difference equations

$$\begin{aligned} &u_{i+1,j} + u_{i-1,j} + u_{i,j+1} + u_{i,j-1} - 4u_{ij} \\ &\quad + \frac{a}{4}[u_{i+1,j+1} - u_{i-1,j+1} - u_{i+1,j-1} + u_{i-1,j-1}] = 0, \end{aligned} \tag{3.2.24}$$

$$i, j = 1, \ldots, N$$

For a red-black ordering of the grid points, as in Figure 3.2-2, it is easy to

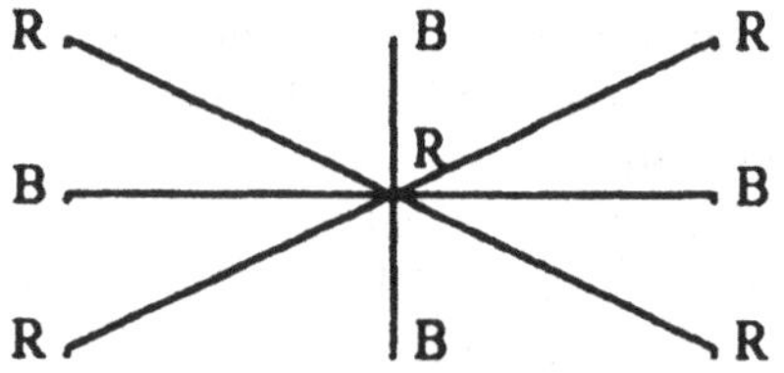

Figure 3.2-7. Red-black ordering for nine-point stencil.

see (Exercise 3.2-8) that the system (3.2.24) may be written in the form

$$\begin{bmatrix} D_R & C \\ C^T & D_B \end{bmatrix} \begin{bmatrix} \mathbf{u}_R \\ \mathbf{u}_B \end{bmatrix} = \begin{bmatrix} \mathbf{b}_1 \\ \mathbf{b}_2 \end{bmatrix} \tag{3.2.25}$$

as was done for Poisson's equation. However, the matrices D_R and D_B in (3.2.25) are no longer diagonal. The problem is that the unknown at the i, j grid point is now coupled with its eight nearest neighbors, some of which have the same color as the center point. This is illustrated in Figure 3.2-7.

The solution to this problem is to introduce more colors as illustrated in Figure 3.2-8. Now, if we write the equations for all the red points first, all the black points next, and so on, the system takes the form

$$\begin{bmatrix} D_1 & B_{12} & B_{13} & B_{14} \\ B_{21} & D_2 & B_{23} & B_{24} \\ B_{31} & B_{32} & D_3 & B_{34} \\ B_{41} & B_{42} & B_{43} & D_4 \end{bmatrix} \begin{bmatrix} \mathbf{u}_R \\ \mathbf{u}_B \\ \mathbf{u}_G \\ \mathbf{u}_W \end{bmatrix} = \begin{bmatrix} \mathbf{b}_1 \\ \mathbf{b}_2 \\ \mathbf{b}_3 \\ \mathbf{b}_4 \end{bmatrix} \tag{3.2.26}$$

where the diagonal blocks D_i are diagonal. The Gauss–Seidel iteration can then be written as

$$\begin{aligned} D_1\mathbf{u}_R^{k+1} &= -B_{12}\mathbf{u}_B^k - B_{13}\mathbf{u}_G^k - B_{14}\mathbf{u}_W^k + \mathbf{b}_1 \\ D_2\mathbf{u}_B^{k+1} &= -B_{21}\mathbf{u}_R^{k+1} - B_{23}\mathbf{u}_G^k - B_{24}\mathbf{u}_W^k + \mathbf{b}_2 \end{aligned} \tag{3.2.27}$$

$\dot{R}$	$\dot{B}$	$\dot{G}$	$\dot{W}$	$\dot{R}$	$\dot{B}$	$\dot{G}$	$\dot{W}$
$\dot{G}$	$\dot{W}$	$\dot{R}$	$\dot{B}$	$\dot{G}$	$\dot{W}$	$\dot{R}$	$\dot{B}$
$\dot{R}$	$\dot{B}$	$\dot{G}$	$\dot{W}$	$\dot{R}$	$\dot{B}$	$\dot{G}$	$\dot{W}$

Figure 3.2-8. A four color ordering.

and so on for the other two colors. Since the D_i are diagonal, the solution of the triangular system to carry out a Gauss-Seidel iteration has again collapsed to just matrix multiplications.

The four-color ordering of Figure 3.2-8 was based on the coupling of grid points illustrated in Figure 3.2-7, and we will call such a pattern a *stencil.* A stencil shows the connection pattern of a grid point to its neighbors and depends on both the differential equation and the discretization used. Some other common stencils are shown in Figure 3.2-9.

The number of colors indicated in Figure 3.2-9 is predicated on the assumption that the given stencil is the same at all points of the grid. Then the criterion for a successful coloring is that when the stencil is put at each point of the grid, the center point has a color different from that of all other points to which it is connected. It is this "local uncoupling" of the unknowns that allows a matrix representation of the problem that in general has the form

$$\begin{bmatrix} D_1 & B_{12} & \cdots & & B_{1c} \\ B_{21} & D_2 & & & \vdots \\ \vdots & & & & B_{c-1,c} \\ B_{c1} & & \cdots & B_{c,c-1} & D_c \end{bmatrix} \begin{bmatrix} \mathbf{u}_1 \\ \mathbf{u}_2 \\ \vdots \\ \mathbf{u}_c \end{bmatrix} = \begin{bmatrix} \mathbf{b}_1 \\ \mathbf{b}_2 \\ \vdots \\ \mathbf{b}_c \end{bmatrix} \tag{3.2.28}$$

in which the diagonal blocks D_i are diagonal. We will call a matrix of the form (3.2.28) a *c-colored* matrix. Note that $c = 4$ in (3.2.26) and $c = 2$ for the red-black ordering. With the system in the form (3.2.28), the Gauss-Seidel iteration can be carried out, analogously to (3.2.27), by

$$\mathbf{u}_i^{k+1} = D_i^{-1}\left[\mathbf{b}_i - \sum_{j<i} B_{ij}\mathbf{u}_j^{k+1} - \sum_{j>i} B_{ij}\mathbf{u}_j^k\right], \qquad i = 1, \ldots, c \tag{3.2.29}$$

and, again, the solution of the triangular system is reduced to Jacobi-type operations.

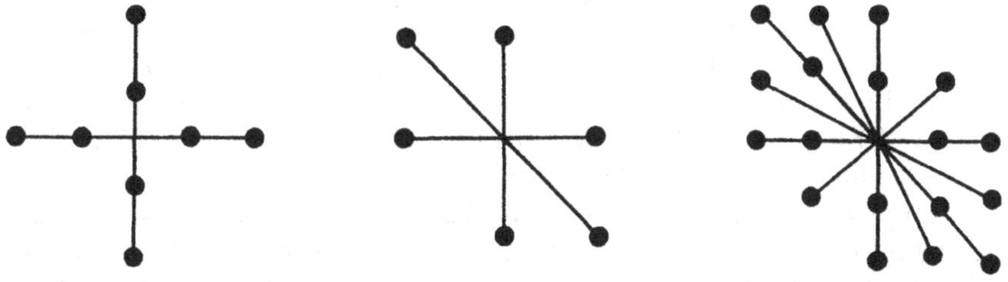

Figure 3.2-9. Some common stencils. (a) 9 point—3 colors; (b) linear elements—3 colors; (c) quadratic elements—6 colors.

G	W	G	W	G	W		R	B	G	R	B	G
R	B	R	B	R	B		B	G	R	B	G	R
G	W	G	W	G	W		G	R	B	G	R	B
R	B	R	B	R	B		R	B	G	R	B	G

Figure 3.2-10. Colorings for Figures 3.2-7 and 3.2-9. (a) Four color ordering; (b) three color ordering.

In general, one wishes to use the minimum number of colors that are necessary to achieve the matrix form (3.2.28). For arbitrary stencils that can vary at each point of the grid and arbitrary grids this is a difficult problem. However, if the stencil is repeated at each grid point it is generally evident how to achieve the minimum number of colors. But the coloring pattern need not be unique, even when the minimum number of colors is used. Figure 3.2.-10 gives another four-color ordering, different from that of Figure 3.2-8, for the stencil of Figure 3.2-7 as well as a three-color ordering suitable for stencils (a) and (b) of Figure 3.2-9. It is left to Exercise 3.2-10 to find a six-color ordering for the stencil (c) of Figure 3.2-9.

We note that for systems of partial differential equations the number of colors will generally be multiplied by the number of equations. Thus, for example, if the grid stencil requires three colors and there are two partial differential equations, then six colors will be required to achieve a c-colored matrix. We note also that the rate of convergence of the Gauss-Seidel and SOR methods depends on the ordering of the equations, and the effect of multicolor orderings on the rate of convergence is not yet completely understood.

Parallel and Vector Implementation

We turn now to the implementation of the Gauss-Seidel and SOR iterations using multicolor orderings. For simplicity, we consider again only a square grid with N^2 interior grid points. We begin with a local memory mesh-connected system with p processors, and assume that $N^2 = cmp$, where c is the number of colors. Thus, each processor will hold mc unknowns. This is illustrated in Figure 3.2-11 for $m = 1$ and $c = 4$, using the color pattern of Figure 3.2-8. The processors first all update their red points and then transmit the new values to the processors that will need them. In Figure 3.2-11 we have used the stencil of Figure 3.2-7 to show a sample communication pattern. Thus, the updated red value in processor P_{12} must be transmitted to processors P_{11}, P_{21}, and P_{22} but not to processors P_{13} and P_{23}. The black values are then all updated, followed by the green and then the white.

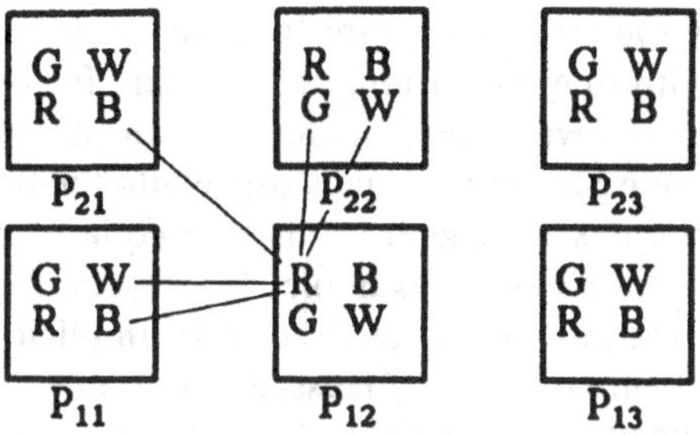

Figure 3.2-11. Processor assignment.

Between each stage there is data transmission and synchronization; alternatively, the iteration could be run asynchronously. For each set of colored values, we do only Jacobi operations, plus the SOR modification using ω. Hence, the iteration is implemented, in essence, by four Jacobi sweeps of the grid, each updating $O(N^2/4)$ points or, in general, c sweeps if c colors are used. Our assumption that $N^2 = cmp$ is based on the tacit assumption that updating at each grid point requires the same amount of work so that the distribution of mc unknowns to each processor balances the overall workload.

We consider next the implementation on vector computers that use vector registers. We assume, for simplicity, that the domain is a square or rectangle, and that the unknowns are stored in c two-dimensional arrays, one for each color, with the ordering of grid points left to right, bottom to top. Boundary values are held in the appropriate positions in these arrays and any forcing function data over the grid are held in a separate array. Then the unknowns of the first color are updated, followed by the second color, etc. The vector operations are of length $O(N/c)$.

As an example, we consider the difference equations (3.2.24) on a square grid with the four-coloring illustrated in Figure 3.2-8. The unknowns will be held in the four arrays *UR*, *UB*, *UG*, *UW*. The top and bottom rows will hold boundary values as will the first and last positions in the other rows. Then the Gauss-Seidel updates of the red points on the ith row will be done by the vector operations

$$\begin{aligned} UR(I,\ ) = 0.25[&UB(I,\ )_{+1} + UW(I,\ )_{-1} + UG(I+1,\ ) \\ &+ UG(I-1,\ )] + 0.0625a[UB(I+1,\ )_{-1} + UB(I-1,\ )_{-1} \\ &+ UW(I+1,\ )_{+1} + UW(I-1,\ )_{+1}] \end{aligned} \tag{3.2.30}$$

where we use the same notation as in (3.2.20). Similar statements will be used to update the black, green, and white points.

For vector computers that require long vector lengths for efficiency, we wish to work with one-dimensional arrays, one for each of the colors, of length $O(N^2/c)$. As was done for the Poisson problem, these vectors will also hold the boundary values, and storage into the boundary positions is assumed to be suppressed. Again we use the equations (3.2.24) and the coloring of Figure 3.2-10 as an example. We reproduce this coloring in Figure 3.2-12 with the grid points ordered. For simplicity of presentation, in the following schematic for the Gauss-Seidel update of the red points, we do not use the special approach of (3.1.16), as was done with the Poisson problem; this is left to Exercise 3.2-15. We also omit multiplication by the constants 0.25 and 0.0625a.

$$\begin{array}{lcccccccccccccccccc} & R_4 & & G_1 & & G_6 & & W_3 & & B_4 & & W_6 & & W_1 & & B_6 & & B_1 \\ & R_5 & & G_2 & & G_7 & & W_4 & & B_5 & & W_7 & & W_2 & & B_7 & & B_2 \\ * & R_6 & & G_3 & & G_8 & & W_5 & & B_6 & & W_8 & & W_3 & & B_8 & & B_3 \\ & R_7 & = & G_4 & + & G_9 & + & W_6 & + & B_7 & + & W_9 & - & W_4 & - & B_9 & + & B_4 \\ & R_8 & & G_5 & & G_{10} & & W_7 & & B_8 & & W_{10} & & W_5 & & B_{10} & & B_5 \\ & R_9 & & G_6 & & G_{11} & & W_8 & & B_9 & & W_{11} & & W_6 & & B_{11} & & B_6 \\ & \vdots & & \vdots & & \vdots & & \vdots & & \vdots & & \vdots & & \vdots & & \vdots & & \vdots \end{array} \tag{3.2.31}$$

Similar computations would be done to update the black, green, and white points. We have indicated by an asterisk in (3.2.31) a spurious computation whose storage into the corresponding boundary position would have to be suppressed. Equation (3.2.31) illustrates the computation for $N = 8$. In general, for this problem, we need N to be of the form $N = 4M$, for some integer M.

Line SOR

We next discuss briefly the parallel and vector implementation of line SOR. Consider first the discrete Poisson equation and the line Gauss-Seidel method (3.2.10) for the equations written in the natural order. The effective parallelization of (3.2.10) has the same difficulty as the point Gauss-Seidel method, and again one approach is a reordering of the equations. This time,

$G8$	$W8$	$R9$	$B9$	$G9$	$W9$	$R10$	$B10$	$G10$	$W10$
$R6$	$B6$	$G6$	$W6$	$R7$	$B7$	$G7$	$W7$	$R8$	$B8$
$G3$	$W3$	$R4$	$B4$	$G4$	$W4$	$R5$	$B5$	$G5$	$W5$
$R1$	$B1$	$G1$	$W1$	$R2$	$B2$	$G2$	$W2$	$R3$	$B3$

Figure 3.2-12. Numbered multicolor ordering.

B	B	B	$\cdots$	B
R	R	R	$\cdots$	R
B	B	B	$\cdots$	B
R	R	R	$\cdots$	R

Figure 3.2-13. Red-black ordering by lines.

however, we color the node points by line as illustrated in Figure 3.2-13. This is sometimes called a "zebra ordering" (replace red by white). With the ordering of Figure 3.2-13, the equations for the unknowns on the ith line couple red points with only black points on the adjacent lines. If we denote the unknowns on the ith red line by $\mathbf{u}_{Ri}$, and similarly for the black unknowns, then a line Gauss-Seidel step for updating the red points is

$$T\mathbf{u}_{Ri}^{k+1} = \mathbf{u}_{Bi-1}^{k} + \mathbf{u}_{Bi}^{k} + \mathbf{b}_i, \qquad i = 1, \ldots, N \tag{3.2.32}$$

and similarly for updating the black points. The tridiagonal systems (3.2.32) can now be solved in parallel or by vectorizing across the systems just as was done with the line Jacobi method. The only difference is that now the vector lengths are $O(N/2)$.

For more general equations and/or discretizations the same principle applies, although additional colors may be needed. Referring to Figure 3.2-9, a red-black coloring by lines still suffices for the stencil (b), but three colors are required for (a) and (c) as illustrated in Figure 3.2-14. The equations using colors by lines can still be represented by (3.2.28) but now the diagonal blocks D_i will have the form

$$D_i = \begin{bmatrix} D_{i1} & & & \\ & D_{i2} & & \\ & & \ddots & \\ & & & D_{ic_i} \end{bmatrix} \tag{3.2.33}$$

G	G	G	$\cdots$	G
B	B	B	$\cdots$	B
R	R	R	$\cdots$	R
G	G	G	$\cdots$	G
B	B	B	$\cdots$	B
R	R	R	$\cdots$	R

Figure 3.2-14. Three-coloring by lines.

where c_i is the number of lines of color i and each D_{ij} is a banded matrix. We call a matrix of the form (3.2.28, 3.2.33) a *block c-colored matrix.*

SSOR

The SSOR iteration can be implemented in exactly the same fashion as SOR using red-black or multicolor orderings. However, a curious thing happens that has the beneficial effect of reducing the necessary computation. Suppose, first, that the red-black ordering is used on the Poisson problem, or any other problem for which the red-black ordering gives a two-colored matrix. Suppose that the pattern of sweeping the grid is

red, black, black (reverse), red (reverse), red, . . .

which would correspond to going through all the grid points and then going through them in the reverse order. However, in this case, the updating of the black points in reverse order uses only red points which have not been changed from the forward sweep. Hence, for the case that $\omega = 1$ the reverse black sweep produces exactly the same updated values as the forward sweep and the first symmetric Gauss-Seidel iteration is really only the three sweeps:

red, black, red (reverse)

The analogous thing happens if c colors $C_1, \ldots, C_c$ are used. Here, the pattern is

$$C_1, \ldots, C_{c-1}, C_c, C_c, C_{c-1}, \ldots, C_1, C_1 \ldots \qquad (3.2.34)$$

and if $\omega = 1$, the two consecutive sweeps for C_c are identical; the same is true for the two consecutive sweeps for C_1. Hence, the symmetric Gauss-Seidel iteration becomes

$$(C_1, \ldots, C_{c-1}, C_c, C_{c-1}, \ldots, C_1)(C_2, \ldots, C_c, \ldots, C_1), \ldots \qquad (3.2.35)$$

and it is reasonable to call the set of sweeps in parentheses the symmetric Gauss-Seidel iterations. The same pattern then persists on subsequent iterations. For two colors, that is, the red-black ordering, (3.2.34) then becomes

$$(R, B, R), \qquad (B, R), \qquad (B, R) \ldots \qquad (3.2.36)$$

where the parentheses define a complete symmetric Gauss-Seidel iteration. Thus, after the first iteration, symmetric Gauss-Seidel reduces to just Gauss-Seidel but with the order of colors reversed from the starting order.

If $\omega \neq 1$, the steps C_c, C_c in (3.2.34) are no longer identical because of the effect of ω. To see what this effect is, let $\mathbf{u}_c^1$ be the SOR result of the first C_c step, let $\mathbf{u}_c^2$ be the result of the second step, and let $\hat{\mathbf{u}}_c^i$ be the corresponding Gauss–Seidel results. Then

$$\mathbf{u}_c^2 = (1-\omega)\mathbf{u}_c^1 + \omega\hat{\mathbf{u}}_c^2 \qquad (3.2.37)$$

But the Gauss–Seidel result depends only on the values at the other colors $1, \ldots, c-1$ which have not changed since the previous Gauss–Seidel result was computed. Hence $\hat{\mathbf{u}}_c^2 = \hat{\mathbf{u}}_c^1$ and substituting into (3.2.37) the expression for $\mathbf{u}_c^1$ in terms of $\hat{\mathbf{u}}_c^1$ and the original value $\mathbf{u}_c^0$ gives

$$\mathbf{u}_c^2 = (1-\omega)[(1-\omega)\mathbf{u}_c^0 + \omega\hat{\mathbf{u}}_c^1] + \omega\hat{\mathbf{u}}_c^1 = (1-\omega)^2\mathbf{u}_c^0$$

$$+ [(1-\omega)\omega + \omega]\hat{\mathbf{u}}_c^1 = (1-\hat{\omega})\mathbf{u}_c^0 + \hat{\omega}\hat{\mathbf{u}}_c^1$$

where $\hat{\omega} = \omega(2-\omega)$ since $(1-\omega)^2 = 1 - \omega(2-\omega)$. Hence, the result of the two consecutive C_c, C_c steps in (3.2.34) with parameter ω is the same as a single SOR step with parameter $\hat{\omega}$. Thus, one can carry out the two C_c, C_c steps with a single Gauss–Seidel sweep (i.e., Jacobi sweep) using the modified value $\hat{\omega}$. The same will also be true for the consecutive C_1, C_1 steps. This, of course, allows considerable reduction in the work required to carry out a complete SSOR iteration.

It should be noted that when the original equations can be written in the red–black form, it is known that the optimal value of ω for the rate of convergence of SSOR is $\omega = 1$. However, the same result is not known for c-colored matrices when $c > 2$.

The Conrad–Wallach Trick

We next describe another way, which we call the *Conrad–Wallach trick*, to save computation in the SSOR iteration. The SSOR iteration (3.2.14) may be written as

$$(D - \omega L)\mathbf{x}^{k+1/2} = (1-\omega)D\mathbf{x}^k + \omega\mathbf{y}^k + \omega\mathbf{b},$$
$$\mathbf{y}^{k+1/2} = L\mathbf{x}^{k+1/2} + \mathbf{b} \qquad (3.2.38a)$$

$$(D - \omega U)\mathbf{x}^{k+1} = (1-\omega)D\mathbf{x}^{k+1/2} + \omega\mathbf{y}^{k+1/2},$$
$$\mathbf{y}^{k+1} = U\mathbf{x}^{k+1} \qquad (3.2.38b)$$

where $\mathbf{y}^0 = U\mathbf{x}^0$. The intent of (3.2.38) is to carry out the SSOR iteration in such a way that the quantities $\mathbf{y}^{k+1/2}$ and $\mathbf{y}^{k+1}$ are obtained with no additional computation. To see how this can be done, we consider the iteration in component form.

At the beginning of the $(k+1)$st stage, let $\mathbf{y}^k = U\mathbf{x}^k$. Then the computation of $\mathbf{x}_i^{k+1/2}$ is given by

$$\hat{x}_i^{k+1/2} = \frac{1}{a_{ii}}\left(\sum_{j<i} l_{ij}x_j^{k+1/2} + y_i^k + b_i\right),$$

$$x_i^{k+1/2} = x_i^k + \omega(\hat{x}_i^{k+1/2} - x_i^k) \tag{3.2.39}$$

In the course of this computation, we replace y_i^k by

$$y_i^{k+1/2} = \sum_{j<i} l_{ij}x_j^{k+1/2} + b_i$$

Hence, at the end of the computation of $\mathbf{x}^{k+1/2}$ we also have $\mathbf{y}^{k+1/2} = L\mathbf{x}^{k+1/2} + \mathbf{b}$. Therefore, at the next half step we compute

$$\hat{x}_i^{k+1} = \frac{1}{a_{ii}}\left(\sum_{i>i} u_{ij}x_j^{k+1} + y_i^{k+1/2}\right),$$

$$x_i^{k+1} = x_i^{k+1/2} + \omega(\hat{x}_i^{k+1} - x_i^{k+1/2}) \tag{3.2.40}$$

During this half-step, we replace $y_i^{k+1/2}$ by

$$y_i^{k+1} = \sum_{j>i} u_{ij}x_j^{k+1} \tag{3.2.41}$$

so that at the end of the computation of x^{k+1} we also have $\mathbf{y}^{k+1} = U\mathbf{x}^{k+1}$ to begin the next stage. Thus, we avoid the computation of $L\mathbf{x}^{k+1/2}$ and $U\mathbf{x}^{k+1}$ except at the outset when we must compute $\mathbf{y}^0 = U\mathbf{x}^0$. Application to the discrete Poisson equation (3.1.5) using both the natural and red-black orderings is left to Exercise 3.2-16.

A Data Flow Approach to SOR

We next consider an approach to the parallel implementation of the SOR algorithm which is seemingly quite different although there is a strong connection to multicolor orderings. We will illustrate this approach by considering first a system of equations that arises from discretizing a partial differential equation with the nine-point grid stencil of Figure 3.2-7. We

old	old	old
new	●	old
new	new	new

Figure 3.2-15. Update pattern.

assume that the grid points are ordered in the natural fashion, left to right, bottom to top.

For a typical grid point, the corresponding unknown can be updated by the SOR algorithm only when its south, west, southeast, and southwest neighbors have already been updated, as illustrated in Figure 3.2-15. The idea of the data flow algorithm is to do the updating as soon as possible at each grid point. This is illustrated in Figure 3.2-16, where the numbers indicate the time at which that unknown is updated.

In Figure 3.2-16, the unknowns at grid points $(1, 1)$ and $(1, 2)$ are updated on the first two time steps. The necessary information is now available to update the unknowns at grid points $(1, 3)$ and $(2, 1)$ and these are done in parallel on the third time step. Similarly, the unknowns at grid points $(1, 4)$ and $(2, 2)$ can be updated on the fourth time step. Now, all the forward neighbors of the $(1, 1)$ grid point have been updated and this unknown can then be updated a second time on the fifth time step, in parallel with the first updates of a number of other unknowns. The pattern should now be clear.

The computation proceeds through the grid in a number of wave fronts, rather similar to those of the data flow formulation of LU decomposition described in Section 2.2. Consider the 11th time step. The unknowns at grid points $(1, 3)$ and $(2, 1)$ are being updated a third time, those at grid points $(4, 1)$, $(3, 3)$, and $(2, 5)$ are being updated a second time, and those of $(6, 1)$, $(5, 3)$, and $(4, 5)$ are being updated the first time. This illustrates that at any given time, once the process has started, a number of unknowns can be updated in parallel and these updates will correspond to different iteration levels.

11, 15, 19	12, 16, 20	13, 17, 21	14, 18, 22	15, 19, 23
9, 13, 17	10, 14, 18	11, 15, 19	12, 16, 20	13, 17, 21
7, 11, 15	8, 12, 16	9, 13, 17	10, 14, 18	11, 15, 19
5, 9, 13	6, 10, 14	7, 11, 15	8, 12, 16	9, 13, 17
3, 7, 11	4, 8, 12	5, 9, 13	6, 10, 14	7, 11, 15
1, 5, 9	2, 6, 10	3, 7, 11	4, 8, 12	5, 9, 13

Figure 3.2-16. Update times.

Semi-iterative Methods

The introduction of the parameter ω in the SOR method is a way to accelerate the basic Gauss–Seidel method. Another acceleration procedure is the following. We start with some basic iterative method (Jacobi, SOR, etc.) written as

$$\mathbf{x}^{k+1} = H\mathbf{x}^k + \mathbf{d}, \qquad k = 0, 1, \ldots \tag{3.2.42}$$

Given the iterates $\mathbf{x}^k$ and $\mathbf{x}^{k+1}$ we attempt to obtain an improved approximation to the solution $\hat{\mathbf{x}}$ by a linear combination of these two iterates. Thus, we define

$$\mathbf{y}^{k+1} = \alpha_1\mathbf{x}^{k+1} + \alpha_2\mathbf{x}^k = \alpha_1(H\mathbf{x}^k + \mathbf{d}) + \alpha_2\mathbf{x}^k \tag{3.2.43}$$

We assume that the method (3.2.42) is consistent, that is, the solution satisfies $\hat{\mathbf{x}} = H\hat{\mathbf{x}} + \mathbf{d}$. (See Appendix 2). We also wish the method defined by (3.2.43) to be consistent. Thus, if we replace $\mathbf{x}^k$ and $\mathbf{y}^{k+1}$ in (3.2.43) by $\hat{\mathbf{x}}$, we require that

$$\hat{\mathbf{x}} = \alpha_1(H\hat{\mathbf{x}} + \mathbf{d}) + \alpha_2\hat{\mathbf{x}} = \alpha_1\hat{\mathbf{x}} + \alpha_2\hat{\mathbf{x}}$$

so that $\alpha_1 + \alpha_2 = 1$. With this constraint on α_1 and α_2, we can write (3.2.43) in terms of a single parameter γ. Also, the iterates that we actually compute will be the $\mathbf{y}^k$ and we write (3.2.43) in the form

$$\mathbf{y}^{k+1} = \gamma(H\mathbf{y}^k + \mathbf{d}) + (1 - \gamma)\mathbf{y}^k \tag{3.2.44}$$

which is known as an extrapolation of the original method (3.2.42) or an *extrapolation method.* At the kth stage, starting with $\mathbf{y}^k$, we do a basic iterative step to form $H\mathbf{y}^k + \mathbf{d}$ and then obtain $\mathbf{y}^{k+1}$ from (3.2.44).

The idea of taking linear combinations of basic iterates can be extended to any number of iterates. Assume that $\mathbf{x}^1, \ldots, \mathbf{x}^m$ have been generated by the basic iterative method (3.2.42) and define

$$\mathbf{y}^{m+1} = \sum_{i=1}^{m} \alpha_{m,i}\mathbf{x}^i \tag{3.2.45}$$

This is known as a *semi-iterative* method. If the basic iterative method (3.2.42) is the Jacobi method, then the corresponding semi-iterative method is called the *Jacobi-SI* method. Similarly, we have the *SOR-SI* and *SSOR-SI* methods.

From the consistency of (3.2.42), the errors $\mathbf{x}^k - \hat{\mathbf{x}}$ satisfy (see Appendix 2)

$$\mathbf{x}^k - \hat{\mathbf{x}} = H^k(\mathbf{x}^0 - \hat{\mathbf{x}}) \tag{3.2.46}$$

and if (3.2.45) is to be consistent we must have

$$\hat{\mathbf{x}} = \sum_{i=1}^{m} \alpha_{m,i}\hat{\mathbf{x}}$$

or

$$\sum_{i=1}^{m} \alpha_{m,i} = 1 \tag{3.2.47}$$

Thus

$$\mathbf{y}^{m+1} - \hat{\mathbf{x}} = \sum_{i=1}^{m} \alpha_{m,i}(\mathbf{x}^i - \hat{\mathbf{x}}) = \sum_{i=1}^{m} \alpha_{m,i}H^i(\mathbf{x}^0 - \hat{\mathbf{x}}) = p(H)(\mathbf{x}^0 - \hat{\mathbf{x}}) \tag{3.2.48}$$

where $p(H)$ is the polynomial

$$p(H) = \sum_{i=1}^{m} \alpha_{m,i}H^i \tag{3.2.49}$$

Because of the role of this polynomial in the error behavior, semi-iterative methods of the type we have been discussing are also known as *polynomial acceleration methods.*

We now wish to choose the $\alpha_{m,i}$ so as to maximize the rate of convergence, and for this we need to minimize the spectral radius of $p(H)$ (see Appendix 2). The condition (3.2.47) is equivalent to

$$p(1) = 1 \tag{3.2.50}$$

and we define $\mathcal{P}_m$ to be the set of polynomials p of degree m for which (3.2.50) holds. Since the eigenvalues of $p(H)$ are $p(\lambda_i)$, $i = 1, \ldots, n$, where $\lambda_1, \ldots, \lambda_n$ are the eigenvalues of H, the minimization problem with which we are faced is

$$\min_{p \in \mathcal{P}_m} \max_{1 \leq i \leq n} |p(\lambda_i)| \tag{3.2.51}$$

The problem (3.2.51) is intractable as stated since we will know the eigenvalues of H only for very special problems; usually, at best, we will only have bounds of some kind. As an example of one way to proceed, we now assume that the eigenvalues of H are real. This is the case for the Jacobi and SSOR iterations if A is symmetric and positive definite (Appendix 2) but not, in general, for the SOR iteration. Let λ_1 and λ_n be the minimum and maximum eigenvalues of H, and let

$$-1 < a \leq \lambda_1 < \lambda_n \leq b < 1 \tag{3.2.52}$$

Then the quantity

$$\min_{m\in\mathcal{P}_m}\ \max_{a\leq\lambda\leq b} |p(\lambda)| \tag{3.2.53}$$

is an upper bound for that of (3.2.51) since the maximum over the eigenvalues has been replaced by a maximum over an interval that contains all the eigenvalues. The minimization problem (3.2.53) is classical and can be solved in terms of Chebyshev polynomials of the first kind. These polynomials may be defined by the recurrence relations

$$\begin{gathered} T_0(\lambda) = 1, \qquad T_1(\lambda) = \lambda, \qquad T_{i+1}(\lambda) = 2\lambda T_i(\lambda) - T_{i-1}(\lambda), \\ i = 1, 2, \ldots, m-1 \end{gathered} \tag{3.2.54}$$

or they can be expressed as

$$T_m(\lambda) = \cos(m \cos^{-1} \lambda), \qquad |\lambda| \leq 1 \tag{3.2.55}$$

The polynomials defined by (3.2.54) solve (3.2.53) when $a = -1$ and $b = 1$. For other intervals it is only necessary to make the linear change of variable that maps $[a, b]$ onto $[-1, 1]$; then the solution of (3.2.53) is given by

$$p_m(\lambda) = T_m\left(\frac{2\lambda - b - a}{b - a}\right) \Big/ T_m\left(\frac{2 - b - a}{b - a}\right) \tag{3.2.56}$$

From (3.2.54), it follows (Exercise 3.2-19) that the polynomials p_m of (3.2.56) satisfy the recurrence relation

$$\begin{gathered} p_0(\lambda) = 1, \qquad p_1(\lambda) = \gamma\lambda - \gamma + 1, \\ p_{i+1}(\lambda) = \rho_{i+1}(\gamma\lambda - \gamma + 1)p_i(\lambda) + (1 - \rho_{i+1})p_{i-1}(\lambda) \end{gathered} \tag{3.2.57}$$

where, with $\beta = (2 - b - a)/(b - a)$,

$$\gamma = 2/(2 - b - a), \qquad \rho_{i+1} = 2\gamma\beta p_i(\beta)/p_{i-1}(\beta) \tag{3.2.58}$$

By again using (3.2.54), it can be shown that the ρ_i also satisfy a recurrence relation, namely,

$$\begin{gathered} \rho_1 = 1, \qquad \rho_2 = 2\beta^2/(2\beta^2 - 1), \\ \rho_{i+1} = 4\beta^2/(4\beta^2 - \rho_i), \qquad i = 2, 3, \ldots \end{gathered} \tag{3.2.59}$$

We could, in principle, obtain the coefficients $\alpha_{m,i}$ of the polynomial p_m and then use (3.2.45). However, it is far more efficient to use the recurrence relations for p_m, to obtain an analogous recurrence relation for the accelerated iterates $\mathbf{y}^m$ of (3.2.45). From (3.2.48) and (3.2.57), with $\mathbf{e}^0 = \mathbf{x}^0 - \hat{\mathbf{x}}$, we have

$$\begin{aligned}\mathbf{y}^{m+1} - \hat{\mathbf{x}} &= p_m(H)\mathbf{e}^0 = \rho_m[\gamma H + (1-\gamma)I]p_{m-1}(H)\mathbf{e}^0 + (1-\rho_m)p_{m-2}(H)\mathbf{e}^0 \\ &= \rho_m[\gamma H + (1-\gamma)I](\mathbf{y}^m - \hat{\mathbf{x}}) + (1-\rho_m)(\mathbf{y}^{m-1} - \hat{\mathbf{x}}) \\ &= \rho_m[\gamma H + (1-\gamma)I]\mathbf{y}^m + (1-\rho_m)\mathbf{y}^{m-1} \\ &\quad - \rho_m[\gamma H + (1-\gamma)I]\hat{\mathbf{x}} - (1-\rho_m)\hat{\mathbf{x}} \end{aligned} \tag{3.2.60}$$

Since $H\hat{\mathbf{x}} = \hat{\mathbf{x}} - \mathbf{d}$, we have

$$\rho_m[\gamma H + (1-\gamma)I]\hat{\mathbf{x}} + (1-\rho_m)\hat{\mathbf{x}} = -\rho_m\gamma\mathbf{d} + \hat{\mathbf{x}}$$

so that (3.2.60) becomes

$$\mathbf{y}^{m+1} = \rho_m[\gamma(H\mathbf{y}^m + \mathbf{d}) + (1-\gamma)\mathbf{y}^m] + (1-\rho_m)\mathbf{y}^{m-1} \tag{3.2.61}$$

This is the basic recurrence relation for the accelerated vectors $\mathbf{y}^i$ and is called the *Chebyshev semi-iterative method* or *Chebyshev acceleration method.*

The procedure is then the following. At the beginning of the $(m+1)$st step, a basic iteration is taken starting from $\mathbf{y}^m$ to give $H\mathbf{y}^m + \mathbf{d}$, and this vector is then combined with $\mathbf{y}^m$ and $\mathbf{y}^{m-1}$ in the linear combination (3.2.61) to give $\mathbf{y}^{m+1}$. Thus, once $H\mathbf{y}^m + \mathbf{d}$ is known, the method requires only scalar times vector multiplications and linked triad operations to obtain $\mathbf{y}^{m+1}$, and is very amenable to vector and parallel computation provided that the basic iteration itself is. A major problem, however, is obtaining good estimates, a and b, for the smallest and largest eigenvalues of H.

Exercises 3.2

1. Verify that (3.2.3) is equivalent to (3.2.1).
2. Verify in detail that (3.2.6) is the matrix representation of the SOR iteration (3.2.4).
3. For a system of three equations in three unknowns, write out the six possible reorderings of these equations by interchanging equations and corresponding unknowns.

4. Write out the equations (3.2.15) explicitly for $N = 3$ and $N = 4$.
5. Do a vector register schematic corresponding to Figure 3.1-6 for the red-black Gauss-Seidel method.
6. Do the computation corresponding to (3.2.21) to obtain new black points from red ones.
7. Assume that N is even and a column of spurious grid points has been added to the grid in order to make the red-black procedure perform correctly. On a vector computer for which $1000 + 10m$ is the timing formula for vectors of length m, estimate the inefficiency caused by these extra grid points as a function of N.
8. Write the equations (3.2.24) in the form (3.2.25) using the red-black ordering and show the structure of the matrices D_R and D_B. Write out the equations explicitly for $N = 4$.
9. Write out the system (3.2.26) for the equations (3.2.24) using the four-color ordering of Figure 3.2-8 with $N = 4$.
10. Find colorings for stencils (a) and (c) of Figure 3.2-9 and verify that the minimum numbers of colors for local uncoupling are those given in the figure.
11. Verify that the colorings of Figure 3.2-10 are suitable for the stencils of Figures 3.2-7 and 3.2.9b, respectively.
12. Do the schematic analogous to (3.2.31) for updating the black, green, and white points. Consider also the case that $N \neq 4M$ and discuss the problems you encounter.
13. Verify that the coloring of Figure 3.2-14 is suitable for a line SOR method for the stencils (a) and (c) of Figure 3.2-9.
14. For the nine-point stencil of Figure 3.2-7 show that the three four-color orderings

GORB	OBOB	GOGO
RBGO	GRGR	RBRB
GORB	BOBO	GOGO
RBGO	RGRG	RBRB

are the only ones (up to permutations of the colors) that decouple the stencil points.
15. Write a pseudocode for carrying out the SOR method with four colors using the special approach of Figure 3.1-8.
16. Apply the Conrad-Wallach trick for $\omega = 1$ to the discrete Poisson equation (3.1.5). Do the same when the equations are reordered using the red-black ordering.
17. Consider the differential equation $u_{xx} + u_{yy} + u_{xy} = 4$ on the unit square with $u(x, y) = x^2 + y^2$ on the boundary. Show that the exact solution is $u(x, y) = x^2 + y^2$. For the discrete equations (3.2.24) with $a = 1$ and the right-hand side equal to $4h^2$ instead of 0, show that the exact solution is $u_{ij} = x_i^2 + y_j^2$. (Note

that these exact solutions are the same as for $u_{xx} + u_{yy} = 4$, as given in Exercise 3.1-16!)

18. For the discrete problem of Exercise 17, write a pseudocode to implement the multicolor SOR method. Estimate the running time per iteration as a function of N.

19. Use (3.2.54) to verify the relation (3.2.57).

References and Extensions 3.2

1. The Gauss–Seidel, SOR, and SSOR iterations, and their block and semi-iterative versions, are classical, and extensive discussions of their mathematical properties are given in Varga [1962] and Young [1971].

2. It is possible to add a relaxation factor to Jacobi's method also, but this is not usually done. However, Schonauer [1983] has reported promising results for a "meander" overrelaxed Jacobi method in which the relaxation parameter varies with the iteration number in a rather complicated way.

3. It was recognized in the early days of parallel computing (see, for example, Ericksen [1972] and Lambiotte [1975]) that the red–black ordering for the discrete Poisson equation allowed a high degree of parallelism in the SOR method. Some years later, several authors independently advocated using more than two colors for more complicated situations; the treatment of multicoloring in the text follows that of Adams and Ortega [1982]. The effect of multicoloring on the rate of convergence is still not completely clear, although Adams and Jordan [1985] have shown that in some situations the asymptotic rate of convergence using certain multicolor orderings is identical to that using the natural ordering. See also Adams *et al.* [1987] for the analysis of rate of convergence of four-color orderings applied to a nine-point discretization of Poisson's equation and Adams [1986] for further discussion of multicolor orderings. Kuo *et al.* [1987] analyze an SOR method using a red–black ordering on a mesh-connected array, and using relaxation factors ω_{ij} that are a function of the grid point. Saltz *et al.* [1987] study communication times in implementing the red-black SOR method on a local memory system. They also show that convergence testing can require an inordinate amount of time on such systems and suggest various statistical tests. The idea of multicoloring has also been used by Berger *et al.* [1982] for the assembly of finite element equations.

4. O'Leary [1984] has proposed other types of multicolor orderings, one of which is illustrated below.

3	3	1	1	3	3	1	2	3	3
3	3	2	2	3	3	2	2	3	1
3	1	2	2	1	1	2	2	1	1
1	1	2	3	1	1	3	3	1	1
1	1	3	3	1	2	3	3	2	2

Here, the nodes are grouped in blocks of five, except at the boundaries. First, all points labeled 1 are ordered, followed by all points labeled 2, then all points labeled 3. The resulting system has the form (3.2.28) with $c = 3$, but now the D_i are block diagonal matrices with blocks that are 5×5 or less. A block SOR iteration can then be carried out with block Jacobi sweeps that involve solving 5×5, or smaller, systems.

5. The Conrad–Wallach trick is given in Conrad and Wallach [1977]. In a later paper (Conrad and Wallach [1979]) they extend the idea to more general "alternating iterations"

$$B_1\mathbf{x}^{k+1/2} = C_1\mathbf{x}^k + \mathbf{b}, \qquad B_2\mathbf{x}^{k+1} = C_2\mathbf{x}^{k+1/2} + \mathbf{b}$$

where $A = B_1 - C_1 = B_2 - C_2$ are splittings of A such that B_1 and B_2 are triangular.

6. The data flow approach to SOR, as discussed in the text, was first implemented by Patel and Jordan [1984]. Subsequently, it was used by Adams and Jordan [1985] as a tool to analyze the rate of convergence of multicolor SOR.

7. For the SOR method, as well as others, it is sometimes suggested that the diagonal elements of A should be scaled to unity before the iteration begins. If D is the diagonal of A, then $D^{-1}A$ will have diagonal elements equal to 1. However, in general, this will destroy the symmetry of A and the scaling $D^{-1/2}AD^{-1/2}$ is usually used when A is symmetric and D has positive diagonal elements. If this scaling is done, then no divisions (or multiplications by D^{-1}) are required during the SOR iteration. However, an analysis for a given problem must be done to indicate whether this savings is greater than the work at the outset to do the scaling. This depends, of course, on the number of iterations, but in many problems, scaling is a worthwhile tactic.

8. Computational results on the CDC CYBER 205 and CRAY-1 for the SOR method using the red–black ordering are reported by Young *et al.* [1985] and Kincaid *et al.* [1986a,b]. Houstis *et al.* [1987] use a block SOR iteration to solve the system of equations resulting from cubic spline collocation discretization of Poisson's equation. Both synchronous and asynchronous versions are considered, and timing results are given on the CYBER 205, an Alliant FX/8 with eight processors, a Flex/32 with seven processors, and a Sequent Balance 21000 with 24 processors. See also Plemmons [1986] for a parallel block SOR method with application to structural analysis problems, and Saad, Sameh, and Saylor [1985] for Chebyshev semi-iterative methods.

9. O'Leary and White [1985] (see also Neumann and Plemmons [1987] and White [1987]), consider *multisplittings* of A of the form

$$A = B_i - C_i, \qquad i = 1, \ldots, k, \qquad \sum_{i=1}^{k} D_i = I \qquad (D_i \geq 0)$$

$$H = \sum_{i=1}^{k} D_i B_i^{-1} C_i, \qquad \mathbf{d} = \left(\sum_{i=1}^{k} D_i B_i^{-1} \right) \mathbf{b}$$

to give the iteration $\mathbf{x}^{k+1} = H\mathbf{x}^k + \mathbf{d}$. A number of standard methods, including the SOR method, can be cast in this form, which leads to another approach to parallelism.

10. Reed, Adams, and Patrick [1987] study data transmission times as a function of processor interconnection, processor assignment, and grid stencil. In particular, they focus on triangular, square, and hexagonal interconnections and five- and nine-point stencils. Their thesis is that all three of these factors must be considered in unison, and consideration of only one or two will likely yield suboptimal results. Their theoretical results include the following: In a message passing environment, hexagonal partitions are best for five-point stencils, provided that small packet size transmissions are possible. If only large packet size transmission is possible, then the reverse conclusion is true. See, also, Patrick *et al.* [1987].
11. A very sophisticated use of the Gauss-Seidel iteration occurs in the *multigrid* method. Assume that a partial differential equation is discretized on a grid of points for which the approximate solution is desired. We call this the *fine* grid and subsets of these grid points are *coarser* grids. A multigrid method takes a number of Gauss-Seidel iterations on the fine grid, then stops and "injects" information from the fine grid to a coarser grid and performs several Gauss-Seidel iterations on this coarser grid. The process is continued by using still coarser grids. Information from these coarser grids is transmitted back to the finer grids by interpolation. There are many important details in this process and many variations on the basic multigrid idea. Properly implemented, multigrid methods are increasingly becoming the method of choice for many problems. For an early basic paper, see Brandt [1977]. For more recent work on parallel and vector implementations, see, for example, Barkai and Brandt [1983], Chan, Saad, and Schultz [1987], Gannon and van Rosendale [1986], Chan and Tuminaro [1987], Kamowitz [1987], and Naik and Ta'asan [1987]. McBryan [1987] studies a number of methods (SOR, conjugate gradient, multigrid) on a 32,000 processor Connection Machine.

3.3. Minimization Methods

If the real $n \times n$ matrix A is symmetric and positive definite, then (Exercise 3.3-1) the solution of the linear system $A\mathbf{x} = \mathbf{b}$ is equivalent to minimizing the quadratic function

$$Q(\mathbf{x}) \equiv \tfrac{1}{2}\mathbf{x}^T A\mathbf{x} - \mathbf{b}^T\mathbf{x} \tag{3.3.1}$$

There is a large number of iterative methods for minimizing the function Q of (3.3.1). Most such methods are of the general form

$$\mathbf{x}^{k+1} = \mathbf{x}^k - \alpha_k \mathbf{p}^k, \qquad k = 0, 1, \ldots \tag{3.3.2}$$

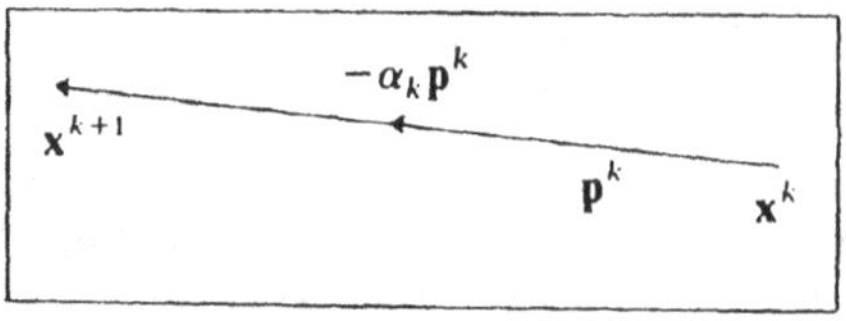

Figure 3.3-1. Moving along direction vector.

where the $\mathbf{p}^k$ are *direction* vectors and the scalars α_k determine the distance to be moved along $\mathbf{p}^k$, as illustrated in Figure 3.3-1. A variety of different methods are possible depending on how the α_k and the $\mathbf{p}^k$ are chosen.

Perhaps the most natural way to choose the α_k is to minimize Q in the direction $\mathbf{p}^k$, so that α_k satisfies

$$Q(\mathbf{x}^k - \alpha_k \mathbf{p}^k) = \min_{\alpha} Q(\mathbf{x}^k - \alpha \mathbf{p}^k) \tag{3.3.3}$$

For fixed $\mathbf{x}^k$ and $\mathbf{p}^k$, (3.3.3) is a minimization problem in a single variable α and can be solved explicitly. For ease of notation, we drop the superscripts on $\mathbf{x}^k$ and $\mathbf{p}^k$. Then

$$\begin{aligned} q(\alpha) \equiv Q(\mathbf{x} - \alpha \mathbf{p}) &= \tfrac{1}{2}(\mathbf{x} - \alpha \mathbf{p})^T A (\mathbf{x} - \alpha \mathbf{p}) - \mathbf{b}^T (\mathbf{x} - \alpha \mathbf{p}) \\ &= \tfrac{1}{2}\mathbf{x}^T A \mathbf{x} - \alpha \mathbf{p}^T A \mathbf{x} + \tfrac{1}{2}\alpha^2 \mathbf{p}^T A \mathbf{p} + \alpha \mathbf{p}^T \mathbf{b} - \mathbf{b}^T \mathbf{x} \\ &= \tfrac{1}{2}\mathbf{p}^T A \mathbf{p} \alpha^2 - \mathbf{p}^T (A\mathbf{x} - \mathbf{b})\alpha + \tfrac{1}{2}\mathbf{x}^T (A\mathbf{x} - 2\mathbf{b}) \end{aligned} \tag{3.3.4}$$

Since A is assumed to be positive definite, $\mathbf{p}^T A \mathbf{p} > 0$ and the quadratic q in α is minimized when $q'(\alpha) = 0$ or, in terms of $\mathbf{x}^k$ and $\mathbf{p}^k$, when

$$\alpha_k = (\mathbf{p}^k)^T (A\mathbf{x}^k - \mathbf{b})/(\mathbf{p}^k)^T A \mathbf{p}^k \tag{3.3.5}$$

This is illustrated in Figure 3.3-2.

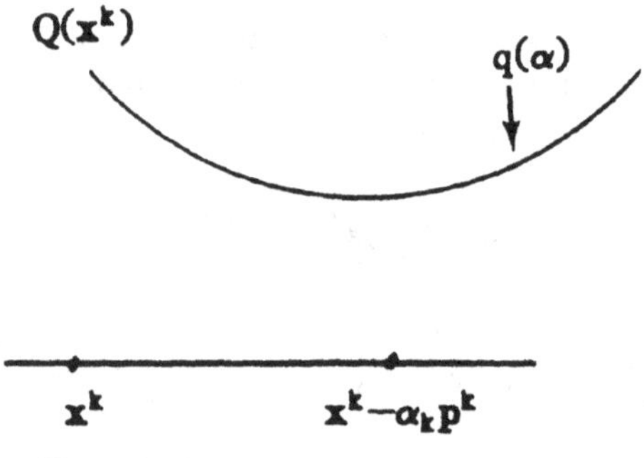

Figure 3.3-2. One-dimensional minimization.

Univariate Relaxation

Let $\mathbf{e}_i$ be the vector with 1 in the ith position and zeroes elsewhere. One of the simplest choices of the direction vectors is $\mathbf{e}_1, \ldots, \mathbf{e}_n$, taken cyclically:

$$\mathbf{p}^0 = \mathbf{e}_1, \qquad \mathbf{p}^1 = \mathbf{e}_2, \qquad \ldots, \qquad \mathbf{p}^{n-1} = \mathbf{e}_n, \qquad \mathbf{p}^n = \mathbf{e}_1, \ldots \tag{3.3.6}$$

Note that $\mathbf{e}_i^T A \mathbf{e}_i = a_{ii}$ and

$$\mathbf{e}_i^T(A\mathbf{x} - \mathbf{b}) = \sum_{j=1}^{n} a_{ij}x_j - b_i$$

Thus, if $\mathbf{p}^k = \mathbf{e}_i$, and α_k is chosen by the minimization principle (3.3.5), the next iterate $\mathbf{x}^{k+1}$ is given by

$$\mathbf{x}^{k+1} = \mathbf{x}^k - \alpha_k \mathbf{e}_i = \mathbf{x}^k - \frac{1}{a_{ii}}\left(\sum_{j=1}^{n} a_{ij}x_j^k - b_i\right)\mathbf{e}_i \tag{3.3.7}$$

In (3.3.7), $\mathbf{x}^{k+1}$ and $\mathbf{x}^k$ differ only in the ith component. Indeed, (3.3.7) is equivalent to minimizing Q in the ith variable x_i with all other variables held constant at their values in $\mathbf{x}^k$.

Now consider the first n steps written for only the components that change and noting that $x_j^k = x_j^0$, until the jth component is changed:

$$x_i^i = x_i^0 - \alpha_i = x_i^0 - \frac{1}{a_{ii}}\left(\sum_{j=1}^{i-1} a_{ij}x_j^j + \sum_{j=i}^{n} a_{ij}x_j^0 - b_i\right)$$

$$= \frac{1}{a_{ii}}\left(b_i - \sum_{j<i} a_{ij}x_j^j - \sum_{j>i} a_{ij}x_j^0\right), \qquad i = 1 \ldots n \tag{3.3.8}$$

The first n steps of univariate relaxation constitute one Gauss–Seidel iteration so that the Gauss–Seidel method is equivalent to combining n successive univariate relaxation steps and calling the result the next Gauss–Seidel iterate.

Overrelaxation

For any method of the form (3.3.2), we can add a relaxation parameter ω to the minimization principle so that α_k is chosen to be

$$\alpha_k = \omega\hat{\alpha}_k \tag{3.3.9}$$

where $\hat{\alpha}_k$ is now the value of α that minimizes Q in the direction $\mathbf{p}^k$. This is illustrated in Figure 3.3-3 for an $\omega > 1$. Thus with an $\omega \neq 1$, the new $\mathbf{x}^{k+1}$ no longer minimizes Q in the direction $\mathbf{p}^k$.

It is clear from Figure 3.3-3 that $Q(\mathbf{x}^k - \omega\hat{\alpha}_k\mathbf{p}^k) < Q(\mathbf{x}^k)$ for $\omega > 0$ until a value of ω is reached for which $Q(\mathbf{x}^k - \omega\hat{\alpha}_k\mathbf{p}^k) = Q(\mathbf{x}^k)$. By the symmetry of a quadratic function in a single variable about its minimum, it follows that this value of ω is 2 as illustrated in the figure. Thus $Q(\mathbf{x}^{k+1}) < Q(\mathbf{x}^k)$ if $0 < \omega < 2$, and $Q(\mathbf{x}^{k+1}) \geq Q(\mathbf{x}^k)$ otherwise (Exercise 3.3-3). It is this descent property for $0 < \omega < 2$ that is the basis of the Ostrowski–Reich Theorem 3.2.3 for the convergence of the SOR iteration.

Steepest Descent

For a function g of n variables, the negative of the gradient vector ∇g evaluated at a point $\mathbf{x}$ gives the direction of maximum local decrease of the function g at $\mathbf{x}$. Hence, a natural choice for the direction vector $\mathbf{p}^k$ of a minimization algorithm is

$$\mathbf{p}^k = \nabla Q(\mathbf{x}^k) = A\mathbf{x}^k - \mathbf{b} \tag{3.3.10}$$

and this defines the *method of steepest descent*

$$\mathbf{x}^{k+1} = \mathbf{x}^k - \alpha_k(A\mathbf{x}^k - \mathbf{b}) \tag{3.3.11}$$

which is also known as *Richardson's* method. Note that if A is normalized to have diagonal elements equal to 1 and $\alpha_k = 1$, then (3.3.11) reduces to the Jacobi iteration (Exercise 3.3-4).

In spite of the fact that moving in the direction of the negative gradient vector gives a maximum local decrease in the function value, the method of steepest descent generally converges very slowly.

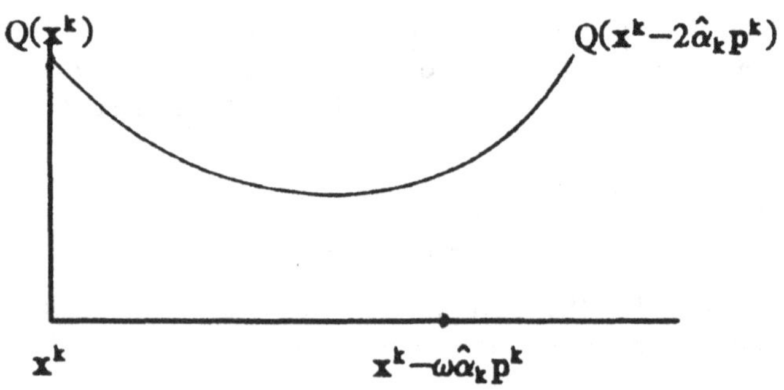

Figure 3.3-3. Overrelaxation.

Conjugate Direction Methods

An extremely interesting and important class of methods, called *conjugate direction* methods, arises when there are n direction vectors $\mathbf{p}^0, \ldots, \mathbf{p}^{n-1}$ that satisfy

$$(\mathbf{p}^i)^T A \mathbf{p}^j = 0, \qquad i \neq j \tag{3.3.12}$$

Such vectors are orthogonal with respect to the inner product $(\mathbf{x}, \mathbf{y}) \equiv \mathbf{x}^T A \mathbf{y}$ defined by A, and are also called *conjugate* with respect to A.

One of the basic properties of conjugate direction methods is given by the following result.

3.3.1. CONJUGATE DIRECTION THEOREM. *If A is a real $n \times n$ symmetric positive definite matrix and $\mathbf{p}^0, \ldots, \mathbf{p}^{n-1}$ are nonzero vectors that satisfy* (3.3.12), *then for any $\mathbf{x}^0$ the iterates $\mathbf{x}^{k+1} = \mathbf{x}^k - \alpha_k \mathbf{p}^k$, where α_k is chosen by the minimization principle* (3.3.5), *converge to the exact solution of $A\mathbf{x} = \mathbf{b}$ in no more than n steps.*

Note that Theorem 3.3.1 guarantees not only that the iterates converge but also that, in the absence of rounding error, they do so in a finite number of steps, no more than n. Thus, conjugate direction methods are really direct methods, but their utility still lies in being treated as iterative methods as will be discussed further shortly.

To see why 3.3.1 should be true, consider first a quadratic function

$$Q(\mathbf{x}) = \frac{1}{2} \sum_{i=1}^{n} a_{ii} x_i^2 - \mathbf{b}^T \mathbf{x} \tag{3.3.13}$$

for which the matrix A is diagonal. It is easy to see (Exercise 3.3-5) that univariate relaxation minimizes the function (3.3.13) in n steps. But $\mathbf{e}_1, \ldots, \mathbf{e}_n$ constitute a set of conjugate directions with respect to a diagonal matrix and thus, in this case, univariate relaxation is equivalent to the conjugate direction method in which $\mathbf{p}^{i-1} = \mathbf{e}_i$, $i = 1, \ldots, n$.

In general, if P is the matrix with columns $\mathbf{p}^0, \ldots, \mathbf{p}^{n-1}$, then (3.3.12) is equivalent to $P^T A P = D$, where D is a diagonal matrix. Hence, with the change of variable $\mathbf{x} = P\mathbf{y}$, the quadratic form (3.3.1) becomes

$$\tfrac{1}{2}(P\mathbf{y})^T A P \mathbf{y} - \mathbf{b}^T P \mathbf{y} = \tfrac{1}{2}\mathbf{y}^T D \mathbf{y} - (P^T \mathbf{b})^T \mathbf{y} \tag{3.3.14}$$

and thus is of the form (3.3.13) in the $\mathbf{y}$ variables. It is easy to see that the conjugate direction method in the original $\mathbf{x}$ variables is equivalent to univariate relaxation in the $\mathbf{y}$ variables (Exercise 3.3-6) and it follows from the previous discussion that the quadratic function will be minimized in at most n steps.

Alternatively, one can give a direct proof of 3.3.1 as follows. First, observe that

$$(A\mathbf{x}^{k+1} - \mathbf{b})^T\mathbf{p}^j = (A\mathbf{x}^k - \alpha_k A\mathbf{p}^k - \mathbf{b})^T\mathbf{p}^j = (A\mathbf{x}^k - \mathbf{b})^T\mathbf{p}^j - \alpha_k(A\mathbf{p}^k)^T\mathbf{p}^j$$

Thus, using the conjugacy of $\mathbf{p}^j$ and $\mathbf{p}^k$ if $j \neq k$ and the definition (3.3.5) of α_k if $j = k$, it follows that

$$\begin{aligned}(A\mathbf{x}^{k+1} - \mathbf{b})^T\mathbf{p}^j &= (A\mathbf{x}^k - \mathbf{b})^T\mathbf{p}^j, \qquad j < k \\ &= 0, \qquad j = k\end{aligned}$$

Therefore

$$(A\mathbf{x}^n - \mathbf{b})^T\mathbf{p}^j = (A\mathbf{x}^{n-1} - \mathbf{b})^T\mathbf{p}^j = \cdots = (A\mathbf{x}^{j+1} - \mathbf{b})^T\mathbf{p}^j = 0$$

for $j = 0, \ldots, n-1$, and since $\mathbf{p}^0, \ldots, \mathbf{p}^{n-1}$ are linearly independent we must have $A\mathbf{x}^n - \mathbf{b} = 0$. It may happen that $A\mathbf{x}^m = \mathbf{b}$ for some $m < n$, in which case we are already at the solution.

In order to utilize a conjugate direction method we must, of course, have the vectors $\mathbf{p}^j$ which satisfy (3.3.12). One classical set of conjugate vectors are the eigenvectors of A. Let $\mathbf{x}_1, \ldots, \mathbf{x}_n$ be n orthogonal eigenvectors with corresponding eigenvalues $\lambda_1, \ldots, \lambda_n$. Then

$$\mathbf{x}_i^T A\mathbf{x}_j = \lambda_j \mathbf{x}_i^T \mathbf{x}_j = 0, \qquad i \neq j$$

so that the $\mathbf{x}_i$ are conjugate with respect to A. This does not provide a practical approach to a conjugate direction method, however, since finding all the eigenvectors of A is a much more substantial problem than solving the linear system.

Another possibility is to orthogonalize a set of linearly independent vectors $\mathbf{y}_1, \ldots, \mathbf{y}_n$ with respect to the inner product $(\mathbf{x}, \mathbf{y}) = \mathbf{x}^T A\mathbf{y}$. This, however, is also too costly.

The Conjugate Gradient Method

The most efficient way, in general, to obtain a set of conjugate direction vectors to be used in solving $A\mathbf{x} = \mathbf{b}$ is the *conjugate gradient method*, which generates the direction vectors in conjunction with carrying out the conjugate direction method. The basic algorithm is given below, in which we use the inner product $(\mathbf{x}, \mathbf{y}) = \mathbf{x}^T\mathbf{y}$, and $\mathbf{r}^k \equiv \mathbf{b} - A\mathbf{x}^k$ is the residual at the kth step. In this form of the algorithm, we have replaced the computation of α_k as given by (3.3.5) by another formulation that is equivalent in the conjugate gradient algorithm. The validity of this replacement is discussed in Appendix 3.

Choose $\mathbf{x}^0$, set $\mathbf{p}^0 = \mathbf{r}^0$, compute $(\mathbf{r}^0, \mathbf{r}^0)$

For $k = 0, 1, \ldots$

$$\alpha_k = -(\mathbf{r}^k, \mathbf{r}^k)/(\mathbf{p}^k, A\mathbf{p}^k) \tag{3.3.15a}$$

$$\mathbf{x}^{k+1} = \mathbf{x}^k - \alpha_k \mathbf{p}^k \tag{3.3.15b}$$

$$\mathbf{r}^{k+1} = \mathbf{r}^k + \alpha_k A\mathbf{p}^k \tag{3.3.15c}$$

$$\text{if } \|\mathbf{r}^{k+1}\|_2^2 \geqslant \varepsilon, \text{ continue} \tag{3.3.15d}$$

$$\beta_k = (\mathbf{r}^{k+1}, \mathbf{r}^{k+1})/(\mathbf{r}^k, \mathbf{r}^k) \tag{3.3.15e}$$

$$\mathbf{p}^{k+1} = \mathbf{r}^{k+1} + \beta_k \mathbf{p}^k \tag{3.3.15f}$$

In the above, (3.3.15c) computes the next residual since

$$\mathbf{r}^{k+1} = \mathbf{b} - A\mathbf{x}^{k+1} = \mathbf{b} - A(\mathbf{x}^k - \alpha_k \mathbf{p}^k)$$

Because $A\mathbf{p}^k$ is already known, this saves the multiplication $A\mathbf{x}^k$. The final two steps compute the next conjugate direction; it is shown in Appendix 3 that these $\mathbf{p}^k$ actually are conjugate. Thus, on the basis of Theorem 3.3.1, the conjugate gradient iterates converge, in exact arithmetic, to the solution of $A\mathbf{x} = \mathbf{b}$ in no more than n steps. We note that there are several other equivalent formulations of the conjugate gradient algorithm; some of these are given in Appendix 3.

The conjugate gradient method is invariably used in conjunction with some form of preconditioning, and this will be the topic of the next section.

Parallel and Vector Implementation

The methods of this section rely heavily on inner products and the matrix-vector multiplication $A\mathbf{p}$. In particular, we next tabulate the overall computational requirements of the conjugate gradient algorithm:

(3.3.15a): $A\mathbf{p}^k$, one inner product, [$(\mathbf{r}^k, \mathbf{r}^k)$ is already known] one divide

(3.3.15b): one linked triad

(3.3.15c): one linked triad ($A\mathbf{p}^k$ is already known)

(3.3.15d): one inner product, one compare

(3.3.15e): one divide [$(\mathbf{r}^{k+1}, \mathbf{r}^{k+1})$ and $(\mathbf{r}^k, \mathbf{r}^k)$ are already known]

(3.3.15f): one linked triad

Thus the total requirements for one iteration are

evaluation of $A\mathbf{p}^k$

two inner products

three linked triads

two scalar divides, one scalar compare

We have used in (3.3.15d) one of many possible convergence tests. The advantage of (3.3.15d) is that it requires virtually no extra work since $(\mathbf{r}^{k+1}, \mathbf{r}^{k+1})$ will be needed on the next step if convergence has not occurred. In contrast, a test on $\|\mathbf{x}^{k+1} - \mathbf{x}^k\| = \|\alpha_k \mathbf{p}^k\|$ requires splitting the linked triad of (3.3.15b) as well as a separate computation of the norm.

For any substantial problem, the computational requirements of the conjugate gradient algorithm will be dominated by the evaluation of $A\mathbf{p}^k$ and it is critical that this computation be done efficiently. For example, if A is a diagonally sparse matrix, it is likely on vector machines that A should be stored by diagonals, and the matrix-vector multiplication-by-diagonals technique of Section 1.3 be used. In those cases where A contains at least some constant diagonals further savings can be made. As an extreme example, consider the matrix (3.1.7) for the discrete Poisson equation on a square. Here, if the vector **p** is partitioned commensurately with A we have

$$A\mathbf{p} = \begin{bmatrix} T & -I & & \\ -I & \ddots & \ddots & \\ & \ddots & \ddots & -I \\ & & -I & T \end{bmatrix} \begin{bmatrix} \mathbf{p}_1 \\ \mathbf{p}_2 \\ \vdots \\ \mathbf{p}_{N-1} \\ \mathbf{p}_N \end{bmatrix} = \begin{bmatrix} T\mathbf{p}_1 - \mathbf{p}_2 \\ T\mathbf{p}_2 - \mathbf{p}_1 - \mathbf{p}_3 \\ \vdots \\ T\mathbf{p}_{N-1} - \mathbf{p}_{N-2} - \mathbf{p}_N \\ T\mathbf{p}_N - \mathbf{p}_{N-1} \end{bmatrix} \quad (3.3.16)$$

The products $T\mathbf{p}_i$ can in turn be evaluated by

$$T\mathbf{p}_i = 4\mathbf{p}_i - \begin{bmatrix} 0 \\ p_{i1} \\ \vdots \\ p_{iN-1} \end{bmatrix} - \begin{bmatrix} p_{i2} \\ \vdots \\ p_{iN} \\ 0 \end{bmatrix} \quad (3.3.17)$$

This evaluates the product in a way analogous to carrying out the Jacobi iteration on a grid using vectors of length N. Indeed, since $A = D(I - H)$, where D is the main diagonal of A and H is the Jacobi iteration matrix, A and H have exactly the same structure with the exception that the main diagonal of H is zero. Hence, multiplication of a vector by A or H involves exactly the same considerations. In particular, carrying out (3.3.16) using vectors of length $O(N^2)$ would require using the same techniques as with Jacobi's method, namely, working with vectors of length $O((N+2)^2)$, which would include the boundary positions, or evaluating $A\mathbf{p}$ by matrix-vector multiplication by diagonals. The details of these approaches are left to Exercise 3.3-7.

The above discussion pertains primarily to the implementation of the conjugate gradient method on vector computers. On parallel systems, the assignment of the components $\mathbf{x}^k$ to the processors also determines the assignment of $\mathbf{p}^k$ and $\mathbf{r}^k$. For example, for the discrete Poisson equation, or a more general equation, the assignment of a grid point to a processor implies that the components of $\mathbf{x}^k$, $\mathbf{p}^k$, and $\mathbf{r}^k$ associated with that grid point are all assigned to the same processor. Then, the multiplication of $A\mathbf{p}^k$ follows exactly the discussion of Jacobi's method in Section 3.1, with $\mathbf{p}^k$ now playing the role of the unknowns. The inner products are done by a fan-in and α_k must then be broadcast to the other processors. The linked triad operations for $\mathbf{x}^{k+1}$, $\mathbf{p}^{k+1}$, and $\mathbf{r}^{k+1}$ are particularly efficient since each processor just updates the components it is assigned. Thus, the key aspect in implementing the conjugate gradient algorithm efficiently on parallel machines is the multiplication $A\mathbf{p}^k$, which depends on the structure of A. However, even if this can be done efficiently, the necessary inner products may degrade the parallel efficiency somewhat.

Domain Decomposition

One of the advantages of the conjugate gradient method is that the coefficient matrix A does not need to be known explicitly as long as the product $A\mathbf{p}$ can be evaluated. We will illustrate this by means of the domain decomposition technique discussed in Section 2.3.

Consider the system (2.3.22), which we rewrite here under the assumption that the coefficient matrix is symmetric so that $C_i = B_i^T$:

$$\begin{bmatrix} A_1 & & & & B_1 \\ & A_2 & & & \vdots \\ & & \ddots & & \\ & & & A_p & B_p \\ B_1^T & & \cdots & B_p^T & A_S \end{bmatrix} \begin{bmatrix} \mathbf{x}_1 \\ \vdots \\ \\ \mathbf{x}_p \\ \mathbf{x}_S \end{bmatrix} = \begin{bmatrix} \mathbf{b}_1 \\ \vdots \\ \\ \mathbf{b}_p \\ \mathbf{b}_S \end{bmatrix} \tag{3.3.18}$$

In order to carry out Step 2 of the domain decomposition algorithm of Figure 2.3-16 we need the system $\hat{A}\mathbf{x}_S = \hat{\mathbf{b}}$, where

$$\hat{A} = A_S - \sum_{i=1}^{p} B_i^T A_i^{-1} B_i, \qquad \hat{\mathbf{b}} = \mathbf{b}_S - \sum_{i=1}^{p} B_i^T A_i^{-1} \mathbf{b}_i \tag{3.3.19}$$

In many problems, the matrices A_i and B_i will be sparse, but that need not be the case for the $B_i^T A_i^{-1} B_i$ and, hence, $\hat{A}$. In order to utilize the original sparsity, we will apply the conjugate gradient method to $\hat{A}\mathbf{x}_S = \hat{\mathbf{b}}$ without explicitly forming $\hat{A}$. Recall that we showed in Section 2.3 that $\hat{A}$ is symmetric positive definite if the coefficient matrix of (3.3.18) is positive definite.

Let $\mathbf{p}$ be any direction vector. Then we can compute $\hat{A}\mathbf{p}$ without forming $\hat{A}$ as shown in Figure 3.3-4. The formation of the vector $\hat{\mathbf{b}}$ is done in a similar way. The solution of the systems in Step 2 could be accomplished by using the Choleski decompositions $A_i = L_i L_i^T$ needed for the remainder of the algorithm of Figure 2.3-16.

Recall that in the algorithm of Figure 2.3-16 the formation of $\hat{A}$ and $\hat{\mathbf{b}}$ and the solution of $\hat{A}\mathbf{x}_S = \hat{\mathbf{b}}$ were the only parts that were not necessarily highly parallel. If we use the conjugate gradient method for $\hat{A}\mathbf{x}_S = \hat{\mathbf{b}}$, with the computation of $\hat{A}\mathbf{p}$ as described above, then the whole algorithm is potentially highly parallel. Assuming that we utilize p processors, each of

Step 1. Form $\mathbf{y}_i = B_i\mathbf{p}$, $i = 1, \ldots, p$
Step 2. Solve the systems $A_i\mathbf{z}_i = \mathbf{y}_i$, $i = 1, \ldots, p$
Step 3. Form $\mathbf{w}_i = B_i^T\mathbf{z}_i$, $i = 1, \ldots, p$.
Step 4. Form $\hat{A}\mathbf{p} = A_S\mathbf{p} - \sum_{i=1}^{p} \mathbf{w}_i$.

Figure 3.3-4. Formation of $\hat{A}\mathbf{p}$.

Steps 1 to 3 in Figure 3.3-4 can be distributed across the processors and done in parallel with no communication. Only Step 4, as well as the computation of the inner products in the conjugate gradient method, will require fan-ins and communication.

Exercises 3.3

1. If A is symmetric and positive definite, verify that the minimum of the quadratic function (3.3.1) is taken on at the solution of $A\mathbf{x} = \mathbf{b}$.
2. Show that (3.3.5) gives the minimum for (3.3.3).
3. If $\hat{\alpha}_k$ is the minimizer of $Q(x^k - \alpha \mathbf{p}^k)$, verify that $Q(\mathbf{x}^k - \omega\hat{\alpha}p^k) < Q(x^k)$ if and only if $0 < \omega < 2$.
4. Show that if A has diagonal elements equal to 1 and $\alpha_k = 1$, then (3.3.11) is the Jacobi iteration.
5. Verify that univariate relaxation minimizes the quadratic function (3.3.13) in n steps.
6. Let $P = (\mathbf{p}^0, \ldots, \mathbf{p}^{n-1})$ where the $\mathbf{p}^i$ are conjugate with respect to A. Note that $P^{-1}\mathbf{p}^{i-1} = \mathbf{e}_i$ and thus a conjugate direction step $\mathbf{x}^i = \mathbf{x}^{i-1} - \alpha_{i-1}\mathbf{p}^{i-1}$ in the variables $\mathbf{y} = P^{-1}\mathbf{x}$ is

$$\mathbf{y}^i = \mathbf{y}^{i-1} - \alpha_{i-1}\mathbf{e}_i$$

   Show that this is identical to the ith univariate relaxation step applied to (3.3.14).
7. Discuss the implementation of (3.3.16) using vectors of length $O((N+2)^2)$ by incorporating the boundary values, and using vectors of length $O(N^2)$ by matrix-vector multiplication by diagonals.

References and Extensions 3.3

1. Minimization methods are discussed (for serial computers) in a variety of books. See, for example, Dennis and Schnabel [1983], which includes nonquadratic problems. The older book by Forsythe and Wasow [1960] contains much information on the classical methods, such as univariate relaxation and steepest descent, for quadratic problems.
2. The conjugate gradient method was developed by Hestenes and Stiefel [1952], who analyzed its basic properties. Since, in exact arithmetic, the conjugate gradient method converges to the exact solution in n steps, it can be viewed as a direct method and an alternative to Choleski factorization. But rounding error destroys this finite convergence property, and it was soon realized that the method was not a viable alternative to factorization for dense systems. Reid [1971], however, following earlier work of Engeli *et al.* [1959], observed that for certain large sparse problems, such as arise from discretized partial differential equations, conjugate gradient methods gave sufficiently good convergence in far less than

n iterations. This spurred a revival of interest in the method, especially when preconditioning is used, as will be discussed in the next section. An annotated bibliography of papers concerning the conjugate gradient method in the period 1948–1976 is given in Golub and O'Leary [1987].

3. It is shown in Appendix 3 that the 2-norms of the error vectors, $\hat{\mathbf{x}} - \mathbf{x}^k$, decrease monotonically. The same is not necessarily true for $\|\mathbf{r}^k\|_2$, the 2-norm of the residuals. Indeed, Hestenes and Stiefel [1952] give an example in which the norms of the residuals increase at every step except the last! Although this is an extreme case, it is not unusual to see $\|\mathbf{r}^k\|_2$ fluctuate as the iteration proceeds. However, in the norm defined by $\|\mathbf{r}\|^2 = \mathbf{r}^T A^{-1}\mathbf{r}$, the residuals do decrease at each iteration. This follows from

$$\mathbf{r}^T A^{-1}\mathbf{r} = (\mathbf{b} - A\mathbf{x})^T A^{-1}(\mathbf{b} - A\mathbf{x}) = \mathbf{b}^T A^{-1}\mathbf{b} - 2\mathbf{x}^T\mathbf{b} + \mathbf{x}^T A\mathbf{x}$$

and it is this quadratic form that the conjugate gradient method decreases at each step.

4. Block conjugate gradient algorithms can be formulated and have the potential of requiring less communication time. See O'Leary [1987] for further discussion and a parallel implementation.

5. Theoretical results on the rate of convergence of the conjugate gradient method are given in van der Sluis and van der Vorst [1986], and Axelsson and Lindskog [1986].

3.4. The Preconditioned Conjugate Gradient Method

The result of the previous section that conjugate direction methods converge in at most n steps is of only theoretical interest, and we wish to view the conjugate gradient algorithm as an iterative method. In this case, an estimate of the rate of convergence is given by

$$\|\mathbf{x}^k - \hat{\mathbf{x}}\|_2 \leq 2\sqrt{\kappa}\,\alpha^k \|\mathbf{x}^0 - \hat{\mathbf{x}}\|_2 \tag{3.4.1}$$

where $\hat{\mathbf{x}}$ is the exact solution of the system,

$$\alpha = (\sqrt{\kappa} - 1)/(\sqrt{\kappa} + 1) \tag{3.4.2}$$

and

$$\kappa = \operatorname{cond}(A) = \|A\|_2 \|A^{-1}\|_2 = \lambda_n/\lambda_1 \tag{3.4.3}$$

In (3.4.3), κ is the condition number of A in the l_2 norm, and it is assumed that A is symmetric positive definite with eigenvalues $\lambda_n \geq \cdots \geq \lambda_1 > 0$. The estimate (3.4.1) is proved in Appendix 3.

Note that $\alpha = 0$ when $\kappa = 1$, and $\alpha \to 1$ as $\kappa \to \infty$. Hence, the larger κ, the closer α will be to 1 and the slower will be the rate of convergence. This leads to the concept of *preconditioning* A by the congruence transformation

$$\hat{A} = SAS^T \tag{3.4.4}$$

where S is a nonsingular matrix chosen so that $\text{cond}(\hat{A}) < \text{cond}(A)$. The system to be solved is then

$$\hat{A}\hat{\mathbf{x}} = \hat{\mathbf{b}} \tag{3.4.5}$$

where $\hat{\mathbf{x}} = S^{-T}\mathbf{x}$ and $\hat{\mathbf{b}} = S\mathbf{b}$.

In principle, we can achieve a perfectly conditioned matrix $\hat{A}$ by the choice $S = A^{-1/2}$ so that $\hat{A} = I$ and the system (3.4.5) is trivial. Of course, this is not a practical approach.

The simplest preconditioning is with a diagonal matrix $S = D$; unfortunately, this will usually not reduce the condition number enough to be useful, and in the sequel we will examine several other types of preconditioners. As opposed to the use of a diagonal matrix, these more complicated preconditioning matrices will tend to destroy the sparsity of the matrix A. For this reason, as well as to avoid the work necessary to carry out the congruence (3.4.4), we will formulate the conjugate gradient method so as to work with the original matrix A, although the sequence of conjugate gradient iterates will be that for the system (3.4.5). To see how this can be done, we first write the conjugate gradient algorithm (3.3.15) for the system (3.4.5):

Choose $\hat{\mathbf{x}}^0$, set $\hat{\mathbf{p}}^0 = \hat{\mathbf{r}}^0$.

For $k = 0, 1, \ldots$

$$\hat{\alpha}_k = -(\hat{\mathbf{r}}^k, \hat{\mathbf{r}}^k)/(\hat{\mathbf{p}}^k)^T\hat{A}\hat{\mathbf{p}}^k \tag{3.4.6a}$$

$$\hat{\mathbf{x}}^{k+1} = \hat{\mathbf{x}}^k - \hat{\alpha}_k\hat{\mathbf{p}}^k \tag{3.4.6b}$$

$$\hat{\mathbf{r}}^{k+1} = \hat{\mathbf{r}}^k + \hat{\alpha}_k\hat{A}\hat{\mathbf{p}}^k \tag{3.4.6c}$$

$$\hat{\beta}_k = (\hat{\mathbf{r}}^{k+1}, \hat{\mathbf{r}}^{k+1})/(\hat{\mathbf{r}}^k, \hat{\mathbf{r}}^k) \tag{3.4.6d}$$

$$\hat{\mathbf{p}}^{k+1} = \hat{\mathbf{r}}^{k+1} + \hat{\beta}_k\hat{\mathbf{p}}^k \tag{3.4.6e}$$

The vectors $\mathbf{x}^k = S^T\hat{\mathbf{x}}^k$ are the preconditioned conjugate gradient iterates expressed in terms of the original variables, and we wish to find the algorithm corresponding to (3.4.6) that the $\mathbf{x}^k$ will satisfy. It suffices to examine the first step ($k = 0$) of (3.4.6). We have

$$\hat{\mathbf{r}}^0 = \hat{\mathbf{b}} - \hat{A}\hat{\mathbf{x}}^0 = S\mathbf{b} - SAS^TS^{-T}\mathbf{x}^0 = S\mathbf{r}^0$$

The vector $\hat{\mathbf{p}}^0$ satisfies $\hat{\mathbf{p}}^0 = S^{-T}\mathbf{p}^0$ and $\hat{\mathbf{p}}^0 = \hat{\mathbf{r}}^0$. Hence

$$(\hat{\mathbf{p}}^0, \hat{A}\hat{\mathbf{p}}^0) = (S^{-T}\mathbf{p}^0)^T SAS^TS^{-T}\mathbf{p}^0 = (\mathbf{p}^0)^T A\mathbf{p}^0$$

and

$$(\hat{\mathbf{r}}^0, \hat{\mathbf{r}}^0) = (S\mathbf{r}^0)^T(S\mathbf{r}^0) = (S^TS\mathbf{r}^0)^T\mathbf{r}^0$$

The last relation suggests that we define a new quantity

$$\tilde{\mathbf{r}}^0 = S^TS\mathbf{r}^0 \tag{3.4.7}$$

and then

$$\hat{\alpha}_0 = -(\tilde{\mathbf{r}}^0, \mathbf{r}^0,)/(\mathbf{p}^0, A\mathbf{p}^0)$$

Multiplying (3.4.6b) by S^T and (3.4.6c) by S^{-1} gives

$$\mathbf{x}^1 = \mathbf{x}^0 - \hat{\alpha}_0\mathbf{p}^0$$

and

$$\mathbf{r}^1 = \mathbf{r}^0 + \hat{\alpha}_0 S^{-1}SAS^TS^{-T}\mathbf{p}^0 = \mathbf{r}^0 + \hat{\alpha}_0 A\mathbf{p}^0$$

For (3.4.6d), we note that

$$(\hat{\mathbf{r}}^i, \hat{\mathbf{r}}^i) = (S\mathbf{r}^i)^T S\mathbf{r}^i = (\tilde{\mathbf{r}}^i)^T\mathbf{r}^i, \qquad i = 0, 1$$

and thus

$$\hat{\beta}_0 = (\tilde{\mathbf{r}}^1, \mathbf{r}^1)/(\tilde{\mathbf{r}}^0, \mathbf{r}^0)$$

Finally, we multiply (3.4.6e) by S^T to obtain

$$\mathbf{p}^1 = S^TS\mathbf{r}^1 + \hat{\beta}_0\mathbf{p}^0 = \tilde{\mathbf{r}}^1 + \hat{\beta}_0\mathbf{p}^0$$

The above formulas give the basis for writing the preconditioned conjugate gradient algorithm in terms of the matrix A. Before stating the algorithm explicitly, however, we discuss the computation of the auxiliary vector $\tilde{\mathbf{r}}$ of (3.4.7). If we knew the preconditioning matrix S, or the matrix S^TS, we could obtain $\tilde{\mathbf{r}}$ by the indicated matrix multiplication. However, our approach to obtaining the preconditioning will be through a symmetric positive definite matrix M that approximates A, and the matrix S is defined only implicitly by

$$(S^TS)^{-1} = M \tag{3.4.8}$$

Since we will usually know M, and not M^{-1}, the computation of the auxiliary vector of (3.4.7) will be obtained by solving the linear system $M\tilde{\mathbf{r}} = \mathbf{r}$. It is in these terms that we give the following *Preconditioned Conjugate Gradient* (*PCG*) method:

Choose $\mathbf{x}^0$. Set $\mathbf{r}^0 = \mathbf{b} - A\mathbf{x}^0$. Solve $M\tilde{\mathbf{r}}^0 = \mathbf{r}^0$. Set $\mathbf{p}^0 = \tilde{\mathbf{r}}^0$.

For $k = 0, 1, \ldots$

$$\alpha_k = -(\tilde{\mathbf{r}}^k, \mathbf{r}^k)/(\mathbf{p}^k, A\mathbf{p}^k) \tag{3.4.9a}$$

$$\mathbf{x}^{k+1} = \mathbf{x}^k - \alpha_k \mathbf{p}^k \tag{3.4.9b}$$

$$\mathbf{r}^{k+1} = \mathbf{r}^k + \alpha_k A\mathbf{p}^k \tag{3.4.9c}$$

Test for convergence (3.4.9d)

$$\text{Solve } M\tilde{\mathbf{r}}^{k+1} = \mathbf{r}^{k+1} \tag{3.4.9e}$$

$$\beta_k = (\tilde{\mathbf{r}}^{k+1}, \mathbf{r}^{k+1})/(\tilde{\mathbf{r}}^k, \mathbf{r}^k) \tag{3.4.9f}$$

$$\mathbf{p}^{k+1} = \tilde{\mathbf{r}}^{k+1} + \beta_k \mathbf{p}^k \tag{3.4.9g}$$

In the above algorithm, we have dropped the caret previously used on the α_k and β_k. Note that if $M = I$, the preconditioned conjugate gradient algorithm reduces to the conjugate gradient algorithm of (3.3.15).

Since the auxiliary system $M\tilde{\mathbf{r}} = \mathbf{r}$ must be solved at each conjugate gradient iteration, it is critical that this system be "easy" to solve. On the other hand, in order that the preconditioning be effective, we want M to be a "good" approximation to A. Clearly, the two requirements are in conflict since the more closely M approximates A, the more likely that the system $M\hat{\mathbf{r}} = \mathbf{r}$ will be nearly as difficult to solve as the system $A\mathbf{x} = \mathbf{b}$.

We next discuss in what sense we wish M to approximate A. By (3.4.4) and (3.4.8), the preconditioned matrix $\hat{A}$ satisfies

$$S^T\hat{A}S^{-T} = S^TSA = M^{-1}A \tag{3.4.10}$$

Therefore, the matrix $M^{-1}A$ is similar to $\hat{A}$ and thus

$$\text{cond}(\hat{A}) = \lambda_{\max}(M^{-1}A)/\lambda_{\min}(M^{-1}A) \tag{3.4.11}$$

the ratio of the maximum and minimum eigenvalues of $M^{-1}A$. Thus, since our goal is to reduce the condition number of $\hat{A}$ as much as possible, the criterion for the approximation of A by M is that the ratio of the largest and smallest eigenvalues of $M^{-1}A$ be as small as possible. In principle, we can make $\text{cond}(\hat{A}) = 1$ by choosing $M = A$, but, of course, this is not a practical choice. We shall consider in the sequel several approaches to obtaining the matrix M, including truncated series expansions and incomplete factorizations. We first give a short discussion of the convergence test (3.4.9d).

If we use the same test, $\|\mathbf{r}^{k+1}\|_2^2 < \varepsilon$, as in the conjugate gradient algorithm (3.3.15), we have to calculate $(\mathbf{r}^{k+1}, \mathbf{r}^{k+1})$ separately since it no longer appears in the algorithm. What does appear is $(\tilde{\mathbf{r}}^{k+1}, \mathbf{r}^{k+1}) = (M^{-1}\mathbf{r}^{k+1}, \mathbf{r}^{k+1})$, which is an inner product defined by M^{-1}. We can consider using this quantity for the convergence test, but it can indicate convergence even though $\|\mathbf{r}^{k+1}\|_2$ is larger than we would like. Therefore, it may be prudent to make an auxiliary check on $\|\mathbf{r}^{k+1}\|_2$ itself once the other test has been passed. In this case, (3.4.9d) would take the form

$$\begin{gathered}\text{If } (\tilde{\mathbf{r}}^{k+1}, \mathbf{r}^{k+1}) \geq \varepsilon, \text{ continue}\\ \text{Otherwise, if } (\mathbf{r}^{k+1}, \mathbf{r}^{k+1}) \geq \varepsilon, \text{ continue}\end{gathered} \tag{3.4.12}$$

This convergence test would be placed after (3.4.9e), which forms $\tilde{\mathbf{r}}^{k+1}$. Note that the use of $(\tilde{\mathbf{r}}^{k+1}, \mathbf{r}^{k+1})$ may cause more iterations than using $(\mathbf{r}^{k+1}, \mathbf{r}^{k+1})$ although this is usually not the case.

Truncated Series Preconditioning

We now consider a rather general approach to preconditioning, which is based on the following series representation of A^{-1}.

3.4.1. THEOREM. *Let A be an $n \times n$ nonsingular matrix and $A = P - Q$ a splitting of A such that P is nonsingular and the largest eigenvalue in magnitude of $P^{-1}Q$ is less than 1. Then, with $H = P^{-1}Q$,*

$$A^{-1} = \left(\sum_{k=0}^{\infty} H^k\right)P^{-1} \tag{3.4.13}$$

PROOF By the Neumann expansion (See Appendix 4), the series for H converges and equals $(I - H)^{-1}$. But $A = P - Q = P(I - H)$ so the result follows. □

On the basis of (3.4.13), we can consider the matrices defined by

$$M = P(I + H + \cdots + H^{m-1})^{-1},$$
$$M^{-1} = (I + \cdots + H^{m-1})P^{-1} \tag{3.4.14}$$

to be approximations to A and A^{-1}, respectively. Thus, the solution of the auxiliary system $M\tilde{\mathbf{r}} = \mathbf{r}$ is effected by

$$\tilde{\mathbf{r}} = M^{-1}\mathbf{r} = (I + H + \cdots + H^{m-1})P^{-1}\mathbf{r} \tag{3.4.15}$$

This is not, however, to be carried out by forming the matrix H and the indicated truncated series. Rather, we recognize (Exercise 3.4-1) that $\tilde{\mathbf{r}}$, as given by (3.4.15), is the result of applying m steps of the iterative method

$$P\mathbf{r}^{i+1} = Q\mathbf{r}^{i} + \mathbf{r}, \qquad i = 0, 1, \ldots, m - 1, \qquad \mathbf{r}^{0} = 0 \tag{3.4.16}$$

and setting $\tilde{\mathbf{r}} = \mathbf{r}^m$. We call (3.4.16) the *subsidiary* iterative method.

We next give some specific preconditioners based on this approach. For the point Jacobi method, P is the diagonal of A and (3.4.16) amounts to taking m Jacobi iterations. This gives the *m-step Jacobi PCG Method* in which (3.4.9e) becomes

$$\text{Do } m \text{ Jacobi iterations on } A\mathbf{r} = \mathbf{r}^{k+1} \text{ to obtain } \tilde{\mathbf{r}}^{k+1} \tag{3.4.17}$$

In (3.4.17) the starting value for the iteration is zero, as in (3.4.16). The solution of $M\tilde{\mathbf{r}}^0 = \mathbf{r}^0$ would be obtained in the same way.

Mechanistically, we can use the Gauss–Seidel and SOR iterations to carry out (3.4.16). However, these methods do not yield a symmetric and positive definite matrix M, as required by the theory. Indeed, for the Gauss–Seidel method and $m = 1$, $M = P = D - L$ where D is the diagonal of A and $-L$ the strictly lower triangular part. Hence, M is not symmetric for $m = 1$ and this property persists for the SOR method and for all $m > 1$ (Exercise 3.4–2). This difficulty can be overcome by use of the SSOR method, and m SSOR iterations gives the *m-step SSOR PCG method.* In this case, the Jacobi iterations (3.4.17) are replaced by SSOR iterations.

We need to verify that use of the SSOR method does indeed give a symmetric positive definite matrix M. This will be a consequence of the following theorem, which will also apply to the Jacobi and other preconditionings. It is stated in terms of the matrix

$$R = (I + H + \cdots + H^{m-1})P^{-1} \tag{3.4.18}$$

which is well defined whenever P^{-1} exists. Note that $M = R^{-1}$ when R is nonsingular.

3.4.2. THEOREM. *Let $A = P - Q$ be symmetric positive definite with P symmetric and nonsingular. With $H = P^{-1}Q$, the matrix R of* (3.4.18) *is symmetric and for any $m \geqslant 1$*

1. *If m is odd, R is positive definite if and only if P is positive definite;*
2. *If m is even, R is positive definite if and only if $P + Q$ is positive definite.*

PROOF. Since A and P are symmetric, Q is also symmetric and it is easy to see (Exercise 3.4-3) that each term of

$$R = P^{-1} + P^{-1}QP^{-1} + P^{-1}QP^{-1}QP^{-1} + \cdots + P^{-1}QP^{-1} \cdots P^{-1}QP^{-1}$$

is symmetric. Thus, R is symmetric.

Since $H = P^{-1}(P - A) = I - P^{-1}A$ and A is positive definite, a result on the eigenvalues of the product of symmetric matrices (See Theorem A.2.7 in Appendix 2) guarantees that the eigenvalues of $P^{-1}A$, and hence those of H, are real. Let

$$T = I + H + \cdots + H^{m-1}$$

and let λ be any eigenvalue of H. Then the corresponding eigenvalue of T is

$$1 + \lambda + \cdots + \lambda^{m-1} = \begin{cases} (1 - \lambda^m)/(1 - \lambda), & \lambda \neq 1 \\ m, & \lambda = 1 \end{cases}$$

and the ratio is positive if m is odd. Hence, for odd m all eigenvalues of T are positive. Assume next that P is positive definite. Then, since $T = RP$, Theorem A.2.7 in Appendix 2 shows that R is positive definite. Conversely, if R is positive definite then, again, A.2.7 shows that P is positive definite and this completes the case of odd m.

Next, assume that m is even. Since $P + PH = P + P(P^{-1})Q = P + Q$, we have that

$$\begin{aligned} R &= P^{-1}(P + PH + PH^2 + PH^3 + \cdots + PH^{m-1})P^{-1} \\ &= P^{-1}[(P + PH) + (P + PH)H^2 + \cdots + (P + PH)H^{m-2}]P^{-1} \\ &= P^{-1}(P + Q)(I + H^2 + \cdots + H^{m-2})P^{-1} \end{aligned}$$

Defining now $T = I + H^2 + \cdots + H^{m-2}$, it follows that the eigenvalues of T contain only even powers of the eigenvalues of H and hence are positive. Set $\hat{R} = PRP = (P + Q)T$. If $P + Q$ is positive definite, then

$T = (P + Q)^{-1}\hat{R}$ and, by A.2.7, $\hat{R}$ is positive definite. Conversely, if $\hat{R}$ is positive definite, then $P + Q$ must be nonsingular and, again, A.2.7 ensures that $P + Q$ is positive definite. But $\hat{R}$ is congruent to R and is positive definite if and only if R is positive definite. □

We next discuss the seemingly strange condition of Theorem 3.4.2 that the matrix $P + Q$ be positive definite. For Jacobi's method, $P = D$, the diagonal of A, and $Q = D - A$. Then the requirement that $P + Q$ be positive definite is just the necessary and sufficient condition that the Jacobi iteration be convergent, as stated in 3.1.2. This convergence result for Jacobi's method is a special case of the following more general convergence theorem for iterations defined by the splitting $A = P - Q$. Recall (see Appendix 2) that the necessary and sufficient condition for the corresponding iteration $\mathbf{x}^{k+1} = P^{-1}Q\mathbf{x}^k + \mathbf{d}$ to be convergent for all $\mathbf{x}^0$ is that the spectral radius $\rho(P^{-1}Q) < 1$. The proof of the following convergence theorem is given in Appendix 2.

3.4.3. THEOREM. *Let $A = P - Q$ and assume that A and P are symmetric and positive definite. Then $\rho(P^{-1}Q) < 1$ if and only if $P + Q$ is positive definite.*

Theorem 3.4.2 showed that the matrix R of (3.4.18) is positive definite for all m if and only if both P and $P + Q$ are positive definite. Thus, on the basis of 3.4.3 we can restate 3.4.2 in the following way.

3.4.4. THEOREM. *Let $A = P - Q$ be symmetric and positive definite and P symmetric and nonsingular. With $H = P^{-1}Q$, the matrix R of* (3.4.18) *is symmetric and positive definite for all $m \geq 1$ if and only if P is positive definite and $\rho(H) < 1$.*

As noted previously, the matrix P must be symmetric in order that R be symmetric for all m. Then, by 3.4.4, for M to be positive definite requires that P be positive definite and that $\rho(H) < 1$, this latter condition implying that the iterative method defined by the splitting $P - Q$ be convergent. In particular, since Jacobi's method can fail to be convergent for positive definite matrices A, the corresponding M need not be positive definite for even m.

On the other hand, for the SSOR method, we can show that the matrix M is always positive definite, assuming as before that A is symmetric positive definite. If $A = D - L - L^T$, it is shown in Appendix 2 that the matrices P and Q for the SSOR iteration are

$$\begin{aligned} P &= [\omega(2-\omega)]^{-1}(D - \omega L)D^{-1}(D - \omega L^T), \\ Q &= [\omega(2-\omega)]^{-1}[(1-\omega)D + \omega L]D^{-1}[(1-\omega)D + \omega L^T] \end{aligned} \tag{3.4.19}$$

Since D is positive definite, P and Q are positive definite for any $0 < \omega < 2$ except for $\omega = 1$ in which case Q is only semidefinite (Exercise 3.4-5). In any case $P + Q$ is positive definite, and we conclude from 3.4.2 that the following result holds.

3.4.5. THEOREM. *If A is symmetric and positive definite and $0 < \omega < 2$, then the matrices R of* (3.4.18) *and M of* (3.4.14) *obtained from the SSOR iteration are positive definite for all m.*

We next examine the effect on the rate of convergence of preconditioners of the form (3.4.14). By (3.4.11), we can estimate $\text{cond}(\hat{A})$ if we can estimate the largest and smallest eigenvalues of $M^{-1}A$. Using (3.4.14) and writing A as $P - Q$ we have

$$\begin{aligned} M^{-1}A &= (I + H + \cdots + H^{m-1})P^{-1}(P - Q) \\ &= (I + H + \cdots + H^{m-1})(I - H) = I - H^m \end{aligned} \tag{3.4.20}$$

If $\lambda_1, \ldots, \lambda_n$ are the eigenvalues of H, it follows that the eigenvalues of $M^{-1}A$ are $1 - \lambda_i^m$, $i = 1, \ldots, n$. In the sequel, we will assume that P is symmetric and positive definite. Then, as in the proof of 3.4.2, the eigenvalues of H are real and we assume that $\lambda_1 \leqslant \cdots \leqslant \lambda_n$. If $\delta = \min|\lambda_i|$, it is easy to show (Exercise 3.4-6) that

$$\text{cond}(\hat{A}) = \frac{\lambda_{\max}(M^{-1}A)}{\lambda_{\min}(M^{-1}A)} = \begin{cases} \dfrac{1 - \lambda_1^m}{1 - \lambda_n^m} & \text{if } \lambda_1 \geqslant 0 \quad \text{or} \quad \lambda_1 < 0 \\ & \quad \text{and} \quad m \text{ odd} \\ \dfrac{1 - \delta^m}{1 - \lambda_n^m} & \text{if } \lambda_1 < 0,\ |\lambda_n| \geqslant |\lambda_1|, \\ & \quad m \text{ even} \\ \dfrac{1 - \delta^m}{1 - \lambda_1^m} & \text{if } \lambda_1 < 0,\ |\lambda_1| \geqslant |\lambda_n|, \\ & \quad m \text{ even} \end{cases} \tag{3.4.21}$$

For SSOR preconditioning we need only the first case of (3.4.21).

3.4.6. THEOREM. *Assume that A is symmetric positive definite and $0 < \omega < 2$. Let $\lambda_1 \leqslant \cdots \leqslant \lambda_n$* be the eigenvalues of the SSOR iteration matrix *H. Then $\lambda_1 \geqslant 0$ and for m-step SSOR preconditioning*

$$\text{cond}(\hat{A}) = \frac{1 - \lambda_1^m}{1 - \lambda_n^m} \tag{3.4.22}$$

which is a strictly decreasing function of m.

PROOF. As previously noted, the matrix P for the SSOR iteration is positive definite and Q is positive definite if $\omega \neq 1$. In this case, by Theorem A.2.7, the eigenvalues of H are positive. In the case that $\omega = 1$, Q is only positive semidefinite and the eigenvalues of H are non-negative (Exercise 3.4-8). In either case, $\lambda_1 \geq 0$ and (3.4.22) follows from the first part of (3.4.21). To show that $\text{cond}(\hat{A})$ is a strictly decreasing function of m we note that, by Theorem A.2.11, the SSOR iteration is convergent, so that $\lambda_n < 1$. Therefore,

$$\frac{1-\lambda_1^{m+1}}{1-\lambda_n^{m+1}} = \frac{(1-\lambda_1)(1+\cdots+\lambda_1^m)}{(1-\lambda_n)(1+\cdots+\lambda_n^m)}$$

$$< \frac{(1-\lambda_1)(1+\cdots+\lambda_1^{m-1})}{(1-\lambda_n)(1+\cdots+\lambda_n^{m-1})} = \frac{1-\lambda_1^m}{1-\lambda_n^m} \qquad (3.4.23)$$

where the proof of the inequality is left to Exercise 3.4-7. □

The proof of Theorem 3.4.6 shows that $\text{cond}(\hat{A})$ is a decreasing function of m for any iterative method for which the eigenvalues of H satisfy $0 \leq \lambda_1 \leq \cdots \leq \lambda_n < 1$. Otherwise, this may not be so, as shown by the following example of m-step Jacobi preconditioning applied to the discrete Poisson equation (3.1.5). By Exercise 3.1-21, the eigenvalues of the Jacobi iteration matrix are

$$\frac{1}{2}\left(\cos\frac{j\pi}{N+1} + \cos\frac{k\pi}{N+1}\right), \qquad j, k = 1, \cdots, N$$

In particular, the largest and smallest eigenvalues satisfy

$$\lambda_n = \cos\frac{\pi}{N+1} = -\cos\frac{N\pi}{N+1} = -\lambda_1,$$

and

$$\delta = \begin{cases} \cos\dfrac{N\pi}{2(N+1)}, & N \text{ even}, \\ 0, & N \text{ odd} \end{cases}$$

Table 3.4-1. Condition Numbers for Jacobi Preconditioning

m	1	2	3	4
cond($\hat{A}$)	830	208	276	104

Thus, by (3.4.21)

$$\text{cond}(\hat{A}) = \begin{cases} \dfrac{1-\lambda_1^m}{1-\lambda_n^m} = \dfrac{1+\lambda_n^m}{1-\lambda_n^m}, & m \text{ odd} \\ \dfrac{1-\delta^m}{1-\lambda_n^m}, & m \text{ even} \end{cases}$$

For example, for $N = 44$, $\lambda_n \doteq 0.9976$ and $\delta \doteq 0$ so that

$$\text{cond}(\hat{A}) \doteq \begin{cases} \dfrac{1+(0.9976)^m}{1-(0.9976)^m}, & m \text{ odd} \\ \dfrac{1}{1-(0.9976)^m}, & m \text{ even} \end{cases}$$

These values are shown in Table 3.4-1 for the first few values of m. We note that the condition number for $m = 1$ is just the condition number for A itself. This is because the main diagonal of A is all 4's and one step of Jacobi preconditioning only scales the matrix by these 4's and has no effect on the condition number. (See Exercise 3.4-10.) As shown in Table 3.4-1, cond($\hat{A}$) does not decrease monotonically as m increases. The effect of this on the m-step Jacobi preconditioned conjugate gradient method applied to the discrete Poisson equation is that, generally, using m steps with m odd results in more iterations than using $m - 1$ steps. For example, Table 3.4-2 shows the number of iterations required for the system when $N = 89$.

Polynomial Preconditioning

The matrix R in (3.4.18) is a particular polynomial in the matrix H, times P^{-1}. This suggests considering more general polynomials in H and defining R by

$$R = (\alpha_0 I + \alpha_1 H + \cdots + \alpha_{m-1} H^{m-1}) P^{-1} \tag{3.4.24}$$

Table 3.4-2. Iterations for m-Step Jacobi PCG

m	0	1	2	3	4	5	6	7	8
Iterations	45	45	23	36	21	30	18	26	16

The idea now is to choose $\alpha_0, \ldots, \alpha_{m-1}$ to retain the positive definiteness of R and to minimize the ratio of the largest and smallest eigenvalues of $RA = M^{-1}A$.

Computationally, the parameters α_i are introduced into the iterative process by accumulating the appropriate linear combinations of the iterates as follows. If, at the kth stage of the PCG method, the subsidiary iterative process is represented by $\mathbf{r}^{i+1} = H\mathbf{r}^i + P^{-1}\mathbf{r}$ with $\mathbf{r}^0 = 0$, the computation of $\tilde{\mathbf{r}}$ is

$$\tilde{\mathbf{r}}^m = (\cdots((\mu_0\mathbf{r}^1) + \mu_1\mathbf{r}^2) + \cdots + \mu_{m-1}\mathbf{r}^m) \tag{3.4.25}$$

where the parentheses indicate that $\tilde{\mathbf{r}}^m$ is accumulated by linked triad operations as the iterates $\mathbf{r}^i$ are produced, and only one additional vector of storage is required. The constants μ_i in (3.4.25) are related to the α_i of (3.4.24) by

$$\mu_i + \mu_{i+1} + \cdots + \mu_{m-1} = \alpha_i, \qquad i = 0, \ldots, m-1 \tag{3.4.26}$$

so that $\mu_{m-1} = \alpha_{m-1}$, $\mu_{m-2} = \alpha_{m-2} - \mu_{m-1}$, and so on. The relation (3.4.26) arises as follows. As noted previously, the representation of $\mathbf{r}^{i+1}$ is $(I + \cdots + H^i)P^{-1}\mathbf{r}$. If we put this into (3.4.25) and equate the coefficients of $H^iP^{-1}\mathbf{r}$ in (3.4.24) and (3.4.25) we obtain (3.4.26). The detailed verification of this is left to Exercise 3.4-12.

We now discuss how to obtain, in principle, the parameters $\alpha_0, \ldots, \alpha_{m-1}$. Under the conditions of 3.4.2, the matrix R of (3.4.24) is symmetric since the α_i do not affect the symmetry argument of 3.4.2. Since $H = I - P^{-1}A$, we can write

$$RA = [\alpha_0 I + \alpha_1(I - P^{-1}A) + \cdots + \alpha_{m-1}(I - P^{-1}A)^{m-1}]P^{-1}A$$

so that RA is a polynomial in $P^{-1}A$. We wish to choose the α_i so that the eigenvalues of RA are positive. Since R is symmetric and A is symmetric positive definite, Theorem A.2.7 then guarantees that R, and hence M, is positive definite. In addition, we wish to choose the α_i so that the eigenvalues of RA are as close to 1 as possible in some sense, and one way to proceed is the following. Let $[a, b]$ be an interval that contains the eigenvalues of $P^{-1}A$ and let q be the polynomial

$$q(\lambda) = [\alpha_0 + \alpha_1(1-\lambda) + \cdots + \alpha_{m-1}(1-\lambda)^{m-1}]\lambda$$

Then $RA = q(P^{-1}A)$ and the spectrum of RA is contained in $\{q(\lambda): \lambda \in [a, b]\}$. Hence, one criterion for choosing the α_i so as to minimize the ratio of the largest and smallest eigenvalues of RA is to minimize $\int_a^b [1 - q(\lambda)]^2\, d\lambda$ over $\alpha_0, \ldots, \alpha_{m-1}$.

To show the effect of polynomial preconditioning, we give in Table 3.4-3 the results of calculations on a "plane stress" problem. In the first column is the number of steps of SSOR preconditioning and the P denotes polynomial preconditioning. I is the number of iterations and T is the running time on a CDC Cyber 203 vector computer. Results are given for three successively larger problems, and as the size of the problem increases, the degree of the polynomial that gives the minimum running time also increases.

The Eisenstat Trick

In Section 3.2, we described the Conrad–Wallach trick for reducing the computation in carrying out the SSOR iteration, and we can use that procedure for SSOR preconditioning. We next describe another way, which we call the *Eisenstat trick*, to reduce the amount of computation. The assumption is that the preconditioning matrix M is of the form

$$M = ST^{-1}S^T \tag{3.4.27}$$

where S is usually lower triangular and T is diagonal. For example, with one-step SSOR preconditioning, we have from (3.4.14) and (3.4.19) that $M = P$ and

$$S = (\hat{D} - L), \qquad \hat{D} = \omega^{-1}D, \qquad T = \omega^{-1}(2 - \omega)D \tag{3.4.28}$$

Table 3.4-3. Polynomial Preconditioning Results

m	I	T	I	T	I	T
0	112	0.133	157	0.213	536	3.293
1	52	0.129	66	0.184	214	2.373
2	38	0.143	50	0.208	152	2.428
$2P$	<u>31</u>	<u>0.116</u>	40	0.167	118	1.885
3	31	0.155	39	0.216	124	2.585
$3P$	24	0.121	30	0.167	88	1.836
4	28	0.176	36	0.249	108	2.780
$4P$	22	0.138	<u>24</u>	<u>0.166</u>	67	1.726
5	25	0.188	33	0.274	97	2.969
$5P$	19	0.143	20	0.167	56	1.716
6	23	0.202	30	0.290	89	3.158
$6P$	18	0.159	18	0.175	47	1.670
$7P$					43	1.739
$8P$					<u>36</u>	<u>1.634</u>

The idea is to consider another preconditioned conjugate gradient method applied to the system

$$\hat{A}\hat{\mathbf{x}} = \hat{\mathbf{b}}, \qquad \hat{A} = S^{-1}AS^{-T}, \qquad \hat{\mathbf{x}} = S^T\mathbf{x}, \qquad \hat{\mathbf{b}} = S^{-1}\mathbf{b} \tag{3.4.29}$$

It is easy to see (Exercise 3.4.9) that the application of the PCG method with the preconditioning matrix M of (3.4.27) is equivalent to the PCG method with preconditioning matrix T^{-1} applied to the system $\hat{A}\hat{\mathbf{x}} = \hat{\mathbf{b}}$. In terms of this new system, the PCG method takes the form

$$\hat{\mathbf{r}}^0 = S^{-1}(\mathbf{b} - A\mathbf{x}^0), \qquad \hat{\mathbf{p}}^0 = \mathbf{q}^0 = T\hat{\mathbf{r}}^0$$

For $k = 0, 1, \ldots$

$$\hat{\alpha}_k = -(\hat{\mathbf{r}}^k, \mathbf{q}^k)/(\hat{\mathbf{p}}^k, \hat{A}\hat{\mathbf{p}}^k)$$

$$\mathbf{x}^{k+1} = \mathbf{x}^k - \hat{\alpha}_k S^{-T}\hat{\mathbf{p}}^k \tag{3.4.30}$$

$$\hat{\mathbf{r}}^{k+1} = \hat{\mathbf{r}}^k + \hat{\alpha}_k \hat{A}\hat{\mathbf{p}}^k$$

$$\mathbf{q}^{k+1} = T\hat{\mathbf{r}}^{k+1}$$

$\hat{\beta}_k$, $\hat{\mathbf{p}}^{k+1}$ as usual

Note that in (3.4.30) we retain the original variables $\mathbf{x}^k$ rather than the $\hat{\mathbf{x}}^k$. We shall return to this point in a moment.

The key consideration now is the evaluation of $\hat{A}\hat{\mathbf{p}}$ in terms of the original matrix A. If $A = D - L - L^T$, then we can write A in the form

$$A = S + S^T - K, \qquad K = S + S^T + L + L^T - D \tag{3.4.31}$$

Setting $\mathbf{t} = S^{-T}\hat{\mathbf{p}}$, we have

$$\hat{A}\hat{\mathbf{p}} = S^{-1}AS^{-T}\hat{\mathbf{p}} = S^{-1}(S + S^T - K)S^{-T}\hat{\mathbf{p}} = \mathbf{t} + S^{-1}(\hat{\mathbf{p}} - K\mathbf{t}) \tag{3.4.32}$$

Thus, the evaluation of $\hat{A}\hat{\mathbf{p}}$ requires the evaluation of $K\mathbf{t}$ plus the solution of the systems

$$S^T\mathbf{t} = \hat{\mathbf{p}}, \qquad S\mathbf{w} = \hat{\mathbf{p}} - K\mathbf{t} \tag{3.4.33}$$

But corresponding systems with coefficient matrices S and S^T need to be solved to carry out the preconditioning at each step by the matrix M of (3.4.27). Hence, the Eisenstat trick will be a more efficient formulation provided that multiplication by K is more efficient than multiplication by A. Note that the quantity $S^{-T}\hat{\mathbf{p}}^k$ in the update of $\mathbf{x}^k$ is simply the current $\mathbf{t}$ computed in (3.4.33). Since this is known, it allows us to work in the original variables $\mathbf{x}^k$ with no additional computation.

In the application of the Eisenstat trick to one-step SSOR preconditioning, S is given by (3.4.28) so that by (3.4.31)

$$K = \hat{D} - L + \hat{D} - L^T + L + L^T - D = \omega^{-1}(2 - \omega)D \qquad (3.4.34)$$

Thus, the additional work for the formation of $\hat{A}\hat{\mathbf{p}}$ requires only a multiplication by a diagonal matrix and two vector additions.

Parallel and Vector Implementation

We next discuss the parallel and vector implementation of the PCG methods considered so far. The primary such method is the m-step SSOR PCG method, but we will begin with the m-step Jacobi PCG method. We have discussed in the previous section the implementation of the basic conjugate gradient method, and in Section 3.1 the implementation of the Jacobi iterations. It is now a question of combining these two.

Consider first a vector computer that requires long vectors for efficiency. Then the Jacobi iterations to carry out the preconditioner should be done using vectors as long as possible. For boundary value problems, we would use the techniques discussed in Section 3.1 to achieve this. As was noted in the previous section, this strategem would also be used for evaluation of the matrix-vector product $A\mathbf{p}^k$ needed for the conjugate gradient iteration.

For SSOR preconditioning, the Jacobi iterations would be replaced by SSOR iterations. We saw in Section 3.2 that in order to do SSOR iterations with long vectors we would use the red-black ordering of the grid points. For more general problems for which the red-black ordering does not suffice, the multicolor orderings of Section 3.2 would be used.

We consider next a local memory parallel system. For either Jacobi or SSOR preconditioning, we distribute the unknowns to the processors as discussed in Section 3.1 and indicated in Figure 3.1-4. We also distribute the vectors $\mathbf{p}$ and $\mathbf{r}$ in the conjugate gradient iteration in the same fashion. The multiplication $A\mathbf{p}^k$ and the computation of the inner products and linked triads in the conjugate gradient iteration is done as discussed in Section 3.3, and the preconditioning is carried out as in Section 3.1 for Jacobi and Section 3.2 for SSOR.

Incomplete Choleski Factorization

We now begin another important approach to preconditioning which is based on *incomplete factorizations* of the matrix A. If LL^T is the Choleski factorization of the symmetric positive definite matrix A and A is sparse, then the factor L is generally much less sparse than A because of fill-in. By an *incomplete Choleski factorization* we shall mean a relation of the form

$$A = LL^T + R \tag{3.4.35}$$

where L is again lower triangular but $R \neq 0$. One way to obtain such incomplete factorizations is to suppress the fill-in, or part of it, that occurs during the Choleski factorization. A simple example is the following. The matrix

$$L = 2^{-1/2}\begin{bmatrix} 2 & & \\ 1 & 3^{1/2} & \\ 1 & -3^{-1/2} & 2^{3/2}3^{-1/2} \end{bmatrix} \tag{3.4.36}$$

is the Choleski factor of

$$A = \begin{bmatrix} 2 & 1 & 1 \\ 1 & 2 & 0 \\ 1 & 0 & 2 \end{bmatrix} \tag{3.4.37}$$

and the (3, 2) element has filled in. If we wish an incomplete factorization that has zeros in the same positions as A, we could set to zero those elements in the Choleski factor in positions corresponding to zero elements in A. Thus, an incomplete factor for (3.4.37) would be the same as the L of (3.4.36) except the (3, 2) element would be zero. This approach has the disadvantage that all of the work of the Choleski decomposition would be done, and it is precisely this work, as well as the need for additional storage, that we wish to avoid. Hence, we desire not to compute any elements of L in positions corresponding to zero elements of A. This leads to the following *incomplete Choleski no-fill factorization* [IC(0)] principle:

$$\begin{aligned} &\text{if } a_{ij} \neq 0, \qquad \text{do the Choleski calculation of } l_{ij} \\ &\text{if } a_{ij} = 0, \qquad \text{set } l_{ij} = 0 \end{aligned} \tag{3.4.38}$$

An algorithm for (3.4.38) is given in Figure 3.4-1. Note that if the "if" statement in Figure 3.4-1 is removed, then this is a complete factorization.

$$l_{11} = a_{11}^{1/2}$$
For $i = 2$ to n
For $j = 1$ to $i - 1$
If $a_{ij} = 0$ then $l_{ij} = 0$ else

$$l_{ij} = \left(a_{ij} - \sum_{k=1}^{j-1} l_{ik}l_{jk}\right) \Big/ l_{jj} \tag{3.4.39}$$

$$l_{ii} = \left(a_{ii} - \sum_{k=1}^{i-1} l_{ik}^2\right)^{1/2}$$

Figure 3.4-1. Incomplete Choleski factorization.

If the incomplete Choleski algorithm of Figure 3.4-1 is applied to the matrix (3.4.37), then the incomplete factor is

$$L = 2^{-1/2}\begin{bmatrix} 2 & & \\ 1 & 3^{1/2} & \\ 1 & 0 & 3^{1/2} \end{bmatrix}$$

Note that the (3, 3) element has now changed, compared with (3.4.36), as a consequence of the (3, 2) element being set to zero.

The no-fill principle is a special case of the following more general way to specify incomplete factorizations. Let $S = \{(i, j)\}$ be a given index set where i and j are between 1 and n. Then (3.4.38) is replaced by

$$\begin{aligned} &\text{if } (i, j) \in S, \text{ do the Choleski calculation of } l_{ij} \text{ by (3.4.39)} \\ &\text{if } (i, j) \notin S, \text{ set } l_{ij} = 0 \end{aligned} \tag{3.4.40}$$

If $S = \{(i, j)\colon a_{ij} \neq 0\}$, then (3.4.40) reduces to the no-fill principle (3.4.38). However, by suitable choice of S, the no-fill principle can be relaxed to allow a certain amount of fill and there are many such possibilities. For example, if A is a diagonally sparse matrix, one common approach is to allow the incomplete factor L to have a few more nonzero diagonals than A itself (counting only the number of diagonals of A on one side of the main diagonal, of course). In particular, for a five-diagonal matrix, such as the Poisson matrix (3.1.7), the *$IC(h, k)$ principle* allows $h + k$ diagonals below the main diagonal of L. This is illustrated in Figure 3.4-2, where it is assumed that A has two nonzero diagonals below the main diagonal. Then, $h - 1$ additional diagonals are allowed to fill adjacent to the first subdiagonal, and $k - 1$ additional diagonals adjacent to the last diagonal. Thus, the IC(1, 1) principle is just the no-fill principle. Several other fill strategies are possible by suitable choices of the set S.

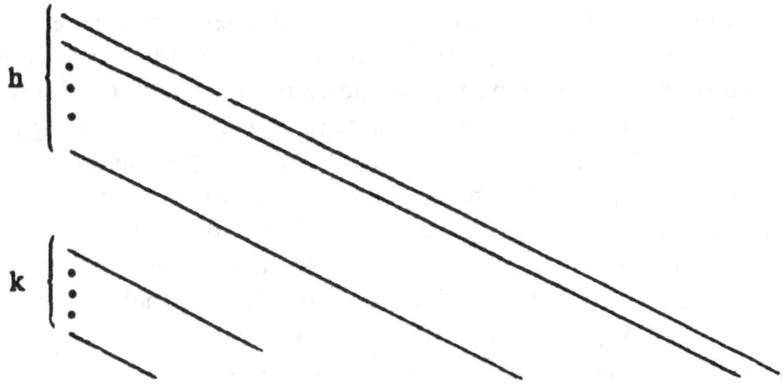

Figure 3.4-2. The IC(h, k) principle.

If LL^T is an incomplete decomposition, then the matrix $R = A - LL^T$ is necessarily nonzero. However, zero elements of R may occur in a predetermined fashion. An incomplete decomposition is *regular* with respect to the set S if $r_{ij} = 0$ whenever $(i, j) \in S$. It is always the case that an incomplete decomposition obtained from (3.4.40) is regular since the specification (3.4.39) for the calculation of l_{ij} implies that

$$r_{ij} = a_{ij} - \sum_{k=1}^{j} l_{ik} l_{jk} = 0 \tag{3.4.41}$$

However, incomplete factorizations that do not come from (3.4.40) need not be regular.

Incomplete Choleski decomposition of a symmetric positive definite matrix cannot necessarily be carried out, in contrast to a complete decomposition. It may fail because the square root of a negative number is required to compute a diagonal element, or, in case of the root-free form LDL^T, the matrix D may not be positive definite. We next state, without proof, a result that guarantees that an incomplete factorization can be carried out. Recall that an M matrix has nonpositive off-diagonal elements and a non-negative inverse (see Appendix 2, Definition A.2-12). A matrix A with positive diagonal elements is an H *matrix* if the matrix $\hat{A}$ with elements $\hat{a}_{ij} = -|a_{ij}|$, $i \neq j$, and $\hat{a}_{ii} = a_{ii}$ is an M matrix.

3.4.7. Theorem. *If A is a symmetric H-matrix, then for any choice of the set S, the incomplete factorization* (3.4.40) *can be carried out.*

In case the conditions of 3.4.7 are not satisfied, the incomplete decomposition may fail for a symmetric positive definite matrix, and there have been several suggested remedies for this. Suppose that at the ith stage

$l_{ii}^2 \leq 0$, which would require the square root of a negative number or would mean that L is singular if $l_{ii}^2 = 0$. One of the simplest ideas is to replace l_{ii}^2 by a positive number; one particular choice for this number is the previous diagonal element $l_{i-1,i-1}^2$. Another strategy is to replace l_{ii}^2 by $(\sum_{j<i} |l_{ij}|)^2$, which ensures that the new ith row of L is diagonally dominant.

A different approach is based on 3.4.7 and called the *shifting strategy*. Define $\hat{A} = \alpha I + A$. Clearly, for some choice of $\alpha > 0$, $\hat{A}$ is strictly diagonally dominant. Since a strictly diagonally dominant matrix with positive diagonal elements and nonpositive off-diagonal elements is an M-matrix (see A.2.16 in Appendix 2), it follows that $\hat{A}$ is an H matrix, and, hence, an incomplete Choleski factorization can be carried out.

Incomplete Decomposition for Special Matrices

In general, an incomplete factorization may require significant computation. In some important special cases, however, it is possible to obtain the factorization very easily. In the following, it will be convenient to work with the root-free form, LDL^T, of the Choleski decomposition, and to assume the no-fill strategy. The incomplete factorization algorithm is then given in Figure 3.4-3.

For $i = 1$ to n

$$d_i = a_{ii} - \sum_{k=1}^{i-1} l_{ik}^2 d_k \tag{3.4.42}$$

For $j = 1$ to $i - 1$

If $a_{ij} = 0$ then $l_{ij} = 0$ else

$$l_{ij} = \left(a_{ij} - \sum_{k=1}^{j-1} l_{ik} d_k l_{jk}\right) \Big/ d_j \tag{3.4.43}$$

Figure 3.4-3. No-fill incomplete LDL^T.

Consider now the block tridiagonal matrix

$$A = \begin{bmatrix} A_1 & B_1^T & & & \\ B_1 & \ddots & \ddots & & \\ & \ddots & \ddots & \ddots & \\ & & \ddots & \ddots & B_{N-1}^T \\ & & & B_{N-1} & A_N \end{bmatrix} \tag{3.4.44}$$

where the A_i are $N \times N$ and tridiagonal and the B_i are $N \times N$ and diagonal; thus, A is a five-diagonal matrix. Recall that this is the form of the discrete matrix for the Poisson equation (3.1.5) as well as the more general matrix (3.1.17). For a no-fill factorization, the matrix L will have nonzero elements only in those subdiagonal positions in which A has nonzero elements. Consider first the element $l_{i,i-N}$ corresponding to an element of a B_j. Since all elements in the ith row of L to the left of $l_{i,i-N}$ are zero, we have from (3.4.43) that

$$l_{i,i-N} = a_{i,i-N}/d_{i-N} \tag{3.4.45}$$

Similarly, by the no-fill strategy, the only nonzero element to the left of $l_{i,i-1}$ is $l_{i,i-N}$ and thus

$$l_{i,i-1} = (a_{i,i-1} - l_{i,i-N}d_{i-N}l_{i-1,i-N})/d_{i-1}$$

But, $l_{i-1,i-N}$ is the element in row $i-1$ directly above the element $l_{i,i-N}$ and must be zero. Hence

$$l_{i,i-1} = a_{i,i-1}/d_{i-1} \tag{3.4.46}$$

The elements of D are given by (3.4.42) as

$$d_i = a_{ii} - l_{i,i-N}^2 d_{i-N} - l_{i,i-1}^2 d_{i-1} \tag{3.4.47}$$

since the only nonzero off-diagonal elements of L in the ith row are $l_{i,i-1}$ and $l_{i,i-N}$. Using (3.4.45) and (3.4.46), we can also write (3.4.47) in the form

$$d_i = a_{ii} - a_{i,i-N}^2/d_{i-N} - a_{i,i-1}^2/d_{i-1} \tag{3.4.48}$$

Thus, in the case of a five-diagonal matrix of the form (3.4.44), the no-fill incomplete factorization is obtained very easily from (3.4.45), (3.4.46), and either (3.4.47) or (3.4.48). We note that the analogous formulas hold for a seven-diagonal matrix arising from a three-dimensional Poisson-type equation (Exercise 3.4-14). On the other hand, they do not hold if the matrices B_i in (3.4.44) are tridiagonal, such as is the case for the equation (3.2.24) (see Exercise 3.4.15).

The subdiagonal elements of L are just the corresponding elements of A, divided by an appropriate element of D. For this reason, it is possible to write the factorization as

$$L_1 D_1 L_1^T, \qquad \operatorname{diag}(L_1) = D_1^{-1} \tag{3.4.49}$$

In this form the subdiagonal elements of L_1 are exactly the corresponding elements of A (Exercise 3.4-16). If (3.4.49) is used, it may be beneficial to scale A so that $D_1 = I$. Then the preconditioning matrix M is just $M = (I + \hat{L})(I + \hat{L}^T)$, where $\hat{L}$ is strictly lower triangular. Details of this scaling are given in Exercise 3.4-17.

Block Methods

We turn next to block incomplete factorizations and assume that A is block tridiagonal as in (3.4.44). It is easy to verify (Exercise 3.4-18) that a (complete) block decomposition of A may be written as

$$A = (D + L)D^{-1}(D + L^T) \tag{3.4.50}$$

where

$$L = \begin{bmatrix} 0 & & & \\ B_1 & \ddots & & \\ & \ddots & & \\ & & B_{N-1} & 0 \end{bmatrix}, \qquad D = \begin{bmatrix} D_1 & & \\ & \ddots & \\ & & D_N \end{bmatrix} \tag{3.4.51}$$

and the D_i are given by

$$D_1 = A_1, \qquad D_i = A_i - B_{i-1}D_{i-1}^{-1}B_{i-1}^T, \qquad i = 2, \ldots, N \tag{3.4.52}$$

Now replace (3.4.52) by

$$D_1 = A_1, \qquad D_i = A_i - B_{i-1}C_{i-1}B_{i-1}^T, \qquad i = 2, \ldots, N \tag{3.4.53}$$

where C_{i-1} is an approximation to D_{i-1}^{-1}. Then, with L again given by (3.4.51),

$$M = (D + L)D^{-1}(D + L^T) \tag{3.4.54}$$

is an approximate, or incomplete, decomposition of A. There are several possible versions of this, depending on how the approximations C_i are made.

We now assume that the A_i are tridiagonal, the B_i are diagonal, A is an M matrix, and

$$\sum_{j \neq k} |a_{kj}| \leq a_{kk}, \qquad k = 1, \ldots, n$$

with strict inequality holding for at least one i. Under these assumptions, we will approximate the inverses of the D_i by tridiagonal matrices C_i in a way to be explained shortly. Then, by (3.4.53), the D_i are also tridiagonal. (The D_i^{-1}, however, will generally be full.) One basis for the approximation of D_i^{-1} is the following theorem, which we state without proof.

3.4.8. THEOREM. *Let T be an $m \times m$ irreducible nonsingular symmetric tridiagonal matrix. Then, there are two vectors* $\mathbf{u}$ *and* $\mathbf{v}$ *such that*

$$T^{-1} = \begin{bmatrix} u_1v_1 & u_1v_2 & \cdots & u_1v_m \\ u_1v_2 & u_2v_2 & \cdots & u_2v_m \\ \vdots & \vdots & & \vdots \\ u_1v_m & u_2v_m & \cdots & u_mv_m \end{bmatrix}$$

Moreover, if T is a strictly diagonally dominant M matrix, then

$$u_1 < u_2 < \cdots < u_m, \qquad v_1 > v_2 > \cdots > v_m \tag{3.4.55}$$

The inequalities (3.4.55) show that the elements T^{-1} decrease as one moves away from the main diagonal, which suggests that a small bandwidth approximation to T^{-1} may be satisfactory. It is possible to give fairly simple recurrence relations for the u_i and v_i but even if we wish to compute only the diagonal part of T^{-1} we need all the u_i and v_i. A simpler approximation is described next.

Assume that the diagonal elements of T are $a_1, \ldots, a_m$ and the off-diagonal elements are $b_1, \ldots, b_{m-1}$. If $T = LL^T$ is the Choleski factorization, then

$$L = \begin{bmatrix} \gamma_1 & & & \\ -\delta_1 & \ddots & & \\ & \ddots & \ddots & \\ & & -\delta_{m-1} & \gamma_m \end{bmatrix} \tag{3.4.56}$$

where

$$\gamma_1^2 = a_1, \qquad \delta_1\gamma_1 = b_1, \qquad \delta_{i-1}^2 + \gamma_i^2 = a_i, \qquad \delta_i\gamma_i = b_i, \qquad i \geq 2$$

Now $T^{-1} = L^{-T}L^{-1}$, and it is easy to verify (Exercise 3.4-19) that the first two diagonals of L^{-1} are

$$\begin{bmatrix} \gamma_1^{-1} & & & \\ \eta_1 & \gamma_2^{-1} & & \\ & \ddots & \ddots & \\ & & \eta_{m-1} & \gamma_m^{-1} \end{bmatrix} \tag{3.4.57}$$

where

$$\eta_i = \frac{\delta_i}{\gamma_i\gamma_{i+1}}, \qquad 1 \leq i \leq m-1$$

Thus, the first two diagonals of L^{-1} are computed relatively easily. If V is the approximation to L^{-1} consisting of these two diagonals, then $C = V^T V$ is tridiagonal and serves as an approximation to T^{-1}.

The Incomplete Choleski Conjugate Gradient Method

We consider next the use of incomplete Choleski factorizations as preconditioners for the conjugate gradient method. Let (3.4.35) be any incomplete factorization with L nonsingular. We then take the preconditioning matrix M of the preconditioned conjugate gradient (PCG) algorithm (3.4.9) to be

$$M = LL^T \tag{3.4.58}$$

Since L is nonsingular, M is symmetric and positive definite. The solution of the systems $M\tilde{\mathbf{r}} = \mathbf{r}$ in the PCG algorithm is carried out by solving the triangular systems

$$L\mathbf{x} = \mathbf{r}, \qquad L^T\tilde{\mathbf{r}} = \mathbf{x} \tag{3.4.59}$$

Note that the incomplete factorization will be done once and for all at the beginning of the PCG iteration and the factor L saved for use in solving the systems (3.4.59) at each step.

The above choice of M defines the general class of *incomplete Choleski preconditioned conjugate gradient* methods, denoted as ICCG methods. The way that the incomplete Choleski factorization is obtained further defines the method. Thus, for example, if the incomplete factorization is obtained by the no-fill principle (3.4.38), the corresponding conjugate gradient method is denoted by ICCG(0), or by ICCG(1, 1) in accord with Figure 3.4-2.

As already discussed, it is sometimes convenient to consider the root-free form of incomplete Choleski decomposition in which (3.4.35) is replaced by

$$A = LDL^T + R \tag{3.4.60}$$

where D is a positive diagonal matrix and L now has 1's on its main diagonal. With $M = LDL^T$,

$$L\mathbf{z} = \mathbf{r}, \qquad D\mathbf{x} = \mathbf{z}, \qquad L^T\tilde{\mathbf{r}} = \mathbf{x} \tag{3.4.61}$$

then replace the forward and back substitutions (3.4.59).

Parallel and Vector Implementation of ICCG

The parallel or vector implementation of the conjugate gradient method itself is the same as in Section 3.3. The issue now is the incomplete factorization and, more importantly, the forward and back solves (3.4.59) or (3.4.61) since these are done on each iteration. The vector and parallel properties of the Choleski factorization algorithms in Chapter 2 are very unsatisfactory for large sparse matrices of the type for which we wish to use the conjugate gradient iteration. Similar implementations of incomplete factorization will share this difficulty, and we wish to examine techniques to circumvent this problem.

We consider first the block tridiagonal matrix (3.4.44). For simplicity, we will assume that all A_i and B_i are $N \times N$, and that the A_i all have the same bandwidth α and the B_i have the same bandwidth β. As we have seen previously, the matrix A for the discrete Poisson equation (3.1.5) is of this form with $\alpha = 1$ and $\beta = 0$, while the matrix of the equations (3.2.24) has $\alpha = \beta = 1$.

We assume that we have obtained a no-fill incomplete factorization LL^T of A. Thus, $L + L^T$ has the same nonzero structure as A and we write L as

$$L = \begin{bmatrix} L_1 & & & \\ K_1 & L_2 & & \\ & \ddots & \ddots & \\ & & K_{N-1} & L_N \end{bmatrix}$$

where the L_i and K_i are all $N \times N$ with semibandwidths α and β, respectively. We have shown in (3.4.45)-(3.4.47) how to obtain such factorizations in the case $\alpha = 1$ and $\beta = 0$, and we concentrate now on solving the systems (3.4.59).

We illustrate the idea by means of the schematic of Figure 3.4-4, where it is assumed that $\alpha = 2$ and $\beta = 1$. The numbers in the column for $\mathbf{x}$ indicate the stage at which the corresponding equation can be solved. At steps 1 and 2 the first two equations are solved. At step 3, the third equation is solved but the $(N+1)$st equation can also be solved simultaneously since the solutions x_1 and x_2 are now available. At step 4, equations 4 and $N+2$ can be solved. Then, at step 5 equations 5, $N+3$, and $2N+1$ can all be solved, and so on. Each two steps an additional equation can be solved in parallel, up to a maximum of $O(N/2)$ equations. Note that we can start solving the second block of equations at step 3, the third block at step 5, and so on up to the Nth block at step $2N-1$. Hence, the solution will be complete after step $3N-2$. Since N^2 equations will have been solved, the average degree of parallelism is $N^2/(3N-2) = O(N/3)$. Exercise 3.4-20 considers the case in which (3.4.44) has M blocks and $N \times N$ matrices.

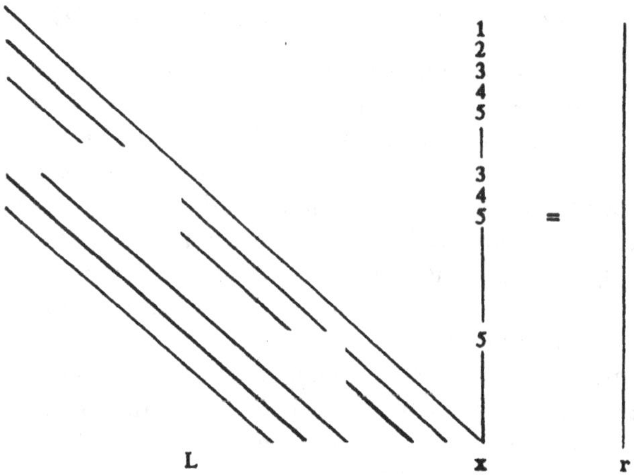

Figure 3.4-4. Solution of $Lx = r$.

The above scheme has been illustrated for bandwidths $\alpha = 2$ and $\beta = 1$. Note that the time at which successive blocks of equations can be started depends only on β and not on α; in particular, new blocks may be started every $\beta + 1$ time steps. For the Poisson equation (3.1.5), $\beta = 0$ so that a new block of equations can be started each time step while for the equations (3.2.24), $\beta = 1$ so a new block can be started every other time step. The key to the process is the uncoupling of the equations of each block after a few unknowns have been computed, and the strategy would not work for a dense banded matrix. Note the similarity of this procedure to the Lawrie-Sameh algorithm of Section 2.3.

The solution of the upper triangular system $L^T\tilde{\mathbf{r}} = \mathbf{x}$ is done in an analogous way, working from bottom to top.

It is useful to interpret the above process in terms of the grid of the differential equation and we will do this for the equation (3.2.24). The grid stencil for the discretization is given in Figure 3.2-7. The lower and upper triangular parts of A correspond to the grid stencils shown in Figure 3.4-5, where P is the center point of the stencil. Since the incomplete factors L and L^T have the same nonzero structure as the lower and upper triangular

Figure 3.4-5. Stencils for L and L^T.

parts of A, we can associate these with the stencils of Figure 3.4-5. In particular, the solution of the equation of $L\mathbf{x} = \mathbf{r}$ corresponding to the grid point P requires that the solution already be known at the west, south, southeast, and southwest neighbors of P. Similarly, the solution of the equation of $L^T\tilde{\mathbf{r}} = \mathbf{x}$ at P requires that the solution be known at the east, north, northeast, and northwest neighbors of P.

Consider now moving through the grid to solve $L\mathbf{x} = \mathbf{r}$, and solving each equation as soon as the necessary prior solutions are available. The order in which these equations can be solved is given in Figure 3.4-6a, where grid points with the same number, say k, imply that the solutions of the corresponding equations can all be done in parallel at the kth step. The solving order for $L^T\tilde{\mathbf{r}} = \mathbf{x}$ is indicated in less detail in Figure 3.4-6b; in this case we move through the grid in the opposite direction. If the grid is $N \times N$, it is clear that the process is equivalent to that described previously in terms of the system of Figure 3.4-4. Note that the solving orders in Figure 3.4-6 are analogous to the update times given in Figure 3.2-16 for the dataflow organization of SOR.

Multicolor Implementation

We next consider the implementation of ICCG algorithms on vector computers that require long vectors. This also yields algorithms with a very high degree of parallelism. For certain problems arising from the discretization of partial differential equations, we can give efficient implementations by again using multicolor orderings of the grid points.

(a)

13	14	15	16	17	18	19
11	12	13	14	15	16	17
9	10	11	12	13	14	15
7	8	9	10	11	12	13
5	6	7	8	9	10	11
3	4	5	6	7	8	9
1	2	3	4	5	6	7

(b)

7	6	5	4	3	2	1
		7	6	5	4	3
				7	6	5
						7

Figure 3.4-6. Solving orders for $Lx = \mathbf{r}$ and $L^T\tilde{\mathbf{r}} = \mathbf{x}$. (a) $L\mathbf{x} = \mathbf{r}$; (b) $L^T\tilde{\mathbf{r}} = \mathbf{x}$.

To illustrate the technique, we assume first that the coefficient matrix A is of the form

$$A = \begin{bmatrix} D_1 & C^T \\ C & D_2 \end{bmatrix} \tag{3.4.62}$$

where D_1 and D_2 are diagonal and C is diagonally sparse. Recall from Section 3.2 that this form of A can arise from a discretization of a partial differential equation using a red–black ordering of the grid points. The root-free form of a complete Choleski factorization of A is then

$$\begin{bmatrix} L_1 & \\ L_3 & L_2 \end{bmatrix}\begin{bmatrix} \hat{D}_1 & \\ & \hat{D}_2 \end{bmatrix}\begin{bmatrix} L_1^T & L_3^T \\ & L_2^T \end{bmatrix} = \begin{bmatrix} D_1 & C^T \\ C & D_2 \end{bmatrix} \tag{3.4.63}$$

where L_1 and L_2 are lower triangular with 1's on the main diagonal, and the $\hat{D}_i$ are diagonal. Equating terms in (3.4.63) gives

$$L_1\hat{D}_1L_1^T = D_1, \qquad L_3\hat{D}_1L_1^T = C, \qquad L_3\hat{D}_1L_3^T + L_2\hat{D}_2L_2^T = D_2 \tag{3.4.64}$$

The first relation of (3.4.64) implies (Exercise 3.4-21) that $L_1 = I$ and $\hat{D}_1 = D_1$. Thus,

$$L_1 = I, \qquad \hat{D}_1 = D_1, \qquad L_3 = CD_1^{-1} \tag{3.4.65}$$

Now consider an IC(0) factorization of (3.4.62) in which we denote the incomplete factorization by

$$M = \begin{bmatrix} L_1 & \\ L_3 & L_2 \end{bmatrix}\begin{bmatrix} \hat{D}_1 & \\ & \hat{D}_2 \end{bmatrix}\begin{bmatrix} L_1^T & L_3^T \\ & L_2^T \end{bmatrix} \tag{3.4.66}$$

Since (3.4.65) shows that a complete Choleski factorization gives L_1 and L_3 with no fill, L_1, L_3, and $\hat{D}_1$ as given by (3.4.65) are also the correct entries for the incomplete factorization (3.4.66). Moreover, L_2 of the incomplete factorization must be the identity since no fill is allowed and thus

$$\hat{D}_2 = \bar{D}_2 \equiv \text{diagonal part of } (D_2 - CD_1^{-1}C^T) \tag{3.4.67}$$

Therefore, the IC(0) factors of (3.4.66) are given by

$$L = \begin{bmatrix} I & \\ CD_1^{-1} & I \end{bmatrix}, \qquad D = \begin{bmatrix} D_1 & \\ & \bar{D}_2 \end{bmatrix} \tag{3.4.68}$$

In the computation of $\tilde{D}_2$ we would only do the computations necessary to obtain the diagonal elements.

If we partition the vectors **r**, **x**, and **z** of the systems (3.4.61) commensurately with A, then (3.4.61) becomes

$$\begin{bmatrix} I & \\ CD_1^{-1} & I \end{bmatrix}\begin{bmatrix} \mathbf{z}_1 \\ \mathbf{z}_2 \end{bmatrix} = \begin{bmatrix} \mathbf{r}_1 \\ \mathbf{r}_2 \end{bmatrix}, \quad \begin{bmatrix} D_1 & \\ & \tilde{D}_2 \end{bmatrix}\begin{bmatrix} \mathbf{x}_1 \\ \mathbf{x}_2 \end{bmatrix} = \begin{bmatrix} \mathbf{z}_1 \\ \mathbf{z}_2 \end{bmatrix},$$

$$\begin{bmatrix} I & D_1^{-1}C^T \\ & I \end{bmatrix}\begin{bmatrix} \tilde{\mathbf{r}}_1 \\ \tilde{\mathbf{r}}_2 \end{bmatrix} = \begin{bmatrix} \mathbf{x}_1 \\ \mathbf{x}_2 \end{bmatrix} \tag{3.4.69}$$

These systems may be solved to give

$$\begin{bmatrix} \mathbf{z}_1 \\ \mathbf{z}_2 \end{bmatrix} = \begin{bmatrix} \mathbf{r}_1 \\ \mathbf{r}_2 - CD_1^{-1}\mathbf{r}_1 \end{bmatrix}, \quad \begin{bmatrix} \mathbf{x}_1 \\ \mathbf{x}_2 \end{bmatrix} = \begin{bmatrix} D_1^{-1}\mathbf{z}_1 \\ \tilde{D}_2^{-1}\mathbf{z}_2 \end{bmatrix},$$

$$\begin{bmatrix} \tilde{\mathbf{r}}_1 \\ \tilde{\mathbf{r}}_2 \end{bmatrix} = \begin{bmatrix} \mathbf{x}_1 - D_1^{-1}C^T\mathbf{x}_2 \\ \mathbf{x}_2 \end{bmatrix}$$

or

$$\tilde{\mathbf{r}}_2 = \tilde{D}_2^{-1}(\mathbf{r}_2 - CD_1^{-1}\mathbf{r}_1), \qquad \tilde{\mathbf{r}}_1 = D_1^{-1}\mathbf{r}_1 - D_1^{-1}C^T\tilde{\mathbf{r}}_2 \tag{3.4.70}$$

Note that the formation of $\tilde{\mathbf{r}}$ requires only multiplication of vectors by diagonal matrices or by diagonally sparse matrices. Thus, the solution of the triangular systems (3.4.61) has been reduced to operations amenable to vector or parallel computation.

If the coefficient matrix cannot be put into the red–black form (3.4.62) but can be put into the form of a c-colored matrix (Section 3.2), the same technique can be applied. Let

$$A = \begin{bmatrix} D_1 & C_{21}^T & \cdots & C_{c1}^T \\ C_{21} & & \ddots & \vdots \\ \vdots & \ddots & & C_{cc-1}^T \\ C_{c1} & \cdots & C_{cc-1} & D_c \end{bmatrix} \tag{3.4.71}$$

where the D_i are diagonal and the C_{ij} are diagonally sparse. Corresponding to (3.4.63), the root-free block Choleski factorization of A is given by

$$A = \begin{bmatrix} L_{11} & & \\ \vdots & \ddots & \\ L_{c1} & \cdots & L_{cc} \end{bmatrix}\begin{bmatrix} \hat{D}_1 & & \\ & \ddots & \\ & & \hat{D}_c \end{bmatrix}\begin{bmatrix} L_{11}^T & \cdots & L_{c1}^T \\ & \ddots & \vdots \\ & & L_{cc}^T \end{bmatrix} \tag{3.4.72}$$

where the L_{ii} have 1's on the main diagonal. It then follows (Exercise 3.4.22) that the L_{ij} and D_i satisfy the relations

$$L_{jj}\hat{D}_jL_{jj}^T = D_j - \sum_{k=1}^{j-1} L_{jk}\hat{D}_kL_{jk}^T, \qquad j = 1, \ldots, c \tag{3.4.73}$$

and

$$L_{ij} = \left(C_{ij} - \sum_{k=1}^{j-1} L_{ik}\hat{D}_kL_{jk}^T\right)(\hat{D}_jL_{jj}^T)^{-1}, \qquad i > j \tag{3.4.74}$$

For a full Choleski decomposition, (3.4.73) requires a Choleski decomposition of the right-hand side of (3.4.73) to obtain the factors L_{jj} and $\hat{D}_j$. However, for an IC(0) decomposition of A, the diagonal factors L_{ii} must be identities and, since $\hat{D}_j$ must be diagonal, (3.4.73) becomes

$$\hat{D}_j = D_j - \text{diagonal part of}\left(\sum_{k=1}^{j-1} L_{jk}\hat{D}_kL_{jk}^T\right), \qquad j = 1, \ldots, c \tag{3.4.75}$$

Because L_{ij} is allowed to be nonzero only in the same diagonals as C_{ij}, the contributions to other diagonals in (3.4.74) are suppressed and we denote this by

$$L_{ij} = \left[C_{ij} - c\text{ diags}\left(\sum_{k=1}^{j-1} L_{ik}\hat{D}_kL_{jk}^T\right)\right]\hat{D}_j^{-1}, \qquad i > j \tag{3.4.76}$$

The equations (3.4.75) and (3.4.76), which generalize (3.4.68), give the IC(0) factorization of A. Note that this factorization is computed using only multiplications of diagonally sparse matrices. Note also that in (3.4.75) only the multiplications that contribute to diagonal elements need be done and, similarly, in (3.4.76) only multiplications that contribute to diagonals that correspond to nonzero diagonals of C_{ij} need be done.

The solution of the triangular systems (3.4.61) can also be carried out using only matrix multiplications. The system $L\mathbf{z} = \mathbf{r}$, with $\mathbf{z}$ and $\mathbf{r}$ partitioned according to L, is

$$\begin{bmatrix} I & & & \\ L_{21} & \ddots & & \\ \vdots & & \ddots & \\ L_{c1} & \cdots & L_{c,c-1} & I \end{bmatrix} \begin{bmatrix} \mathbf{z}_1 \\ \vdots \\ \mathbf{z}_c \end{bmatrix} = \begin{bmatrix} \mathbf{r}_1 \\ \vdots \\ \mathbf{r}_c \end{bmatrix} \tag{3.4.77}$$

since the diagonal blocks are identities. Thus

$$\mathbf{z}_j = \mathbf{r}_j - \sum_{k=1}^{j-1} L_{jk}\mathbf{z}_k, \qquad j = 1, \ldots, c$$

so that the computation of $\mathbf{z}$ requires only multiplication of vectors by diagonally sparse matrices. The solution of $L^T\tilde{\mathbf{r}} = \mathbf{x}$ is accomplished in a similar way.

Consider now the implementation on a vector computer. We assume that the matrix A is stored by diagonals, with only the nonzero diagonals of each C_{ij} (and D_j) being stored. The factor L is stored the same way. If A arose from a two-dimensional problem on an $N \times N$ grid, then A is $N^2 \times N^2$. Thus, the vector lengths in the incomplete decomposition and solution of the triangular systems are no more than $O(N^2/c)$, and diminish in length the farther a diagonal of C_{ij} or L_{ij} is removed from the main diagonal. For most problems this decrease in length will not be too bad, and as a working number we assume an average vector length of $l = O(N^2/2c)$. If $N = 100$, then $l = O(2500)$ for $c = 2$, the red-black ordering. For larger c, l is of course smaller, but for $c = 6$, l is still close to 1000.

In conjunction with the conjugate gradient method, the evaluation of $A\mathbf{p}$ may be done using still longer vector lengths if the nonzero diagonals of A line up across the C_{ij}. For example, the main diagonal of A is of length N^2.

The Eisenstat Trick

The Eisenstat trick, previously discussed in conjunction with SSOR, can also be used with incomplete Choleski preconditioning. We assume now that A has been scaled so that its main diagonal is the identity. Then the incomplete Choleski factors (3.4.68) for the case of the red-black ordering become

$$L = \begin{bmatrix} I & \\ C & I \end{bmatrix}, \qquad D = \begin{bmatrix} I & \\ & \bar{D}_2 \end{bmatrix}$$

The matrix K of (3.4.31) is then

$$K = L + L^T - \begin{bmatrix} & \\ C & \end{bmatrix} - \begin{bmatrix} & C^T \\ & \end{bmatrix} - I = I$$

Thus, in this case, the multiplication $K\mathbf{t}$ of the Eisenstat trick disappears, and we can obtain $A\hat{\mathbf{p}}^k$ with virtually no work beyond that already required for the preconditioning. As the number of colors increases, however, the situation becomes less favorable. In general, only the first block column of K will be zero off the main diagonal and the relative efficiency of the Eisenstat trick decreases as the number of colors increases.

Block Jacobi Preconditioning and Domain Decomposition

We can use the block (or line) Jacobi iteration as the subsidiary iterative method (3.4.16) and so obtain the *m-step block Jacobi* PCG method (Exercise 3.4-4); similarly for SSOR. We next relate block Jacobi preconditioning to domain decomposition in the following way. Suppose that the domain of a partial differential equation is decomposed as shown, for example, in Figure 3.1-14. As discussed in Section 3.1, we assume that all grid points are in some subdomain; that is, there is no separator set. If $A = (A_{ij})$ is the block form of the coefficient matrix corresponding to this domain decomposition, and there are p subdomains, the preconditioning matrix for the one-step block Jacobi PCG method is $M = \operatorname{diag}(A_{11}, \ldots, A_{pp})$. We may interpret this block Jacobi preconditioning as a simple form of *domain decomposition preconditioning*, in which the preconditioning consists of solving the subdomain problems with the unknowns in the other subdomains held at their values from the previous conjugate gradient iteration.

This approach to preconditioning has potentially excellent parallel and vector properties provided that the structure of the problem is suitable. For example, as we discussed in Section 3.1, the computation of a block Jacobi step can be done by "vectorizing across the systems." This implies that the matrices A_{ii} are all the same size and have the same structure (for example, tridiagonal). For parallel computation we would choose the subdomains so that the effort in solving the subdomain problems was roughly balanced.

Although the one-step block Jacobi preconditioned conjugate gradient method has potentially excellent parallel properties, the rate of convergence may be disappointingly poor. For example, for the Poisson problem and the one-step Jacobi line preconditioner, Exercise 3.4-11 shows that the condition number is reduced by only a factor of 2. Hence, it may be useful to use larger domains, for example, the subsquares of Figure 3.1-14. But, then, problems of the same nature as the original must be solved on each subdomain. Thus, if the original grid is, say, 1000×1000 and there are 16 subdomains as in Figure 3.1-14, then each subdomain will be 250×250 and the solution of these subproblems can be very costly. One approach to this problem is to obtain only approximate solutions to the subdomain problems by means of incomplete factorizations $L_i L_i^T$ of the A_{ii}. Then, in the preconditioning step of the PCG, we would solve the systems

$$L_i \mathbf{x}_i = \mathbf{r}_i, \qquad L_i^T \tilde{\mathbf{r}}_i = \mathbf{x}_i, \qquad i = 1, \cdots, p$$

with one set of systems being solved in each processor.

Exercises 3.4

1. Show that the $\tilde{\mathbf{r}}$ of (3.4.15) is given by $\mathbf{r}^m$ of (3.4.16) with $\mathbf{r}^0 = 0$.
2. For the SOR method, show that the matrix M of (3.4.14) is, in general, not symmetric for all $m \geq 1$ and all $0 < \omega < 2$.
3. Let B and C be symmetric $n \times n$ matrices. Show that the products $B(CB)^m$ are symmetric for any positive integer m.
4. Formulate the m-step block Jacobi PCG method analogous to (3.4.17).
5. If D is positive definite and $0 < \omega < 2$, show that the matrices P and Q of (3.4.19) are symmetric positive definite except for $\omega = 1$, in which case Q is only semidefinite.
6. Verify (3.4.21).
7. If a, b, c, and d are real numbers such that $cb < ad$, show that

$$\frac{a+c}{b+d} < \frac{a}{b}$$

Apply this to prove the inequality in (3.4.23) when $0 \leq \lambda_1 \leq \lambda_n$.

8. Under the assumptions of 3.4.6, show that the eigenvalues of the SSOR iteration matrix are non-negative if $\omega = 1$.
9. Show that the preconditioned conjugate gradient method applied to $A\mathbf{x} = \mathbf{b}$ with the preconditioning matrix M of (3.4.27) is equivalent to applying the PCG method to the system $\hat{A}\hat{\mathbf{x}} = \hat{\mathbf{b}}$ of (3.4.29) with preconditioning matrix T^{-1}.
10. Assume that the one-step Jacobi PCG method is applied to $A\mathbf{x} = \mathbf{b}$ with A given by (3.1.7). Show that the rate of convergence is the same as with no preconditioning. (Hint: Show first that the method is the same as CG, with no preconditioning, applied to the system $\hat{A}\mathbf{x} = \hat{\mathbf{b}}$, where if D is the main diagonal of A, $\hat{A} = D^{-1}A$ and $\hat{\mathbf{b}} = D^{-1}\mathbf{b}$. Then show that, since D is a constant times the identity, the condition numbers of A and $\hat{A}$ are the same.)
11. Consider the one-step block Jacobi PCG method for $A\mathbf{x} = \mathbf{b}$ when A is the discrete Poisson matrix (3.1.7). In this case

$$B = M^{-1}A = \begin{bmatrix} I & -T^{-1} & & \\ -T^{-1} & \ddots & \ddots & \\ & \ddots & \ddots & -T^{-1} \\ & & -T^{-1} & I \end{bmatrix} = I + C$$

where C is the Kronecker product $(T - 4I) \otimes T^{-1}$. Use Exercise 3.1-19 to show that the eigenvalues of T^{-1} and $T - 4I$ are $(4 - 2\cos kh)^{-1}$ and $-2\cos kh$, $k = 1, \ldots, N$, respectively, where $h = \pi/(N+1)$. Then use the fact (see, for example, Ortega [1987a, p. 237]) that the eigenvalues of $(T - 4I) \otimes T^{-1}$ are the products of the eigenvalues of $T - 4I$ and T^{-1} to conclude that the eigenvalues of B are

$$\frac{2 \cos jh}{-4 + 2 \cos kh}, \qquad j, k = 1, \ldots, N.$$

From this, show that cond(B), the ratio of the largest and smallest eigenvalues, is

$$\text{cond}(B) = 1/(1 - \cos h) \doteq 2h^{-2}$$

where the approximation holds for small h. Conclude that the condition number of the preconditioned matrix is only a factor of 2 less than the condition number of A, as $h \to 0$.

12. Verify in detail the relation (3.4.26).
13. Show that if the algorithm of Figure 3.4-1 is applied to a tridiagonal matrix the result is a complete Choleski decomposition. More generally, show that if the algorithm is applied to a banded matrix that has no zeros within the band, the result is again a complete Choleski decomposition.
14. Let

$$A = \begin{bmatrix} A_1 & C_1 & & \\ C_1 & \ddots & \ddots & \\ & \ddots & \ddots & C_{N-1} \\ & & C_{N-1} & A_N \end{bmatrix},$$

$$A_i = \begin{bmatrix} A_{i1} & B_{i1} & & \\ B_{i1} & \ddots & \ddots & \\ & \ddots & \ddots & B_{iN-1} \\ & & B_{iN-1} & A_{iN} \end{bmatrix}$$

where each A_{ij} is $N \times N$ and tridiagonal, each B_{ij} is $N \times N$ and diagonal, and each C_i is $N^2 \times N^2$ and diagonal. Thus, A is $N^3 \times N^3$ and 7-diagonal. Show that the IC(0) incomplete factors L and D satisfy

$$l_{i,i-1} = a_{i,i-1}/d_{i-1}, \qquad l_{i,i-N} = a_{i,i-N}/d_{i-N},$$

$$l_{i,i-N^2} = a_{i,i-N^2}/d_{i-N^2}, \qquad d_i = a_{ii} - l_{i,i-N^2}^2 d_{i-N^2} l_{i,i-1}^2 d_{i-1}$$

15. Assume that the matrices B_i in (3.4.44) are tridiagonal. Show that (3.4.46) is no longer valid.

16. Let LDL^T, with $\text{diag}(L) = I$, be a root-free Choleski decomposition (complete or incomplete) and let $L_1 D_1 L_1^T$ with $\text{diag}(L_1) = D_1^{-1}$ be the same decomposition. Show that $D_1 = D^{-1}$ and $LD^{1/2} = L_1 D_1^{1/2}$. Use this to show that the incomplete decomposition for the matrix of (3.4.44) can be written in the form (3.4.49), where the subdiagonal elements of L_1 are the corresponding subdiagonal elements of A.
17. Let $L_1 D_1 L_1^T$ be the decomposition of Exercise 16. Show that the corresponding decomposition $\hat{L}_1 \hat{D}_1 \hat{L}_1^T$ of the matrix $\hat{A} = D_1^{1/2} A D_1^{1/2}$ has the property that $\hat{D}_1 = I$.
18. Verify that (3.4.50)-(3.4.52) give the complete block Choleski decomposition of the matrix A of (3.4.44).
19. Show that the first two diagonals of L^{-1} of (3.4.56) are given by (3.4.57).
20. Assume that the matrix of (3.4.44) has M blocks of size $N \times N$ so that A is $MN \times MN$. Show that the scheme of Figure 3.4-4 starts the mth block at step $2M - 1$ and completes the solution at step $2M + N - 2$ so that the average degree of parallelism is $MN/(2M + N - 2)$.
21. Show that if L is a lower triangular matrix such that LL^T is diagonal, then L is diagonal. Conclude from this that the first relation of (3.4.64) implies that $L = I$ and $\hat{D}_1 = D_1$.
22. Verify the relations (3.4.73) and (3.4.74).

References and Extensions 3.4

1. Although the idea of preconditioning goes back to Hestenes [1956], most of the research on preconditioning has been done since the potential value of the conjugate gradient method as an iterative method was recognized in the early 1970s. A seminal paper on preconditioning was that of Concus, Golub, and O'Leary [1976]. See, also, Axelsson [1976].
2. The truncated series approach to preconditioning on vector and parallel computers was initiated by Dubois *et al.* [1979] for the case that the matrix P of (3.4.15) is the main diagonal of A, that is, for Jacobi's method as the subsidiary iteration. Johnson *et al.* [1983] then considered polynomial preconditioning, again for the case that P is the main diagonal of A. Adams [1982, 1983, 1985] studied truncated series preconditioning in the context of m steps of a subsidiary iterative method including, in particular, the Jacobi and SSOR iterations. Theorems 3.4.2, 3.4.5, and 3.4.6 are based on this work. Adams also treated polynomial preconditioning for more general P, including that of SSOR, and Table 3.4-2 is taken from her work. See also Saad [1985] for a general analysis of polynomial preconditioning methods and Chen [1982] for a detailed study of scaling with application to polynomial preconditioning. Vaughan and Ortega [1987] describe an implementation of SSOR PCG on an Intel iPSC hypercube.
3. The "Eisenstat trick" is given in Eisenstat [1981]. A related idea is presented by Bank and Douglas [1985]. An analysis and comparison of the Bank–Douglas,

Eisenstat, and Conrad-Wallach procedures is given in Ortega [1987c], both for stationary iterative methods as well as the conjugate gradient method.

4. The idea of incomplete factorization dates back at least to Varga [1960]. Meijerink and van der Vorst [1977] gave a detailed treatment of the ICCG method, including the IC(h, k) formulation. The concept of a regular incomplete factorization is given in Robert [1982]. An incomplete "twisted" factorization is given in van der Vorst [1987].

5. Theorem 3.4.7 was proved for M matrices by Meijerink and van der Vorst [1977] and extended to H matrices by Manteuffel [1980]. This latter paper also discusses the shifting strategy and notes that it is not always necessary to choose α so large that $\alpha I + A$ is diagonally dominant.

6. Kershaw [1978] suggested the strategy of replacing the current l_{ii} in an incomplete decomposition by $\sum|l_{ij}|$ to ensure diagonal dominance. A related idea was given by Gustafsson [1978], who called it the modified ICCG method (MICCG). The modified method can be formulated in terms of a parameter α that ranges from zero (unmodified) to one (modified). The rate of convergence will many times be optimal for an α slightly less than one. See Ashcraft and Grimes [1987] and Axelsson and Lindskog [1986] for further discussion.

7. The treatment (3.4.45)-(3.4.48) of incomplete decomposition of the matrix (3.4.44) is based on van der Vorst [1982], who also gave the relation (3.4.49).

8. The block method discussion (3.4.50)-(3.4.57) is based on Concus, Golub, and Meurant [1985]. Meurant [1984] gives some corresponding vectorizations. A large number of other papers treat various block incomplete factorizations, usually under the assumption that A is block tridiagonal; see, for example, Axelsson [1985, 1986], Eisenstat *et al.* [1984], T. Jordan [1982], Kershaw [1982], Reiter and Rodrigue [1984], and Rodrigue and Wolitzer [1984]. The latter four papers were directed primarily toward efficient algorithms for CRAY computers. See also Axelsson and Polman [1986].

9. The approach of Figure 3.4-4 for solving $L\mathbf{x} = \mathbf{r}$ is due to van der Vorst [1983] and extended by Ashcraft [1985a].

10. The use of multicoloring in ICCG was suggested by Schreiber and Tang [1982]. It was further developed in Poole [1986] and Poole and Ortega [1987]. Nodera [1984] has also applied the idea to both incomplete Choleski and SSOR preconditioning. Although multicoloring can give a very high degree of parallelism, it may degrade the rate of convergence, compared with the natural ordering.

11. Incomplete factorization to approximate the one-step block Jacobi PCG algorithm was suggested by Ashcraft [1987b], who gives results on various experiments. Block Jacobi preconditioning was also studied by Kowalik and Kumar [1982]. In the text, we have identified this block Jacobi preconditioning with domain decomposition, but most work on domain decomposition uses separator sets and starts from the equations written in the arrowhead form (3.3.18). There are then two main possibilities: the PCG method can be applied to the system (3.3.18) or to the reduced Schur complement system $\hat{A}\mathbf{x}_s = \hat{\mathbf{b}}$, where $\hat{A}$ and $\hat{\mathbf{b}}$ are given by (3.3.19). For an excellent review of these two

approaches, plus others and additional references, see Keyes and Gropp [1987]. This paper also reports on experiments on an Intel iPSC hypercube. For other work on domain decomposition, see Lichnewsky [1984], who uses multicoloring within the subdomains; Gonzalez and Wheeler [1987], who consider a generalized Poisson equation with Neumann boundary conditions; Nour-Omid and Park [1987], who report on experiments on a hypercube for a plane stress problem; and Rodrigue [1986], who discusses a domain decomposition called the Schwartz process.

12. A number of other approaches to preconditioning have been considered. McBryan and van de Velde [1985] use fast Poisson solvers based on the Fast Fourier Transform and the ADI iteration as preconditioners. Nour-Omid and Parlett [1987] use "element preconditioning," which is potentially useful in finite-element analysis.

13. Several other papers have reported numerical results and comparisons of different methods. Kightley and Jones [1985] give numerical results on the CRAY-1 for several preconditionings applied to four three-dimensional test problems. Two of these problems are the Poisson equation, one with Dirichlet boundary conditions and one with Neumann boundary conditions. An interesting aspect of these two problems was that simple diagonal scaling of A was the best of all the preconditioners in running time. The other two test problems were from fluid dynamics. On one problem, diagonal scaling again did very well, being beaten only by a version of ICCG and even then only by about 10%. Knightley and Thompson [1987] compare a number of multigrid codes and an ICCG method on a CRAY-1. Here, the test problems were two-dimensional Poisson equations on a square with Dirichlet boundary conditions. The multigrid methods showed better performance. Chan [1985] compares SSOR preconditioning with the multigrid method and a direct sparse matrix method for two-dimensional problems. Seager [1986a,b] considers the overhead in multitasking (large grain) and microtasking (small grain) approaches to preconditioned conjugate gradient on the four-processor CRAY X-MP.

14. As discussed in Section 3.3, the conjugate gradient method can be considered a minimization method and is, thus, inherently restricted to symmetric matrices. However, there have been many attempts to extend the method to nonsymmetric matrices, and, in particular, to devise methods that retain as many desirable properties of the conjugate gradient method as possible Some of these methods have been tested on vector computers. For example, Oppe and Kincaid [1987] report on tests of various preconditioned conjugate gradient methods run on five sample reservoir simulation problems. Of these five problems, only one had a symmetric positive definite coefficient matrix; two others were almost symmetric, and the other two were highly nonsymmetric. The preconditioners included point and block Jacobi, SSOR, polynomial, incomplete Choleski, and modified incomplete Choleski. Also included were several semi-iterative methods. The codes were run on a CYBER 205 and a CRAY X-MP. See also Kincaid *et al.* [1986*a*,*b*].

Appendices

Appendix 1

The *ijk* Forms of *LU* and Choleski Decomposition

We give in this appendix more details of the *ijk* forms of *LU* and Choleski factorization discussed in Chapter 2. These forms are based on the generic triply nested For loop shown in Figure A.1-1.

We assume that A admits a stable LU decomposition so that pivoting is not required. Choleski decomposition will be expressed in the usual LL^T form as well as the root-free Choleski or symmetric Gaussian elimination (SGE) form LDL^T, where L is unit lower triangular. The LDL^T form provides a natural transition between the LU and Choleski codes. For Choleski, or SGE, we assume that only the lower triangle of A is stored and this will be overwritten by the factors L (and D for SGE).

Vector Computers

The *kij* and *kji* codes for LU decomposition are given in Figures 2.1-1 and 2.1-2. Mathematically, the *kij* and *kji* updates can be written as subtractions of *outer products* and, therefore, are sometimes called *outer product* forms of LU decomposition. This is seen by writing the first stage of the LU decomposition as

$$A = \begin{bmatrix} a_{11} & \mathbf{a}_1^T \\ \hat{\mathbf{a}}_1 & A_2 \end{bmatrix} = \begin{bmatrix} 1 & 0 \\ \mathbf{l}_1 & I \end{bmatrix} \begin{bmatrix} 1 & 0 \\ 0 & \hat{A}_2 \end{bmatrix} \begin{bmatrix} a_{11} & \mathbf{u}_1 \\ 0 & I \end{bmatrix} = \begin{bmatrix} a_{11} & \mathbf{u}_1 \\ a_{11}\mathbf{l}_1 & \hat{A}_2 + \mathbf{l}_1\mathbf{u}_1 \end{bmatrix}$$

Thus, the updating of the submatrix A_2 is accomplished (mathematically) by subtracting the outer product $\mathbf{l}_1\mathbf{u}_1$ of the first column of L and first row of U. The *kij* and *kji* forms both compute L by column and U by row; that is, at the kth stage the kth column of L and the $(k + 1)$st row of U are computed (the first row of U is just the first row of A). The exact way this is done differs in the two algorithms, however. The *kji* form computes rows

For ______
  For ______
    For ______
      $a_{ij} = a_{ij} - l_{ik}a_{kj}$

Figure A.1-1. The generic For loop for LU decomposition.

of U by vector operations and elements of L by scalar operations. In the *kji* form the columns of L can be computed by vector operations whereas the elements of rows of U are computed one at a time as the result of vector operations on columns.

The SGE and Choleski *kij* and *kji* Forms

The codes are in Figure A.1-2. We have given the SGE algorithms and then indicated in parentheses the changes to convert the SGE algorithms to the corresponding Choleski algorithm.

We are assuming in these codes that only the lower half of A is stored. Thus, the basic update statement changes from $a_{ij} = a_{ij} - l_{ik}a_{kj}$ in full storage LU decomposition to $a_{ij} = a_{ij} - l_{ik}a_{jk}$ in SGE. In the Choleski codes, l_{jk} plays the role of a_{jk} in this basic arithmetic statement. Although not explicitly indicated in the codes, the elements of L can overwrite the corresponding elements of A in the Choleski code. In SGE, however, these overwrites may need to be postponed until the original elements of A are no longer needed; the different *ijk* forms of SGE have different requirements in this regard. In the *kji* form of Figure A.1-2, the entire kth column of A must be used for the updates before it can be overwritten by the kth column of L. Note that whereas the Choleski code stores the full factor L, the SGE code stores only the strictly lower triangular part, and the diagonal of A will contain the elements of D at completion. Regardless of when the overwrites of L onto A are performed in SGE, we will assume that L and A have the same

(a)

($l_{11} = a_{11}^{1/2}$)
For $k = 1$ to $n - 1$
  For $i = k + 1$ to n
    $l_{ik} = a_{ik}/a_{kk}$ (a_{ik}/l_{kk})
    For $j = k + 1$ to i
      $a_{ij} = a_{ij} - l_{ik}a_{jk}$ ($a_{ij} - l_{ik}l_{jk}$)
  ($l_{k+1,k+1} = a_{k+1,k+1}^{1/2}$)

(b)

($l_{11} = a_{11}^{1/2}$)
For $k = 1$ to $n - 1$
  For $s = k + 1$ to n
    $l_{sk} = a_{sk}/a_{kk}$ (a_{sk}/l_{kk})
  For $j = k + 1$ to n
    For $i = j$ to n
      $a_{ij} = a_{ij} - l_{ik}a_{jk}$ ($a_{ij} - l_{ik}l_{jk}$)
  ($l_{k+1,k+1} = a_{k+1,k+1}^{1/2}$)

Figure A.1-2. The *kij* and *kji* forms of SGE and Choleski. (a) *kij*; (b) *kji*.

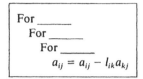

storage structure. Thus, in the inner loop of the *kij* SGE algorithm the ith row of A is updated using the kth column of A while in the Choleski code the ith row of A and jth column of L are used. In both cases, rows and columns of the data are required. For the *kji* codes, access is by columns of both A and L.

As with full storage LU decomposition, the *kij* and *kji* forms of SGE and Choleski are immediate update algorithms. The inner loop vector instruction in all four cases is again a linked triad, although the average vector lengths are shorter. The average vector length for all four versions is $O(n/3)$, as given in (2.1.17).

The *kij* and *kji* forms are also outer product forms since for Choleski, for example, the first stage can be written as

$$A = \begin{bmatrix} a_{11} & \mathbf{a}_1^T \\ \mathbf{a}_1 & A_2 \end{bmatrix} = \begin{bmatrix} a_{11}^{1/2} & 0 \\ \mathbf{l}_1 & I \end{bmatrix} \begin{bmatrix} 1 & 0 \\ 0 & \hat{A}_2 \end{bmatrix} \begin{bmatrix} a_{11}^{1/2} & \mathbf{l}_1^T \\ 0 & I \end{bmatrix}$$

so that the updated submatrix $\hat{A}_2$ is obtained from A_2 by subtracting the outer product $\mathbf{l}_1\mathbf{l}_1^T$. George and Liu [1981] call the *kij* and *kji* forms *submatrix Choleski.* Both the *kij* and *kji* forms compute L a column at a time. The data access patterns for the codes of Figure A.1-2 were given in Figure 2.1-11.

Delayed Updating: The LU *ikj* and *jki* Forms

The *ikj* form of LU decomposition is analogous to the *kij* form except that updates to subsequent rows of A are delayed until that row receives final processing. The same relation holds between the *jki* and *kji* forms; thus, the *ikj* and *jki* forms are called *delayed update* algorithms. The codes are given in Figure A.1-3. (Recall that the *jki* code was also given in Figure 2.1-3.)

At the ith stage of the *ikj* algorithm, all updates are performed on the ith row of A to produce the ith rows of L and U. Thus, the ith row of U is computed as the linear combination $\mathbf{u}_i = \sum_{k=1}^{i-1} l_{ik}\mathbf{u}_k$ of the previous rows of U (from those positions needed for the ith row of U). Access in the inner loop is by rows of A while the elements of L give the multipliers in

(a)	(b)
For $i = 2$ to n	For $j = 2$ to n
For $k = 1$ to $i - 1$	For $s = j$ to n
$l_{ik} = a_{ik}/a_{kk}$	$l_{sj-1} = a_{sj-1}/a_{j-1,j-1}$
For $j = k + 1$ to n	For $k = 1$ to $j - 1$
$a_{ij} = a_{ij} - l_{ik}a_{kj}$	For $i = k + 1$ to n
	$a_{ij} = a_{ij} - l_{ik}a_{kj}$

Figure A.1-3. The *ikj* and *jki* forms of LU decomposition. (a) *ikj*; (b) *jki*.

the linear combination. The *jki* form is the corresponding column-oriented algorithm. Access now is by columns of A and columns of L. The basic operation is again a linear combination with the a_{kj} playing the role of multipliers in the linear combination. At the jth stage, the jth columns of L and U are computed after all the required updates to A are made. The access patterns of the *ikj* and *jki* forms were shown in Figure 2.1-4. We note that the average vector lengths of the inner loop operations in the *ikj* and *jki* forms are again $O(\frac{2}{3}n)$.

The SGE and Choleski *ikj* and *jki* Forms

The codes for these forms are given in Figure A.1-4; the access patterns were given in Figure 2.1-11.

In the *ikj* and *jki* algorithms, the basic operation is again a linear combination, and the average vector lengths are $O(\frac{1}{3}n)$. In the *ikj* Choleski algorithm, the inner loop updates the ith row of A using columns of L; thus, both row and column access is required. The same is true of SGE although it is the rows of A, stored as columns by symmetry, that are required. Note that in SGE, L cannot be overwritten onto A since the original A is needed for the future updates. L is being computed by rows, and this is one form of what is called *row Choleski* in George and Liu [1981]. The algorithm can be based on bordering; that is, if $A_{i-1} = \hat{L}_{i-1}\hat{L}_{i-1}^T$ is the decomposition of the $(i-1)$st principal submatrix, then the decomposition of A_i is

$$A_i = \begin{bmatrix} A_{i-1} & \mathbf{a}_i \\ \mathbf{a}_i^T & a_{ii} \end{bmatrix} = \begin{bmatrix} \hat{L}_{i-1} & 0 \\ \mathbf{l}_i^T & l_{ii} \end{bmatrix} \begin{bmatrix} \hat{L}_{i-1}^T & \mathbf{l}_i \\ 0 & l_{ii} \end{bmatrix}$$

Thus, the new ith row of L is obtained from $\hat{L}_{i-1}\mathbf{l}_i = \mathbf{a}_i$, $l_{ii} = (a_{ii} - \mathbf{l}_i^T\mathbf{l}_i)^{1/2}$.

In the *jki* form, access is by columns of both A and L. In SGE, the a_{jk} are the multipliers in the linear combination. They are the elements of the

(a)	(b)
$(l_{11} = a_{11}^{1/2})$	$(l_{11} = a_{11}^{1/2})$
For $i = 2$ to n	For $j = 2$ to n
For $k = 1$ to $i-1$	For $s = j$ to n
$l_{ik} = a_{ik}/a_{kk}\ (a_{ik}/l_{kk})$	$l_{sj-1} = a_{sj-1}/a_{j-1,j-1}\ (a_{sj-1}/l_{j-1,j-1})$
For $j = k+1$ to i	For $k = 1$ to $j-1$
$a_{ij} = a_{ij} - l_{ik}a_{jk}\ (a_{ij} - l_{ik}l_{jk})$	For $i = j$ to n
$(l_{ii} = a_{ii}^{1/2})$	$a_{ij} = a_{ij} - l_{ik}a_{jk}\ (a_{ij} - l_{ik}l_{jk})$
	$(l_{jj} = a_{jj}^{1/2})$

Figure A.1-4. The *ikj* and *jki* forms of SGE and Choleski. (a) *ikj*; (b) *jki*.

jth row of A, and L can only overwrite that portion of A up to the jth row. The columns of L are computed one at a time, and this is one form of what is called *column Choleski* by George and Liu [1981].

The *LU ijk* and *jik* Forms

These forms are based on explicit LU decomposition using inner products. The codes are given in Figure A.1-5. Note that the j loop in the *ijk* form splits into two parts. The first computes the elements of the ith row of L and then the second computes the elements of the ith row of U. The inner loop computations are inner products of the ith row of L and columns of A. Similarly, in the *jik* form, the first i loop computes the jth column of U and the second i loop updates the remainder of the jth column of A. The basic vector operation is an inner product of rows of L and the jth column of U. The access pattern of the two forms was given in Figure 2.1-4. Note that all necessary updating is done at the stage where the current row (or column) is being computed; thus, these are also delayed update algorithms. The *ijk* form computes L and U by rows, whereas the *ikj* form computes L and U by columns. Finally, the average vector lengths for the inner product are again $O(\frac{2}{3}n)$.

The SGE and Choleski *ijk* and *jik* Forms

The codes for these forms are given in Figure A.1-6 and the access patterns were given in Figure 2.1-11.

In the *ijk* form, the inner loop is an inner product of the ith and jth rows of L for Choleski and the ith row of L and jth row of A for SGE. Since the rows of L are being computed one at a time, *ijk* Choleski is another form of row Choleski. Note that in SGE all previous rows of A are needed for the updating at the ith stage so that we cannot overwrite L

```
For i = 2 to n
  For j = 2 to i
    l_{ij-1} = a_{ij-1}/a_{j-1,j-1}
    For k = 1 to j - 1
      a_{ij} = a_{ij} - l_{ik}a_{kj}
  For j = i + 1 to n
    For k = 1 to i - 1
      a_{ij} = a_{ij} - l_{ik}a_{kj}
```

```
For j = 2 to n
  For s = j to n
    l_{sj-1} = a_{sj-1}/a_{j-1,j-1}
  For i = 2 to j
    For k = 1 to i - 1
      a_{ij} = a_{ij} - l_{ik}a_{kj}
  For i = j + 1 to n
    For k = 1 to j - 1
      a_{ij} = a_{ij} - l_{ik}a_{kj}
```

Figure A.1-5. The *ijk* and *jik* forms of *LU* decomposition. (a) *ijk*; (b) *jik*.

(a)	(b)
$(l_{11} = a_{11}^{1/2})$	$(l_{11} = a_{11}^{1/2})$
For $i = 2$ to n	For $j = 2$ to n
For $j = 2$ to i	For $s = j$ to n
$l_{ij-1} = a_{ij-1}/a_{j-1,j-1}$ $(a_{ij-1}/l_{j-1,j-1})$	$l_{sj-1} = a_{sj-1}/a_{j-1,j-1}$ $(a_{sj-1}/l_{j-1,j-1})$
For $k = 1$ to $j-1$	For $i = j$ to n
$a_{ij} = a_{ij} - l_{ik}a_{jk}$ $(a_{ij} - l_{ik}l_{jk})$	For $k = 1$ to $j-1$
$(l_{ii} = a_{ii}^{1/2})$	$a_{ij} = a_{ij} - l_{ik}a_{jk}$ $(a_{ij} - l_{ik}l_{jk})$
	$(l_{jj} = a_{jj}^{1/2})$

Figure A.1-6. The *ijk* and *jik* forms of SGE and Choleski. (a) *ijk*; (b) *jik*.

on to A. In the *jik* form, the inner loop is an inner product of the ith row of L and the jth row of L or A, the same as in the *ijk* form. However, L is being computed a column at a time so that this is another form of column Choleski. Note that in SGE the jth row of A is needed at the jth stage so that L cannot overwrite A except in those positions before the jth row. Both the *ijk* and *jik* forms are delayed update algorithms and the average vector length for the inner products is $O(\frac{1}{3}n)$.

Parallel Computers

We next discuss the *ijk* forms for parallel systems whose p processors may or may not have vector capability. We will consider only local memory systems with row or column wrapped interleaved storage. In the following, P_i will denote the ith processor and $P(i)$ will denote the processor holding the ith row (or column) of A. We will begin with the LU decomposition.

LU Decomposition

The basic codes for the *kij* and *kji* forms of LU factorization were given in Figures 2.1-1 and 2.1-2, but they need to be interpreted suitably in order to be useful for parallel systems. Consider first the *kij* code. On a vector (or serial) machine, there is a sequential order inherent in this code that is inappropriate for parallel systems. The essence of the *kij* form is that rows (as opposed to columns) are updated as soon as possible, and the intent is to do in parallel as many of these tasks as possible. For example, in Figure 2.1-1, the kth stage is completed before the $(k+1)$st stage begins, but this is too restrictive for a parallel code. Indeed, some processors may be free to begin the $(k+1)$st stage while others are still completing the kth stage; for maximum efficiency, these processors should be allowed to begin. Hence, processors will be allowed to proceed immediately to later stages after all of their computation in the current stage is complete. We now discuss the individual forms in more detail.

The LU–kij,r Form

We will denote the *kij* form of *LU* factorization with row interleaved storage by *LU–kij,r* and similarly for the other forms. For the *LU–kij,r* form, a straightforward pseudocode for each processor is given in Figure A.1-7 where *myrows* is the set of indices for the rows assigned to each processor. With row-interleaved storage, each processor calculates a multiplier and then updates a row that it holds. All processors can do this in parallel until the last $p \times p$ submatrix, when processors start to drop out one by one. In order to perform the updates at the kth stage, each processor requires row k, and hence row k must be broadcast to all processors before stage k can begin.

The algorithm given in Figure A.1-7 automatically synchronizes the processors at each stage, since $P(k+1)$ does not finish stage k before any other processor, and must make the next broadcast of information. This is undesirable since it causes processors to become idle while waiting for the next pivot row. Thus, we will allow $P(k+1)$ to broadcast row $k+1$ as soon as that row has been updated, before continuing to update its other rows. Using this send-ahead strategy, it is unlikely that contention for communication resources will exist, since row $k+1$ is not ready to be sent until after row k has been received and used. The pseudocode for this algorithm, which we consider the basic implementation of *LU–kij,r*, is given in Figure A.1-8.

The algorithm in Figure A.1-8 might be improved by beginning computation of the multipliers while the remainder of a pivot row is being received. For example, the computation of the multipliers l_{i1} could begin as soon as a_{11} is received, rather than waiting for the entire first row. In any case, communication delays seem to be very satisfactory. On parallel-vector

```
for k = 1 to n - 1 do
  if (k in myrows) then
    broadcast(row k)
  else
    receive(row k)
  for all rows i > k in myrows do
    compute(l_ik)
    update(row i)
```

Figure A.1-7. Naive *LU–kij,r* code,for each processor.

```
broadcast(row 1)
for k = 1 to n - 1 do
  if (k not in myrows) then
    receive(row k)
  for all rows i > k in myrows do
    l_ik = a_ik / a_kk
    for j = k + 1 to n do
      a_ij = l_ij - a_ik a_kj
    if ((i = k + 1) and (i ≠ n)) then
      broadcast(row k + 1)
```

Figure A.1-8. *LU–kij,r* code for each processor.

machines, the updates would proceed by vector operations on the rows. This would necessitate, of course, that all elements of the required rows be available. The vectors have full length of $n - k$ at the kth stage; this will be in contrast to some of the other forms, which will have vector lengths $O((n - k)/p)$.

The LU–kij,c Form

Next, consider the *kij* form with column interleaved storage, which we denote by *LU–kij,c*. At the kth stage all multipliers will be computed in $P(k)$. According to the algorithm of Figure 2.1-1, each multiplier is used to update the corresponding row before the next multiplier is computed. However, it is clear that unless $P(k)$ gives priority to computing the entire kth column of multipliers before updating the rest of its columns, delays will be incurred by other processors. The multipliers could be computed and broadcast in segments; a segment length of 1 corresponds to broadcasting each multiplier as it is computed. While this would allow other processors to start updating as soon as possible, the communication cost would be much greater than that for the *LU–kij,r* algorithm.

At the other extreme, the entire column of multipliers could comprise a segment. This would cause delays at each stage while the multipliers were being computed, but a further modification of the *LU–kij,c* algorithm to allow compute-and-send-ahead would alleviate this problem except for the first stage. Specifically, when the kth column of multipliers is received, $P(k + 1)$ should give priority to computing and sending the $(k + 1)$st column of multipliers. This requires a further deviation from the *kij* paradigm, in that column $k + 1$ would be fully updated before $P(k + 1)$ updates the rest of the submatrix by rows. This variant of the *LU–kij,c* algorithm is much more natural in the context of the *kji* form.

Finally, on vector processors, the formation of an entire column of multipliers could be done with a vector divide. However, since each row in the *kij,c* form is distributed across the processors, the vector lengths for the row operations will be divided by p. We call these *partial* vector lengths. As noted above, the *kij,r* form allows full vector lengths for all updating operations.

The LU–kji,r Form

The *kji* form differs from the *kij* form in that updates are done by column rather than by row. Again, we first assume that we have row-interleaved storage. We can adapt the code in Figure 2.1-2 to a parallel version in the following way. At the kth stage, an entire column of multipliers is computed in parallel by all the processors. Then the remaining submatrix of A is updated column by column. The calculation of the multipliers and the updating requires that row k be available to all processors, and hence $P(k)$ must broadcast row k prior to the beginning of stage k. The communication cost is identical to the naive form of *LU–kij,r*; in fact, the total cost is the same, since within each stage the processors are doing exactly the same operations on the same elements in a different order.

In order to eliminate unnecessary delays while processors wait for data, we would again use a compute-and-send-ahead strategy. At the start of stage k, $P(k+1)$ would update and broadcast all of row $k+1$ before updating the rest of its columns. There is no reason to prefer this to the *LU–kij,r* algorithm, since their execution times would be identical. In addition, the code would be slightly more complicated, as the entries in row $k+1$ are updated in a different order than the rest of the coefficient matrix. And, on vector machines, the *kji,r* form is at a disadvantage since vector lengths are only partial.

The LU–kji,c Form

In its simplest form, the *LU–kji,c* algorithm suffers from the same difficulty that the naive form of *LU–kij,r* does: unwanted synchronization at the end of each stage. However, we can use a strategy analogous to that used for the *LU–kij,r* form. At stage k, after $P(k+1)$ has updated column $k+1$, it computes and broadcasts the $(k+1)$st column of multipliers before continuing to update its remaining columns. For each stage except the first, this will reduce the amount of delay time for processors waiting to receive the next column of multipliers. Since vector lengths are full, we conclude that, although there is a delay at the outset, both the scalar and vector forms of *kji,c* look promising.

The *ikj* and *jki* Forms of *LU* Factorization: Delayed Updates

The codes for the *ikj* and *jki* forms were given in Figure A.1-3. The essence of the *ikj* form is to delay the updates of rows until the time that the row is to receive final processing. The same is true for the *jki* form using columns in place of rows. We summarize this in the prescriptions shown in Figure A.1-9, which we now discuss in more detail.

The LU–ikj,r Form

Since storage is by rows, if we interpret the delayed update strategy strictly, only one processor will be active at a time: first P_2 updates the second row and transmits to all processors, then P_3 updates the third row, and so on. To alleviate this problem, all processors could begin updating other rows. When P_2 completes row 2, it is transmitted to all processors and P_3 gives priority to completing the third row and transmitting to all processors. Thus, each processor gives priority to the delayed update strategy but updates other rows while waiting for data. On vector machines, the vector lengths will be full.

A variation on this theme is the following: $P(1)$ broadcasts row 1, and then all other processors update their ith row with row 1, while $P(1)$ updates row $p + 1$. Next, $P(2)$ broadcasts the new row 2, and all other processors update the next p rows with row 2 while $P(2)$ updates row $p + 2$ with row 1, and so on. The effect is to have a band of p rows being updated at any given time, and as rows are completed at the top of the band, new rows are included at the bottom, so that the band "migrates" through the matrix. While this strategy allows processors to proceed in parallel, it has a serious defect. As new rows are included at the bottom of the band, they must be updated by all previous rows. Hence, rows with small indices must either be stored in each processor, or rebroadcast each time they are needed. In either case, there is a large overhead for extra storage or communication.

It is clear that the *ikj,r* form has no merit if the delayed update strategy is strictly obeyed. With the modifications discussed above, it becomes more like the *kij,r* form, except that the coding is more complicated. On some vector processors, delayed updates will have the advantage of fewer store operations, and on other machines there may also be an advantage of fewer

For $i = 2$ to n	For $j = 2$ to n
Compute ith row of L	Compute $(j - 1)$st column of L
Do all updates for *ith* row of **A**	Do all updates for jth column of L

Figure A.1-9. Parallel *ijk* and *jki* forms of *LU* factorization.

index computations and storage accesses. But it is unlikely that this will outweigh the increased complexity.

The LU–ikj,c Form

In this form, there is delayed update by rows and storage by columns. During stage i, processor 1 first calculates l_{i1} and sends it to all other processors. Each of these then updates their portion of row i with row 1, whereupon processor 2 calculates and broadcasts l_{i2} and then all processors update their portion of row i with row 2. This process continues until row i has been completely updated. Each update on row i is done in parallel by all processors, but there are communication delays to broadcast the multipliers.

An alternative organization is to compute and send the multipliers as soon as possible before updating the remainder of the row. Here, the computation and transmission of multipliers are overlapped with the updating of the remainder of the row; this is a slight deviation from the delayed update strategy. The code for this modification is clearly more complicated, and on vector machines, vector lengths are only partial. We conclude that this form has little merit.

The LU–jki,r Form

The *jki* form does delayed updates by column. On parallel systems with storage by rows, the algorithm proceeds as follows. At stage j, the entire $(j-1)$st column of multipliers is computed in parallel (requiring all processors to have access to the diagonal element). Then, as k is increased from 1 to $j-1$, $P(k)$ broadcasts a_{kj}, which is used as a multiplier by all processors to update the jth column in parallel. As soon as $P(k+1)$ has updated element $a_{k+1,j}$, it broadcasts this new element before proceeding to update any other elements of column j it may contain. While this form exhibits a high degree of parallelism, the communication is high since each element of U is broadcast as a multiplier for some linear combination of columns. Moreover, on vector processors, the vector lengths are only partial.

The LU–jki,c Form

Since storage is by columns, a strict adherence to the delayed update prescription would render this form useless because all but one processor would be idle while a column is updated. The only way the form could be viable is to deviate rather drastically from the delayed update philosophy. For example, at the first stage, multipliers would be computed in P_1 and broadcast to all other processors. All processors would begin updating their columns until P_2 has updated its second column, computed its multipliers, and sent them. Then P_3 could concentrate on the final update of columns, and so on. Thus, priority would be given to the delayed final updates, but in the meantime other processors would be doing immediate updates. This is the same situation as the *ikj,r* form and, as with that form, we can also create a *migrating band* version of the algorithm. The vector lengths are full and we conclude, as with the *ikj,r* form, that only for some vector processors would this form be potentially viable.

The *ijk* and *jik* inner product forms

The pseudocodes for the *ijk* and *jik* forms were given in Figure A.1-5. We interpret these forms as in Figure A.1-10.

The LU–ijk,r Form

Since A is stored by rows, an inner product of a row of L and column of U will require data from one processor for the row, and a number of processors for the column. This requires transmitting the necessary elements of the row of L to the correct processors before computing the partial inner products within each processor, and then doing a fan-in across the processors to complete the inner product. This requires a prohibitive amount of communication, and this form seems to have little merit. (There also is very poor load balancing at the beginning; for example, in computing the second row of U only the first processor is used. However, the load balancing is good at the end.)

The LU–ijk,c Form

The inner products now involve a column of U from one processor and a row of L distributed across several processors. Again, we would transmit the necessary portions of the column to the other processors and

For $i = 2$ to n Compute ith row of L and U with inner products of ith row of L and columns of U	For $j = 2$ to n Compute $(j-1)$st column of L and U with inner products of ith row of L and columns of U

Figure A.1-10. Parallel *ijk* and *jik* forms of *LU* factorization.

then proceed as in the *ijk,r* form. Thus this form has the same problems as the *ijk,r* form.

The LU–jik,r, LU–jik,c Forms

These two forms have the same difficulties as the two *ijk* forms.

Recall that the properties of the *LU* forms on parallel computers were summarized in Table 2.2-1.

Choleski Factorization

We next consider the Choleski factorization $A = LL^T$. Thus, CH–*kij,r* or CH–*kij,c* will denote the *kij* form of Choleski with row or column interleaved storage, and similarly for the other forms. We now discuss the various forms in more detail. The pseudocodes for the *kij* and *kji* immediate update submatrix forms were given in Figure A.1-2.

The CH–kij,r Form

In this form, storage is by interleaved rows. At the kth stage, $P(k)$ computes and broadcasts l_{kk}. For each row i, $P(i)$ computes l_{ik} and updates the ith row of A. This updating requires $l_{k+1,k}, \ldots, l_{ik}$ so that each processor will need access to most of the kth column of L. This is considerable communication. However, it may be possible to overlap at least some of the communication with computation as follows. When the processors receive l_{kk}, they can all compute in parallel their elements of the kth column of L and then broadcast them. While waiting to receive these data, they can begin the updates of their rows, using the elements of the kth column that they possess. Note that all processors will attempt to broadcast at almost the same time so that on some architectures there will be severe contention for the communication resources.

After the first stage, additional savings can potentially be achieved by the following compute-and-send-ahead strategy. All processors first compute and broadcast the next column of L before completing the current update. That is, at the kth stage, $P(k+1)$ computes and broadcasts $l_{k+1,k+1}$ as soon as possible, and then all processors compute and broadcast their elements of the $(k+1)$st column of L before completing the updates of the kth stage. This send-ahead strategy is a rather large deviation from the *kij* paradigm and is done more naturally in the context of the *kji,r* form, to be discussed shortly. On vector processors, the *kij,r* form can use vectors or full length. However, unless the compute-ahead strategy and overlapping of computation and communication can be achieved, this form will be inferior to some of the others.

The CH−kij,c Form

Next, assume that storage is by interleaved columns. At the kth stage, $P(k)$ computes and broadcasts the elements, l_{ik}, of the kth column of L, and there are different ways that this can be done. If the l_{ik} are broadcast one at a time, other processors can begin updating their portions of the rows as soon as the necessary l_{ik} are received; as with the *kij,r* form, the elements $l_{k+1,k}, \ldots, l_{j,k}$ are needed to update the jth row. If the l_{ik} are broadcast one at a time, $O(n^2)$ broadcasts are needed, and this will be excessive. On the other hand, we can deviate somewhat from the *kij* paradigm and compute and broadcast several l_{ik} at once. This will decrease the number of broadcasts but at the cost of possible additional delays while processors wait for data. At the extreme, all of the kth column of L can be broadcast at once, and this may be the best strategy in conjunction with a send-ahead as in the *kij,r* form; that is, at the kth stage, $P(k+1)$ will compute and broadcast all of the $(k+1)$st column of L before completing the updates of the kth stage. Again, this is a rather large deviation from the *kij* paradigm and the same effect can be obtained in the *kji* form, to be discussed next. On vector processors, there will be further delays at the first stage to obtain sufficient multipliers, but this can perhaps be handled at subsequent stages by the compute-ahead strategy. Vector lengths are only partial, however.

The CH−kji,r Form

The *kji* form also does immediate updates but these are now by column. The *kji,r* form proceeds as follows. At the first stage, $P(1)$ computes and broadcasts l_{11}, and then all other processors can compute in parallel their portion of the first column of L. There are now two communication strategies. Since the update of the jth column requires that each processor hold l_{j1} in addition to the elements of the jth column it already holds, we could broadcast the elements of the first column one by one. Thus, $P(2)$ broadcasts l_{21} and then all processors can update their portion of the second column while $P(3)$ is broadcasting l_{31}, and so on. This will require a total of $O(n^2)$ broadcasts.

The second strategy is for all processors to broadcast at one time their portions of the kth column; this will require a total of $O(pn)$ broadcasts. As with the *kij,r* form, we can use a compute-ahead strategy and compute and broadcast the elements of the $(k+1)$st column of L before the updating of the kth stage is completed. Again, if computation and communication can be overlapped, this can be quite satisfactory. Note that this is a deviation from the *kji* paradigm, but less so than for the *kij* form since updates are by column. Vector lengths will only be partial in the *kji,r* form.

The CH–kji,c Form

The discussion of the *kji,c* form, with storage by columns, mirrors that of the *kij,c* form, except that now the update of the $(k + 1)$st column is no longer as much of a deviation from the *kji* paradigm; indeed, this is only a rearrangement of the communication, not the computation. As with the previous forms, it will be highly desirable to use a send-ahead strategy, and update and broadcast the $(k + 1)$st column of L as soon as possible during the kth stage. There will be full vector lengths for vector processors. It is clear that the *kji,c* form is the best of the *kij* and *kji* forms.

The Delayed Update *ikj* and *jki* Forms

The codes for the *ikj* and *jki* forms were given in Figure A.1-4. The *ikj* form is delayed update by rows while the *jki* form is delayed update by columns. We now discuss them in more detail.

The CH–ikj,r Form

As with *LU* factorization, we will have to deviate rather drastically from the delay prescription in order to have reasonable load balancing. The "migrating band" approach discussed for *LU* factorization can also be formulated here, but, again, at best we would achieve an algorithm no better than the *kij,r* form. The only exception would be on vector processors for which delayed updating is important.

The CH–ikj,c Form

With storage by columns, the *ikj* form is somewhat better since all processors are involved in updating row i. In particular, the products $l_{ik}l_{jk}$ can be performed in parallel. However, these products must be subtracted from a_{ij}, which lies in $P(j)$, so that a high degree of communication is required. Thus, this is an unattractive form.

The CH–jki,r Form

This is delayed update by columns with row storage. It mirrors the *kji,r* form except that all updates to the jth column are done at the jth stage. The kth update requires the kth column of L (from the element l_{jk} on). Hence, the elements of the jth row of L may be broadcast at the outset of the stage before the updates begin, or broadcast one by one and the updates begun as soon as the next multiplier is available. The latter possibility will require more communication time. Vector lengths are only partial.

The CH–jki,c Form

If storage is by columns, we have essentially the same problem as with the *ikj,r* form in that we must deviate considerably from the delayed updating in order to obtain good load balancing.

The *ijk* and *jik* Inner Product Forms

The codes for these forms were given in Figure A.1-6. The *ijk* form is delayed update by rows, in which the inner loop is an inner product of two rows of L.

The CH–ijk,r Form

At the ith stage of the CH–*ijk,r* algorithm $P(i)$ subtracts from elements of the ith row the inner products of rows 1 through $i - 1$ with the current ith row. Since the ith row is being continually updated, these inner products cannot be done in parallel, and, hence, at most two processors will be active at a given time in performing the updates. If we allow deviation from the form so that other processors can proceed to later stages, this will require that each row either be rebroadcast when needed to update a row of higher index or be saved in each processor. This would drastically increase either communication or storage costs.

The CH–ijk,c Form

With storage by interleaved columns, the situation is only slightly better. Now the rows are distributed across the processors and partial inner products can be done in parallel. However, these partial inner products must then be summed by a fan-in and the communication cost becomes prohibitive. We conclude that neither the *ijk,r* nor the *ijk,c* form can be competitive.

The CH–jik,r and CH–jik,c Forms

The *jik* form also computes inner products of the rows of L, but now L is computed by columns rather than by rows. At the jth stage, column j of L is computed and inner products of row j of L with all succeeding rows are needed. Consider first storage by interleaved rows. The jth row of L must first be broadcast to all processors and then the inner products may be done in parallel. This is exactly the same data pattern as the *jki,r* form. The difference is that the *jki* form updates the jth column by a linear combination of columns while the *jik* form updates by inner products of rows. On scalar machines, these are equivalent. However, on vector processors, the *jik,r* form will use inner products with full vector lengths compared with the partial vector lengths of the *jki,r* form. In a similar way, it is easy to see that the *jik,c* form with storage by interleaved columns has the same difficulties as the *jki,c* form.

Recall that the properties of the parallel Choleski forms were summarized in Table 2.2-2.

Appendix 2

Convergence of Iterative Methods

In this appendix, we discuss some basic convergence theorems for iterative methods. Most of these results are classical and may be found in Varga [1962] or Young [1971]. We consider first the iterative method

$$\mathbf{x}^{k+1} = H\mathbf{x}^k + \mathbf{d}, \qquad k = 0, 1, \ldots \tag{A.2.1}$$

for approximating solutions of the linear system

$$A\mathbf{x} = \mathbf{b} \tag{A.2.2}$$

We assume that the $n \times n$ matrix A is nonsingular and that $\hat{\mathbf{x}}$ is the unique solution of (A.2.2). Then the iterative method (A.2.1) is said to be *consistent* with (A.2.2) if

$$\hat{\mathbf{x}} = H\hat{\mathbf{x}} + \mathbf{d} \tag{A.2.3}$$

For a consistent method we can subtract (A.2.3) from (A.2.1) to obtain the basic error equation

$$\mathbf{e}^{k+1} = H\mathbf{e}^k, \qquad k = 0, 1, \ldots \tag{A.2.4}$$

where $\mathbf{e}^i = \mathbf{x}^i - \hat{\mathbf{x}}$ is the error at the ith step. This equation is equivalent to

$$\mathbf{e}^k = H^k\mathbf{e}^0, \qquad k = 1, 2, \ldots \tag{A.2.5}$$

If we require that (A.2.1) converge for any $\mathbf{x}^0$, then this is equivalent to requiring that $\mathbf{e}^k \to 0$ as $k \to \infty$ for any $\mathbf{e}^0$. By choosing $\mathbf{e}^0$ successively equal to the coordinate vectors $\mathbf{e}_1, \mathbf{e}_2, \ldots$, where $\mathbf{e}_i$ is zero except for a 1 in the ith position, we see that $\mathbf{e}^k \to 0$ as $k \to \infty$ for any $\mathbf{e}^0$ is equivalent to $H^k \to 0$ for $k \to \infty$. If $\lambda_1, \ldots, \lambda_n$ are the eigenvalues of H and $\rho(H) = \max_i|\lambda_i|$ is the spectral radius of H, we then have the following basic result, whose proof is given, for example, in Ortega [1987a; Theorem 5.3.4].

A.2.1. THEOREM. *If H is an $n \times n$ matrix, then $H^k \to 0$ as $k \to \infty$ if and only if $\rho(H) < 1$. Thus, the consistent iterative method* (A.2.1) *converges for any $\mathbf{x}^0$ to the unique solution of* (A.2.2) *if and only if $\rho(H) < 1$.*

Consistent iterative methods arise naturally in the following way. Let

$$A = P - Q \tag{A.2.6}$$

be a splitting of A, and assume that P is nonsingular. Then it is easy to see that

$$\mathbf{x}^{k+1} = P^{-1}Q\mathbf{x}^k + P^{-1}\mathbf{b}, \qquad k = 0, 1, \ldots \tag{A.2.7}$$

is a consistent iterative method. For such methods, the question of convergence reduces to ascertaining if $\rho(P^{-1}Q) < 1$. A useful tool for this in certain cases is given by the following result, whose proof is given, for example, in Ortega [1987a; Theorem 5.4.2].

A.2.2. STEIN'S THEOREM. *If H is an $n \times n$ real matrix, then $\rho(H) < 1$ if and only if there is a symmetric positive definite matrix B such that $B - H^TBH$ is positive definite.*

We will say that a real, not necessarily symmetric, matrix C is *positive definite* if $\mathbf{x}^TC\mathbf{x} > 0$ for all real $\mathbf{x} \neq 0$. This is equivalent to the symmetric part of C, $(C + C^T)/2$, being positive definite in the usual sense. We will use this concept in the following way.

A.2.3. DEFINITION. The splitting $A = P - Q$ is *P-regular* if P is nonsingular and $P + Q$ is positive definite.

We can now give the following convergence theorem.

A.2.4. *P*-REGULAR SPLITTING THEOREM. *If A is symmetric positive definite and $A = P - Q$ is a P-regular splitting, then $\rho(P^{-1}Q) < 1$.*

PROOF. Let $H = P^{-1}Q$ and $C = A - H^TAH$. Then, since $P^{-1}Q = I - P^{-1}A$, we have

$$\begin{aligned} C &= A - (I - P^{-1}A)^TA(I - P^{-1}A) \\ &= (P^{-1}A)^TA + AP^{-1}A - (P^{-1}A)^TAP^{-1}A \\ &= (P^{-1}A)^T(P + P^T - A)P^{-1}A = (P^{-1}A)^T(P^T + Q)(P^{-1}A) \end{aligned} \tag{A.2.8}$$

By assumption, $P + Q$ is positive definite and therefore $P^T + Q$ is positive definite. Thus, since C is congruent to $P^T + Q$, it is also positive definite. It then follows from Stein's Theorem A.2.2 that if A is positive definite we have $\rho(H) < 1$. □

There are two different converses associated with A.2.4, each useful in certain situations. The first is as follows:

A.2.5. First Converse of P-Regular Splitting. *Assume that A is symmetric and nonsingular, $A = P - Q$ is a P-regular splitting, and $\rho(P^{-1}Q) < 1$. Then A is positive definite.*

Proof. Again let $H = P^{-1}Q$, so that $\rho(H) < 1$. Then, for any $\mathbf{x}^0$, by A.2.1 the sequence $\mathbf{x}^k = H\mathbf{x}^{k-1}$, $k = 1, 2, \ldots$, converges to zero. Now suppose that A is not positive definite. Then there is some $\mathbf{x}^0 \neq 0$ so that $(\mathbf{x}^0)^T A\mathbf{x}^0 \leq 0$, and

$$\mathbf{y}^0 = P^{-1}A\mathbf{x}^0 \neq 0$$

Thus, from (A.2.8),

$$(\mathbf{x}^0)^T C\mathbf{x}^0 = (\mathbf{y}^0)^T(P^T + Q)\mathbf{y}^0 > 0$$

by the assumption of a P-regular splitting. Moreover, as shown by (A.2.8), C is positive definite, so that, for any $k \geq 0$,

$$0 \leq (\mathbf{x}^k)^T C\mathbf{x}^k = (\mathbf{x}^k)^T A\mathbf{x}^k - (\mathbf{x}^{k+1})^T A\mathbf{x}^{k+1}$$

and we have shown that strict inequality holds for $k = 0$. Thus,

$$(\mathbf{x}^{k+1})^T A\mathbf{x}^{k+1} \leq (\mathbf{x}^k)^T A\mathbf{x}^k \leq \cdots \leq (\mathbf{x}^1)^T A\mathbf{x}^1 < (\mathbf{x}^0)^T A\mathbf{x}^0 \leq 0$$

But this contradicts the fact that $\mathbf{x}^k \to 0$ as $\mathbf{k} \to \infty$ so A must be positive definite. □

The second converse of A.2.4 is applicable when P itself is symmetric positive definite. In this case, convergence implies not only that A must be positive definite but that the splitting must be P-regular. Note that A.2.4 and A.2.6 contain the result 3.4.3 stated in the text.

A.2.6. Second Converse of P-Regular Splitting. *Assume that $A = P - Q$ is symmetric and nonsingular, P is symmetric positive definite, and $\rho(P^{-1}Q) < 1$. Then A and $P + Q$ are positive definite.*

In order to prove A.2.6 we need the following result about the eigenvalues of products of symmetric matrices; for a proof, see, e.g., Ortega [1987a; Theorem 6.2.3]

A.2.7. THEOREM. *Let B and C be real symmetric matrices. If either is positive definite, then BC has real eigenvalues. If both B and C are positive definite, then BC has positive eigenvalues. Conversely, if BC has positive eigenvalues and either B or C is positive definite, then both are positive definite.*

PROOF OF A.2.6. Again, set $H = P^{-1}Q = I - P^{-1}A$. Since P^{-1} is positive definite, A.2.7 ensures that the eigenvalues $\lambda_1, \ldots, \lambda_n$ of H are real and, since $\rho(H) < 1$, we must have

$$-1 < \lambda_i < 1, \qquad i = 1, \ldots, n \tag{A.2.9}$$

Thus the eigenvalues of $P^{-1}A$ are positive and, again by A.2.7, A is positive definite. Moreover, $(I - H)^{-1}$ exists and the matrix $G = (I - H)^{-1}(I + H)$ has eigenvalues $(1 + \lambda_i)/(1 - \lambda_i)$, $i = 1, \ldots, n$, which are positive by (A.2.9). We can write G as

$$G = (I - P^{-1}Q)^{-1}(I + P^{-1}Q) = [P^{-1}(P - Q)]^{-1}P^{-1}(P + Q)$$
$$= A^{-1}(P + Q)$$

and then A.2.7 shows that $P + Q$ is positive definite since A^{-1} is positive definite. □

We note that it is an open question as to whether A.2.6 holds without the assumption that P is symmetric.

We now apply the above general results to some particular iterative methods. We first note that Theorem 3.1.2 is an immediate consequence of A.2.4 and A.2.6. Here, $P = D$ and $Q = B$.

A.2.8. JACOBI ITERATION CONVERGENCE. *If $A = D - B$ is symmetric and nonsingular and the diagonal D of A is positive definite, then the Jacobi iteration converges for any $\mathbf{x}^0$ if and only if both A and $D + B$ are positive definite.*

We next prove Theorem 3.2.3 in a somewhat strengthened form.

A.2.9. OSTROWSKI–REICH THEOREM. *If A is symmetric and nonsingular with positive diagonal elements and $\omega \in (0, 2)$, then the SOR iteration converges for every $\mathbf{x}^0$ if and only if A is positive definite.*

PROOF. We will first apply Theorem A.2.4. If $A = D - L - L^T$, the SOR iteration matrix is

$$H_\omega = (D - \omega L)^{-1}[(1 - \omega)D + \omega L^T] \tag{A.2.10}$$

and it is easy to verify that P and Q are given by

$$P = \omega^{-1}(D - \omega L), \qquad Q = \omega^{-1}[(1 - \omega)D + \omega L^T]$$

Since D has positive diagonal elements, P is nonsingular and it only remains to verify that $P + Q$ is positive definite. The symmetric part of $P + Q$ is

$$\frac{1}{2}(P + P^T) + \frac{1}{2}(Q + Q^T) = \frac{1}{2\omega}(2D - \omega L - \omega L^T)$$

$$+ \frac{1}{2\omega}[2(1 - \omega)D + \omega L + \omega L^T] = \frac{2 - \omega}{\omega} D$$

which is positive definite if $\omega \in (0, 2)$. The converse statement follows immediately from A.2.5. □

Theorem A.2.9 gives the full range of allowable real ω for the SOR iteration. This is a consequence of the following result, which does not assume that A is necessarily symmetric.

A.2.10. KAHAN'S LEMMA. *Assume that A has nonzero diagonal elements. Then the spectral radius of the SOR iteration matrix* (A.2.10) *with* $L^T = U$ *satisfies*

$$\rho(H_\omega) \geqslant |\omega - 1| \tag{A.2.11}$$

PROOF. Because L is strictly lower triangular, $\det D^{-1} = \det(D - \omega L)^{-1}$ and we have

$$\det H_\omega = \det D^{-1} \det[(1 - \omega)D + \omega U]$$

$$= \det[(1 - \omega)I + \omega D^{-1}U] = (1 - \omega)^n$$

since $D^{-1}U$ is strictly upper triangular. But $\det H_\omega$ is the product of the eigenvalues of H_ω and therefore (A.2.11) must hold. □

Theorem A.2.4 also applies to the SSOR iteration. In order to find the correct splitting $A = P - Q$ in which P is symmetric, we examine the more general alternating iteration

$$S\mathbf{x}^{k+1/2} = (S - A)\mathbf{x}^k + \mathbf{b} \tag{A.2.12a}$$

$$S^T\mathbf{x}^{k+1} = (S^T - A)\mathbf{x}^{k+1/2} + \mathbf{b} \tag{A.2.12b}$$

Combining the two halves of (A.2.12) gives the single step iteration

$$\mathbf{x}^{k+1} = (I - S^{-T}A)(I - S^{-1}A)\mathbf{x}^k + [(I - S^{-T}A)S^{-1} + S^{-T}]\mathbf{b} \tag{A.2.13}$$

If this iteration is assumed to arise from a splitting $A = P - Q$, then we must have

$$P^{-1} = [(I - S^{-T}A)S^{-1} + S^{-T}] = S^{-T}(S + S^T - A)S^{-1}$$

or

$$P = S(S + S^T - A)^{-1}S^T \tag{A.2.14}$$

This P is clearly symmetric, and the corresponding Q is

$$Q = P - A = S(S + S^T - A)^{-1}S^T - A \tag{A.2.15}$$

The P and Q given by (A.2.14) and (A.2.15) satisfy

$$\begin{aligned} P^{-1}Q &= I - P^{-1}A = I - S^{-T}(S + S^T - A)S^{-1}A \\ &= I - S^{-T}A - S^{-1}A + S^{-T}AS^{-1}A = (I - S^{-T}A)(I - S^{-1}A) \end{aligned}$$

which is the iteration matrix of (A.2.13), as expected.

For the SSOR iteration $S = \omega^{-1}D - L$ so that (A.2.12a) becomes

$$\begin{aligned} (\omega^{-1}D - L)\mathbf{x}^{k+1/2} &= [\omega^{-1}D - L - D + L + L^T]\mathbf{x}^k + \mathbf{b} \\ &= [(\omega^{-1} - 1)D + L^T]\mathbf{x}^k + \mathbf{b} \end{aligned}$$

and similarly for (A.2.12b). Note that in the definition of S, ω has been factored from the familiar $D - \omega L$ so that $\mathbf{b}$ is not multiplied by ω in

(A.2.12). With this S, (A.2.14) becomes

$$P = (\omega^{-1}D - L)[\omega^{-1}D - L + \omega^{-1}D - L^T - D + L + L^T]^{-1}(\omega^{-1}D - L^T)$$

$$= \omega^{-2}(D - \omega L)[(2\omega^{-1} - 1)D]^{-1}(D - \omega L^T)$$

$$= \frac{1}{\omega(2-\omega)}(D - \omega L)D^{-1}(D - \omega L^T) \tag{A.2.16}$$

and it is easy to verify that the corresponding Q of (A.2.15) is

$$Q = \frac{1}{\omega(2-\omega)}[(1-\omega)D + \omega L]D^{-1}[(1-\omega)D + \omega L^T] \tag{A.2.17}$$

We note that the P and Q of (A.2.16, 17) can also be obtained from the iteration matrix

$$H = (D - \omega L^T)^{-1}[(1-\omega)D + \omega L](D - \omega L)^{-1}$$
$$\times [(1-\omega)D + \omega L^T] \tag{A.2.18}$$

of the SSOR iteration. The middle two terms of (A.2.18) can be written as

$$[(1-\omega)D + \omega L](D - \omega L)^{-1} = [(1-\omega)I + \omega LD^{-1}](I - \omega LD^{-1})^{-1}$$
$$= (I - \omega LD^{-1})^{-1}[(1-\omega)I + \omega LD^{-1}]$$
$$= D(D - \omega L)^{-1}[(1-\omega)D + \omega L]D^{-1}$$

since products of the form $(I + B)^{-1}(aI + bB)$ commute. Thus

$$H = (D - \omega L^T)^{-1}D(D - \omega L)^{-1}[(1-\omega)D + \omega L]D^{-1}[(1-\omega)D + \omega L^T]$$

This displays the factors P^{-1} and Q with the exception of the constant $\omega(2-\omega)$ which cancels out.

If A is positive definite and $\omega \in (0, 2)$, then the matrix P of (A.2.16) is positive definite, and the matrix Q of (A.2.17) is positive definite unless $\omega = 1$, in which case Q is positive semidefinite. In either case, $P + Q$ is positive definite so that $A = P - Q$ is a P-regular splitting. Theorems A.2.4 and A.2.5 both apply and we can summarize the convergence properties of the SSOR iteration as follows.

A.2.11. SSOR CONVERGENCE. *If A is symmetric and nonsingular with positive diagonal elements and $0 < \omega < 2$, then the SSOR iteration converges for every $\mathbf{x}^0$ if and only if A is positive definite.*

We note that if A is symmetric positive definite the eigenvalues of the SSOR iteration matrix are real, and positive if $\omega \neq 1$. This follows from A.2.7 since P and Q are positive definite. (If $\omega = 1$, the eigenvalues are only nonnegative.) Similarly, A.2.7 shows that the eigenvalues of the Jacobi iteration matrix are real.

Regular Splittings and Diagonal Dominance

The previous results have depended on the coefficient matrix A being symmetric and positive definite. The other standard approach to convergence theorems for the Jacobi and Gauss–Seidel iterations is when A is an M matrix or is diagonally dominant. In these cases, symmetry is not necessary. We recall the following definitions, which will be used in the sequel.

A.2.12. DEFINITIONS. The real $n \times n$ matrix A is

a. *Diagonally dominant* if

$$|a_{ii}| \geq \sum_{j \neq i} |a_{ij}|, \qquad i = 1, \ldots, n \tag{A.2.19}$$

and *strictly diagonally dominant* if strict inequality holds in (A.2.19) for all i.

b. *Reducible* if there is a permutation matrix P such that

$$PAP^T = \begin{bmatrix} B_{11} & B_{12} \\ 0 & B_{22} \end{bmatrix}$$

and *irreducible* if it is not reducible.

c. *Irreducibly diagonally dominant* if it is diagonally dominant, irreducible, and strict inequality holds in (A.2.19) for at least one i.

d. *Nonnegative*, denoted by $A \geq 0$, if all elements are nonnegative, and *positive*, denoted by $A > 0$, if all elements are positive.

e. *An M matrix* if $a_{ij} \leq 0$, for all $i \neq j$, and $A^{-1} \geq 0$.

We will first consider the following classes of splittings.

A.2.13. DEFINITION. $A = P - Q$ is a *weak regular splitting* if P is nonsingular, $P^{-1} \geq 0$, and $P^{-1}Q \geq 0$. It is a *regular splitting* if $P^{-1} \geq 0$ and $Q \geq 0$.

Clearly a regular splitting is a weak regular splitting. The basic convergence theorem for these splittings is the following.

A.2.14. WEAK REGULAR SPLITTING THEOREM. Assume that A is nonsingular with $A^{-1} \geq 0$ and that $A = P - Q$ is a weak regular splitting. Then $\rho(P^{-1}Q) < 1$.

PROOF. Set $H = P^{-1}Q$. Then $H \geq 0$ and by the relations

$$(I + H + \cdots + H^m)(I - H) = I - H^{m+1}, \qquad P^{-1} = (I - H)A^{-1}$$

we have, since $A^{-1} \geq 0$,

$$0 \leq (I + H + \cdots + H^m)P^{-1} = (I - H^{m+1})A^{-1} \leq A^{-1}$$

for all $m \geq 0$. Since $P^{-1} \geq 0$, each row of P^{-1} must contain at least one positive element and it follows that the elements of $I + H + \cdots + H^m$ are bounded above as $m \to \infty$. Therefore, since $H \geq 0$, the sum converges and consequently $H^k \to 0$ as $k \to \infty$. Thus, by A.2.1, $\rho(H) < 1$. □

We now apply A.2.14 to the Jacobi and Gauss-Seidel iterations in the case that A is an M matrix. Let

$$A = D - L - U, \qquad B = L + U \tag{A.2.20}$$

where D is the diagonal part of A, $-L$ the strictly lower triangular part and $-U$ the strictly upper triangular part. If A is an M matrix, then $B \geq 0$ and

$$I = (D - B)A^{-1} = DA^{-1} - BA^{-1} \leq DA^{-1}$$

which shows that the diagonal elements of D are positive. Therefore, the Jacobi and Gauss-Seidel iterations are well defined.

A.2.15. THEOREM. *Let A be an M matrix. Then the Jacobi and Gauss-Seidel iterates converge for any $\mathbf{x}^0$ to the unique solution of $A\mathbf{x} = \mathbf{b}$.*

PROOF. For the Jacobi iteration, $A = D - B$ is clearly a regular splitting so that A.2.14 applies. For the Gauss-Seidel iteration, the splitting is $A = (D - L) - U$. Since D is nonsingular, $D - L$ is nonsingular and

$$(D - L)^{-1} = [I + D^{-1}L + (D^{-1}L)^2 + \cdots + (D^{-1}L)^{n-1}]D^{-1} \geq 0 \tag{A.2.21}$$

where the series terminates because $D^{-1}L$ is strictly lower triangular. Hence $A = (D - L) - U$ is a regular splitting and, again, A.2.14 applies. □

We next give convergence theorems that apply when A is diagonally dominant. We first need the following result about M matrices.

A.2.16. LEMMA. *Let A be strictly or irreducibly diagonally dominant and assume that $a_{ii} > 0$, $i = 1, \ldots, n$, and $a_{ij} \leq 0$, $i \neq j$. Then A is an M matrix.*

PROOF. *Let* $H = I - D^{-1}A$ be the Jacobi iteration matrix. Then by Ortega [1987a; Theorem 6.1.6], A is an M matrix if $\rho(H) < 1$. If A is strictly diagonally dominant, then $\rho(H) \leq \|H\|_\infty < 1$, while if A is irreducibly diagonally dominant, $\rho(H) < 1$ follows from Ortega [1987a; Theorem 6.1.10]. □

A.2.17. DIAGONAL DOMINANCE THEOREM. *Let A be strictly or irreducibly diagonally dominant. Then the Jacobi and Gauss-Seidel iterates both converge for any* $\mathbf{x}^0$.

PROOF. Let

$$\hat{A} = |D| - |L| - |U|$$

where $|L|$ denotes the matrix whose elements are the absolute values of the elements of L, and similarly for $|D|$ and $|U|$. Clearly, $\hat{A}$ is also strictly or irreducibly diagonally dominant if A is. Hence, by A.2.16, $\hat{A}$ is an M matrix so that by A.2.15

$$\rho[|D|^{-1}(|L| + |U|)] < 1, \qquad \rho[(|D| - |L|)^{-1}|U|] < 1$$

But

$$|D^{-1}(L + U)| \leq |D|^{-1}(|L| + |U|)$$

and

$$|(D - L)^{-1}U| \leq (|D| - |L|)^{-1}|U|$$

where the second inequality follows from (A.2.21). It then follows from comparison theorems on spectral radii (if $|B| \leq C$, then $\rho(B) \leq \rho(C)$; see, for example, Varga [1962]) that

$$\rho[D^{-1}(L + U)] \leq \rho[|D|^{-1}(|L| + |U|)] < 1$$

$$\rho[(D - L)^{-1}U] \leq \rho[(|D| - |L|)^{-1}|U|] < 1. \qquad \square$$

ADI convergence

We next prove Theorem 3.1.3 on convergence of the ADI iteration

$$(\alpha I + H)\mathbf{x}^{k+1/2} = (\alpha I - V)\mathbf{x}^k - \mathbf{b}, \qquad k = 0, 1, \ldots \quad \text{(A.2.22a)}$$

$$(\alpha I + V)\mathbf{x}^{k+1} = (\alpha I - H)\mathbf{x}^{k+1/2} + \mathbf{b}, \qquad k = 0, 1, \ldots \quad \text{(A.2.22b)}$$

A.2.18. ADI Convergence. *Let A, H, and V be symmetric positive definite matrices such that $A = H + V$, and let $\alpha > 0$. Then, the iterates (A.2.22) are well defined and converge to the unique solution of $A\mathbf{x} = \mathbf{b}$.*

Proof. The iteration matrix for (A.2.22) is

$$S = (\alpha I + V)^{-1}(\alpha I - H)(\alpha I + H)^{-1}(\alpha I - V)$$

and it suffices to show that $\rho(S) < 1$. Since H and V are positive definite and $\alpha > 0$, the matrices $\alpha I + H$ and $\alpha I + V$ are nonsingular and the iterates are well defined. Let

$$F = (\alpha I - H)(\alpha I + H)^{-1}, \qquad G = (\alpha I - V)(\alpha I + V)^{-1}$$

If $\lambda_n \geq \cdots \geq \lambda_1 > 0$ are the eigenvalues of H, then $(\alpha - \lambda_i)/(\alpha + \lambda_i)$ are the eigenvalues of F and are clearly all less than 1 in absolute value. Since $(\alpha I - H)$ and $(\alpha I + H)^{-1}$ commute, F is symmetric, and in the l_2 norm

$$\|F\|_2 = \max_i \frac{|\alpha - \lambda_i|}{\alpha + \lambda_i} < 1$$

In the same way, we obtain $\|G\|_2 < 1$. Hence

$$\|FG\|_2 \leq \|F\|_2\|G\|_2 < 1$$

so that the spectral radius of FG satisfies $\rho(FG) < 1$. But S is similar to FG since

$$S = (\alpha I + V)^{-1}FG(\alpha I + V)$$

and thus $\rho(S) < 1$. □

Rate of Convergence

For the iteration (A.2.1) with $\rho(H) < 1$, the *asymptotic convergence factor* is defined as

$$\alpha = \sup_{x^0} \{\limsup_{k\to\infty} \|\mathbf{x}^k - \hat{\mathbf{x}}\|^{1/k}\} \qquad \text{(A.2.23)}$$

where $\hat{\mathbf{x}}$ satisfies $\hat{\mathbf{x}} = H\hat{\mathbf{x}} + \mathbf{d}$.

In order to understand (A.2.23) better, consider a single sequence and let

$$\beta = \limsup_{k\to\infty} \|\mathbf{x}^k - \hat{\mathbf{x}}\|^{1/k}$$

Since $\mathbf{x}^k \to \hat{\mathbf{x}}$ as $k \to \infty$, clearly $\beta \leq 1$ and for any $\varepsilon > 0$, there is a k_0 such that

$$\|\mathbf{x}^k - \hat{\mathbf{x}}\| \leq (\beta + \varepsilon)^k, \qquad k \geq k_0$$

Hence, if $\beta < 1$ we may choose ε such that $\beta + \varepsilon < 1$ and then, asymptotically, $\|\mathbf{x}^k - \hat{\mathbf{x}}\|$ tends to zero at least as rapidly as the geometric sequence $(\beta + \varepsilon)^k$. The supremum in (A.2.23) is taken to reflect the worse possible behavior of any individual sequence.

The basic theorem for the asymptotic convergence factor for the iteration (A.2.22) is the following.

A.2.19. THEOREM. *The asymptotic convergence factor* (A.2.23) *in any norm equals* $\rho(H)$.

For a formal proof of this theorem, see, for example, Ortega [1972]. We will indicate in the following a less formal development that will be illustrative.

First, note that A.2.19 implies that, in any norm, for any sequence $\{\mathbf{x}^k\}$ and $\varepsilon > 0$ such that $\rho(H) + \varepsilon < 1$ there is a k_0 such that

$$\|\mathbf{x}^k - \hat{\mathbf{x}}\| \leq [\rho(H) + \varepsilon]^k, \qquad k \geq k_0 \tag{A.2.24}$$

Hence, asymptotically, the errors are decreasing almost as rapidly as $\rho(H)^k$. It is important to note that this error reduction is, in general, only asymptotic. Consider, for example,

$$H = \begin{bmatrix} 0.5 & a \\ 0 & 0 \end{bmatrix}$$

so that $\rho(H) = 0.5$. But

$$H^k = \begin{bmatrix} (0.5)^k & a(0.5)^{k-1} \\ 0 & 0 \end{bmatrix}$$

so that with $\mathbf{e}^k = \mathbf{x}^k - \hat{\mathbf{x}}$ and $\mathbf{e}^0 = (0, 1)^T$, we have $\mathbf{e}^k = H^k\mathbf{e}^0 = (a(0.5)^{k-1}, 0)^T$. Suppose that $a = 2^p$. Then

$$\|\mathbf{e}^k\|_2 = 2^{p-k+1} \geqslant \|\mathbf{e}^0\|_2 \qquad \text{for } k \leqslant p+1$$

so that the first p errors, in the 2-norm, are actually greater than the initial error. This illustrates that $\rho(H)$ need not be a measure of the rate of convergence, as measured in some usual norm, in the initial stages of the iteration.

We next illustrate A.2.19 in the following way. Assume that H has n linearly independent eigenvectors $\mathbf{v}_1, \ldots, \mathbf{v}_n$ corresponding to the n eigenvalues $|\lambda_1| \geqslant |\lambda_2| \geqslant \cdots \geqslant |\lambda_n|$. Then, for any sequence $\mathbf{x}^k$ generated by (A.2.1), the errors $\mathbf{e}^k = \mathbf{x}^k - \hat{\mathbf{x}}$ satisfy

$$\mathbf{e}^k = H^k\mathbf{e}^0 = \alpha_1\lambda_1^k\mathbf{v}_1 + \cdots + \alpha_n\lambda_n^k\mathbf{v}_n = \lambda_1^k\left[\alpha_1\mathbf{v}_1 + \sum_{i=2}^{n}\left(\frac{\lambda_i}{\lambda_1}\right)^k\mathbf{v}_i\right] \qquad \text{(A.2.25)}$$

where $\mathbf{e}^0 = \alpha_1\mathbf{v}_1 + \cdots + \alpha_n\mathbf{v}_n$. Now suppose that $|\lambda_1| > |\lambda_2|$. Then

$$\frac{\mathbf{e}^k}{\lambda_1^k} \to \alpha_1\mathbf{v}_1 \qquad \text{as } k \to \infty. \qquad \text{(A.2.26)}$$

The interpretation of (A.2.26) is that the error vectors $\mathbf{e}^k$ tend to the direction $\mathbf{v}_1$ and that asymptotically the errors behave as $\lambda_1^k\alpha_1\mathbf{v}_1$. Thus, again asymptotically, the errors are reduced by the factor $\rho(H) = |\lambda_1|$ at each iteration.

Note that if $\alpha_1 = 0$, then $|\lambda_2| < \rho(H)$ determines the rate of convergence of the sequence. However, this is of little consequence since it is extremely unlikely that an initial $\mathbf{x}^0$ would be such that $\alpha_1 = 0$. Even if it were, rounding error in the computation would have the effect of making $\alpha_1 \neq 0$ in later iterations.

Suppose, next, that $|\lambda_1| = |\lambda_2| > |\lambda_3|$. In this case

$$\mathbf{e}^k = \alpha_1\lambda_1^k\mathbf{v}_1 + \alpha_2\lambda_2^k\mathbf{v}_2 + \text{lower-order terms}$$

If $\lambda_1 = \lambda_2$, then $\mathbf{e}^k$ tends to the direction $\alpha_1\mathbf{v}_1 + \alpha_2\mathbf{v}_2$. Otherwise, $\mathbf{e}^k$ need not tend to a fixed direction but, rather, tends to the subspace spanned by $\mathbf{v}_1$ and $\mathbf{v}_2$. For example, if $\lambda_1 = -\lambda_2$, then

$$\mathbf{e}^k = \lambda_1^k(\alpha_1\mathbf{v}_1 + (-1)^k\alpha_2\mathbf{v}_2) + \text{lower-order terms}$$

Similarly, if $|\lambda_1| = \cdots = |\lambda_p| > |\lambda_{p+1}|$, then $\mathbf{e}^k$ tends to the subspace spanned by $\mathbf{v}_1, \ldots, \mathbf{v}_p$. In any case, the errors are still decreasing asymptotically by the factor $\rho(H)$.

Now suppose that H does not have a diagonal Jordan form; in particular, suppose that $\lambda_1 = \cdots = \lambda_p$ and that λ_1 is associated with a $p \times p$ Jordan block. Let $\mathbf{v}_1$ be an eigenvector associated with λ_1, and $\mathbf{v}_2, \ldots, \mathbf{v}_p$ generalized eigenvectors such that

$$H\mathbf{v}_i = \lambda_1 \mathbf{v}_i + \mathbf{v}_{i-1}, \qquad i = 2, \ldots, p \tag{A.2.27}$$

(See, e.g., Ortega [1987a; Section 3.2].) It follows from (A.2.27) that

$$H^k\mathbf{v}_i = \lambda_1^k \mathbf{v}_i + k\lambda_1^{k-1}\mathbf{v}_{i-1} + \cdots + \binom{k}{i-1}\lambda_1^{k-i+1}\mathbf{v}_1 \tag{A.2.28}$$

where $\binom{k}{j}$ is the binomial coefficient $k!/(k-j)!j!$.

Now, for simplicity, consider the case $p = 2$ so that $|\lambda_1| = |\lambda_2| > |\lambda_3| \geq \cdots \geq |\lambda_n|$. Then using (A.2.28) for $i = 2$ we have

$$\begin{aligned} \mathbf{e}^k = H^k\mathbf{e}^0 &= \alpha_1\lambda_1^k\mathbf{v}_1 + \alpha_2(\lambda_1^k\mathbf{v}_2 + k\lambda_1^{k-1}\mathbf{v}_1) + \sum_{i=3}^{n} \alpha_i H^k \mathbf{v}_i \\ &= \lambda_1^k\left[\left(\alpha_1 + \alpha_2\frac{k}{\lambda_1}\right)\mathbf{v}_1 + \alpha_2\mathbf{v}_2 + \frac{1}{\lambda_1^k}\sum_{i=3}^{n}\alpha_i H^k\mathbf{v}_i\right] \end{aligned} \tag{A.2.29}$$

where, again, $\mathbf{e}^0 = \alpha_1\mathbf{v}_1 + \cdots + \alpha_n\mathbf{v}_n$, and $\mathbf{v}_3, \ldots, \mathbf{v}_n$ are either eigenvectors or generalized eigenvectors. Since $|\lambda_1| > |\lambda_i|$, $i = 3, \ldots, n$, it follows from

$$\binom{k}{j}\left|\frac{\lambda_i}{\lambda_1}\right|^k \to 0 \quad \text{as } k \to \infty, \qquad i = 3, \ldots, n$$

that

$$\lambda_1^{-k}H^k\mathbf{v}_i \to 0 \qquad \text{as } k \to \infty, \qquad i = 3, \ldots, n$$

Hence, asymptotically, the error behaves as

$$\mathbf{e}^k \sim \lambda_1^k\left[\left(\alpha_1 + \alpha_2\frac{k}{\lambda_1}\right)\mathbf{v}_1 + \alpha_2\mathbf{v}_2\right] \sim \alpha_2 k\lambda_1^{k-1}\mathbf{v}_1 \tag{A.2.30}$$

This shows that the error vectors are tending to the direction of the eigenvector $\mathbf{v}_1$, but because of the k term the errors are no longer decreasing asymptotically by the factor $|\lambda_1| = \rho(H)$. However, $\rho(H)$ is still the best *single* indicator of the rate of convergence since for any $\delta > 0$

$$\frac{k\lambda_1^k}{(|\lambda_1| + \delta)^k} \to 0 \qquad \text{as } k \to \infty$$

That is, the errors are going to zero asymptotically at least as fast as μ^k, where μ is arbitrarily close to $\rho(H)$.

The general result is similar. If $\lambda_1 = \cdots = \lambda_p$ is associated with a $p \times p$ Jordan block and $|\lambda_p| > |\lambda_{p+1}|$, then it may be shown, by proceeding as above, that

$$\mathbf{e}^k \sim c k^{p-1} \lambda_1^k \mathbf{v}_1$$

Since

$$\frac{k^{p-1}\lambda_1^k}{(|\lambda_1| + \delta)^k} \to 0 \qquad \text{as } k \to \infty$$

for any $\delta > 0$, it is again the case that the errors go to zero at least as fast as $[\rho(H) + \delta]^k$ for any $\delta > 0$. If there are several Jordan blocks of the same size associated with the eigenvalue of largest modulus, the same result is true, although now the error tends to the subspace spanned by the corresponding eigenvectors.

On the basis of Theorem A.2.19, the asymptotic rate of convergence of the iterative method (A.2.1) is faster the smaller $\rho(H)$ is. Consider now the problem of choosing the parameter ω to minimize $\rho(H_\omega)$, where H_ω is the SOR iteration matrix given by (A.2.10). In general, this is very difficult, but by a beautiful theory due to Frankel and Young in the early 1950s (see Varga [1962] and Young [1971] for a full exposition) there is a solution when A is the coefficient matrix (3.1.7) of the discrete Poisson matrix or more generally, when A is consistently ordered (see Young [1971]). The basic theorem is as follows:

A.2.20. THEOREM. *Assume that A is symmetric positive definite and consistently ordered, and that H_ω is the SOR iteration matrix* (A.2.10). *Let $\mu = \rho(J)$, where J is the Jacobi iteration matrix. Then there is a unique $\omega \in (0, 2)$ that minimizes $\rho(H_\omega)$ and is given by*

$$\omega_0 = \frac{2}{1 + (1 - \mu^2)^{1/2}} \tag{A.2.31}$$

Moreover,

$$\rho(H_\omega) = \omega - 1, \qquad \omega_0 \leqslant \omega \leqslant 2 \tag{A.2.32a}$$

and

$$\rho(H_\omega) = \tfrac{1}{4}\{\omega\mu + [\omega^2\mu^2 - 4(\omega - 1)]^{1/2}\}^2, \qquad 0 \leqslant \omega \leqslant \omega_0 \tag{A.2.32b}$$

On the basis of (A.2.32), we can plot $\rho(H_\omega)$ as a function of ω as shown in Figure A.2-1. The slope of this curve to the right of ω_0 is 1, but at ω_0 the slope of the curve on the left is infinite. Thus, it is best to overestimate ω_0 rather than underestimate it.

An immediate consequence of (A.2.32b) is that

$$\rho(H_1) = \mu^2 \tag{A.2.33}$$

which states that the asymptotic rate of convergence of the Gauss-Seidel method is exactly twice that of the Jacobi method, under the conditions of the theorem.

The formulas (A.2.31) and (A.2.32) require knowledge of μ, and in general this will not be available. However, for the $N^2 \times N^2$ Poisson matrix (3.1.7) it can be shown (from Exercise 3.1-21) that

$$\mu = \cos \frac{\pi}{N+1} \tag{A.2.34}$$

For example, with $N = 44$, we have

$$\mu = 0.99756, \qquad \rho(H_1) = 0.99513, \qquad \omega_0 = 1.87, \qquad \rho(H_{\omega_0}) = 0.87$$

Since $\rho(H_{\omega_0}) \doteq \rho(H_1)^{30}$, the asymptotic rate of convergence with ω_0 is approximately 30 times as fast as for Gauss-Seidel. In general, for this Poisson problem, it follows from (A.2.32b) and (A.2.34) that the asymptotic rate of convergence of SOR with ω_0 is approximately $0.63N$ as fast as Gauss-Seidel.

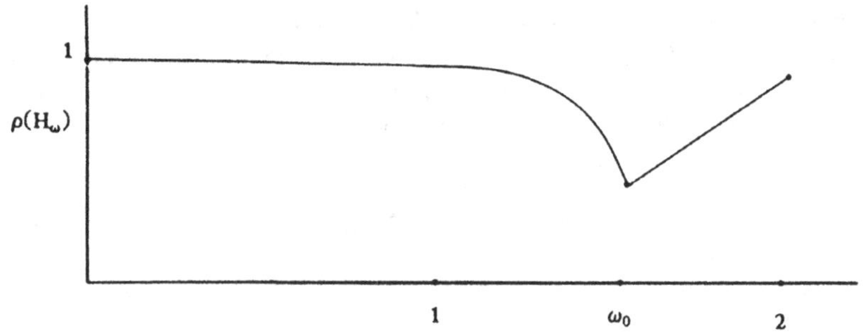

Figure A.2-1. SOR spectral radius.

Appendix 3

The Conjugate Gradient Algorithm

We consider in this appendix various theoretical results about the conjugate gradient algorithm. We assume throughout that the coefficient matrix A is symmetric positive definite. We wish to show primarily two things: that the vectors $\mathbf{p}^k$ generated by the conjugate gradient algorithm are, in fact, conjugate directions; and the error estimate (3.4.1).

We first write the algorithm in a form slightly different from that given in (3.3.15). The difference is in the definition of β_k, and we will show later that the two forms are equivalent. We also use the definition of α_k as given by (3.3.5) and show that this is equivalent to that used in (3.3.15a). For ease of notation, we will write the iteration number as a subscript throughout this appendix. With these changes, the algorithm is as follows:

Choose $\mathbf{x}_0$. Set $\mathbf{p}_0 = \mathbf{r}_0 = \mathbf{b} - A\mathbf{x}_0$

For $k = 0, 1, \ldots$

$$\alpha_k = -\mathbf{r}_k^T\mathbf{p}_k/\mathbf{p}_k^T A\mathbf{p}_k \tag{A.3.1a}$$

$$\mathbf{x}_{k+1} = \mathbf{x}_k - \alpha_k\mathbf{p}_k \tag{A.3.1b}$$

$$\mathbf{r}_{k+1} = \mathbf{r}_k + \alpha_k A\mathbf{p}_k \tag{A.3.1c}$$

$$\beta_k = -\mathbf{p}_k^T A\mathbf{r}_{k+1}/\mathbf{p}_k^T A\mathbf{p}_k \tag{A.3.1d}$$

$$\mathbf{p}_{k+1} = \mathbf{r}_{k+1} + \beta_k\mathbf{p}_k \tag{A.3.1e}$$

A.3.1. THEOREM. *Let A be an $n \times n$ symmetric positive definite matrix and $\hat{\mathbf{x}}$ the solution of the system $A\mathbf{x} = \mathbf{b}$. Then the vectors $\mathbf{p}_k$ generated by (A.3.1) satisfy*

$$\mathbf{p}_k^T A\mathbf{p}_j = 0, \qquad 0 \leq j < k, \qquad k = 1, \ldots, n-1 \tag{A.3.2}$$

and $\mathbf{p}_k \neq 0$ unless $\mathbf{x}^k = \hat{\mathbf{x}}$. Hence $\mathbf{x}^m = \hat{\mathbf{x}}$ for some $m \leq n$.

PROOF. As a companion relation to (A.3.2), we will show that the residuals $\mathbf{r}_j = \mathbf{b} - A\mathbf{x}_j$ satisfy

$$\mathbf{r}_k^T\mathbf{r}_j = 0, \qquad 0 \leq j < k, \qquad k = 1, \ldots, n-1 \tag{A.3.3}$$

We first note that by the definitions (A.3.1a) and (A.3.1d) of α_j and β_j and by (A.3.1c) and (A.3.1e), we have

$$\mathbf{p}_j^T\mathbf{r}_{j+1} = \mathbf{p}_j^T\mathbf{r}_j + \alpha_j\mathbf{p}_j^T A\mathbf{p}_j = 0, \qquad j = 0, 1, \ldots \tag{A.3.4a}$$

$$\mathbf{p}_j^T A\mathbf{p}_{j+1} = \mathbf{p}_j^T A\mathbf{r}_{j+1} + \beta_j\mathbf{p}_j^T A\mathbf{p}_j = 0, \qquad j = 0, 1, \ldots \tag{A.3.4b}$$

Now assume, as an induction hypothesis, that (A.3.2) and (A.3.3) hold for some $k < n-1$. Then we will show that they hold for $k+1$. Since $\mathbf{p}_0 = \mathbf{r}_0$, (A.3.4) shows that they hold for $k = 1$. For any $j < k$, using (A.3.1c, e) we have

$$\begin{aligned}\mathbf{r}_j^T\mathbf{r}_{k+1} &= \mathbf{r}_j^T(\mathbf{r}_k + \alpha_k A\mathbf{p}_k) = \mathbf{r}_j^T\mathbf{r}_k + \alpha_k\mathbf{p}_k^T A\mathbf{r}_j \\ &= \mathbf{r}_j^T\mathbf{r}_k + \alpha_k\mathbf{p}_k^T A(\mathbf{p}_j - \beta_{j-1}\mathbf{p}_{j-1}) = 0\end{aligned}$$

since all three terms vanish by the induction hypothesis. Moreover, using (A.3.1e), (A.3.4a), and then (A.3.1c) we have

$$\begin{aligned}\mathbf{r}_k^T\mathbf{r}_{k+1} &= (\mathbf{p}_k - \beta_{k-1}\mathbf{p}_{k-1})^T\mathbf{r}_{k+1} \\ &= -\beta_{k-1}\mathbf{p}_{k-1}^T\mathbf{r}_{k+1} = -\beta_{k-1}\mathbf{p}_{k-1}^T(\mathbf{r}_k + \alpha_k A\mathbf{p}_k) = 0\end{aligned}$$

since the last two terms are zero by (A.3.4). Therefore, we have shown that (A.3.3) holds for $k+1$.

Next, we have for any $j < k$, using (A.3.1e), the induction hypothesis, (A.3.1c) and then (A.3.2)

$$\mathbf{p}_j^T A\mathbf{p}_{k+1} = \mathbf{p}_j^T A(\mathbf{r}_{k+1} + \beta_k\mathbf{p}_k) = \mathbf{p}_j^T A\mathbf{r}_{k+1} = \alpha_j^{-1}(\mathbf{r}_{j+1} - \mathbf{r}_j)^T\mathbf{r}_{k+1} = 0$$

Note that we have assumed here that $\alpha_j \neq 0$; we shall return to this point in a moment. By (A.3.4.b), we also have that $\mathbf{p}_k^T A\mathbf{p}_{k+1} = 0$. Therefore, (A.3.2) holds for $k+1$ and the induction argument is complete.

We now show that the $\mathbf{p}_k$ are nonzero unless we are at the solution. Suppose that $\mathbf{p}_m = 0$ for some $m < n$. Then, using (A.3.1e) we have

$$\begin{aligned}0 = \mathbf{p}_m^T\mathbf{p}_m &= (\mathbf{r}_m + \beta_{m-1}\mathbf{p}_{m-1})^T(\mathbf{r}_m + \beta_{m-1}\mathbf{p}_{m-1}) \\ &= \mathbf{r}_m^T\mathbf{r}_m + 2\beta_{m-1}\mathbf{r}_m^T\mathbf{p}_{m-1} + \beta_{m-1}^2\mathbf{p}_{m-1}^T\mathbf{p}_{m-1} \geq \mathbf{r}_m^T\mathbf{r}_m\end{aligned}$$

since $\mathbf{r}_m^T\mathbf{p}_{m-1} = 0$ by (A.3.4a). Hence $\mathbf{r}_m = \mathbf{b} - A\mathbf{x}_m = 0$ so that $\mathbf{x}_m = \hat{\mathbf{x}}$. On the other hand, if $\mathbf{p}_0, \ldots, \mathbf{p}_{n-1}$ are all nonzero, then $\mathbf{x}^n = \hat{\mathbf{x}}$ by the Conjugate Direction Theorem 3.3.1.

Finally, we return to the assumption that $\alpha_j \neq 0$. By (A.3.1e) and (A.3.4b) we have

$$\mathbf{r}_j^T\mathbf{p}_j = \mathbf{r}_j^T(\mathbf{r}_j + \beta_{j-1}\mathbf{p}_{j-1}) = \mathbf{r}_j^T\mathbf{r}_j \tag{A.3.5}$$

Hence, the definition of α_j in (A.3.1a) is equivalent to

$$\alpha_j = -\mathbf{r}_j^T\mathbf{r}_j/\mathbf{p}_j^TA\mathbf{p}_j \tag{A.3.6}$$

Therefore, if $\alpha_j = 0$, then $\mathbf{r}_j = 0$ and, as above, $\mathbf{x}_j = \hat{\mathbf{x}}$ so that the process stops with $\mathbf{x}_j$. □

Next, we wish to show that the definition of β_k used in (A.3.1d) is equivalent to the one given in Section 3.3. We have from (A.3.1c), (A.3.4b), (A.3.1e), and (A.3.3) that

$$\mathbf{r}_{k+1}^T\mathbf{p}_{k+1} = (\mathbf{r}_k + \alpha_kA\mathbf{p}_k)^T\mathbf{p}_{k+1} = \mathbf{r}_k^T\mathbf{p}_{k+1} = \mathbf{r}_k^T(\mathbf{r}_{k+1} + \beta_k\mathbf{p}_k) = \beta_k\mathbf{r}_k^T\mathbf{p}_k$$

Thus, using (A.3.5), we obtain

$$\beta_k = \mathbf{r}_{k+1}^T\mathbf{p}_{k+1}/\mathbf{r}_k^T\mathbf{p}_k = \mathbf{r}_{k+1}^T\mathbf{r}_{k+1}/\mathbf{r}_k^T\mathbf{r}_k \tag{A.3.7}$$

which is the form of β_k used in (3.3.15e). The definitions (A.3.6) and (A.3.7) of α and β are the ones preferred for computation since only the inner product $\mathbf{r}_k^T\mathbf{r}_k$ is required at each step. The definitions given in (A.3.1a,d) are sometimes useful for theoretical purposes.

We next give some basic relations that will be needed in proving the error estimate (3.4.1), and which also give additional insight into the conjugate gradient method. Recall that $\text{span}(\mathbf{y}_1, \ldots, \mathbf{y}_m)$ is the subspace generated by all linear combinations of $\mathbf{y}_1, \ldots, \mathbf{y}_m$.

A.3.2. THEOREM. *Let $\mathbf{p}_0, \ldots, \mathbf{p}_{n-1}$ be the direction vectors generated by the conjugate gradient algorithm and let $\mathbf{r}_0, \ldots, \mathbf{r}_{n-1}$ be the residual vectors. Then*

$$A\mathbf{p}_i \in \text{span}(\mathbf{p}_0, \ldots, \mathbf{p}_{i+1}), \qquad i = 0, \ldots, n-2 \tag{A.3.8}$$

$$\mathbf{r}_i \in \text{span}(\mathbf{p}_0, \ldots, \mathbf{p}_i), \qquad i = 0, \ldots, n-1 \tag{A.3.9}$$

$$\text{span}(\mathbf{p}_0, \ldots, \mathbf{p}_i) = \text{span}(\mathbf{p}_0, A\mathbf{p}_0, \ldots, A^i\mathbf{p}_0)$$

$$= \text{span}(\mathbf{r}_0, A\mathbf{r}_0, \ldots, A^i\mathbf{r}_0), \qquad i = 0, \ldots, n-1 \qquad \text{(A.3.10)}$$

PROOF. We will prove (A.3.8) and (A.3.9) together by induction. By (A.3.1c) and (A.3.1e)

$$\mathbf{p}_1 = \mathbf{r}_1 + \beta_0\mathbf{p}_0 = \mathbf{r}_0 + \alpha_0 A\mathbf{p}_0 + \beta_0\mathbf{p}_0$$

Thus, since $\mathbf{r}_0 = \mathbf{p}_0$,

$$A\mathbf{p}_0 = \alpha_0^{-1}(\mathbf{p}_1 - \mathbf{p}_0 - \beta_0\mathbf{p}_0)$$

so that (A.3.8) holds for $i = 0$. Since $\mathbf{r}_0 = \mathbf{p}_0$, (A.3.9) also holds for $i = 0$.

Now assume that (A.3.8) and (A.3.9) hold for $i = 0, \ldots, k < n - 2$. By (A.3.1c) and the induction hypothesis we have

$$\mathbf{r}_{k+1} = \mathbf{r}_k + \alpha_k A\mathbf{p}_k = \sum_{j=0}^{k} \nu_j\mathbf{p}_j + \alpha_k \sum_{j=0}^{k+1} \eta_j\mathbf{p}_j$$

Thus, $\mathbf{r}_{k+1} \in \text{span}(\mathbf{p}_0, \ldots, \mathbf{p}_{k+1})$. Then, from (A.3.1e) and (A.3.1c),

$$\mathbf{p}_{k+2} = \mathbf{r}_{k+2} + \beta_{k+1}\mathbf{p}_{k+1} = \mathbf{r}_{k+1} + \alpha_{k+1}A\mathbf{p}_{k+1} + \beta_{k+1}\mathbf{p}_{k+1}$$

Since $\mathbf{r}_{k+1} \in \text{span}(\mathbf{p}_0, \ldots, \mathbf{p}_{k+1})$, it follows that $A\mathbf{p}_{k+1} \in \text{span}(\mathbf{p}_0, \ldots, \mathbf{p}_{k+2})$. This completes the induction except to show that (A.3.9) also holds for $\mathbf{r}_{n-1}$; this follows as before.

To prove (A.3.10), we again use induction. It is trivially true for $i = 0$ since $\mathbf{p}_0 = \mathbf{r}_0$. Assume that it holds for $k < n - 1$. Then, by the induction hypothesis and (A.3.8), we have

$$A^{k+1}\mathbf{p}_0 = A(A^k\mathbf{p}_0) = A\left(\sum_{j=0}^{k} \nu_j\mathbf{p}_j\right) = \sum_{j=0}^{k} \nu_j A\mathbf{p}_j \in \text{span}(\mathbf{p}_0, \ldots, \mathbf{p}_{k+1})$$

Now, for any η_j,

$$\sum_{j=0}^{k+1} \eta_j A^j\mathbf{p}_0 = \eta_{k+1}A^{k+1}\mathbf{p}_0 + \sum_{j=0}^{k} \eta_j A^j\mathbf{p}_0$$

The first term on the right is in $\text{span}(\mathbf{p}_0, \ldots, \mathbf{p}_{k+1})$ by the previous equation, and the second term by the induction hypothesis. Hence, we have shown that

$$\text{span}(\mathbf{p}_0, A\mathbf{p}_0, \ldots, A^{k+1}\mathbf{p}_0) \subset \text{span}(\mathbf{p}_0, \mathbf{p}_1, \ldots, \mathbf{p}_{k+1})$$

To prove the reverse inclusion we first write

$$\sum_{j=0}^{k+1} \eta_j \mathbf{p}_j = \eta_{k+1}\mathbf{p}_{k+1} + \sum_{j=0}^{k} \eta_j \mathbf{p}_j$$

The second term is in span($\mathbf{p}_0, \ldots, A^k\mathbf{p}_0$) by the induction hypothesis. The first term may be written, by (A.3.1e) and (A.3.1c), as

$$\eta_{k+1}\mathbf{p}_{k+1} = \eta_{k+1}(\mathbf{r}_{k+1} + \beta_k \mathbf{p}_k) = \eta_{k+1}(\mathbf{r}_k + \alpha_k A\mathbf{p}_k + \beta_k \mathbf{p}_k)$$

The first and third terms on the right of this equation are in span($\mathbf{p}_0, \ldots, \mathbf{p}_k$) by (A.3.9), and hence in span($\mathbf{p}_0, \ldots, A^k\mathbf{p}_0$) by the induction hypothesis. In the second term, $A\mathbf{p}_k$ may be written, using (A.3.8) and the induction hypothesis, as

$$A\mathbf{p}_k = A \sum_{j=1}^{k} \nu_j A^j \mathbf{p}_0 = \sum_{j=1}^{k} \nu_j A^{j+1} \mathbf{p}_0$$

so that it is in span($\mathbf{p}_0, \ldots, A^{k+1}\mathbf{p}_0$). Hence, we have shown that

$$\text{span}(\mathbf{p}_0, \ldots, \mathbf{p}_{k+1}) \subset \text{span}(\mathbf{p}_0, \ldots, A^{k+1}\mathbf{p}_0)$$

and the first equality in (A.3.10) is proved. The second equality is trivial since $\mathbf{r}_0 = \mathbf{p}_0$. □

A subspace of the form span($\mathbf{p}_0, \ldots, A^i\mathbf{p}_0$) is known as a *Krylov subspace.* We next show that the conjugate gradient iterates minimize the A-norm of the error over a translated (affine) Krylov subspace. Recall that the A-norm is defined by $\|\mathbf{y}\|_A^2 = \mathbf{y}^T A\mathbf{y}$.

A.3.3. Minimizing Property of Conjugate Gradient. *For each* $k = 0, 1, \ldots, n-1$, *the conjugate gradient iterate* $\mathbf{x}_{k+1}$ *minimizes* $\|\hat{\mathbf{x}} - \mathbf{x}\|_A$ *over*

$$S_k = \mathbf{x}_0 + \text{span}(\mathbf{p}_0, \ldots, \mathbf{p}_k) = \mathbf{x}_0 + \text{span}(\mathbf{p}_0, A\mathbf{p}_0, \ldots, A^k\mathbf{p}_0)$$

Proof. For given k, let $\mathbf{x} = \mathbf{x}_0 + \sum_{j=0}^k \nu_j \mathbf{p}_j$ be in S_k. Since

$$\mathbf{r}_0 = \mathbf{b} - A\mathbf{x}_0 = \mathbf{b} - A\mathbf{x}_0 - (\mathbf{b} - A\hat{\mathbf{x}}) = A(\hat{\mathbf{x}} - \mathbf{x}_0),$$

we have

$$\hat{\mathbf{x}} - \mathbf{x} = \hat{\mathbf{x}} - \mathbf{x}_0 - \sum_{j=0}^{k} \nu_j \mathbf{p}_j = A^{-1}\mathbf{r}_0 - \sum_{j=0}^{k} \nu_j \mathbf{p}_j$$

Therefore, using the conjugacy of the $\mathbf{p}_j$,

$$\|\hat{\mathbf{x}} - \mathbf{x}\|_A^2 = (\hat{\mathbf{x}} - \mathbf{x})^T A(\hat{\mathbf{x}} - \mathbf{x}) = \left(A^{-1}\mathbf{r}_0 - \sum_{j=0}^{k} \nu_j \mathbf{p}_j\right)^T A\left(A^{-1}\mathbf{r}_0 - \sum_{j=0}^{k} \nu_j \mathbf{p}_j\right)$$

$$= \mathbf{r}_0^T A^{-1}\mathbf{r}_0 - 2\mathbf{r}_0^T \sum_{j=0}^{k} \nu_j \mathbf{p}_j + \sum_{j=0}^{k} \nu_j^2 \mathbf{p}_j^T A \mathbf{p}_j$$

This is a diagonal quadratic form in the ν_j and the minimum is taken on when

$$\nu_j = \mathbf{r}_0^T \mathbf{p}_j / \mathbf{p}_j^T A \mathbf{p}_j, \qquad j = 0, \ldots, k$$

Applying (A.3.1c) of the conjugate gradient algorithm repeatedly, we obtain

$$\mathbf{r}_j = \mathbf{r}_{j-1} + \alpha_{j-1} A \mathbf{p}_{j-1} = \cdots = \mathbf{r}_0 + \sum_{i=0}^{j-1} \alpha_i A \mathbf{p}_i$$

so that, by the conjugacy of the $\mathbf{p}_i$, we have $\mathbf{r}_j^T \mathbf{p}_j = \mathbf{r}_0^T \mathbf{p}_j$. Hence, by (A.3.1a), $\nu_j = -\alpha_j$. It follows that the conjugate gradient iterate $\mathbf{x}_{k+1}$ is

$$\mathbf{x}_{k+1} = \mathbf{x}_k - \alpha_k \mathbf{p}_k = \cdots = \mathbf{x}_0 - \sum_{i=0}^{k} \alpha_i \mathbf{p}_i = \mathbf{x}_0 + \sum_{i=0}^{k} \nu_i \mathbf{p}_i$$

and this is the minimizer of $\|\hat{\mathbf{x}} - \mathbf{x}\|_A^2$ over S_k. □

We can phrase the result A.3.3 in an equivalent way that will be useful in the sequel. By (A.3.10),

$$S_{k-1} = \mathbf{x}_0 + \operatorname{span}(\mathbf{r}_0, A\mathbf{r}_0, \ldots, A^{k-1}\mathbf{r}_0)$$

so that elements of S_{k-1} may be written as $\mathbf{x}_0 + \sum_{j=0}^{k-1} q_j A^j \mathbf{r}_0$. By A.3.3 the conjugate gradient iterate $\mathbf{x}_k$ satisfies

$$\|\hat{\mathbf{x}} - \mathbf{x}_k\|_A^2 = \min_{q_0, \ldots, q_{k-1}} Q(q_0, \ldots, q_{k-1})$$

where

$$Q = \left(\hat{\mathbf{x}} - \mathbf{x}_0 - \sum_{j=0}^{k-1} q_j A^j \mathbf{r}_0\right)^T A\left(\hat{\mathbf{x}} - \mathbf{x}_0 - \sum_{j=0}^{k-1} q_j A^j \mathbf{r}_0\right)$$

Since, as before, $A(\hat{\mathbf{x}} - \mathbf{x}_0) = \mathbf{r}_0$, we have

$$Q = \left(\mathbf{r}_0 - \sum_{i=0}^{k-1} q_j A^{j+1} \mathbf{r}_0\right)^T A^{-1}\left(\mathbf{r}_0 - \sum_{j=0}^{k-1} q_j A^{j+1} \mathbf{r}_0\right)$$
$$= [R_k(A)\mathbf{r}_0]^T A^{-1} [R_k(A)\mathbf{r}_0]$$

where $R_k(A) = I - \sum_{j=0}^{k-1} q_j A^{j+1}$ is the matrix polynomial corresponding to the scalar polynomial $1 - \sum_{j=0}^{k-1} q_i \lambda^{j+1}$. Hence we can state the result A.3.3 in the equivalent form:

$$\|\hat{\mathbf{x}} - \mathbf{x}_k\|_A^2 = \min_{R_k \in \mathcal{R}_k} \mathbf{r}_0^T R_k(A)^T A^{-1} R_k(A) \mathbf{r}_0 \tag{A.3.11}$$

where $\mathcal{R}_k$ is the set of polynomials of degree k with $R_k(0) = 1$.

The representation (A.3.11) will allow us to obtain estimates of the error at the kth step. We first need to develop some properties of the polynomials R_k. Let $\lambda_1, \ldots, \lambda_n$ and $\mathbf{v}_1, \ldots, \mathbf{v}_n$ be the eigenvalues and corresponding orthonormal eigenvectors of A, and let $\mathbf{r}_0 = \sum_{j=1}^n \eta_j \mathbf{v}_j$. Then

$$R_k(A)\mathbf{r}_0 = \sum_{j=1}^n \eta_j R_k(A)\mathbf{v}_j = \sum_{j=1}^n \eta_j R_k(\lambda_j)\mathbf{v}_j$$

Thus

$$\mathbf{r}_0^T R_k(A)^T A^{-1} R_k(A)\mathbf{r}_0 = \left[\sum_{j=1}^n \eta_j R_k(\lambda_j)\mathbf{v}_j\right]^T \left[\sum_{j=1}^n \eta_j R_k(\lambda_j)\lambda_j^{-1}\mathbf{v}_j\right]$$

$$= \sum_{j=1}^n \eta_j^2 R_k(\lambda_j)^2 \lambda_j^{-1}$$

by the orthonormality of the $\mathbf{v}_j$. Using this in (A.3.11), where the minimum is still over all polynomials in $\mathcal{R}_k$, we have

$$\|\hat{\mathbf{x}} - \mathbf{x}_k\|_A^2 = \min \sum_{j=1}^n \eta_j^2 R_k(\lambda_j)^2 \lambda_j^{-1} \leq \min \max_{1 \leq j \leq n} |R_k(\lambda_j)|^2 \sum_{j=1}^n \eta_j^2 \lambda_j^{-1} \tag{A.3.12}$$

Now

$$\sum_{j=1}^n \eta_j^2 \lambda_j^{-1} = \left(\sum_{j=1}^n \eta_j \mathbf{v}_j\right)^T A^{-1} \left(\sum_{j=1}^n \eta_j \mathbf{v}_j\right)$$

$$= \mathbf{r}_0^T A^{-1} \mathbf{r}_0 = (\hat{\mathbf{x}} - \mathbf{x}_0)^T A (\hat{\mathbf{x}} - \mathbf{x}_0) \tag{A.3.13}$$

Thus, combining (A.3.12) and (A.3.13),

$$\|\hat{\mathbf{x}} - \mathbf{x}_k\|_A^2 \leq \gamma_k^2 \|\hat{\mathbf{x}} - \mathbf{x}_0\|_A^2 \tag{A.3.14}$$

where

$$\gamma_k = \min_{R_k \in \mathcal{R}_k} \max_{1 \leq j \leq n} |R_k(\lambda_j)| \tag{A.3.15}$$

Therefore, we have obtained an estimate of the error at the kth step in terms of the initial error. The problem now is to obtain bounds for the γ_k.

Clearly, if λ_1 and λ_n are the minimum and maximum eigenvalues of A, then

$$\gamma_k \leq \min_{R_k \in \mathcal{R}_k} \max_{\lambda_1 \leq \lambda \leq \lambda_n} |R_k(\lambda)| \tag{A.3.16}$$

This is the classical Chebyshev minimization problem whose solution is

$$\hat{R}_k(\lambda) = T_k((\lambda_1 - 2\lambda + \lambda_n)/(\lambda_1 - \lambda_n))/T_k((\lambda_n + \lambda_1)/(\lambda_1 - \lambda_n))$$

where $T_k(z)$ is the kth Chebyshev polynomial [see (3.2.54)]. From the Chebyshev theory, it can be shown that

$$\min_{R_k \in \mathcal{R}_k} \max_{\lambda_1 \leq \lambda \leq \lambda_n} |R_k(\lambda)| \leq 2(1 - \sqrt{\nu})^k/(1 + \sqrt{\nu})^k, \qquad \nu = \lambda_1/\lambda_n \tag{A.3.17}$$

Since A is symmetric positive definite, its condition number with respect to the l_2 norm is $\kappa = 1/\nu$. Hence, if we combine (A.3.14), (A.3.16), and (A.3.17), we obtain the error bound

$$\|\hat{\mathbf{x}} - \mathbf{x}_k\|_A \leq 2\alpha^k \|\hat{\mathbf{x}} - \mathbf{x}_0\|_A, \qquad \alpha = (\sqrt{\kappa} - 1)/(\sqrt{\kappa} + 1) \tag{A.3.18}$$

This is the standard error estimate for the conjugate gradient method in terms of the A-norm.

We can also write (A.3.18) in terms of the 2-norm by means of the inequalities

$$\|\mathbf{x}\|_2^2/\|A^{-1}\|_2 = \lambda_1 \mathbf{x}^T\mathbf{x} \leq \mathbf{x}^T A \mathbf{x} \leq \lambda_n \mathbf{x}^T \mathbf{x} = \|A\|_2 \|\mathbf{x}\|_2^2$$

Applying this to (A.3.18) yields

$$\begin{aligned} \|\hat{\mathbf{x}} - \mathbf{x}_k\|_2^2 &\leq \|A^{-1}\|_2 \|\hat{\mathbf{x}} - \mathbf{x}_k\|_A^2 \leq (2\alpha^k)^2 \|A^{-1}\|_2 \|\hat{\mathbf{x}} - \mathbf{x}_0\|_A^2 \\ &\leq (2\alpha^k)^2 \|A^{-1}\|_2 \|A\|_2 \|\hat{\mathbf{x}} - \mathbf{x}_0\|_2^2 \end{aligned}$$

or

$$\|\hat{\mathbf{x}} - \mathbf{x}_k\|_2 \leq 2\sqrt{\kappa}\,\alpha^k \|\hat{\mathbf{x}} - \mathbf{x}_0\|_2 \tag{A.3.19}$$

We summarize the above error estimates in the following result.

A.3.4. THEOREM. *The kth conjugate gradient iterate satisfies*

$$\|\hat{\mathbf{x}} - \mathbf{x}_k\|_A \leq 2\alpha^k \|\hat{\mathbf{x}} - \mathbf{x}_0\|_A$$

and

$$\|\hat{\mathbf{x}} - \mathbf{x}_k\|_2 \leq 2\sqrt{\kappa}\,\alpha^k \|\hat{\mathbf{x}} - \mathbf{x}_0\|_2$$

where $\kappa = \text{cond}(A)$ *and* $\alpha = (\sqrt{\kappa} - 1)/(\sqrt{\kappa} + 1)$.

The error estimate (A.3.19) does not necessarily imply that the errors actually decrease at each step. This important property is a consequence of the next theorem.

A.3.5. THEOREM. *The conjugate gradient iterates satisfy*

$$\|\hat{\mathbf{x}} - \mathbf{x}_k\|_2 < \|\hat{\mathbf{x}} - \mathbf{x}_{k-1}\|_2 \tag{A.3.20}$$

unless $\mathbf{x}_{k-1} = \hat{\mathbf{x}}$.

PROOF. We first note that

$$\begin{aligned}
\|\hat{\mathbf{x}} - \mathbf{x}_{k-1}\|_2^2 &= (\hat{\mathbf{x}} - \mathbf{x}_k + \mathbf{x}_k - \mathbf{x}_{k-1})^T(\hat{\mathbf{x}} - \mathbf{x}_k + \mathbf{x}_k - \mathbf{x}_{k-1}) \\
&= (\hat{\mathbf{x}} - \mathbf{x}_k, \hat{\mathbf{x}} - \mathbf{x}_k) + 2(\hat{\mathbf{x}} - \mathbf{x}_k, \mathbf{x}_k - \mathbf{x}_{k-1}) \\
&\quad + (\mathbf{x}_k - \mathbf{x}_{k-1}, \mathbf{x}_k - \mathbf{x}_{k-1})
\end{aligned}$$

or

$$\|\hat{\mathbf{x}} - \mathbf{x}_{k-1}\|_2^2 = \|\hat{\mathbf{x}} - \mathbf{x}_k\|_2^2 + 2(\hat{\mathbf{x}} - \mathbf{x}_k, \mathbf{x}_k - \mathbf{x}_{k-1}) + \|\mathbf{x}_k - \mathbf{x}_{k-1}\|_2^2 \tag{A.3.21}$$

The last quantity on the right is positive unless $\mathbf{x}_k = \mathbf{x}_{k-1}$. As noted previously, $\mathbf{x}_k = \mathbf{x}_{k-1}$ implies that $\mathbf{x}_{k-1} = \hat{\mathbf{x}}$. Thus, if $\mathbf{x}_k \neq \mathbf{x}_{k-1}$, it suffices to show that the second term on the right of (A.3.21) is non-negative.

Let $\mathbf{x}_m = \hat{\mathbf{x}}$. Then, since

$$\mathbf{x}_m - \mathbf{x}_k = \mathbf{x}_m - \mathbf{x}_{m-1} + \mathbf{x}_{m-1} - \cdots - \mathbf{x}_{k+1} + \mathbf{x}_{k+1} - \mathbf{x}_k$$

we have, using (A.3.1b),

$$(\hat{\mathbf{x}} - \mathbf{x}_k)^T(\mathbf{x}_k - \mathbf{x}_{k-1}) = (\alpha_{m-1}\mathbf{p}_m^T\mathbf{p}_{k-1} + \cdots + \alpha_k\mathbf{p}_k^T\mathbf{p}_{k-1})\alpha_{k-1} \tag{A.3.22}$$

By (A.3.6), the α_i are all nonpositive; hence, it suffices to show that $\mathbf{p}_j^T\mathbf{p}_{k-1} \geq 0$, $j \geq k$. Applying (A.3.1e) repeatedly, we obtain

$$\mathbf{p}_j = \mathbf{r}_j + \beta_{j-1}\mathbf{r}_{j-1} + \cdots + (\beta_{j-1}\cdots\beta_k)\mathbf{r}_k + (\beta_{j-1}\cdots\beta_{k-1})\mathbf{p}_{k-1} \tag{A.3.23}$$

In particular, for $k = 1$, (A.3.23) shows that $\mathbf{p}_j \in \text{span}(\mathbf{r}_0, \ldots, \mathbf{r}_j)$, and by the orthogonality of the $\mathbf{r}_i$, (A.3.3), we have that $\mathbf{r}_j^T\mathbf{p}_{k-1} = 0$, $j \geq k$. Thus, from (A.3.23) and (A.3.7) we obtain

$$\mathbf{p}_j^T\mathbf{p}_{k-1} = \beta_{j-1}\cdots\beta_{k-1}\mathbf{p}_{k-1}^T\mathbf{p}_{k-1} = \mathbf{r}_j^T\mathbf{r}_j\mathbf{p}_{k-1}^T\mathbf{p}_{k-1}/\mathbf{r}_{k-1}^T\mathbf{r}_{k-1} \geq 0 \qquad \square$$

The above results do not take into account any special properties of the matrix A. In particular, the following result is of interest.

A.3.6. THEOREM. *If A has only m distinct eigenvalues, then the conjugate gradient iterates will converge in at most m iterations.*

PROOF. This is an almost immediate consequence of the basic error relation (A.3.11). Let $\lambda_1, \ldots, \lambda_m$ be the distinct eigenvalues of A, necessarily positive since A is positive definite, and define the polynomial of degree m

$$R_m(\lambda) = \prod_{j=1}^{m}(\lambda_j - \lambda)\Big/\prod_{j=1}^{m}\lambda_j$$

Clearly, $R_m(0) = 1$. Moreover, $R_m(A) = 0$ since if $A = PDP^T$, where D is diagonal and P is orthogonal, then $R_m(A) = PR_m(D)P^T$ and $R_m(D)$ is a product of diagonal matrices such that for any i, at least one of the diagonal matrices is zero in position i. The relation (A.3.11) then ensures that $\hat{\mathbf{x}} - \mathbf{x}_m = 0$. $\square$

Three-Term Recurrence Relation

We end this Appendix by showing that the conjugate gradient iterates satisfy a three-term recurrence relation of the form

$$\mathbf{x}_{k+1} = \rho_{k+1}(\delta_{k+1}\mathbf{r}_k + \mathbf{x}_k) + (1 - \rho_{k+1})\mathbf{x}_{k-1} \tag{A.3.24}$$

where, if α_k and β_{k-1} are the quantities in (A.3.1),

$$\rho_{k+1} = 1 + \alpha_k\beta_{k-1}/\alpha_{k-1}, \qquad \delta_{k+1} = -\alpha_k/\rho_{k+1} \tag{A.3.25}$$

In order to obtain (A.3.24), we first note that from (A.3.1b, e)

$$\mathbf{x}_{k+1} = \mathbf{x}_k - \alpha_k \mathbf{p}_k = \mathbf{x}_k - \alpha_k(\mathbf{r}_k + \beta_{k-1}\mathbf{p}_{k-1}) \tag{A.3.26}$$

We now substitute $\mathbf{p}_{k-1} = -\alpha_{k-1}^{-1}(\mathbf{x}_k - \mathbf{x}_{k-1})$, obtained from (A.3.1b), into (A.3.26), which gives

$$\begin{aligned} \mathbf{x}_{k+1} &= \mathbf{x}_k - \alpha_k \mathbf{r}_k + \alpha_k \beta_{k-1}(\mathbf{x}_k - \mathbf{x}_{k-1})/\alpha_{k-1} \\ &= \left(1 + \frac{\alpha_k \beta_{k-1}}{\alpha_{k-1}}\right)\mathbf{x}_k - \alpha_k \mathbf{r}_k - \frac{\alpha_k \beta_{k-1}}{\alpha_{k-1}}\mathbf{x}_{k-1} \end{aligned} \tag{A.3.27}$$

which is (A.3.24).

We next replace $\mathbf{r}_k$ in (A.3.24) by $\mathbf{b} - A\mathbf{x}_k$ to give

$$\begin{aligned} \mathbf{x}_{k+1} &= \rho_{k+1}[\delta_{k+1}(\mathbf{b} - A\mathbf{x}_k) + \mathbf{x}_k] + (1 - \rho_{k+1})\mathbf{x}_{k-1} \\ &= \rho_{k+1}\{\delta_{k+1}[(I - A)\mathbf{x}_k + \mathbf{b}] + (1 - \delta_{k+1})\mathbf{x}_k\} + (1 - \rho_{k+1})\mathbf{x}_{k-1} \end{aligned} \tag{A.3.28}$$

If A is scaled so that its main diagonal is the identity, then the Jacobi iteration is

$$\mathbf{y}_{k+1} = (I - A)\mathbf{y}_k + \mathbf{b}$$

Hence (A.3.28) is an acceleration of the Jacobi method of the same form as the semi-iterative method (3.2.61), with the exception that δ_{k+1} is now allowed to be variable. It may be shown that if we use this conjugate gradient acceleration of Jacobi's method, we obtain the one-step Jacobi PCG method. Similarly, if we accelerate the SSOR iteration, we obtain the one-step SSOR PCG method.

Appendix 4

Basic Linear Algebra

We review in this appendix, without proof, some fundamentals of linear algebra that are used in the text. For a full treatment, see, for example, Ortega [1987a]. We deal only with real vectors and matrices. It is assumed that the reader is familiar with the most elementary parts of linear algebra.

If A is an $n \times n$ matrix, then the following are equivalent:

$\det A \neq 0$
There is an $n \times n$ matrix A^{-1} such that $AA^{-1} = A^{-1}A = I$
$A\mathbf{x} = \mathbf{b}$ has a unique solution for any $\mathbf{b}$
$A\mathbf{x} = 0$ has only the solution $\mathbf{x} = 0$
The row or columns of A are linearly independent.

If A satisfies any of these conditions (and, hence, all) it is *nonsingular* and A^{-1} is its inverse.

The *rank* of a matrix is the number of linearly independent rows (or, equivalently, columns). Hence, the last statement above may be replaced by "A has rank n." An important class of matrices have rank one and may be written in the form $\mathbf{u}\mathbf{v}^T$ for two column vectors $\mathbf{u}$ and $\mathbf{v}$.

A matrix P is *orthogonal* if $PP^T = I$. The columns $\mathbf{p}_i$ of an orthogonal matrix are *orthogonal* vectors: $\mathbf{p}_i^T\mathbf{p}_j = 0$, $i \neq j$, and also *orthonormal*: $\mathbf{p}_i^T\mathbf{p}_i = 1$. Inverses and products of orthogonal matrices are also orthogonal. An important type of orthogonal matrix is a *permutation* matrix in which each row and column has exactly one 1 and the other elements are zero. The effect of the multiplication PA, where P is permutation matrix, is to interchange the rows of A. AP interchanges the columns.

An eigenvalue of A is a scalar for which the equation

$$A\mathbf{x} = \lambda\mathbf{x}$$

has a nonzero solution $\mathbf{x}$, called an *eigenvector*. An $n \times n$ matrix has exactly n eigenvalues (counting multiplicities). These are the roots of the characteristic equation $\det(A - \lambda I) = 0$, which is a polynomial of degree n. An eigenvalue may be complex, even though A is real, and the corresponding eigenvector is then necessarily complex. The set of eigenvalues is the *spectrum* of A and the maximum eigenvalue in absolute value is the *spectral radius*, denoted by $\rho(A)$.

If $p(\gamma) = a_0 + a_1\gamma + \cdots + a_m\gamma^m$ is a polynomial of degree m, then $p(A) = a_0 = a_0 + a_1 A + \cdots + a_m A^m$ is the corresponding *matrix polynomial.* If λ and $\mathbf{x}$ are any eigenvalue and eigenvector pair of A, then $p(\lambda)$ and $\mathbf{x}$ are an eigenvalue and eigenvector of $p(A)$. In particular, if A has eigenvalues $\lambda_1, \ldots, \lambda_n$, then $\alpha I + A$ has eigenvalues $\alpha + \lambda_1, \ldots, \alpha + \lambda_n$ and the same eigenvectors as A. Also, A is nonsingular if and only if $\lambda_i \neq 0$, $i = 1, \ldots, n$, in which case A^{-1} has eigenvalues λ_i^{-1} and the same eigenvectors as A.

The matrix A is *symmetric* if it equals its transpose: $A = A^T$. A symmetric matrix has only real eigenvalues and the corresponding eigenvectors $\mathbf{x}_i$ are orthogonal. A symmetric matrix may be written as

$$A = PDP^T \tag{A.4.1}$$

where $D = \operatorname{diag}(\lambda_1, \ldots, \lambda_n)$ is a diagonal matrix whose diagonal entries are the eigenvalues of A, and P is an orthogonal matrix whose columns are eigenvectors of A.

A *principal submatrix* of A is any submatrix obtained by deleting rows and corresponding columns of A. A *leading principal* submatrix of size $m \times m$ is obtained by deleting all rows and columns $m + 1, \ldots, n$.

A symmetric matrix is *positive definite* if any of the following equivalent conditions are true:

$\mathbf{x}^T A\mathbf{x} > 0$ for all vectors $\mathbf{x} \neq 0$
The eigenvalues of A are all positive
The leading principal submatrices of A all have positive determinant.
There is a Choleski factorization $A = LL^T$.

A symmetric positive definite matrix A is nonsingular and A^{-1} is also symmetric positive definite. A symmetric positive definite matrix has a *square root* which can be defined using (A.4.1) by $A^{1/2} = PD^{1/2}P^T$, where $D^{1/2}$ is the diagonal matrix containing the positive square roots of the eigenvalues of A.

A symmetric matrix is *positive semidefinite* if all of its eigenvalues are non-negative, or equivalently if $\mathbf{x}^T A\mathbf{x} \geq 0$ for all $\mathbf{x}$. More generally, if A is a symmetric matrix with eigenvalues $\lambda_1 \leq \lambda_2 \leq \cdots \leq \lambda_n$, then

$$\lambda_1 \mathbf{x}^T\mathbf{x} \leq \mathbf{x}^T A\mathbf{x} \leq \lambda_n \mathbf{x}^T\mathbf{x}$$

for all vectors $\mathbf{x}$.

If P is a nonsingular matrix, then PAP^{-1} is a *similarity* transformation, and PAP^T is a *congruence.* Similarity transformations preserve eigenvalues; that is, A and PAP^{-1} have the same eigenvalues. Congruences, in general, change the eigenvalues but preserve their signs: if A is a symmetric matrix, then A and PAP^T have the same number of positive eigenvalues and the same number of negative eigenvalues. In particular, if A is positive definite, so is PAP^T.

Equation (A.4.1) shows that a symmetric matrix is similar to a diagonal matrix. In general, a matrix A will be similar to a diagonal matrix if and only if it has n linearly independent eigenvectors. If this is not the case, the best that can be done is that A is similar to a matrix whose diagonal elements are the eigenvalues of A, there is one or more 1 in the diagonal above the main diagonal, and the rest of the matrix is zero. This is the *Jordan canonical form* of A.

A *norm*, denoted by $\| \ \|$, on the space R^n of n-vectors satisfies

$$\|\mathbf{x}\| \geq 0 \quad \text{and} \quad \|\mathbf{x}\| = 0 \text{ only if } \mathbf{x} = 0$$

$$\|\alpha\mathbf{x}\| = |\alpha| \, \|\mathbf{x}\| \text{ for all scalars } \alpha \tag{A.4.2}$$

$$\|\mathbf{x} + \mathbf{y}\| \leq \|\mathbf{x}\| + \|\mathbf{y}\|$$

Common norms are the l_∞ (or max) norm

$$\|\mathbf{x}\|_\infty = \max_{1 \leq i \leq n} |x_i|$$

and the l_p norms

$$\|\mathbf{x}\|_p = \left(\sum_{i=1}^{n} |x_i|^p \right)^{1/p}$$

especially for $p = 1$ and $p = 2$. The l_2 norm is the usual Euclidean distance. In this norm, orthogonal matrices have the important property that $\|P\mathbf{x}\|_2 = \|\mathbf{x}\|_2$. Other norms can be defined by

$$\|\mathbf{x}\|_B = (\mathbf{x}^T B\mathbf{x})^{1/2}$$

where B is a symmetric positive definite matrix. This is an *inner product* norm since $(\mathbf{x}, \mathbf{y})_B \equiv \mathbf{x}^T B\mathbf{y}$ defines an inner product.

Norms of matrices can be defined by means of vector norms as

$$\|A\| = \max_{x \neq 0} \frac{\|A\mathbf{x}\|}{\|\mathbf{x}\|} = \max_{\|\mathbf{x}\|=1} \|A\mathbf{x}\|$$

Such matrix norms satisfy the properties of vector norms as well as

$$\|AB\| \leqslant \|A\| \, \|B\|$$

If $\|A\| < 1$ is some norm [or, equivalently, if $\rho(A) < 1$], then the following geometric series, also called the *Neumann expansion*, is valid:

$$(I - A)^{-1} = \sum_{k=0}^{\infty} A^k$$

Bibliography

An extensive bibliography on numerical methods for parallel and vector computers is given in Ortega and Voigt [1987]. It is our intention to keep this bibliography up to date and available on computer networks. For information on access, contact ICASE, MS132C, NASA-Langley Research Center, Hampton, Virginia 23665, 804-865-2513.

In the following, certain conference proceedings and anthologies that have been published in book form are listed under the name of the editor (or editors) and then individual articles are referenced by a pointer back to the whole volume; for example, the reference

Brandt, A. [1981]. "Multigrid Solvers on Parallel Computers," in Schultz [1981], pp. 39–83.

refers to the article by Brandt in the volume listed under Schultz [1981].

Abu-Shomays, I. [1985]. "Comparison of Methods and Algorithms for Tridiagonal Systems and for Vectrorization of Diffusion Computation," in Numrich [1985], pp. 29–56.

Abu-Sufah, W., and Malony, A. [1986]. "Vector Processing on the Alliant FX/8 Multiprocessor," Proc. 1986 Int. Conf. Parallel Processing, pp. 559–566.

Adams, L. [1982]. "Iterative Algorithms for Large Sparse Linear Systems on Parallel Computers," Ph.D. dissertation, Applied Mathematics, University of Virginia; also published as NASA CR-166027, NASA Langley Research Center.

Adams, L. [1983]. "An *M*-Step Preconditioned Conjugate Gradient Method for Parallel Computation," Proc. 1983 Int. Conf. Parallel Processing, pp. 36–43.

Adams, L. [1985]. "*M*-Step Preconditioned Conjugate Gradient Methods," *SIAM J. Sci. Stat. Comput.* **6**, 452–463.

Adams, L. [1986]. "Reordering Computations for Parallel Execution," *Commun. Appl. Numer. Math.* **2**, 263–271.

Adams, L., and Jordan, H. [1985]. "Is SOR Color-Blind?" *SIAM J. Sci. Stat. Comput.* **7**, 490–506.

Adams, L., LeVeque, R., and Young, D. [1987]. "Analysis of the SOR Iteration for the 9-Point Laplacian," *SIAM J. Numer. Anal.* To appear.

Adams, L., and Ong, E. [1987]. "Additive Polynomial Preconditioners for Parallel Computers," *Parallel Comput.*, to appear.

Adams, L., and Ortega, J. [1982]. "A Multi-Color SOR Method for Parallel Computation," Proc. 1982 Int. Conf. Parallel Processing, pp. 53-56.

Adams, L., and Voigt, R. [1984]. "A Methodology for Exploiting Parallelism In the Finite Element Process," in Kowalik [1984], pp. 373-392.

Alaghband, G., and Jordan, H. [1985]. "Multiprocessor Sparse L/U Decomposition with Controlled Fill-In," ICASE Report No. 85-48, NASA Langley Research Center.

Amdahl, G. [1967]. "The Validity of the Single Processor Approach to Achieving Large Scale Computing Capabilities," AFIPS Conf. Proc. 30, pp. 483-485.

Andrews, G., and Schneider, F. [1983] "Concepts and Notations for Concurrent Programming," *Comput. Surveys* **15**, 3-43.

Ashcraft, C. [1985a]. "Parallel Reduction Methods for the Solution of Banded Systems of Equations," General Motors Research Lab. Report No. GMR-5094.

Ashcraft, C. [1985b]. "A Moving Computation Front Approach for Vectorizing ICCG Calculations," General Motors Research Lab. Report No. GMR-5174.

Ashcraft, C. [1987a]. "A Vector Implementation of the Multifrontal Method for Large Sparse, Symmetric Positive Definite Linear Systems," Applied Mathematics Technical Report ETA-TR-51, Boeing Computer Services.

Ashcraft, C. [1987b]. "Domain Decoupled Incomplete Factorizations," Applied Mathematics Technical Report ETA-TR-49, Boeing Computer Services.

Ashcraft, C., and Grimes, R. [1987]. "On Vectorizing Incomplete Factorization and SSOR Preconditioners," Applied Mathematics Technical Report ETA-TR-41, Boeing Computer Services, *SIAM J. Sci. Stat. Comput.* To appear.

Axelrod, T. [1986]. "Effects of Synchronization Barriers on Multiprocessor Performance," *Parallel Comput.* **3**, 129-140.

Axelsson, O. [1976]. "A Class of Iterative Methods for Finite Element Equations," *Comput. Methods Appl. Mech. Eng.* **9**, 123-137.

Axelsson, O. [1985]. "A Survey of Vectorizable Preconditioning Methods for Large Scale Finite Element Matrix Problems," *BIT* **25**, 166-187.

Axelsson, O. [1986]. "A General Incomplete Block-Matrix Factorization Method," *Lin. Alg. Appl.* **74**, 179-190.

Axelsson, O., and Lindskog, G. [1986]. "On the Rate of Convergence of the Preconditioned Conjugate Gradient Method," *Numer. Math.* **48**, 499-523.

Axelsson, O., and Polman, B. [1986]. "On Approximate Factorization Methods for Block Matrices Suitable for Vector and Parallel Processors," *Lin. Alg. Appl.* **77**, 3-26.

Bank, R., and Douglas, C. [1985]. "An Efficient Implementation for SSOR and Incomplete Factorization Preconditionings." *Appl. Numer. Math.* **1**, 489-492.

Barkai, D., and Brandt, A. [1983]. "Vectorized Multigrid Poisson Solver for the CDC Cyber 205," *Appl. Math. Comp.* **13**, 215-228.

Barlow, J., and Ipsen, I. [1984]. "Parallel Scaled Givens Rotations for the Solution of Linear Least Squares Problems," Department of Computer Science Report RR-310, Yale University.

Barlow, R., and Evans, D. [1982]. "Synchronous and Asynchronous Iterative Parallel Algorithms for Linear Systems," *Comput. J.* **25**, 56-60.

Baudet, G. [1978]. "Asynchronous Iterative Methods for Multiprocessors," *J. ACM* **25**, 226-244.

Berger, M., and Bokhari, S. [1985]. "A Partitioning Strategy for PDE's Across Multiprocessors," Proc. 1985 Int. Conf. Parallel Processing, pp. 166-170.

Berger, M., and Bokhari, S. [1987]. "A Partitioning Strategy for Non-Uniform Problems on Multiprocessors," *IEEE Trans. Comput.* **TC36**, 570-580.

Berger, P., Brouaye, P., and Syre, J. [1982]. "A Mesh Coloring Method for Efficient MIMD Processing in Finite Element Problems," Proc. 1982 Int. Conf. Parallel Processing, pp. 41-46.

Bini, D. [1984]. "Parallel Solution of Certain Toeplitz Linear Systems," *SIAM J. Comput.* **13**, 368–476.

Birkhoff, G., and Schoenstadt, A. (eds.) [1984]. *Elliptic Problem Solvers*, Academic Press, New York.

Bischof, C., and Van Loan, C. [1987]. "The WY Representation for Products of Householder Matrices," *SIAM J. Sci. Stat. Comput.* **8**, s2–s13.

Bjorstad, P. [1987]. "A Large Scale, Sparse, Secondary Storage, Direct Linear Equation Solver for Structural Analysis and its Implementation on Vector and Parallel Architectures," *Parallel Comput.* **5**, 3–12.

Bojanczyk, A., Brent, R., and Kung, H. [1984]. "Numerically Stable Solution of Dense Systems of Linear Equations using Mesh-Connected Processors," *SIAM J. Sci. Stat. Comput.* **5**, 95–104.

Bokhari, S. [1981]. "On the Mapping Problem," *IEEE Trans. Comput.* **C-30**, 207–214.

Bokhari, S. [1985]. "Partitioning Problems in Parallel, Pipelined and Distributed Computing," ICASE Report No. 85-54, NASA Langley Research Center. To appear in IEEE Trans. Comput.

Book, D., [1981]. *Finite Difference Techniques for Vectorized Fluid Dynamics Calculation*, Springer-Verlag, New York.

Bowgen, G., and Modi, J. [1985]. "Implementation of QR Factorization on the DAP Using Householder Transformations," *Comput. Phys. Commun.* **37**, 167–170.

Brandt, A. [1977]. "Multigrid Adaptive Solutions to Boundary Value Problems," *Math. Comp.* **31**, 333–390.

Brandt, A. [1981], "Multigrid Solvers on Parallel Computers," in Schultz [1981], pp. 39–83.

Bucher, I. [1983]. "The Computational Speed of Supercomputers," Proc. ACM Sigmetrics Conf. on Measurement and Modeling of Computer Systems, pp. 151–165.

Buzbee, B. [1973]. "A Fast Poisson Solver Amenable to Parallel Computation," *IEEE Trans. Comput.* **C-22**, 793–796.

Buzbee B. [1983]. "Remarks for the IFIP Congress '83 Panel on How to Obtain High Performance for High-Speed Processors," Los Alamos National Laboratory Report No. LA-UR-83-1392.

Buzbee, B. [1985]. "Two Parallel Formulations of Particle-in-Cell Models," in Snyder *et al.* [1985], pp. 223–232.

Calahan, D. [1985]. "Task Granularity Studies on a Many-Processor CRAY X-MP," *Parallel Comput.* **2**, 109–118.

Calahan, D. [1986]. "Block-Oriented, Local-Memory-Based Linear Equation Solution on the CRAY-2: Uniprocessor Algorithms," Proc. 1986 Int. Conf. Parallel Processing, pp. 375–378.

Chamberlain, R. [1987]. "An Alternative View of LU Factorization with Partial Pivoting on a Hypercube Multiprocessor," in Heath [1987], pp. 569–575.

Chan, T. [1985]. "Analysis of Preconditioners for Domain Decomposition," Department of Computer Science Report RR-408, Yale University.

Chan, T. [1987]. "On the Implementation of Kernel Numerical Algorithms for Computational Fluid Dynamics on Hypercubes," in Heath [1987], pp. 747–755.

Chan, T., and Resasco, D. [1987a]. "A Domain-Decomposed Fast Poisson Solver on a Rectangle," *SIAM J Sci. Stat. Comput.* **8**, s14–s26.

Chan, T., and Resasco, D. [1987b]. "Hypercube Implementation of Domain Decomposed Fast Poisson Solvers," in Heath [1987], pp. 738–746.

Chan, T., Saad, Y., and Schultz, M. [1987]. "Solving Elliptic Partial Differential Equations on the Hypercube Multiprocessor," *Appl. Numer. Methods* **3**, 81–88.

Chan, T., and Tuminaro, R. [1987]. "Implementation of Multigrid Algorithms on Hypercubes," in Heath [1987], pp. 730–737.

Chazan, D., and Miranker, W. [1969]. "Chaotic Relaxation," *J. Lin. Alg. Appl.* **2**, 199-222.

Chen, S. [1982]. "Polynomial Scaling in the Conjugate Gradient Method and Related Topics in Matrix Scaling," Ph.D. dissertation, Department of Computer Science, Pennsylvania State University.

Chen, S. [1984]. "Large-Scale and High-Speed Multiprocessor System for Scientific Applications: CRAY X-MP-2 Series," in Kowalik [1984], pp. 59-67.

Cheng, K., and Sahni, S. [1987] "VLSI Systems for Band Matrix Multiplication," *Parallel Comput.* **4**, 239-258.

Chu, E., and George, A. [1987]. "Gaussian Elimination with Partial Pivoting and Load Balancing on a Multiprocessor," *Parallel Comput.* **5**, 65-74.

Cleary, A., Harrar, D., and Ortega, J. [1986]. "Gaussian Elimination and Choleski Factorization on the FLEX/32," Applied Mathematics Report RM-86-13, University of Virginia.

Clementi, E., Detrich, J., Chin, S., Corongiu, G., Folsom, D., Logan, D., Caltabiano, R., Carnevali, A., Helin, J., Russo, M., Gnudi, A., and Palamidese, P. [1987]. "Large-Scale Computations on a Scalar, Vector and Parallel 'Supercomputer'," *Parallel Comput.* **5**, 13-44.

Concus, P., Golub, G., and Meurant, G. [1985], "Block Preconditioning for the Conjugate Gradient Method," *SIAM J. Sci. Stat. Comput.* **6**, 220-252.

Concus, P., Golub, G., and O'Leary, D. [1976]. "A Generalized Conjugate Gradient Method for the Numerical Solution of Elliptic Partial Differential Equations," in *Sparse Matrix Computations*, J. Bunch and D. Rose (eds.), Academic Press, New York, pp. 309-322.

Conrad, V., and Wallach, Y. [1977]. "A Faster SSOR Algorithm," *Numer. Math.* **27**, 371-372.

Conrad, V., and Wallach, Y. [1979]. "Alternating Methods for Sets of Linear Equations," *Numer. Math.* **27**, 371-372.

Cosnard, M., and Robert, Y. [1986]. "Complexity of Parallel QR Factorization," *J. ACM* **33**, 712-723.

Cowell, W., and Thompson, C. [1986]. "Transforming Fortran DO Loops to Improve Performance on Vector Architectures," *ACM Trans. Math. Software* **12**, 324-353.

Dave, A., and Duff, I. [1987]. "Sparse Matrix Calculations on the CRAY-2," *Parallel Comput.* **5**, 55-64.

Davis, G. [1986]. "Column LU Factorization with Pivoting on a Hypercube Multiprocessor," *SIAM J. Algebraic Discrete Methods* **7**, 538-550.

Delosme, J.-M., and Ipsen, I. [1987]. "Efficient Systolic Arrays for the Solution of Toeplitz Systems: An Illustration of a Methodology for the Construction of Systolic Architectures in VLSI," in *Systolic Arrays*, Adam Hilger Ltd., Bristol, pp. 37-46.

Deminet, J. [1982]. "Experience with Multiprocessor Algorithms," *IEEE Trans. Comput.* **C-31**, 278-288.

Dennis, J., and Schnabel, R. [1983]. *Numerical Methods for Unconstrained Optimization and Nonlinear Equations*, Prentice-Hall, Englewood Cliffs, New Jersey.

Dongarra, J., DuCroz, J., Hammarling, S., and Hanson, R. [1986]. "An Update Notice on the Extended BLAS." *ACM Signum Newslett.* **21**(4), 2-4.

Dongarra, J., and Eisenstat, S. [1984]. "Squeezing the Most out of an Algorithm in CRAY-FORTRAN," *ACM Trans. Math. Softw.* **10**, 221-230.

Dongarra, J., Gustavson, F., and Karp, A. [1984]. "Implementing Linear Algebra Algorithms for Dense Matrices on a Vector Pipeline Machine," *SIAM Rev.* **26**, 91-112.

Dongarra, J., and Hewitt, T. [1986]. "Implementing Dense Linear Algebra Algorithms Using Multitasking on the CRAY X-MP-4 (or approaching the gigaflop)," *SIAM J. Sci. Stat. Comput.* **7**, 347-350.

Dongarra, J., and Hinds, A. [1979]. "Unrolling Loops in FORTRAN," *Software Pract. Exper.* **9**, 219-229.

Dongarra, J., and Hinds, A. [1985]. "Comparison of the CRAY X-MP-4, Fujitsu VP-200 and Hitachi S-810/20. An Argonne Perspective," Argonne National Laboratory Report No. ANL-8579.

Dongarra, J., and Johnsson, L. [1987]. "Solving Banded Systems on a Parallel Processor," *Parallel Comput.* **5**, 219-246.

Dongarra, J., Kaufman, K., and Hammarling, S. [1986]. "Squeezing the Most Out of Eigenvalue Solvers on High Performance Computers," *Linear Alg. Appl.* **77**, 113-136.

Dongarra, J., and Sameh, A. [1984]. "On Some Parallel Banded System Solvers," Argonne National Laboratory Report No. ANL/MCS-TM-27.

Dongarra, J., Sameh, A., and Sorensen, D. [1986]. "Implementation of Some Concurrent Algorithms for Matrix Factorization," *Parallel Comput.* **3**, 25-34.

Dongarra, J., and Sorensen, D. [1987]. "A Portable Environment for Developing Parallel FORTRAN Programs," *Parallel Comput.* **5**, 175-186.

Dubois, M., and Briggs, F. [1982]. "Performance of Synchronized Iterative Processes in Multiprocessor Systems," *IEEE Trans. Software Eng.* **SE-8**, 419-431.

Dubois, P., Greenbaum, A., and Rodrigue, G. [1979]. "Approximating the Inverse of a Matrix for Use in Iterative Algorithms on Vector Processors," *Computing* **22**, 257-268.

Duff, I. [1984]. "The Solution of Sparse Linear Equations on the CRAY-1," in Kowalik [1984], pp. 293-309.

Duff, I. [1986]. "Parallel Implementation of Multifrontal Schemes," *Parallel Comput.* **3**, 193-209.

Dunigan, T. [1987]. "Hypercube Performance", in Heath [1987], pp. 178-192.

Eisenstat, S. [1981]. "Efficient Implementation of a Class of Conjugate Gradient Methods," *SIAM J. Sci. Stat. Comput.* **2**, 1-4.

Eisenstat, S., Elman, H., and Schultz, M. [1984]. "Block-Preconditioned Conjugate Gradient-Like Methods for Numerical Reservoir Simulation", Department of Computer Science Report RR-346, Yale University.

Eisenstat, S., Heath, M., Henkel, C., and Romine, C. [1987]. "Modified Cyclic Algorithms for Solving Triangular Systems on Distributed Memory Multiprocessors." *SIAM J. Sci. Stat. Comput.*, to appear.

Engeli, H., Ginsburg, T., Rutishauser, H., and Stiefel, E. [1959]. "Refined Iterative Methods for Computation of the Solution and the Eigenvalues of Self-adjoint Boundary Value Problems." *Mitteilungen aus dem Institut fur Angewandte Mathematik*, 8, Birkhauser Verlag, Basel.

Ericksen, J., [1972]. "Iterative and Direct Methods for Solving Poisson's Equation and Their Adaptability to ILLIAC IV," Center for Advanced Computation Document No. 60, University of Illinois.

Fergusson, W. [1986]. "The Rate of Convergence of a Class of Block Jacobi Schemes." *SIAM J. Numer. Anal.* **23**, 297-303.

Fernbach, S. (ed.) [1986]. *Supercomputers*, North-Holland, Amsterdam.

Flynn, M. [1966]. "Very High Speed Computing Systems," *Proc. IEEE.* **54**, 1901-1909.

Fong, K., and Jordan, T. [1977]. "Some Linear Algebraic Algorithms and Their Performance on the CRAY-1," Los Alamos National Laboratory Report No. LA-6774.

Forsythe, G., and Wasow, W. [1960]. *Finite Difference Methods for Partial Differential Equations*, Wiley, New York.

Fox, G., and Furmanski, W. [1987]. "Communication Algorithms for Regular Convolutions and Matrix Problems on the Hupercube," in Heath [1987], pp. 223-238.

Fox, G., Kowala, A., and Williams, R. [1987]. "The Implementation of a Dynamic Load Balancer," in Heath [1987], pp. 114-121.

Fox, G., Otto, S., and Hey, A. [1987]. "Matrix Algorithms on a Hypercube I. Matrix Mutliplication," *Parallel Comput.* **4**, 17-32.

Funderlic, R., and Geist, A. [1986]. "Torus Data Flow for Parallel Computation of Missized Matrix Problems," *Lin Alg. Appl.* **77**, 149-163.

Gallivan, K., Jalby, W., Meier, U., and Sameh, A. [1987]. "The Impact of Hierarchical Memory Systems on Linear Algebra Algorithm Design," Center for Supercomputing Research and Development Report. No. 625, Univ. of Illinois.

Gannon, D. [1980]. "A Note on Pipelining a Mesh Connected Multiprocessor for Finite Element Problems by Nested Dissection," Proc. 1980 Int. Conf. Parallel Processing, pp. 197-204.

Gannon, D. [1981]. "On Mapping Non-Uniform PDE Structures and Algorithms onto Uniform Array Architectures," Proc. 1981 Int. Conf. Parallel Processing, pp. 100-105.

Gannon, D. [1986]. "Restructuring Nested Loops on the Alliant Cedar Cluster: A Case Study of Gaussian Elimination of Banded Matrices," Center for Supercomputing Research and Development Report No. 543, University of Illinois.

Gannon, D., and Van Rosendale, J. [1984]. "On the Impact of Communication Complexity in the Design of Parallel Numerical Algorithms," *IEEE Trans. Comput.* **C-33**, 1180-1194.

Gannon, D., and Van Rosendale, J. [1986]. "On the Structure of Parallelism in a Highly Concurrent PDE Solver," *J. Par. Dist. Comput.* **3**, 106-135.

Gao, G. [1986]. "A Pipelined Solution Method of Tridiagonal Linear Equation Systems," Proc. 1986 Int. Conf. Parallel Processing, pp. 84-91.

Gao, G. [1987]. "A Stability Classification Method and Its Application to Pipelined Solution of Linear Recurrences," *Parallel Comput.* **4**, 305-321.

Geist, A., and Heath, M. [1986]. "Matrix Factorization on a Hypercube Multiprocessor," in Heath [1986], pp. 161-180.

Geist, G., and Romine, C. [1987]. "LU Factorization Algorithms on Distributed-Memory Multiprocessor Architectures," Oak Ridge National Laboratory Report No. ORNL/TM-10383.

Gentleman, W. [1975]. "Error Analysis of the QR Decomposition by Givens Transformations," *Lin. Alg. Appl.* **10**, 189-197.

Gentleman, W. [1978]. "Some Complexity Results for Matrix Computations on Parallel Processors," *J. ACM* **25**, 112-115.

George, A. [1977]. "Numerical Experiments Using Dissection Methods to Solve *n* by *n* Grid problems," *SIAM J. Numer. Anal.* **14**, 161-179.

George, A., and Chu, E. [1987]. "Gaussian Elimination with Partial Pivoting and Load Balancing on a Multiprocessor," Oak Ridge National Laboratory Report No. ORNL/TM-10323.

George, A., Heath, M., and Liu, J. [1986]. "Parallel Cholesky Factorization on a Shared Memory Multiprocessor," *Lin. Alg. Appl.* **77**, 165-187.

George, A., Heath, M., Liu, J., and Ng. E. [1986]. "Sparse Cholesky Factorization on a Local Memory Multiprocessor," Oak Ridge National Laboratory Report No. ORNL/TM-9962.

George, A., Heath, M., Liu, J., and Ng, E. [1987a]. "Solution of Sparse Positive Definite Systems on a Shared-Memory Multiprocessor," Oak Ridge National Laboratory Report No. ORNL/TM-10260.

George, A., Heath, M., Ng, E., and Liu, J. [1987b]. "Symbolic Cholesky Factorization on a Local-Memory Multiprocessor," *Parallel Comput.* **5**, 85-96.

George, A., and Liu, J. [1981]. *Computer Solution of Large Sparse Positive Definite Systems*, Prentice-Hall, Englewood Cliffs, New Jersey.

George, A., Liu, J., and Ng, E. [1987]. "Communication Reduction in Parallel Sparse Cholesky Factorization on a Hypercube," in Heath [1987], pp. 576-586.

George, A., Poole, W., and Voigt, R. [1978]. "Analysis of Dissection Algorithms for Vector Computers," *Comput. Math. Appl.* **4**, 287-304.

Gohberg, I., Kailath, T., Koltracht, I., and Lancaster, P. [1987]. "Linear Complexity Parallel Algorithms for Linear Systems of Equations with Recursive Structure," *Lin. Alg. Appl.* **88**, 271-316.

Golub, G., and O'Leary, D. [1987]. "Some History of the Conjugate Gradient and Lanczos Algorithms: 1948-1976," Department of Computer Science Report TR-87-20, University of Maryland.

Golub, G., Plemmons, R., and Sameh, A. [1986]. "Parallel Block Schemes for Large Scale Least Squares Computations," Center for Supercomputing Research and Development Report No. 574, University of Illinois.

Golub, G., and van Loan, C. [1983]. *Matrix Computations.* Johns Hopkins University Press, Baltimore.

Gonzalez, R., and Wheeler, M. [1987]. "Domain Decomposition for Elliptic Partial Differential Equations with Neumann Boundary Conditions," *Parallel Comput.* **5**, 257-263.

Gottlieb, A., Grishman, R., Kruskal, C., McAuliffe, K., Rudolph, L., and Snir, M. [1983]. "The NYU Ultracomputer—Designing an MIMD Shared Memory Parallel Computer," *IEEE Trans. Comput.* **C-32**, 175-189.

Grear, J., and Sameh, A. [1981]. "On Certain Parallel Toeplitz Linear System Solvers," *SIAM J. Sci. Stat. Comput.* **2**, 238-256.

Greenbaum, A. [1986a]. "Synchronization Costs on Multiprocessors," New York University Ultracomputer Note No. 98.

Greenbaum, A. [1986b]. "Solving Sparse Triangular Linear Systems Using Fortran with Parallel Extensions on the NYU Ultracomputer Prototype," New York University Ultracomputer Note No. 99.

Gropp, W. [1986]. "Dynamic Grid Manipulation for PDE's on Hypercube Parallel Processors," Department of Computer Science Report RR-458, Yale University.

Gustafsson, I. [1978]. "A Class of First Order Factorization Methods," *BIT* **18**, 142-156.

Hack, J. [1986]. "Peak vs. Sustained Performance in Highly Concurrent Vector Machines," *Computer* **19**(9), 11-19.

Hay, R., and Gladwell, I. [1985]. "Solving Almost Block Diagonal Linear Equations on the CDC Cyber 205," University of Manchester Numerical Analysis Report No. 98.

Hayes, L., and Devloo, P. [1986]. "A Vectorized Version of a Sparse Matrix-Vector Multiply," *Int. J. Num. Met. Eng.* **23**, 1043-1056.

Heath, M. [1985]. "Parallel Cholesky Factorization in Message-Passing Multiprocessor Environments," Oak Ridge National Laboratory Report No. ORNL-6150.

Heath, M. (ed.) [1986]. *Hypercube Multiprocessors,* 1986, Society for Industrial and Applied Mathematics, Philadelphia.

Heath, M. (ed.) [1987]. *Hypercube Multiprocessors,* 1987, Society for Industrial and Applied Mathematics, Philadelphia.

Heath, M., and Romine, C. [1987]. "Parallel Solution of Triangular Systems on Distributed-Memory Multiprocessors," Oak Ridge National Laboratory Report No. ORNL/TM-10384.

Heath, M., and Sorensen, D. [1986]. "A Pipelined Givens Method for Computing the QR Factorization of a Sparse Matrix," *Lin Alg. Appl.* **77**, 189-203.

Heller, D. [1976]. "Some Aspects of the Cyclic Reduction Algorithm for Block Tridiagonal Linear Systems," *SIAM J. Numer. Anal.* **13**, 484-496.

Heller, D. [1978]. "A Survey of Parallel Algorithms in Numerical Linear Algebra," *SIAM Rev.* **20**, 740-777.

Heller, D., Stevenson, D., and Traub, J. [1976]. "Accelerated Iterative Methods for the Solution of Tridiagonal Linear Systems on Parallel Computers," *J. ACM* **23**, 636-654.

Hestenes, M. [1956]. "The Conjugate Gradient Method for Solving Linear Systems". *Proc. Sixth Symp. Appl. Math.*, McGraw-Hill, New York, 83-102.

Hestenes, M., and Stiefel, E. [1952]. "Methods of Conjugate Gradients for Solving Linear Systems." *J. Res. Natl. Bur. Stand. Sect. B* **49**, 409-436.

Hockney, R. [1965]. "A Fast Direct Solution of Poisson's Equation Using Fourier Analysis," *J. ACM* **12**, 95-113.

Hockney, R. [1970]. "The Potential Calculation and Some Applications." *Meth. Comput. Phys.* **9**, 135-211.

Hockney, R. [1987]. "Parametrization of Computer Performance," *Parallel Comput.* **5**, 97-104.

Hockney, R., and Jesshope, C. [1981]. *Parallel Computers: Architecture, Programming and Algorithms*, Adam Hilger, Ltd., Bristol.

Houstis, E., Rice, J., and Vavalis, E. [1987]. "Parallelization of a New Class of Cubic Spline Collocation Methods," in Vichnevetsky and Stepleman [1987].

Hwang, K., and Briggs, F. [1984]. *Computer Architecture and Parallel Processing*, McGraw-Hill, New York.

Ipsen, I. [1984]. "A Parallel QR Method Using Fast Givens' Rotations," Department of Computer Science Report RR-299, Yale University.

Ipsen, I. [1987]. "Systolic Algorithms for the Parallel Solution of Dense Symmetric Positive-Definite Toeplitz Systems," Department of Computer Science Report RR-539, Yale University.

Ipsen, I., Saad, Y., and Schultz, M. [1986]. "Complexity of Dense Linear System Solution on a Multiprocessor Ring," *Lin. Alg. Appl.* **77**, 205-239.

Jalby, W., and Meier, U. [1986]. "Optimizing Matrix Operations on a Parallel Multiprocessor with a Memory Hierarchy," Center for Supercomputing Research and Development Report No. 555, University of Illinois.

Jesshope, C., and Hockney, R. (eds.). [1979]. *Infotech State of the Art Report: Supercomputers*, Vols. 1 & 2, Infotech Int. Ltd., Maidenhead.

Johnson, O., Micchelli, C., and Paul, G. [1983]. "Polynomial Preconditioners for Conjugate Gradient Calculations," *SIAM J. Numer. Anal.* **20**, 362-376.

Johnsson, L. [1985a]. "Data Permutations and Basic Linear Algebra Computations on Ensemble Architectures," Department of Computer Science Report RR-367, Yale University.

Johnsson, L. [1985b]. "Solving Narrow Banded Systems on Ensemble Architectures," *ACM Trans. Math. Software* **11**, 271-288.

Johnsson, L. [1987a]. "Communication Efficient Basic Linear Algebra Computations on Hypercube Architectures," *J. Par. Dist. Comp.* **4**, 133-172.

Johnsson, L. [1987b]. "Solving Tridiagonal Systems on Ensemble Architectures," *SIAM J. Sci. Stat. Comput.* **8**, 354-392.

Jordan, H. [1986]. "Structuring Parallel Algorithms in an MIMD, Shared Memory Environment," *Parallel Comput.* **3**, 93-110.

Jordan, T. [1982]. "A Guide to Parallel Computation and some CRAY-1 Experiences," in Rodrigue [1982], pp. 1-50.

Kamowitz, D. [1987]. "SOR and MGR[$\dot{\nu}$] Experiments on the Crystal Multicomputers," *Parallel Comput.* **4**, 117-142.

Kapur, R., and Browne, J. [1984]. "Techniques for Solving Block Tridiagonal Systems on Reconfigurable Array Computers," *SIAM J. Sci. Stat. Comput.* **5**, 701-719.

Kascic, M. [1979]. "Vector Processing on the CYBER 200," in Jesshope and Hockney [1979], pp. 237-270.

Kershaw, D. [1978]. "The Incomplete Choleski-Conjugate Gradient Method for the Iterative Solution of Systems of Linear Equations," *J. Comp. Phys.* **26**, 43-65.

Kershaw, D. [1982], "Solution of Single Tridiagonal Linear Systems and Vectorization of the ICCG Algorithm on the CRAY-1," in Rodrigue [1982], pp. 85-89.

Keyes, D., and Gropp, W. [1987]. "A Comparison of Domain Decomposition Techniques for Elliptic Partial Differential Equations and Their Parallel Implementation," *SIAM J. Sci. Stat. Comput.* **8**, s166-s202.

Kightley, J., and Jones, I. [1985]. "A Comparison of Conjugate Gradient Preconditionings for Three-Dimensional Problems in a CRAY-1," *Comput. Phys. Commun.* **37**, 205-214.

Kightley, J., and Thompson, C. [1987]. "On the Performance of Some Rapid Elliptic Solvers on a Vector Processor," *SIAM J. Sci. Stat. Comput.* **8**, 701-715.

Kincaid, D., Oppe, T., and Young, D. [1986a]. "Vector Computations for Sparse Linear Systems," *SIAM J. Algebraic Discrete Methods* **7**, 99-112.

Kincaid, D., Oppe, T., and Young, D. [1986b]. "Vectorized Iterative Methods for Partial Differential Equations," *Commun. Appl. Numer. Math.* **2**, 789–796.

Kogge, P. [1981]. *The Architecture of Pipelined Computers*, McGraw-Hill, New York.

Kowalik, J. (ed.) [1984]. *Proceedings of the NATO Workshop on High Speed Computations*, West Germany, NATO ASI Series, vol. F-7, Springer-Verlag, Berlin.

Kowalik, J., and Kumar, S. [1982]. "An Efficient Parallel Block Conjugate Gradient Method for Linear Equations," Proc. 1982 Int. Conf. Parallel Processing, pp. 47–52.

Kuck, D. [1976]. *Parallel Processing of Ordinary Programs*, Advances in Computers 15, Academic Press, New York, pp. 119–179.

Kuck, D. [1977]. "A Survey of Parallel Machine Organization and Programming," *ACM Comput. Surv.* **9**, 29–59.

Kuck, D. [1978]. *The Structure of Computers and Computation*, Wiley, New York.

Kuck, D., Lawrie, D., and Sameh, A., (eds.) [1977]. *High Speed Computer and Algorithm Organization*, Academic Press, New York.

Kumar, S., and Kowalik, J. [1984]. "Parallel Factorization of a Positive Definite Matrix on an MIMD Computer," Proc. 1984 Int. Conf. Parallel Processing, pp. 410–416.

Kumar, S., and Kowalik, J. [1986]. "Triangularization of a Positive Definite Matrix on a Parallel Computer," *J. Par. Dist. Comp.* **3**, 450–460.

Kung, H. [1976]. "Synchronized and Asynchronous Parallel Algorithms for Multi-processors," *Algorithms and Complexity*, J. Traub (ed.), Academic Press, New York, 153–200.

Kung, H. [1980]. "The Structure of Parallel Algorithms," *Advances in Computers* 19, M. Yovitts (ed.), Academic Press, New York, pp. 65–112.

Kung, H. [1982]. "Why Systolic Architectures?" *Computer* **15**(1), 37–46.

Kung, H. [1984]. "Systolic Algorithms," in Parter [1984], pp. 127–140.

Kung, S. [1984]. "On Supercomputers with Systolic/Wavefront Array Processors," *Proc. IEEE* **72**, 867–884.

Kuo, J., Levy, B., and Muskus, B. [1987]. "A Local Relaxation Method for Solving Elliptic PDEs on Mesh Connected Arrays," *SIAM J. Sci. Stat. Comput.* **8**, 550–573.

Lakshmivarahan, S. and Dhall, S. [1987]. "A Lower Bound on the Communication Complexity in Solving Linear Tridiagonal Systems on Cube Architectures," in Heath [1987], pp. 560–568.

Lambiotte, J. [1975]. "The Solution of Linear Systems of Equations on a Vector Computer," Ph.D. dissertation, University of Virginia.

Lambiotte, J., and Voigt, R. [1975]. "The Solution of Tridiagonal Linear Systems on the CDC STAR-100 Computer," *ACM Trans. Math. Software* **1**, 308–329.

Larson, J. [1984]. "Multitasking on the CRAY X-MP-2 Multiprocessor," *Computer* **17**(7), 62–69.

Lawrie, D., and Sameh, A. [1984]. "The Computation and Communication Complexity of a Parallel Banded System Solver," *ACM Trans. Math. Software* **10**, 185–195.

LeBlanc, T. [1986]. "Shared Memory versus Message Passing in a Tightly Coupled Multiprocessor: A Case Study," Computer Science Department Report, University of Rochester.

Lewis, J., and Simon, H. [1986]. "The Impact of Hardware Gather/Scatter on Sparse Gaussian Elimination," Proc. 1986 Int. Conf. Parallel Processing, pp. 366–368.

Li, G., and Coleman, T. [1987a]. "A Parallel Triangular Solver for a Hypercube Multiprocessor," in Heath [1987], pp. 539–551.

Li, G., and Coleman, T. [1987b]. "A New Method for Solving Triangular Systems on Distributed Memory Message-Passing Multiprocessors," Computer Science Report TR 87-812, Cornell University.

Lichnewsky, A. [1984]. "Some Vector and Parallel Implementations for Preconditioned Conjugate Gradient Algorithms," in Kowalik [1984], pp. 343–359.

Lim, D., and Thanakij, R. [1987]. "A Survey of ADI Implementations on Hypercubes," in Heath [1987], pp. 674–679.

Lincoln, N. [1982]. "Technology and Design Tradeoffs in the Creation of a Modern Supercomputer," *IEEE Trans. Comput.* **C-31**, 349-362.

Liu, J. [1986]. "Computational Models and Task Scheduling for Parallel Sparse Cholesky Factorization," *Parallel Comput.* **3**, 327-342.

Liu, J. [1987]. "Reordering Sparse Matrices for Parallel Elimination," Department of Computer Science Report No. CS-87-01, York University, Ontario, Canada.

Lord, R., Kowalik, J., and Kumar, S. [1980]. "Solving Linear Algebraic Equations on a MIMD Computer," Proc. 1980 Int. Conf. Parallel Processing, pp. 205-210.

Louter-Nool, M. [1987]. "Basic Linear Algebra Subprograms (BLAS) on the CDC CYBER 205," *Parallel Comput.* **4**, 143-166.

Luk, F. [1986]. "A Rotation Method for Computing the QR-Decomposition," *SIAM J. Sci. Stat. Comput.* **7**, 452-459.

Madsen, N., Rodrigue, G., and Karush, J. [1976]. "Matrix Multiplication by Diagonals on a Vector/Parallel Processor," *Inf. Proc. Lett.* **5**, 41-45.

Manteuffel, T. [1980]. "An Incomplete Factorization Technique for Positive Definite Linear Systems," *Math. Comput.* **34**, 473-497.

Mattingly, B., Meyer, C., and Ortega, J. [1987]. "Orthogonal Reduction on Vector Computers," *SIAM J. Sci. Stat. Comput.* To appear.

McBryan, O. [1987]. "Numerical Computation on Massively Parallel Hypercubes," in Heath [1987], pp. 706-719.

McBryan, O., and van de Velde, E. [1985]. "Parallel Algorithms for Elliptic Equations," *Commun. Pure Appl. Math.* **38**, 769-795.

McBryan, O., and van de Velde, E. [1986a]. "Elliptic Equation Algorithms on Parallel Computers," *Commun. Appl. Numer. Methods* **2**, 311-316.

McBryan, O., and van de Velde, E. [1986b]. "Hypercube Programs for Computational Fluid Dynamics," in Heath [1986], pp. 221-243.

McBryan, O., and van de Velde, E. [1987a]. "Hypercube Algorithms and Implementations," *SIAM J. Sci. Stat. Comput.* **8**, s227-s287.

McBryan, O., and van de Velde, E. [1987b]. "Matrix and Vector Operations on Hypercube Parallel Processors," *Parallel Comput.* **5**, 117-126.

Meier, U. [1985]. "A Parallel Partition Method for Solving Banded Systems of Linear Equations," *Parallel Comput.* **2**, 33-43.

Meijerink, J., and van der Vorst, H. [1977]. "An Iterative Solution for Linear Systems of Which the Coefficient Matrix is a Symmetric M-Matrix," *Math. Comput.* **31**, 148-162.

Meijerink, J., and van der Vorst, H. [1981]. "Guidelines for the Usage of Incomplete Decompositions in Solving Sets of Linear Equations as They Occur in Practical Problems", *J. Comput. Phys.* **44**, 134-155.

Melhem, R. [1987a]. "Determination of Stripe Structures for Finite Element Matrices," *SIAM J. Numer. Anal.* **24**, 1419-1433.

Melhem, R. [1987b]. "Parallel Solution of Linear Systems with Striped Sparse Matrices," *Parallel Comput*, to appear.

Meurant, G. [1984]. "The Block Preconditioned Conjugate Gradient Method on Vector Computers," *BIT* **24**, 623-633.

Miranker, W. [1971]. "A Survey of Parallelism in Numerical Analysis," *SIAM Rev.* **13**, 524-547.

Modi, J., and Clarke, M. [1984]. "An Alternative Givens Ordering," *Numer. Math.* **43**, 83-90.

Moler, C. [1972]. "Matrix Computations with Fortran and Paging." *Commun. ACM* **15**, 268-270.

Moler, C. [1986]. "Matrix Computation on Distributed Memory Multiprocessors," in Heath [1986]. pp. 181-195.

Morison, R., and Otto, S. [1987]. "The Scattered Decomposition for Finite Elements," *J. Sci. Comput.* **2**, 59-76.

Naik, V., and Ta'asan, S. [1987]. "Performance Studies of the Multigrid Algorithms Implemented on Hypercube Multiprocessor Systems," in Heath [1987], pp. 720-729.

Neta, B., and Tai, H.-M. [1985]. "LU Factorization on Parallel Computers," *Comput. Math. Appl.* **11**, 573-580.

Neumann, M., and Plemmons, R. [1987]. "Convergence of Parallel Multisplitting Iterative Methods for M-Matrices," *Lin. Alg. Appl.* **88**, 559-575.

Nodera, T. [1984]. "PCG Method for the Four Color Ordered Finite Difference Schemes," in Vichnevetsky and Stepleman [1984], pp. 222-228.

Noor, A., Kamel, H., and Fulton, R. [1978]. "Substructuring Techniques—Status and Projections," *Comput. Structures* **8**, 621-632.

Nour-Omid, B., and Park, K. [1987]. "Solving Structural Mechanics Problems on the Caltech Hypercube," *Comput. Methods Appl. Mech. Eng.* **61**, 161-176.

Nour-Omid, B., and Parlett, B. [1987]. "Element Preconditioning Using Splitting Techniques," *SIAM J. Sci. Stat. Comput.* **6**, 761-770.

O'Leary, D. [1984]. "Ordering Schemes for Parallel Processing of Certain Mesh Problems," *SIAM J. Sci. Stat. Comput.* **5**, 620-632.

O'Leary, D. [1987]. "Parallel Implementation of the Block Conjugate Gradient Algorithm," *Parallel Comput.* **5**, 127-140.

O'Leary, D., and Stewart, G. [1985]. "Data-Flow Algorithms for Parallel Matrix Computations," *Commun. ACM* **28**, 840-853.

O'Leary, D., and White R. [1985]. "Multi-splittings of Matrices and Parallel Solution of Linear Systems," *SIAM J. Alg. Discrete Methods* **6**, 630-640.

Onaga, K., and Takechi, T. [1986]. "A Wavefront Algorithm for LU Decomposition of a Partitioned Matrix on VLSI Processor Arrays, *J. Par. Dist. Comput.* **3**, 137-157.

Oppe, T., and Kincaid, D. [1987]. "The Performance of ITPACK on Vector Computers for Solving Large Sparse Linear Systems Arising in Sample Oil Reservoir Simulation Problems," *Commun. Appl. Numer. Math.* **3**, 23-30.

Opsahl, T., and Parkinson, D. [1986]. "An Algorithm for Solving Sparse Sets of Linear Equations with an Almost Tridiagonal Structure on SIMD Computers," Proc. 1986 Int. Conf. Parallel Processing, pp. 369-374.

Ortega, J. [1972]. *Numerical Analysis: A Second Course*, Academic Press, New York.

Ortega, J. [1987a]. *Matrix Theory: A Second Course*, Plenum Press, New York.

Ortega, J. [1987b]. "The *ijk* Forms of Factorization Methods I. Vector Computers," *Parallel Comp.*, to appear.

Ortega, J. [1987c]. "Efficient Implementations of Certain Iterative Methods," Applied Mathematics Report No. RM-87-02, University of Virginia.

Ortega, J., and Romine, C. [1987]. "The *ijk* Forms of Factorization Methods II. Parallel Computers. Applied Mathematics Report No. RM-87-01, University of Virginia.

Ortega, J., and Voigt, R. [1985]. "Solution of Partial Differential Equations on Vector and Parallel Computers," *SIAM Rev.* **27**, 149-240.

Ortega, J., and Voigt, R. [1987]. "A Bibliography on Parallel and Vector Numerical Algorithms," ICASE Report I-3, NASA-Langley Research Center.

Paker, Y. [1983]. *Multi-Microprocessor Systems*, Academic Press, New York.

Parkinson, D. [1987]. "Organizational Aspects of Using Parallel Computers," *Parallel Comput.* **5**, 75-84.

Parter, S. (Ed.) [1984]. *Large Scale Scientific Computation*, Academic Press, Orlando, Florida.

Parter, S., and Steuerwalt, S. [1980]. "On *k*-line and $k \times k$ Block Iterative Schemes for a Problem Arising in 3-D Elliptic Difference Equations," *SIAM J. Numer. Anal.* **17**, 823-839.

Parter, S., and Steuerwalt, M. [1982]. "Block Iterative Methods for Elliptic and Parabolic Difference Equations," *SIAM J. Numer. Anal.* **19**, 1173-1195.

Patel, N., and Jordan, H. [1984]. "A Parallelized Point Rowwise Successive Over-Relaxation Method on a Multiprocessor," *Parallel Comput.* **1**, 207-222.

Patrick, M., Reed, D., and Voigt, R. [1987]. "The Impact of Domain Partitioning on the Performance of a Shared Memory Multiprocessor," *Parallel Comput.* **5**, 211-218.

Peters, F. [1984]. "Parallel Pivoting Algorithms for Sparse Symmetric Matrices," *Parallel Comput.* **1**, 99-110.

Pfister, G., Brantley, W., George, D., Harvey, S., Kleinfelder, W., McAuliffe, K., Melton, E., Norton, V., and Weiss, J. [1985]. "The IBM Research Parallel Processor Prototype (RP3): Introduction and Architecture," Proc. 1985 Int. Conf. Parallel Processing, pp. 764-771.

Plemmons, R. [1986]. "A Parallel Block Iterative Scheme Applied to Computations in Structural Analysis," *SIAM J. Algebraic Discrete Methods* **7**, 337-347.

Poole, E. [1986]. "Multicolor Incomplete Cholesky Conjugate Gradient Methods on Vector Computers," Ph.D. dissertation, Applied Mathematics, University of Virginia.

Poole, E., and Ortega, J. [1987]. "Multicolor ICCG Methods for Vector Computers," *SIAM J. Numer. Anal.* **24**, 1394-1418.

Pothen, A., Jha, S., and Vemulapati, U. [1987]. "Orthogonal Factorization on a Distributed Memory Multiprocessor," in Heath [1987], pp. 587-596.

Reed, D., Adams, L., and Patrick, M. [1987]. "Stencils and Problem Partitionings: Their Influence on the Performance of Multiple Processor Systems," *IEEE Trans. Comput.* **TC 36**, 845-858.

Reed, D., and Patrick, M. [1984]. "A Model of Asynchronous Iterative Algorithms for Solving Large Sparse Linear Systems," Proc. 1984 Int. Conf. Parallel Processing, pp. 402-409.

Reed, D., and Patrick, M. [1985a]. "Parallel Iterative Solution of Sparse Linear Systems: Models and Architectures," *Parallel Comput.* **2**, 45-67.

Reed, D., and Patrick, M. [1985b]. "Iterative Solution of Large Sparse Linear Systems on a Static Data Flow Architecture: Performance Studies," *IEEE Trans. Comput.* **C-34**, 874-881.

Reid, J. [1971]. "On the Method of Conjugate Gradients for the Solution of Large Sparse Systems of Linear Equations," *Proc. Conf. Large Sparse Sets of Linear Equations*, Academic Press, New York.

Reiter, E., and Rodrigue, G. [1984]. "An Incomplete Choleski Factorization by a Matrix Partition Algorithm," in Birkhoff and Schoenstadt [1984], pp. 161-173.

Robert, I. [1982]. "Regular Incomplete Factorizations of Real Positive Definite Matrices," *Lin. Alg. Appl.* **48**, 105-117.

Rodrigue, G. (Ed.) [1982]. *Parallel Computations*, Academic Press, New York.

Rodrigue, G. [1986]. "Some Ideas for Decomposing the Domain of Elliptic Partial Differential Equations in the Schwarz Process," *Commun. Appl. Numer. Method* **2**, 245-249.

Rodrigue, G., and Wolitzer, D. [1984]. "Preconditioning by Incomplete Block Cyclic Reduction," *Math. Comput.* **42**, 549-565.

Romine, C. [1986]. "Factorization Methods for the Parallel Solution of Linear Systems," Ph.D. dissertation, Applied Mathematics, University of Virginia.

Romine, C., and Ortega, J. [1988]. "Parallel Solution of Triangular Systems of Equations," *Parallel Comput.* **6**, 109-114.

Ronsch, W. [1984]. "Stability Aspects in Using Parallel Algorithms," *Parallel Comput.* **1**, 75-98.

Saad, Y. [1985]. "Practical Use of Polynomial Preconditionings for the Conjugate Gradient Method," *SIAM J. Sci. Stat. Comput.* **6**, 865-882.

Saad, Y. [1986a]. "Communication Complexity of the Gaussian Elimination Algorithm on Multiprocessors," *Lin. Alg. Appl.* **77**, 315-340.

Saad, Y. [1986b]. "Gaussian Elimination on Hypercubes," Department of Computer Science Report RR-462, Yale University.

Saad, Y., Sameh, A., and Saylor, P. [1985]. "Solving Elliptic Difference Equations on a Linear Array of Processors," *SIAM J. Sci. Stat. Comput.* **6**, 1049-1063.

Saad, Y., and Schultz, M. [1985]. "Topological Properties of Hypercubes," Department of Computer Science Report RR-389, Yale University.

Saad, Y., and Schultz, M. [1986]. "Data Communications in Parallel Architectures," Department of Computer Science Report RR/461, Yale University.

Saad, Y., and Schultz, M. [1987]. "Parallel Direct Methods for Solving Banded Linear Systems," *Lin. Alg. Appl.* **88**, 623-650.

Saied, F., Ho, C-T., Johnsson, L., and Schultz, M. [1987]. "Solving Schrodinger's Equation on the Intel iPSC by the Alternating Direction Method," in Heath [1987], pp. 680-691.

Saltz, J., Naik, V., and Nicol, D. [1987]. "Reduction of the Effects of the Communication Delays in Scientific Algorithms on Message Passing MIMD Architectures," *SIAM J. Sci. Stat. Comput.* **8**, s118-s138.

Sameh, A. [1985]. "On Some Parallel Algorithms on a Ring of Processors," *Comput. Phys. Commun.* **37**, 159-166.

Sameh, A. and Kuck, D. [1978]. "On Stable Parallel Linear System Solvers," *J. ACM* **25**, 81-91.

Schnendel, U. [1984]. *Introduction to Numerical Methods for Parallel Computers* (translator, B. W. Conolly), Halsted Press.

Schonauer, W. [1983]. "Numerical Experiments with Instationary Jacobi-OR Methods for the Iterative Solution of Linear Equations," ZAMM 63, pp. T380-T382.

Schreiber, R. [1986]. "On Systolic Array Methods for Band Matrix Factorizations," *BIT* **26**, 303-316.

Schreiber, R., and Tang, W. [1982]. "Vectorizing the Conjugate Gradient Method," in Control Data Corp. [1982] in Proceedings Symposium .CYBER 205 Applications, Fort Collins, Colorado.

Seager, M. [1986a]. "Overhead Considerations for Parallelizing Conjugate Gradient," *Commun. Appl. Numer. Math.* **2**, 273-279.

Seager, M. [1986b]. "Parallelizing Conjugate Gradient for the CRAY X-MP," *Parallel Comput.* **3**, 35-48.

Seitz, C. [1985]. "The Cosmic Cube," *Commun. ACM* **28**, 22-33.

Shanehchi, J., and Evans, D. [1982]. "Further Analysis of the QIF Method," *Int. J. Comput. Math.* **11**, 143-154.

Snyder, L., Jamieson, L., Gannon, D., and Siegel, H. (eds.) [1985]. *Algorithmically Specialized Parallel Computers*, Academic Press, Orlando, Florida.

Sorensen, D. [1984]. "Buffering for Vector Performance on a Pipelined MIMD Machine," *Parallel Comput.* **1**, 143-164.

Sorensen, D. [1985]. "Analysis of Pairwise Pivoting in Gaussian Elimination," *IEEE Trans. Comput.* **C-34**, 274-278.

Stewart, G. W. [1973]. *Introduction to Matrix Computations*, Academic Press, New York.

Stone, H. [1973]. "An Efficient Parallel Algorithm for the Solution of a Tridiagonal Linear System of Equations," *J. SCM* **20**, 27-38.

Stone, H. [1975]. "Parallel Tridiagonal Equation Solvers," *ACM Trans. Math. Software* **1**, 289-307.

Stone, H. [1987]. *High-Performance Computer Architecture*, Addison-Wesley, Reading, MA.

Storaasli, O., Peebles, S., Crockett, T., Knott, J., and Adams, L. [1982]. "The Finite Element Machine: An Experiment in Parallel Processing," Proc. of Conf. on Res. in Structures and Solid Mech., NASA Conf. Pub. 2245, NASA Langley Research Center, pp. 201-217.

Swarztrauber, P. [1979]. "A Parallel Algorithm for Solving General Tridiagonal Equations," *Math. Comput.* **33**, 185-199.

Traub, J. [1974]. "Iterative Solution of Tridiagonal Systems on Parallel or Vector Computers," in Traub, [1974], pp. 49-82.

Traub, J., (ed). [1974]. *Complexity of Sequential and Parallel Numerical Algorithms*, Academic Press, New York.

Uhr, L. [1984]. *Algorithm Structured Computer Arrays and Networks*, Academic Press, Orlando, Florida.

van der Sluis, A., and van der Vorst, H. [1986]. "The Rate of Convergence of Conjugate Gradients," *Numer. Math.* **48**, 543-560.

van der Vorst, H. [1982]. "A Vectorizable Variant of Some ICCG Methods," *SIAM J. Sci. Stat. Comput.* **3**, 350-356.

van der Vorst, H. [1983]. "On the Vectorization of Some Simple ICCG Methods," First Int. Conf. Vector and Parallel Computation in Scientific Applications, Paris, 1983.

van der Vorst, H. [1986]. "Analysis of a Parallel Solution Method for Tridiagonal Systems," Department of Mathematics and Information Report No. 86-06, Delft University of Technology.

van der Vorst, H. [1987]. "Large Tridiagonal and Block Tridiagonal Linear Systems on Vector and Parallel Computer," *Parallel Comput.* **5**, 45-54.

Varga, R. [1960]. "Factorization and Normalized Iterative Methods," in *Boundary Problems in Differential Equations* (Rudolph E. Langer, [ed.]), University of Wisconsin Press, Madison, pp. 121-142.

Varga, R. [1962]. *Matrix Iterative Analysis.* Prentice Hall, Englewood Cliffs, New Jersey.

Vaughan, C., and Ortega, J. [1987]. "SSOR Preconditioned Conjugate Gradient on a Hypercube," in Heath [1987], pp. 692-705.

Veen, A. [1986]. "Dataflow Machine Architecture," *ACM Comput. Surveys* **18**, 365-396.

Vichnevetsky, R., and Stepleman, R. (eds.) [1987]. "Advances in Computational Methods for Partial Differential Equations—VI," Proc. of the Sixth IMACS International Symposium, IMACS, New Brunswick, Canada.

Voigt, R. [1977]. "The Influence of Vector Computer Architecture on Numerical Algorithms," in Kuck *et al.* [1977], pp. 229-244.

Wang, H. [1981]. "A Parallel Method for Tridiagonal Equations," *ACM Trans. Math. Software* **7**, 170-183.

Wachspress, E. [1984]. "Navier-Stokes Pressure Equation Iteration," in Birkhoff and Schoenstadt [1984], pp. 315-322.

Ware, W. [1973]. "The Ultimate Computer," *IEEE Spect.* **10**(3), 89-91.

White, R. [1987]. "Multisplittings of a Symmetric Positive Definite Matrix," *Comput. Meth. Appl. Mech. Eng.* **64**, 567-578.

Wing, O., and Huang, J. [1977]. "A Parallel Triangulation Process of Sparse Matrices," Proc. 1977 Int. Conf. Parallel Processing, pp. 207-214.

Wing, O., and Huang, J. [1980]. "A Computational Model of Parallel Solutions of Linear Equations," *IEEE Trans. Comput.* **C-29**, 632-638.

Young, D. [1971]. *Iterative Solution of Large Linear Systems,* Academic Press, New York.

Young, D., Oppe, T. Kincaid, D., and Hayes, L. [1985]. "On the Use of Vector Computers for Solving Large Sparse Linear Systems," Center for Numerical Analysis Report No. CNA-199, University of Texas at Austin.

Index

9 780306 428623